Clan Kinsella's
History of Ireland

Clan Kinsella's History of Ireland

by John and James Kinsella

Published by
Old Baldy Press
Rochester, NY
First edition, 2004
Second edition, paperback,
2008

For more information on the Kinsellas, visit www.kinsella.org

Second Printing

ISBN 978-0-9761157-1-7

Library of Congress Control Number: 2008921703

Front cover image copyright © 2008
Jennifer Lee Farina Haseloff

Contents

"Remember the people from whom you descend"

Old Irish proverb

Preface to the Second Edition

The first, hardcover edition of *Clan Kinsella's History of Ireland* was published in 2004 and quickly sold out. In this second edition the text has been reset with small editorial changes made throughout. The major revision is inclusion of an appendix describing the impact of DNA studies. Over the last decade these studies have precipitated wholesale review of our understanding of ancient Ireland, its people, and its culture. In future editions we will continue to relate insights offered by this intriguing and growing body of information.

Acknowledgements

This book represents the love and thoughtfulness of others who allowed us the time to complete it. We'd like to thank Lucille Kinsella and Jill Kinsella for their patience and editing skills. The other editors, who were wonderful, include Susan Kinsella, Beth Sakanishi, Tom Kinsella and Ken Ballou. A special thank you for his exceptional editing job must go to Gordon Gensler . . . you have never seen an editing job until you've seen Gordon's.

We'd be remiss if we didn't thank Dan and Tom Kinsella for help in brainstorming through countless dilemmas as well as Susan Kinsella who is wholly responsible for researching and choosing the recycled paper used for this book.

John and James Kinsella

Introduction

"We shall not depart from the paths of our ancestors, the old pleasant custom, for it is the plainest, as follows. The place, time, author, and cause of writing this book, are:"[1]

This book was completed in Rochester, New York in the United States of America 2004 years after the birth of Christ. The authors are James Kinsella and his father John Kinsella, the son of Daniel Kinsella, the son of Daniel Kinsella, the son of Martin Kinsella, the son of John Kinsella, historians of Ui Cinnsealaigh (anglicized Hy Kinsella). This book will propagate knowledge of our clan, describing the history of Hy Kinsella, a powerful ruling clan in southern Leinster from the 4th until the 16th century, when Irish culture was forever transformed by the English. To properly understand the people described and the decisions they made, special attention is given to describing their culture and the events that affected them. Since the people of Clan Kinsella played a key role in Irish history from the arrival of the Celts until the present, this clan's history contains much of Ireland's history.

The primary sources for early history are the Irish annals and *Keating's History of Ireland*. Ever since the arrival in Ireland of St. Patrick, who introduced not only Christianity but also writing,[2] the Irish have been avid writers. Many monasteries wrote their own chronicles, called annals, which described some of the important events that occurred each year. Although many of these annals have been lost, no other culture in West-

---

[1] As written in 1650 by Duald MacFirbis, one of the last of an ancient line of learned men, in the introduction to the *Book of Genealogies*.

[2] While both claims are disputed, St. Patrick was certainly a driving force for the overwhelming acceptance of both.

ern Europe can boast of so many books written before the 10th century.

The pure Gaelic (early Irish) society lasted, gradually changing with time, into the 16th century. By then the English government had strengthened its hold on Ireland to such an extent that Gaelic culture and language went into decline. Realizing this, Irishmen like Geoffrey Keating began collecting and saving Ireland's ancient manuscripts. In 1630, Keating began visiting monasteries to transcribe and redact into English whatever ancient documents he could find. One eminent Irish historian said of Keating, "He invents nothing, embroiders little. What he does not find before him, he does not relate." Keating knew that much of what he was reading was pure myth but he faithfully copied everything. Known as *Keating's History of Ireland*, his compilation was completed around 1633.

Much of the material the authors researched from the 12th - 19th centuries was derived from both Irish and English sources. The enmity between the Irish natives and the English settlers was so great that accounts by the two sides of the same event differ widely, and it is difficult to determine what was factual and what was propaganda.

As England's power grew in Ireland from the 17th to the 19th centuries, the importance of the ancient sources was disparaged by "experts." The ruling English elite's disdain for Irish writings was absolute and continued well into the 19th century. A clear example is the occasion when Dr. Petrie, an Irish historian addressing the Royal Irish Academy, reported on the Tara Brooch and commented that there was evidence of similar early workmanship in the Irish annals. Dr. Brinkley, the President of the Academy, said with incredulous astonishment, "Surely, sir, you do not mean to tell us that there exists the slightest evidence to prove that the Irish had any acquaintance with the arts of civilized life before the arrival of the English in Ireland."

With the passing of time, and England's control, archaeologists and historians alike have uncovered the fact that early Irish society, far from being backward and primitive, was more advanced in many ways than other cultures on the European continent at the time.

The purpose of this book is to share knowledge of this culture and Kinsella history, but the work is unfinished. This book contains stories that have been passed down from generation to generation about the Kinsellas in Ireland, but there are surely more. If you have such a story about the Kinsellas in Ireland, no matter how small or insignificant, email the Kinsella webpage at *www.kinsella.org* so it can be included in future editions for the benefit of all. What follows is a history of Clan Kinsella as we know it today.

Glossary

Ard Righ, "ard ree": The position of Ard Righ belonged in theory to the strongest **provincial righ**. Two titles existed: Ard Righ with Opposition, which meant three or four of the **provincial righs** had submitted, and Ard Righ without Opposition, which meant all the **provincial righs** had submitted. The Ard Righ gained recognition as the strongest ruler in Ireland but was given no other rights.

bannrigh, "ban-ree": An Irish queen. In Gaelic, "bann" means female, and "righ" means ruler.

Beltane, "BELL-tinnuh" (May 1): The first day of summer, often marked by festivals with huge bonfires. On Beltane, the cows would be brought up to the mountains for pasturing.

black rent: A rent exacted for "protection" by the Irish on the English settlers of the **Pale.**

boaire, "bo-ahreh": A "strong" farmer of the freeman class. He ranked above the **ocaire** in wealth and just below the nobility.

Boruma, "bow-room-ah": A tribute in cattle, especially the legendary tribute imposed on Leinster by the Hy Neill.

brehon, "bree-hon": An Irish **file** who, like today's lawyer, specialized in law. The top ranking brehons acted as judges.

Brehon law: The law that governed Irish society. These laws were believed to have been first written down by a **file** under the supervision of St. Patrick, several **righs**, and **brehons**.

Chief Governor of Ireland: The government of England's supreme judge, head of the civil administration, and chief military commander in Ireland. He could declare war, could call on the king's nobles to help him, and had an army at his disposal. His office was itinerant: he asserted his authority by traveling around the **Pale**, administering justice as he went. A council made up of the great Normans of Ireland advised him.

derbfine, "durb-fine": A legal term for all males who had the same great-grandfather (that is, up to and including second cousins), together with their families. This family unit was important for legal purposes in **Brehon law**.

druid: A learned class who were the receptacles of knowledge in Celtic society. They may have acted as priests for their pagan beliefs and were certainly believed to have magical capabilities. They were considered sacred and could not be harmed.

eric fee: The fine or compensation paid for homicide according to **Brehon law**.

Fianna, "fee-on-a": The royal band of warriors whose elected leader followed the orders of the Ard Righ. The most famous leader of the Fianna was Finn mac Cool of the 3rd century. Later, the name was adopted by a political organization founded to create an Irish republic.

file, "fill-uh" (pl. **filid**, "feely"): The intellectuals of Gaelic society who acted as a **righ**'s advisors and promoters. Like druids, they were considered sacred and could not be harmed for any reason.

Gael, "gale": A Celtic group who, according to Irish myth, arrived in Ireland with the sons of Milesius from northern Spain around 1000 B.C. Today's Irish are their descendants.

Home Rule: The right of Ireland to manage her internal affairs while still allowing England supreme control over trade, the army and navy, foreign policy and all imperial matters.

honor price: The measure of a person's social status on which punishments were based. For example, injuring someone required payment of a designated fraction of that person's honor price. Injuring a **righ** was much more costly than injuring a slave.

Imbolc, "IM-bulk" (February 1): The first day of spring, marking the beginning of the growth cycle for plants and animals; also, St. Brigid's feast day. Imbolc was a day to clean out the house and farmyard.

land reform: In the late 19th century, political activists fought under this title for such tenant-farmers' rights as fair rents and the right to change landlords.

Lughnasa, "LOO-nah-sah" (August 1): The first day of fall. Lughnasa was when the first crops began coming in and when temporary marriages, which could be ended on May 1 (**Beltane**) by either partner, might be set up.

ocaire, "oc-ahreh": A "small" farmer of the freeman class. He ranked below the **boaire** in wealth.

ollamh, "ull-uv": The top rank a **file** could attain; roughly equivalent to a modern Ph.D. An ollamh had to earn several subordinate degrees and then complete twelve years of study ("seven degrees of wisdom") in history, law, medicine, music, poetry, grammar and divinity. He had to know by heart 350 historical tales and certain poetical structures and be able to improvise a poem at a moment's notice. He had to be perfectly familiar with the pedigrees and locations of the principal families, etymologies of Irish names, and important events at home and abroad.

Pale: The area, centered at Dublin and spreading along the coast of Leinster, settled by the English after the Norman incursion during the 12th century. This area, where the customs and language of England largely prevailed, grew and contracted with the rise and fall of Irish power.

pattern: Outdoor pilgrimage to a religious location, usually on the feast day of a local saint, that could attract thousands of people. The rituals carried out at a pattern, often of pagan origin, didn't require the presence of a priest.

provincial righ: The man owed tribute by all the tuaths in a province. He could rarely control events in territories outside his own except in times of war. Then, rather than being controlled by him, the other territories were in alliance with this man.

rath: A circular enclosure or **ring fort** used to protect either families and their lodgings or animals from attack, usually by predators. Some enclosures were of stone while others were mounds of piled dirt with palisades on top.

righ, "ree": An Irish king or ruler. A righ's powers were far more limited than those of a traditional European king and there were several levels of rulership. The least powerful was a righ who ruled over a **tuath**. An over-righ ruled over a territory (several tuatha). A **provincial righ** ruled over a province, such as Leinster, which comprised several territories. Finally, the **Ard Righ** ruled over all the people of Ireland.

ring fort: See **rath**.

Samhain, "sow-in" (November 1): The first day of winter was the time when the boundary between our world and the otherworld was believed to be weakest. At night the ancestors and Sidh were believed to wander the earth; we remember this today as Halloween.

seanchie "shenuchy": An Irish **file** who specialized in history. The seanchie fulfilled the same role as today's U.S. presidential historian.

Sidh "shee": When the Gaels defeated the Tuatha De Danann, whom they call the Sidh, they drove them underground. The Gaels believe this magic people still survive today in 'fairy mounds' which they come out of at night. Given their magical capability, the Tuatha De Danann should be placated rather than provoked. Numerous maladies were blamed on them ranging from poor health to droughts.

tuath, "too-u" (pl. **tuatha**): This literally means 'people.' By extension, it refers to the primary political unit of early Ireland (similar to the concept of a kingdom), which was ruled by a **righ**. Each tuath had one ruling clan and normally several subject clans. This could provide from 700 to 3000 soldiers in an emergency.

Maps

Early Medieval Ireland

+ = Religious sites
■ = Towns/raths
Leinster = Province
Ossory = Territory

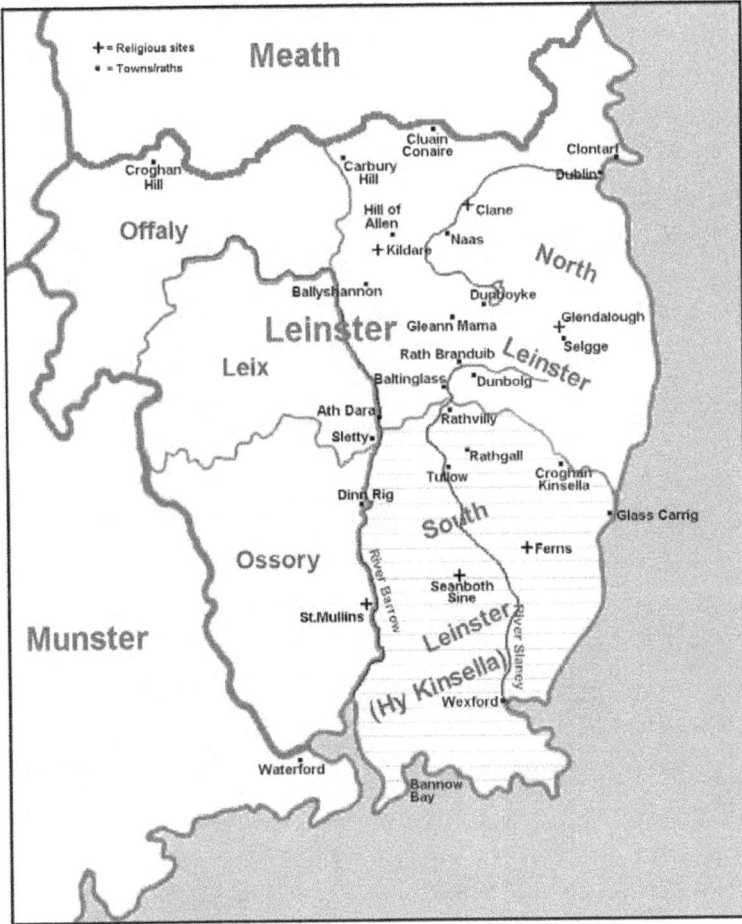

Early Medieval Ireland (Detail)

Ireland After 1200

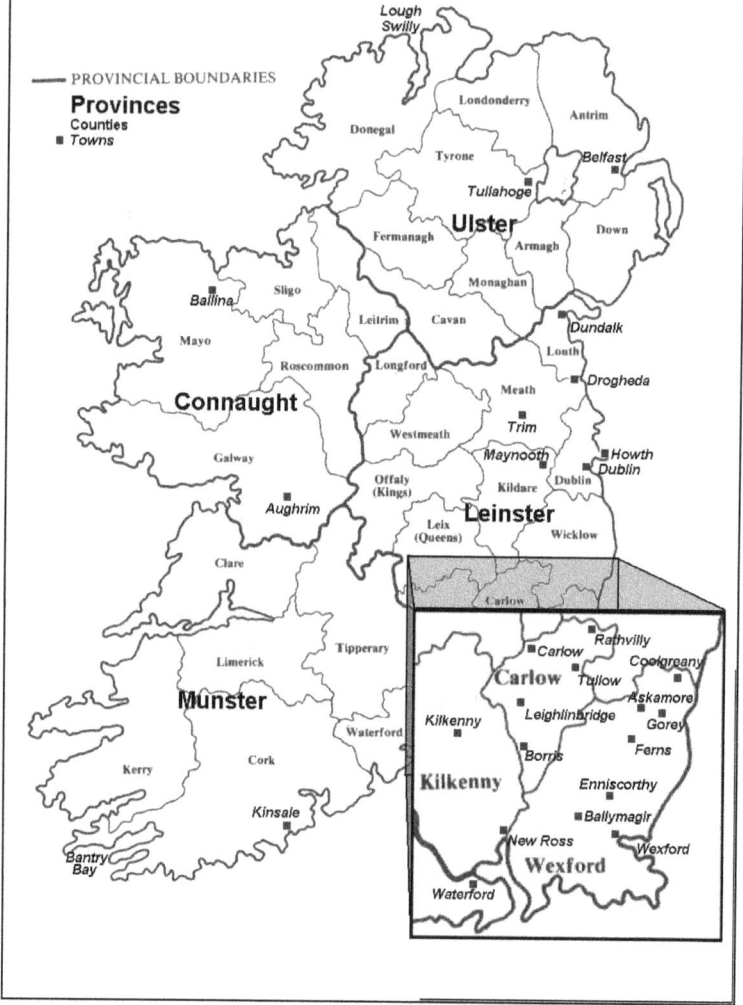

Lough
Swilly

PROVINCIAL BOUNDARIES

Provinces
Counties
■ Towns

Londonderry

Antrim

Donegal

Tyrone

Belfast ■

Tullahoge ■

Ulster

Down

Fermanagh

Armagh

Monaghan

Ballina ■

Sligo

Leitrim

Cavan

Dundalk ■

Mayo

Louth

Roscommon

Longford

Drogheda ■

Connaught

Meath

Westmeath

Trim ■

Galway

Maynooth ■

Howth ■

Offaly
(Kings)

Dublin ■ Dublin

Aughrim ■

Kildare

Leinster

Leix
(Queens)

Wicklow

Clare

Carlow

Rathvilly ■

Carlow ■

Coolgreany ■

Tipperary

Carlow

Tullow

Askamore ■

Limerick

Leighlinbridge ■

Gorey ■

Kilkenny ■

Ferns ■

Munster

Waterford

Borris ■

Kerry

Cork

Kilkenny

Enniscorthy ■

Kinsale ■

Ballymaglr ■

Bantry
Bay

New Ross ■

Wexford ■

Wexford

Waterford ■

The Peopling of Ireland

he last ice sheet retreated from northern Europe around 11,000 B.C. Shortly after, woolly mammoths, bears and reindeer wandered into this previously frozen land, closely followed by Stone Age hunters. After the retreat of the ice flows, Ireland developed a mild and agreeable climate similar to today's. In the modern climate, moisture picked up from the warm Gulf Stream bathes the island in the form of rain. This rain cannot escape from the saucer-like interior, cut off from the sea by the mountain barrier that (except for a fifty-mile stretch of beach on the east coast) entirely rims Ireland. As a result rivers and lakes spread a watery web over the country-side, giving it the lushest pasturelands in Europe. The ocean winds that bring the rain also blow it away, usually within a few minutes, as no part of the island is more than seventy miles from the sea, and sunlight glitters over the wet world. Because of this moist climate, winters are milder and summers are cooler than on the European Continent.

The first evidence of people in Ireland is from about 8,500 B.C. These people lived in the north of Ireland, opposite Scotland, from where archaeologists surmise they migrated. The sea level then was so low that Ire-

Shalwy Court Tomb

23

land, Scotland and England were connected by land. These people lived by hunting, fishing and collecting oysters, mussels, nuts and fruits.

By 4,000 B.C., a farming people had arrived in Ireland. These aboriginal people built wooden homes with thatched roofs and buried their dead in court tombs, giant stone edifices, many of which still survive. Evidence of these peasant farmers is apparent all across the north of Ireland.

The people who followed farmed light soil in lowland areas and built the passage graves of Newgrange, Knowth, and Dowth at the bend of the Boyne River in County Meath, magnificent mounds decorated with intricate art forms that still resist decipherment.

Entrance stone at Newgrange and "roof box" above

Newgrange, the most spectacular passage grave in northern Europe, was constructed around 3,200 B.C. Professor Michael O'Kelly, during an archaeological study of the site in 1967, discovered that the entrance to the tomb had been closed by a large, highly decorated stone (found buried near the entrance-way). The opening led to a 60-foot passageway at the end of which was a cross-shaped burial chamber with three recesses, each containing large stone basins. Oral tradition held that at sunrise on the winter solstice (the shortest day of the year, December 21st) the sun's rays penetrated into the back of the tomb. The following year O'Kelly tested the theory. December 21st was a clear day. As he waited in the dark recesses of the tomb, he hoped for the best, but the tomb remained completely dark. So much for oral tradition, he thought.

But in 1969, while clearing debris, Professor O'Kelly discovered a rectangular opening directly above the entrance that became known as the "roof box." He theorized that this newly discovered opening might be high enough to allow the sun's rays to enter the tomb on the winter solstice. The following year he waited anxiously in the rear of the chamber as sunrise approached. Then, in the words of another witness, "suddenly, a sharply defined beam of rose-gold dawn light from the roof box aperture appeared on the chamber floor, illuminating the entire chamber and revealing the impressive corbelled roof above. As suddenly as it appeared, the light slowly receded, leaving us inside with a sense of awe and wonderment at one of the world's oldest and most dramatic architectural devices."

Today Newgrange is recognized as one of the earliest architectural monuments built to mark the winter solstice. The site, like the more modern Stonehenge, had religious overtones tied to marking the middle of winter. Why ancient people worked so hard to identify the winter solstice is still hotly debated.

Around 2,500 B.C. a new group of people appeared in southwest Ireland, possibly proto-Celtic (pronounced "keltic"). Unlike previous Irish people who had raised cattle for milk and dairy products, they raised cattle for beef. They knew how to

smelt copper and build wedge
tombs, burial places like court
tombs but with a different
design. Archaeologists have
named them the Bell Beaker
people for the type of pottery
they created.

Typical Bell Beaker pottery

The Celts, Ancestors of the Gaels

Today's Irish are descendants of a Celtic group named
Gaels. The Celts were a loose association of people with
similar languages and cultures. Celtic society began in Austria
and Switzerland around 1,000 B.C. Their development was
spectacular after they mastered the smelting of iron. They exploded out of their Germanic homelands, expanding their territory to include Spain and northern Italy to the south and
Galatia (modern-day Turkey) to the east. Recent archaeological excavations indicate that they may have ventured as far
east as China. They also expanded north and west to occupy
England, Scotland, Wales and Ireland. By 600 B.C. their sway
extended over all of modern Europe with the exception of the
Scandinavian countries. Their presence is evident in the names
of such major European rivers as the Thames, Seine and
Danube and such major cities as London, Paris and Milan.

Rather than a written language, the Celts had a strong oral
tradition, which allowed them to pass down through generations a vast store of Celtic history, philosophy, law, genealogy,
and science. Their religious leaders, the druids, were not illit-

erate (in public and private business they used Greek characters), but they believed that a carefully cultivated memory was superior to written documents for preserving such important information.[1]

The first written references to the Celts occur in the 6th and 5th centuries B.C. when they encountered Greeks and Romans. The Greeks called them Keltoi, the Romans called them Gauls. Julius Caesar commented that they referred to themselves as Celtae. Roman and Greek historians had much to say about these "northern barbarians" who often raided their lands, including descriptions that were therefore understandably seldom complimentary:

> Almost all Gauls are of tall stature, fair and ruddy, terrible for the fierceness of their eyes, fond of quarreling and of over-bearing insolence.

> Physically the Gauls are terrifying in appearance. The Gallic women are not only equal to their husbands in stature but rival them in strength as well.

> The way they dress is astonishing. They wear cloaks fastened at the shoulder with a broach. These cloaks are brightly colored, striped and checkered in design (that is, tartans).

> The Celts are exceedingly fond of wine and drink it greedily. When they become drunk they fall into a stupor or into a maniacal disposition.

---

[1] Strict rules were enforced in verbal agreements requiring a number of people supporting each side of the agreement to be present. This made it virtually impossible to falsify an agreement. A written agreement, on the other hand, could be and often was altered or simply forged.

They frequently exaggerate with the aim of extolling themselves and diminishing the status of others. They are boasters and threateners and given to bombastic self-dramatization, and yet quick of mind and with good natural ability for learning.

In conversations they use very few words and speak in riddles, for the most part hinting at things and leaving a great deal to be understood. To believe that we can penetrate the Celtic mind, and share the Celt's psychological condition and feelings, is a pure waste of time.

Because the Celts left no written accounts, history books mention little of their military prowess, even though their achievements were formidable, particularly in the 4th and 3rd centuries B.C. Here is a partial list of their accomplishments:

They served as mercenaries in Egyptian armies and aided the Pharaohs in winning countless battles.

They marched with Hannibal's army when he crossed the Alps and invaded Italy. Although they made up 50% of the army, they accounted for 75% of the casualties because in every battle Hannibal put his Celtic troops front and center.

They defeated the Greek army at Thermopylae and sacked Greece's most sacred temple at Delphi.

They defeated the Roman army and sacked Rome.

Caesar irrevocably changed Celtic culture in continental Europe when he waged his famous Gallic Wars against them (in modern-day France) in the 1st century B.C. A famous

Roman historian,[2] after becoming familiar with the Celts' fighting style of charging completely naked at the enemy in hopes of overcoming by individual strength alone, wrote:

Fighting retail, they were beaten wholesale.
Had they been inseparable,
they would have been insuperable.

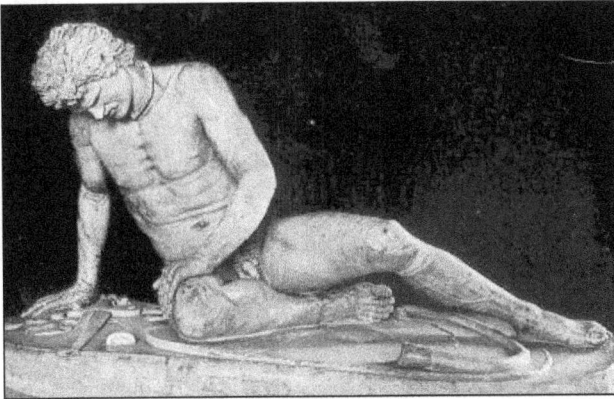

***The Dying Gaul**, a Celtic warrior*

After Caesar's victories over the Celts in Gaul, Roman language, law and customs eventually supplanted Celtic culture. The continental Celts (except for those in Brittany) became, in effect, Romans. Fortunately, some Celts had migrated to Ireland centuries before, carrying their oral traditions with them and preserving irreplaceable information for future generations.

The Celts who arrived in Ireland brought with them their culture and language. Archaeology identifies several waves of

---

[2] Publius Cornelius Tacitus (born in 55 A.D.) observed the Celts' fighting style in England.

migrations for these early Celts who displaced the Bell Beaker people:

1) The first group of Celts, coming primarily from Northern Britain where they were known as Picts, took over the northern parts of Ireland.

2) The next group, the Fir Bolg,[3] a group belonging to the Belgae Celts of continental Europe and England, invaded Ireland and overthrew the Picts sometime between the 6th and 4th century B.C.

3) The Laigin, whose invasion-legend has survived and will be related later, described themselves as Celts who invaded Ireland from Gaul.[4] This resulted in the conquest of considerable parts of Leinster and Connacht around 300 B.C.

4) The final group of Celts, the Gaels, reached Ireland directly from England, arriving around 50 B.C.

These people intermixed to such an extent that they all began to call themselves Gaels. They were to create the culture we consider Irish. This archaeological settlement history can be compared to that held to be true by the ancient Irish as described in the next chapter by their Mythological Cycle.[5]

---

[3] Also known as the Erainn or Iverni.
[4] The section of western France known as Amorica.
[5] DNA studies have recently called the settlement history described above into question. See Appendix G.

The Gaels of Ireland

eltic society included a learned religious class called druids whose duty was to preserve the traditions, laws, pedigrees and history of their race. In prehistoric times they passed on this information by word of mouth. When Christianity came to Ireland in the 5th century, the monks replaced the druids as the keepers of knowledge and fortunately wrote down much of this ancient information. Although they may have doubted the accuracy of some of the ancient stories, they recorded them faithfully. Of the unknown number of vellum manuscripts stored in Irish monasteries, many were undoubtedly lost over the centuries due to warfare, Viking raids, fire, and plain neglect. However, the surprising number that did survive and the oral tradition that is still alive in Ireland preserve the earliest history of the Gaels.

The Gaels understood that they were not the first to inhabit Ireland. They believed others had come before, and they communicated this belief through their myths and legends. Telling these tales is part of Celtic tradition and cannot be divorced from their culture. The stories were thought to bring blessing and good fortune to all who heard them.

The following is a summary of the Gaelic Mythological Cycle describing the five invasions of Ireland. (As in all myths, actual dates are vague or absent.)

31

Gaelic Mythological Cycle

First Invasion[1]

Partholan, the son of the king of Greece, fled after murdering his own father and mother. Accompanied by his wife Dealgnaid and a group of followers, they reached Ireland on Beltane[2] after wandering for seven years. They soon conquered the aboriginal inhabitants, the Fomorians, who were a race of misshapen people. The defeat of the Fomorians probably represented the replacement of the aboriginal gods by the Partholanian gods. The Partholanians were wiped out by a mysterious plague 300 years after arriving.

The Gaels would learn of them and the subsequent invasions from a sage named Fintan who retained his memory through many reincarnations.

Second Invasion

The next migration to arrive was Nemed and his followers from Scythia. Like the Partholanians before them, they battled against the Fomorians. Though the Nemedians were at first successful, winning four decisive victories against the Fomorians, a pestilence suddenly decimated the population until less than two thousand Nemedians survived.

The Nemedians then had to suffer from Fomorian tyranny and oppression, paying heavy tributes to their overlords. Later three Nemedian chieftains led their people in revolt. They attacked the Fomorian stronghold of Tory Island. Though the Nemedians managed to kill one of the Fomorian kings and captured one of the towers, the Nemedians were almost totally

---

[1] Some versions describe six invasions. They begin with Cesair, granddaughter of Noah, and her people, all of who died out before the invasion by Partholan.

[2] Beltane was the Gaelic season of summer starting on May 1.

annihilated when the Fomorians received reinforcement. Only thirty Nemedians survived the battle. Among these survivors were two of Nemed's descendants, Britain Máel and Semeon.

Britain Máel fled to Alba (Scotland) where he founded a colony; eventually the whole island was named after him. Semeon fled to Greece where he became a slave. His descendants, known as the Fir Bolg, would later escape servitude and return to Ireland as the next group of invaders.

Third Invasion

The Fir Bolg escaped from servitude in Greece and invaded Ireland next. They were the first to build ring forts, often called raths. Over 30,000 such structures remain in Ireland.

A typical small farmer's ring fort

Fourth Invasion

The fourth invaders were the Tuatha De Danann, also known as the children of the goddess Danu. They came from the sky and brought the magical Lia Fail, the sacred coronation stone that roared when a legitimate successor to the throne stood on it. Known as the Sidh, they would later be regarded as Celtic deities by the pagan Irish and as fairies to the Christians. They defeated the Fir Bolg at the first battle of Magh Tuireadh, causing the surviving Fir Bolg to flee to the islands off the coast of Ireland. One, Aengus, built a famous fort, Dun Aengus, in the most isolated part of the Aran Islands.

The Tuatha De Danann then dwelt in peace until a previous people, the Fomorians, rose up only to be eventually defeated by the Tuatha De Danann in the second battle of Magh Tuireadh.[3]

Dun Aengus

Fifth Invasion[4]

The last group of invaders was led by the sons of Milesius who arrived with their people, the Gaels, from northern Spain around 1,000 B.C., according to the Irish annals.[5] The Gaels, fighting with iron weapons, won a series of battles against the

---

[3] The Fomorians fought the Partholanians, Nemedians and Tuatha Dé Danann. They were possibly nothing more than pirates or raiders, since they never settled in Ireland, and were never considered a Celtic people (Irish). The Fomorians, a race of strange ugly, misshapen giants, lived on Tory Island. They were cruel, violent and oppressive.

[4] Five was one of the magical numbers of the Celts as evidenced by the division of Ireland into five (often fictitious) parts.

[5] The Irish scholar T. F. O'Rahilly believes the correct date to be around 100 B.C. Cultures often rewrite their history to make it appear their founding was more ancient than reality suggests.

bronze-wielding Tuatha De Danann. Rather than continuing the war, the Tuatha De Danann (also called the Sidh) agreed to split the rule of Ireland; they chose to move underground in mounds and rule by night. These Sidh would, over time, become today's fairies and leprechauns. The victorious Gaels divided the island between Milesius' nephew, Lug, and Milesius' three surviving sons, Heremon, Heber and Ir. All the prominent clans of Ireland can trace their lineage from these four with Heremon founding the most distinguished line. This included the righs and nobility of the ancient provinces of Leinster (where the Kinsellas ruled), Connacht, Meath and Ulster. One genealogical list that details the ancestors of Milesius before the Gaels arrived in Ireland traces them all the way back to Adam![6]

These invasions of Ireland are considered to be pure myth, but recently modern scientific methods have shown that the basis for them could lie in fact. For years historians have denied that the Gaels came to Ireland from northern Spain because of the great distance over water, yet a recent DNA study by scientists at Trinity College found a high correlation between the DNA of living Irishmen and the DNA of people living in northern Spain. The correlation was the highest in Connacht (98.3%) and dropped in eastern Ireland, presumably due to Norman, Norse, and English DNA mixing with Gaelic Irish DNA.

---

[6] See *Appendix B: Kinsella Genealogy Listing* for a genealogy that was put together by some speculative early monks.

Early Gaelic Ireland's Culture

o better understand the history of Hy Kinsella and the people who created it, it's important to understand the culture of the people living 2,000 years ago. Ancient Irish culture was based largely on raising cattle. (Even today high rainfall levels preclude intensive crop cultivation.) Society stratified people into social ranks based on their possessions, with each rank having certain well-defined responsibilities. The more important and the wealthier the person, the greater the demands made upon him or her; the greater the demands a person met, the more prestige that person commanded. Nobles, led by the Irish equivalent of a king called a righ,[1] held the highest rank. Below the nobility was the majority of the population, the common freemen. At the lowest rank were the unfree, those cast out of their clan or captured in war. Each rank included several levels, and people moved freely up or down in rank depending on their gain or loss of material goods. Differences between the homes of a noble and a freeman were relatively small and lay mainly in quality rather than size. For example, a noble would have a 30-foot house, a door frame made of yew, and cups and plates fashioned from yew or oak; a freeman would have a 27-foot house, a door frame of ash, and cups and plates of ash. Before looking at the social ranks in detail, however, one should understand the prevalent values with which the Irish of every rank were indoctrinated.

---

[1] The term "righ" had quite a different meaning to the Gaelic Irish than more familiar terms like chief, prince or king have today. This will be discussed later.

"The person who lost his propriety and his manners lost all he had."

Gaelic proverb about honor

Gaelic culture was built around the concept of honor. Every person in Gaelic society had a rank, corresponding to today's social class, and an honor price associated with that rank. The honor price was the monetary sum owed to a person in certain legal situations, such as when he or she was falsely accused of a crime and thus dishonored.

While a person's wealth or skills determined his social rank, Gaelic law stipulated that one dishonorable deed could strip him of his rank. Since honor helped define a person's place in society, he not only had to act honorably but also had to continually defend his honor against insult and attack. Honor was most important to a noble, who faced many situations in which it could be lost: unfairness to tenants, refusal of hospitality to guests, sheltering fugitives from the law, tolerating insults, or eating stolen food. A noble without honor was replaced.[2] Gaelic nobles constantly hosted feasts to increase their honor and status, demonstrating that they were effective in defending, winning, and distributing wealth to their people. During these occasions people were seated carefully according to their rank, reinforcing each person's standing among their peers.

Honor also regulated warfare. An Irish noble pursued warfare not to create a larger kingdom but either to cleanse or to increase his honor. In Gaelic Ireland nothing could be gained by battling an enemy of low status or by conquering all one's enemies, who were needed to maintain fame. The mentality of

---

[2] A righ who had lost his honor would also lose most of his followers. They would force the dishonored righ out, perhaps through a military engagement, and elect a new righ.

warfare among the Irish was closer to the concept of competi-
tion enjoyed by today's sports teams, who attempt to defeat but
not vanquish opponents.   Honor, which stressed personal
prowess, determined even the weapons allowed. Bows were
rarely used by the Irish, even after their effectiveness was
proven by Viking and later Norman foes, because with them a
coward could effectively kill a stronger man. Upon the advent
of gunpowder, a Gaelic noble said, "The warrior's day is over;
the weak man is now as good as the strong man."[3]

The story of Ailill, a Connacht righ, resonated with the ancient Irish:

> Ailill waged a terrible battle in which he was severely injured.
> As he was carried from the field in his chariot he asked his
> charioteer, "Look behind and see whether the slaying is great...."
>
> The charioteer looked and replied, "The slaying with which
> your people are slain is unendurable."
>
> Ailill said, "Not then their own guilt falls on them, but the
> guilt of my pride and untruthfulness. Turn thou the chariot
> towards the enemy, for my own slaying will be the saving of the
> multitude." So he faced the pursuers and gave his life to arrest
> the slaughter.[4]

*"I would give him food and lodging for the night even if he had
a man's head under his arm."*
                            Gaelic proverb about hospitality

Among the Gaels, another cultural trait closely tied to
honor was hospitality. It was the duty of every freeman to be
hospitable. To refuse someone (other than a criminal) food and
shelter required compensating the injured party according to

---

[3] Domhnall Cam ma Dhughaill.
[4] A battle often ended abruptly with the slaying of a Gaelic leader.

his rank. Even causing someone else to refuse hospitality (by not returning borrowed food on time, for example) required paying the honor price of the embarrassed host.

Hospitality was so highly regarded that some wealthy men opened inns that charged overnight guests nothing. What the host lost in payment he gained in honor, for the greatest inn-keepers held a rank equivalent to righ. In an old Irish story a traveler to medieval England returned with the most extraordinary news: the English people, he related, actually charged for the food, drink and bed provided to a stranger! Few in ancient Ireland would have believed his tale.

> Of all virtues their hospitality was the most extensive; every door and every hearth was open to the stranger and to the fugitive; to those they were particularly human and generous, vied with one another who would use them best, and looked on the person who sought their protection as a sacred depositum, which on immemorial custom, before the thoughts of men were contracted by weights and measures, and reckoned so far a sacred obligation as to think themselves bound to entertain the man.[5]

The Gaels used oral tradition to teach morals as well as to perpetuate culture. The Irishman most famous for his hospitality was the 7th-century Connacht righ, Guaire the Hospitable, whose story all Irish ancestors would have known. The following tale illustrates both honor and hospitality, and listeners were expected to strive to emulate this example:

> The Meath Righ, Dermot, was marching to attack Guaire when a messenger arrived with a request that, since Connacht wasn't fully prepared for battle, Dermot should not cross the river he was beside for another twenty-four hours.

---

[5] Thomas Pennant writing in 1772 about his journey through the Gaelic Highlands.

"I gladly grant his request," said Dermot, "and would have granted him much greater had he asked it."

Shortly after, the battle ensued and Guaire was defeated. As a form of submission, Guaire was made to kneel with the point of Dermot's sword between his teeth. Dermot decided to test Guaire's famed hospitality. First Dermot had one of his druids ask Guaire for a gift in honor of the druid's vast learning. The humiliated Guaire made no response. Next Dermot had a leper ask a gift for God's sake, to which Guaire, with his teeth still closed upon the sword point, gave the gold brooch from his mantle. At the secret instigation of Dermot, one of his people took the brooch from the leper, who at once complained of his loss to the kneeling Guaire. Immediately the Connacht righ un-linked the golden girdle that bound his waist and gave it to the leper. The gift was again taken from the leper, who returned a third time to Guaire. Realizing the man's distress and knowing that he had nothing more to give, tears streamed from Guaire's eyes.

"Arise, Guaire," said Dermot, "and do homage only to God!" A peace treaty was ratified between the two righs, who kept it ever after.

A grasp of the Irish social structure provides further insights into Gaelic culture. While most of continental Europe divided people into three classes – the nobleman, the cleric, and the common man – Ireland had a fourth class, the file or educated man. (The nobility ranged from knight to king, clerics ranged from monk to pope, and filid from apprentice to ollamh.)

Nobleman

The Irish nobleman had clients, people who farmed his lands and took care of his cattle. If he gained clients, he rose in social status; if he lost them, he fell. Maintaining his honor was essential for social status. A man with a good reputation could attract many clients, raise his honor price and have more power and influence. A nobleman who lost all his clients became a common man and had to farm and raise cattle himself.

The Gaelic emphasis on honor explains the prevalence of conflicts. A man had to assert his status and defend his reputation. In early Ireland, "saving face" cannot be underestimated as the motive for political and military action. A Gaelic noble chose death before dishonor.

Warriors all came from the nobility. The ideal destiny for a noble was everlasting fame in song and story. A heroic death helped ensure fame, as illustrated by the Gaelic proverb, *"Fame is more lasting than life."* A noble's worst fear was shame or ridicule, as indicated by the proverb, *"A person may live after his harassment, but he will not survive his disgrace."* The type of heated debates an attack on one's honor could provoke are not so difficult to imagine. They occur today whenever men sit together and begin boasting of their adventures.

A druid who prophesied to the Irish warrior Cuchulainn[6] in his youth that he would not live long was given the answer: "If it makes me famous, a single day of life would be enough." But men could not acquire fame through deeds alone; there had to be people who would report the deeds – the filid.

To inculcate this concept of fame and honor, the Gaels retold stories, such as when a spirit appeared at the court of the Ulster righ. The spirit proposed to three outstanding champions, including Cuchulainn, that they strike off its head, provided it could do the same to them the next day. The three agreed to make the attempt. They indeed cut through the

---

[6] Cuchulainn is perhaps Ireland's most famous warrior. Some of his deeds will be described later.

monster's throat, but without killing it, whereupon two of them fled, refusing to accept the role of victim.

Cuchulainn was different. Since the ghost's head grew again on its shoulders, even after Cuchulainn's terrible blow, the next day the warrior laid his head on the block. To universal surprise the spirit struck with the blunt and not the sharp edge of the weapon, declaring there to be in all Ireland no greater warrior than Cuchulainn, to who was to be given, from then on and wherever he went, the hero's portion.[7] This story drove home the concept that it was not just the number of feats that entitled a man to the highest honor; he also had to be prepared to keep his word, even at the cost of his life. In Gaelic society the man with the greatest honor also had the greatest social rank – the leader of the kingdom.

Ireland was divided into kingdoms called tuatha. Each tuath had one ruling clan and normally several subject clans who had been defeated by the ruling clan during previous conflicts. The ruler of each tuath, called a righ rather than a king, was the highest-ranking noble. From the 5th through the 12th centuries Ireland had approximately 180 tuatha with areas roughly equivalent to today's Irish baronies.

A righ had very limited power in comparison to what would later be wielded by a European king. He presided over his people and their lands without owning them and with his use of them strictly constrained by law. His main responsibilities were upholding the law (which he did not create) and waging war. In peacetime he held little more power than any other noble. This is much different from the feudal concept of kingship, which did not develop in Europe until the 11th century. During the 4th and 5th centuries when the Roman Empire was crumbling, the rest of Europe consisted of groups of peo-

---

[7] At feasts the best warrior was given the choicest parts of the animal being cooked, thus "the hero's portion."

ple held together by kinship ties. Their leaders' power was severely restricted. Ireland's political structure at this time was therefore similar to that of continental Europe.

The righ, especially in early Irish history, was the military leader. He and his chief nobles, usually his close kin, were expected to fight in times of danger and to sacrifice their lives defending their followers. Since the righ's strength lay in the men under his command, he needed to look after them. He

Aileach was the fort of the northern Hy Neill righs

postponed or even canceled rents in times of scarcity and attended to the needs of the poor: "Gentlemen are very charitable to the poor: some will have twenty or more people at every meal in the house."[8]

To rule was considered an obligation as well as a privilege. The righ and his people were equal partners in a mutually beneficial relationship that revolved around the principle of

---

[8] John L. Campbell, *A Collection of Highland Rites and Customs* (London, 1975).

reciprocity. An Irish righ was expected to perform a balancing act between authority and responsibilities, in which various forces were threatening to tip him over. He had to act as leader of his people, for whom he maintained order, and on whose behalf he made treaties, submission or war. A prudent righ kept an eye on potentially troublesome kinsmen, descendants and noblemen, placated or punished other tuatha with the military, legal or economic means at his disposal, and tried not to offend clerics and filid. He had to display royal qualities such as generosity and valor, judge justly, and avoid actions that caused harm to his personal stature in any sense of the word. If a righ managed to keep all these things in check, he was entitled to the obedience and material benefits of his people. But one who failed risked losing his position. If he disregarded his responsibilities he could be sanctioned by his clients or people, and if his transgression were dire, God would unleash vengeful forces on him and his tuath.

Royal succession was a frequent cause of conflict because Ireland, like the rest of Europe, had no strict rules for inheriting the throne. Primogeniture, inheritance by the firstborn, did not become the rule until the 13th century. The Gaelic system allowed anyone whose grandfather or father had been a righ to contend for succession. Theoretically, election by all the freemen of the clan determined the new righ, but often contenders disputed the result and started a dynastic feud.

A nobleman who became a tuath righ had only just begun his political ascent. He could now try to move up the hierarchy among righs. Each tuath was ruled by a righ. An over-righ, such as the Hy Kinsella righ, ruled several tuatha, called a territory, by submission of tuath righs. A provincial righ, such as the Leinster righ, ruled several territories, called a province, by submission of territorial righs. The Ard Righ, the political apogee, theoretically ruled all of Ireland. In fact, until the 11th century, the Ard Righ was a provincial righ with delusions of grandeur.

File

Before Christianity came to Ireland in the 5th century, druids were the religious and intellectual leaders of Gaelic society. As druids slowly disappeared, clerics and filid (plural of file) assumed their social duties. The filid became the intellectuals of Gaelic society and, like druids, they were considered sacred and could not be harmed for any reason. In return, the filid could not harm another for any reason without losing their social status.

A file received an elaborate education with seven distinct levels. The top rank a file could attain, that of ollamh, corresponded to today's Ph.D. An ollamh had to earn several subordinate degrees and then complete twelve years of study in history, law, medicine, music, poetry, grammar, and divinity (the "seven degrees of wisdom"). He had to know by heart 350 historical tales and certain poetical structures and be able to improvise a poem at a moment's notice. He had to be perfectly familiar with the pedigrees and locations of the principal families of Ireland, etymologies of Irish names, and important events at home and abroad. At the end of his studies a candidate was examined by one or more eminent ollamhs. If they judged him favorably the righ formally conferred the degree.

A file could choose to specialize in law, earning the title brehon, or specialize in history, earning the title seanchie. A brehon was equivalent to today's judge and a seanchie to today's presidential historian. The ollamh who chose not to specialize fulfilled the duty of advisor to the righ.

The file fulfilled numerous duties for the nobles and the whole clan. The ollamh file acted as the righ's counselor and composed poetry for significant events such as births, marriages, deaths, and warfare. He was given land along with special gifts and privileges and was exempt from the customary dues of dependents.

The righ paid fees to his file[9] for songs or poems of praise that spread his fame and recorded his lineage in order to prove his worthiness for royal office. As public relations agent, the file often exaggerated the greatness of his lord (within limits), but he also withheld or understated unmerited praise. An over-eager file who spread falsehoods, such as over-exaggerated praise, was fined. The purpose of the file's praise was not always to increase the prestige of his righ; sometimes it was to prescribe ideals for his righ to achieve.

A file was free to do and say what he pleased, within proscribed bounds, because he possessed the terrible weapon of satire. To insult someone and cause him to lose honor was a serious matter in a society that esteemed honor so highly. The following poem, which we consider innocuous, significantly decreased the status of the righ described:

The Boorish Patron

I have heard that he does not give a horse for songs of praise;
He gives what is natural to him – a cow.[10]

The Irish believed that satire had magical abilities, including the power to raise facial blemishes (a terrible dishonor) and the power to kill. If satire revealed someone's truly dishonorable deed, he lost all rank and was ostracized. We might be skeptical that a community would reject someone simply be-

---

[9] The term "bard" was used for simple musicians and storytellers with no formal education. They were held in much lower esteem than filid.

[10] Horses were revered by the Irish and owning any improved a person's status. Cows, though important, were commonplace. Anonymous 9th-century author.

cause of words, but clerics to this day have a similar weapon – excommunication.

A file also acted as an ambassador, taking his righ's pleas to another righ's court. He could sue for peace and prevent unwise bloodshed or he could agitate for war. A file traveled freely, heard what was said in the tuath, and relayed it to the righ in the form of wise counsel. A file considered himself a spokesman not only of the righ but also of the community, voicing its concerns and convictions. He played a central, highly practical and functional role in the smooth operation of society, maintaining the social order, expressing the feelings and concerns of his tuath, and celebrating the many events of its life cycle. Filid were instrumental in maintaining the identity and unity of the Gaels and their culture.

Cleric

From ancient Celtic times, the Irish treated the religious man with great respect. Before the arrival of St. Patrick, the Irish worshiped the sun and the earth, and druids acted as priests. After the arrival of Patrick, Irish Christianity thrived. Only clerics and filid could travel freely throughout the country and expect a warm welcome wherever they went. Religious establishments sprang up throughout Ireland and practiced a particularly demanding and intellectual form of monasticism compared with the rest of Europe. In the centuries following the disintegration of the Roman Empire, during Europe's Dark Ages, Ireland underwent a religious, intellectual and artistic renaissance. Irish monks, using newly-learned writing skills, copied whatever biblical, Greek and Latin texts came their way and saved them from the destruction that occurred on the continent. Most material that survives from medieval Europe came from Irish monasteries.

Irish Christianity was similar to that practiced throughout Europe except that power was decentralized and concentrated in individual monasteries. On the Continent, bishops governed geographical areas containing several monasteries, headed by abbots who were subordinate to the bishops. In Ireland, bishops held no such power and served mainly to ordain priests. The pope's inability to control the Irish abbots through the bishops led eventually to the elimination of this distinctively Irish form of church organization.

Common Man

The life of the Irish common man combined farming with cattle raising. He owned some clan land, cattle and movable goods. If he wanted more, he became a client by renting from a noble of his choice. In the winter he grazed some of his cattle on rented land and the rest on the clan's common land. In the summer he brought his cattle into the hills and lived in a makeshift hut while the cattle fed on the surrounding grasses. Periodically he left his women and children in the hills to care for the animals while he returned home to ensure the survival of the crops planted before leaving.[11]

Festivals were a major diversion from the predictability of this repetitive lifestyle and Ireland celebrated many. Often taking place at hilltops on holy days, festivals were a chance for the clan to come together and celebrate. All the local people made their way to a traditional hilltop during the day, often collecting wood for a bonfire that night. ("Bonfire" came from "bonefire" because bones were thrown into the fire.) Together they ate, watched local entertainers, listened to music, and heard the filid relate stories about the clan's history.

---

[11] This summer migration, called "booleying" from the Irish "buaile" (cattle-enclosure), still occurred in Ireland up to the 20th century.

Fairs, which were called at the righ's whim for economic and political reasons, served numerous purposes. They assembled the clans to promote a common identity and provided education in the law, created a temporary trading center for foreigners, and allowed matchmaking for the younger generation. In the centuries following St. Patrick, fairs became less and less common, as the monasteries gained dominance over education and trade, eroding some of the righ's power.

The frequent skirmishes in Ireland described in the annals rarely disrupted the common man's life. He could be called on to fight for his righ only every few years for a period of about six weeks.[12] Raiding usually took place in the spring when cattle were weak from lack of food during the winter and could not be driven far. A typical raid consisted of walking into a neighboring tuath, locating some unattended cattle, and driving them back across the border as fast as possible. The common men were responsible for herding the cattle. If the owners realized what was occurring, they called on their nobles to ride after the cattle and take them back. If a fight occurred it involved nobles, not common men.

Battles, which occurred between provinces in the summer when cattle were at their prime, were a different matter. The common men were expected to fight, although the nobles took the brunt of the attack and therefore the honor. Battles were uncommon in early Ireland, but they became more frequent as the political situation intensified with the consolidation of power in just a few families and as the Irish worked towards forging an overall monarchy.

In general, the common man in Ireland had a better life than the serf, his counterpart in continental Europe. He owned some of his own land and cattle, could choose which noble to

---

[12] This varied depending on the power of the righ and the agreements set up when a tuath submitted to an over-righ.

rent more land or cattle from, and could annul that choice later. He rarely suffered the starvation that often threatened the life of a serf because Ireland was a lush land with a low population density. He could not be over-taxed by the special fees that drove many serfs to their deaths because an Irish righ could not make laws.

Irish Provinces

The Celts liked to think Ireland's provinces numbered a magical five: Ulster, Meath, Leinster, Munster and Connacht. Reality was rarely this simple. The borders of the provinces changed constantly depending on the strength of provincial righs, and the tuatha in these regions eventually considered themselves sub-provinces, owing allegiance to no one. Ossory, between Munster and Leinster, was one such case. When Ossory's righ was weak, Munster or Leinster claimed it; when Ossory's righ was strong, it was subordinate to neither. Breifne held a similar position as a buffer between Connacht, Ulster and Meath.

Hy Kinsella

Early in its history, during the 7th century, Leinster was divided into South and North Leinster, each controlled by a ruling family who then competed for the throne of the entire province. South Leinster, referred to as the territory of Hy Kinsella, contained more than a dozen tuatha, each with its own righ. North Leinster consisted of several territories, each with a number of tuatha.

The territory of Hy Kinsella includes 75 miles of mostly sandy coastline with numerous bays, the major ones being Wexford Bay and Bannow Bay. The territory has some of the most spectacular scenery in Ireland and enjoys more hours of sunshine than any other part of the country. Its climate, temperate because of the Atlantic Gulf Stream, is mild in winter and cool in summer with a consistently high humidity. Until the late medieval period it was densely forested, except where it had been cleared for cultivation. The plains watered by the Slaney and Barrow Rivers are among the richest agricultural lands in Ireland. The territory is also rich in minerals; from antiquity it has been mined for copper, lead, silver and gold. The rolling countryside in the south and east gives way to hills and eventually to rugged mountains, the Blackstairs on the western border and the Wicklow Mountains on the northern border, which form a strong natural defense against invaders.

Geographical areas such as the territory of Hy Kinsella had no fixed borders and fluctuated in size. A powerful Hy Kinsella righ would raid and collect tribute from neighboring tuatha. If they were not strong enough to rebel and refuse tribute, after a few generations they became a subordinate tuath in the territory or province. The opposite could also happen; a weak righ could lose a tributary tuath. This occurred along both the boundaries of provinces and of territories making up provinces.

In the case where a ruler of Hy Kinsella gained the submission of all the tuatha in Leinster, he became the Leinster righ. Hy Kinsella did not expand, however, to include all of Leinster. The ruler simply had an army strong enough to impose his will on the North Leinster territories and extract tribute and military support from them. When the ruler died, tuatha outside Hy Kinsella could refuse to pay tribute to the new ruler, and he would have to regain their submission. If he succeeded, these tuatha might eventually be absorbed into Hy Kinsella and be considered part of the territory.

The Origins of the Leinstermen

previous chapter recounted how the sons of Milesius invaded Ireland and defeated the Tuatha De Danann. This chapter relates the genealogy of Heremon, a son of Milesius and the founder of the most distinguished Irish lineage.

According to the annals, Heremon was succeeded as Ard Righ of Ireland by his son, Irial. Information about the next several generations is meager. We are told only their names, that they were Ard Righs of Ireland, and how they died, usually in battle. During the reign of Tighernmas, the 13th Ard Righ of Ireland, we are told gold was first smelted in Ireland. In the 18th century, gold was discovered in County Wexford on Croghan Kinsella,[1] the second highest mountain in Ireland, and the area seems to have been mined in prehistoric times. Since Tighernmas' domain was the province of Leinster, Croghan Kinsella may have been the source of Ireland's ancient gold. Incidentally, Croghan Kinsella is well known to sailors coming across the Irish Sea as the first landfall they see.

Ugaine Mor, the 66th Ard Righ of Ireland, is the next major personage mentioned in the line of Heremon. The annals say he was killed in 588 B.C. and was survived by his two sons, Laeghaire Lorc and Cobthach. The Kinsellas trace their ances-

---

[1] Maps made pre-1900 list the mountain as Croghan Kinsella; on current maps it is simply Croghan.

53

try from Laeghaire. They would all be familiar with the following origin story of the Leinstermen.

Dinn Rig in southern County Carlow

Laeghaire Lorc was given the "lands about the River Liffey in Leinster" and became the 68th Ard Righ of Ireland. His brother, Cobthach, deeply disappointed that the throne had not been given to him, devised a plan to kill Laeghaire. On the advice of his druid, Cobthach feigned death, and when Laeghaire came to the bier to pay his respects, Cobthach rose up and stabbed him to death.[2] He then killed Laeghaire's son, Oilill Aine, and considered killing his grandson, Maon. When he discovered the boy could not speak, Cobthach spared him since he was no threat to the throne – no Gael with a blemish could be righ. The Hy Neill, the bitter enemies of the Kinsellas, trace their ancestry through Cobthach.

---

[2] Cobthach was actually sick, having contracted a wasting disease caused by envying his brother. Magh Breagh was the name of the place where he lay sick so, after committing his crime, he was referred to as Cobthach Coal-mBreagh.

Maon left Ireland after his father and grandfather had been killed by Cobthach and traveled to France,[3] his grandmother's country, with a party of nine. The king of the French made Maon the leader of his household guards through which many victories were gained. Maon became so successful that his fame lured many Irishmen to France where they obeyed him as the true heir to Ireland's throne. Back in Ireland Cobthach ruled as Ard Righ for 30 years.

Moiriath, daughter of the Munster Righ, fell in love with Maon after hearing countless stories of his courage and fame. She sent Craiftine the harper to him with many presents and a ballad in which she set forth the intensity of her passion for him. When Craiftine arrived in France, he sang the lay for Maon. Maon was so inspired by the song that he asked the king of France for an auxiliary force so that he might go and regain Ireland. The king did so and they sailed to Wexford.

Maon marched to Dinn Rig where Cobthach resided with many of his nobles and attacked the fortress, killing all his enemies. It was then that a druid who was in the fortress inquired who had executed the slaughter. "The mariner" (An loingseach), replied a man outside. "Does the mariner speak?" asked the druid. "He speaks" (Labhraidh), said the other. And hence the name Labhraidh Loingseach clung to Maon ever since.[4]

The origin of the name Laigin, another name for the people of Leinster, refers to the spears with wide green-blue iron heads (laighne) carried by Labraid's army. According to an ancient poem:

> Two hundred and twenty hundred foreigners,
> With broad spears they came over;

---

[3] Another version of this story has him travel to Munster.
[4] The story is abbreviated from Myles Dillon, *The Cycle of the Kings* (Dublin, 1994).

From these spears without flaw
The Leinstermen are called Laigin.[5]

Some historians believe that the attack by Labraid Loing-sech is actually a folk recollection of an invasion of Leinster by the continental Celts who had previously invaded England and whose descendants fought Caesar there. The story of Maon's being originally from Ireland and returning to reclaim his rightful throne is thought to have been fabricated so that the leaders of the invading army could effectively graft their gene-alogy onto that of the original Irish clans. In any event, all the ancient genealogies agree that Labraid Loingsech was a direct descendant of Heremon.

Labraid Loingsech may have brought more than just soldiers to Ireland when he recaptured his throne. After his arrival the earliest LaTene art (the winding, entwining art closely associated with Celtic art) reached Ireland. The celebrated Turoe stone in County Galway is one early example of LaTene art. On

Turoe stone

the top of this intricately carved stone is a collection of repeat-ing patterns such as trumpets and stylized heads of animals. LaTene art, found on stones, drawings, clothes, weapons and jewelry, became part of Gaelic culture.

[5] An anonymous 9th-century author.

56

Inner ring of Rathgall in County Wicklow

Labraid Loingsech and his followers probably also built Rathgall, a huge triple-ringed fort near Tullow in County Wicklow. The outer ring encloses an area 315 meters in diameter. The inner ring, a stone wall 5.4 meters wide and 2.5 meters high, encloses an area 45 meters across. Based on traces of Iron Age activity, recent excavations reveal that it was in continual use from the 8th century B.C. until around 265 A.D. This important structure has been identified as Dunam, one of the sites marked on an ancient Greek map of Ireland known as the Ptolemy Map. From this fort the South Leinster righs, those of Hy Kinsella, ruled.

Dermot MacMurrough, one of Labraid's descendants, born some fifty generations after him, was well aware of the story of foreign mercenaries coming to Ireland to retrieve a throne. His attempt to duplicate this feat in the 12th century brought disaster to Ireland. The mercenaries stayed and were followed by the English, who over the next several centuries succeeded in transforming the Gaelic culture that had existed in Ireland for over two thousand years.

Ancient Irish Tales

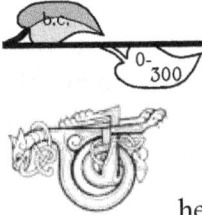

he ancient Gaels passed tradition from one generation to the next through oral tales. The heroes and heroines of the tales often exemplified cultural ideals that the Irish wanted to emulate. At every festival and feast these tales were told, and the greatest festival of all was Samhain.[1] The Gaels believed there was an otherworld, where the dead dwelled, that could be reached at certain times of the year. The first night of Samhain, the beginning of winter for the Irish, was the time when the boundary between our world and the otherworld was weakest. Few dared travel on this night for fear of encountering those long dead. The Irish were not afraid of meeting their ancestors but instead the enemies of their ancestors, who might choose to settle old scores.

People set out food for deceased family members before nightfall and then hurried to a central meeting place, usually a noble's house, to spend the first night of Samhain. A great feast began at dusk, followed in traditional Celtic style by games, music, dancing and storytelling. Masked children ran around collecting overdue offerings on behalf of the Sidh (fairy folk) in gratitude for a good harvest.[2] The first night of Samhain was the greatest celebration of the year.

---

[1] Pronounced "sow-in"; Halloween today. It was a season that started at dusk on October 31.

[2] Whence the origin of modern trick-or-treaters.

Later in the evening the Irish gathered in the great hall and listened to a file tell stories. The most advanced filid, called ollamhs, had memorized word for word hundreds of tales, which they passed on to the next generation during these frequent gatherings. The tales featured fantastic characters who exemplified, often in exaggerated ways, the most honorable aspects of Gaelic culture. These characters taught the next generation which cultural attributes were desirable and which were not.

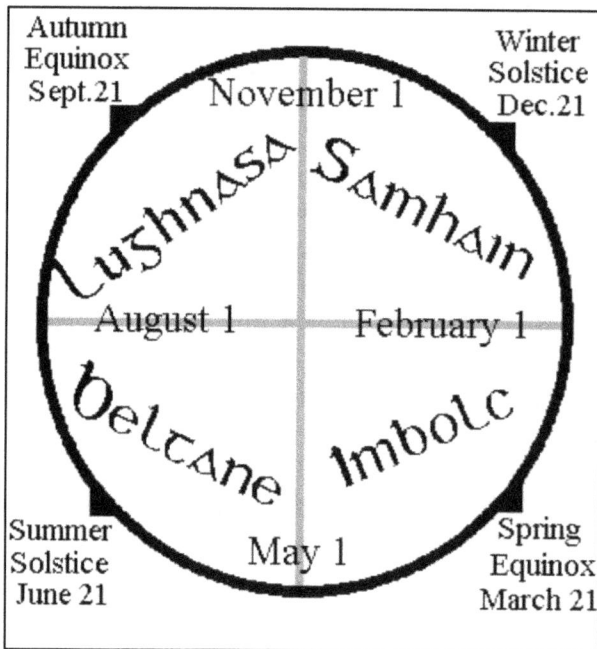

Gaelic Seasons

The tales provide a fuller understanding of who the people of Hy Kinsella were and why they made the decisions they did. Out of the thousands to choose from, a handful are included here. The second story, *The Cattle Raid of Cooley*, comes from the 12th-century *Book of Leinster* commissioned by Dermot MacMurrough, a direct ancestor of all Kinsellas. The original language of the story is Gaelic, and the best English translation was done in the middle of the 20th century by Thomas Kinsella.

Let us imagine a gathering during the 7th century (when monks were just beginning to record oral tales) in southern Leinster, the land of Hy Kinsella: [3]

Tuath righ's rath

It's the beginning of Samhain and, with the end of feasting signaled by the servants who start cleaning up, people turn to dancing, music, and games. The Samhain feast began at dusk in the house of Connor, the tuath righ, after a host of people from the surrounding countryside arrived with their winter tribute for him.

---

[3] Your authors have chosen to focus on battle stories (rather than the equally popular saints' stories) because they were common to the whole island. Saints' stories were specific to individual tuatha, each having its own local saint.

Much of the tribute had been consumed by those present that very night.

An elderly man, the royal file named Irial, sits by Connor and Mor, the bannrigh (female righ or queen). He looks around the circular assembly hall, lighted by torches on the walls and two fires full of glowing embers in the center of the room. These fires served to cook the meal, one still heating a great cauldron of stew while the other holds the remains of a roasting bull Connor had ordered butchered that day. Surrounding these fires, in a huge U shape, are long tables. Behind these are more tables, reaching all the way to the circular walls of the assembly hall. Near one of the two entrances to the hall sits the steward. As he pulls his green woolen cloak closer about him, he surveys all in the hall to ensure everything continues smoothly.

Activity teems amidst this collection of furniture and cookware. Children bob for apples in buckets of water to Irial's right. To his left a group sings songs while swaying back and forth. In front of him two fiddlers and a whistler play tunes beside the cook fires as a crowd dances around them. Farther back is the only settled area, where a group has gathered around to hear a lone harpist. Weaving throughout, hordes of little children run, faces disguised behind masks, pleading food for the Sidh, the fairy folk. "Little of that food will be seen by the fairies tonight," Irial thinks as he watches a child lift her mask to chew an apple.

"He's certainly entranced by something," Irial hears someone near him say. He turns to see Connor and Mor laughing. Mor pushes up the slight gold crown that sits on her brown hair, like the one her husband wears. She motions to one of the cup-bearers standing nearby, dressed in a green cloak, to fill up her husband's horn of wine.

"I said," Connor manages between chuckles, "don't you think it's time for a tale or two?" The righ, a man in his late forties, has long golden hair with only occasional gray showing. With skin as white as milk and eyes as blue as the sky, he looks the perfect Gaelic leader. Connor reaches over and picks up one of the last pieces of beef from the plate he has shared with Irial.

"I think it's past time," replies Irial. He quaffs some of the wine from the horn he shares with Connor and repeats, "It's past time, indeed." It was customary for the royal file and the tuath righ to share their food and drink. Irial stands up, carrying a branch from which numerous little silver bells hang, and slowly walks around the tables until he reaches the center of the room, between the two fires of glowing embers. The main cook and his two young helpers, each wearing leather aprons, vacate their positions by the fires to give him room. Once there, Irial rings the small bells, producing a wonderfully sweet sound, so that a hush envelops the room as people move to join their families, either on a bench or on the floor in the central U shape.

"Let the most beautiful choose the first tale tonight," says Irial as he turns to smile at bannrigh Mor. "What would you have, my bannrigh?"

She smiles coyly at the old man before sinking into thought. "Shall we start with a brief story? I'd like to hear about our own Leinster. Perhaps it wouldn't be out of place to hear about the Boruma tribute?"

"So it shall be," says Irial as he asks for a drinking horn and takes a sip from one of the many proffered. Immediately he begins the tale. "Long ago, Tuathal Techtmhar was Ard Righ of Ireland (76-106 A.D.) and he had two very pretty daughters, Fithir and Dairine. Now, before we go any further, let me make it perfectly clear that the Leinster righ at the time, Eochaidh Aaincheann, was not from Hy Kinsella."

Snickers arise from the audience for, already familiar with the story, they realize why Irial is disavowing any involvement by Hy Kinsella in this tale.

"It was this Leinster Righ who asked for the hand of Dairine. Tuathal, the Ard Righ, agreed, so the Leinster Righ married the Ard Righ's daughter and took her to his fortress. Unfortunately he soon tired of her and decided that her sister, Fithir, would be a better match for him. He brazenly returned to Tara, told Tuathal that Dairine had died and that he would like to ask for the hand of his other daughter, Fithir.

"Tuathal again agreed, so Eochaidh married Fithir and took her back to Leinster. How long this charade continued is not known, but one day Fithir discovered the evil truth that her sister, Dairine, was still alive but being kept as a servant. The shock of this discovery and all the shame it brought upon Fithir resulted in the poor girl's death. Upon hearing of Fithir's death, Dairine also died.

Fithir and Dairine
Two daughters of princely Tuathal;
Fithir died of shame,
Dairine died of her grief.[4]

"When Tuathal learned of the death of his two daughters and was informed that Eochaidh was the cause of their death, he became enraged. Preparations were made for a huge army to plunder and despoil the people of Leinster. Unfortunately for Eochaidh's people, Ulster and Connacht aided the Ard Righ in plundering, so Leinster was devastated. At the end of a year, the province finally submitted, and Eochaidh sent a messenger to Tuathal offering tribute in perpetuity to Tuathal and each Ard Righ who should succeed him as retribution for the death of the two ladies. The tribute, which was to be paid every other year, was exceedingly large:

Three score hundred[5] kine [cows]
Three score hundred ounces of silver
Three score hundred fine mantles
Three score hundred large hogs
Three score hundred wethers [rams]
Three score hundred braxen [brass] caldrons

Lowering his head, Irial finishes the tale by saying, "This tribute, called the Boruma tribute, is still in force today. Some years the Leinstermen pay the tribute submissively, but at other times they refuse and then much strife and conflict breaks out."

---

[4] An anonymous 9th-century author.
[5] "Three score hundred" equals 6,000.

Muted applause begins but quickly dies out. This tale of shame never goes over well in Leinster. With the opening tale completed, all those in the rath have reached the hall and filled it nearly to bursting.

"As you are all aware," Irial says surveying the crowd, "Tonight is the start of Samhain. Outside the walls of this rath spirits from the otherworld roam freely. Spirits such as those I will speak of tonight. Woe to anyone who comes across the spirit of one such as, say, Cuchulainn tonight!"

Excitement fills the air. Rarely does Irial tell such an important tale so early in the night. Of all the stories the highest grade of file, an ollamh, has to memorize (350 in all), the Ulster Cycle, which features the warrior Cuchulainn, is the most important. The Ulster Cycle, a series of over a dozen stories, describes the situation between Ulster and Connacht around the time of Christ. Among the nobles, it's a favorite.

"Early one morning, in the bedroom of the righ and bannrigh of Connacht, the bannrigh Maeve suddenly boasted she was more important than her husband Ailill, because she owned more material goods.[6] Ailill violently disagreed with this statement." Smiling at the audience, Irial says as an aside, "But we all know about bannrigh Maeve's competitive nature and temper."

Irial continues, "Of course bannrigh Maeve immediately, and I mean that very instant, ordered an inventory of all their belongings. Servants counted up their jewels, fine clothing and household items." Shrugging his shoulders, Irial says, "They had the same amount. When the servants counted the horses, sheep and pigs, they had the same amount.

However," and here Irial spreads his hands wide, emphasizing the reason for the tale, which the audience already knows, "Ailill had one thing bannrigh Maeve didn't, Finnbennach the white horned bull!" One almost feels the frustration bannrigh Maeve felt when she was bested by her husband. Irial describes the white horned bull as

---

[6] In Celtic countries (unlike elsewhere in Europe) women could amass more wealth and therefore more power than men.

"an amazing bull so big and strong that its like had never been seen before in Connacht."

Maeve on the Irish pound

Raising the pitch of his voice, Irial imitates bannrigh Maeve, "'Find me a bull better than the white horned bull,' she screamed at her servants. 'And do it quickly!'

"Well, it wasn't long before she discovered a better bull than the white horned one," Irial continues in his own voice again, "but this one lived in eastern Ulster, in the territory of Cooley. It was known as the brown bull of Cooley. Again, Maeve immediately sent out her servants, this time to ask the owner, a man named Daire, for the loan of his bull for a year. For this she would pay handsomely."

Connor lifts his bull horn for a sip of wine but spills some on his white linen tunic. Mor rolls her eyes at him and covers the stain with his red silk cloak. To keep it in place she adjusts the gold brooch on his shoulder. Connor simply grins back at her

High ranking noble's brooch

66

before turning to look around at his people. They are well fed, he muses, and quite content. To his right, lounging on couches facing Irial are Connor's hostages, the sons of nobles, along with guards. Just behind them are nine pipe players, each wearing a speckled glossy cloak with fine silver embroidery, who have already been busy today. On the other side of the hall sit the jugglers with their balls of silver and long darts. Just behind them sits one of the door-keepers, straining to hear all Irial has to say. Nearer to the fire are Connor's three jesters, wearing cloaks of gray. They are the only ones Irial has to fear for they are impudent enough to interrupt even the royal file. Just in front of the righ is his champion, still chewing on the hero's portion of beef, and beside him sits the local abbot staring very intently at the royal file. The abbot has spent the last several years copying down tales Irial has told him.

"When Daire heard of Maeve's proposition, he considered it most generous and accepted the offer," Irial continues while reaching for a flagon of beer. He takes a small sip as ripples of laughter crisscross the room. It's customary for Gaels to seal any deal with a drink. "If bannrigh Maeve's messengers had left then, this tale would never have been composed, but they didn't. They stayed at Daire's house overnight and during the ensuing discussion mentioned that it was fortunate Daire had accepted the offer because, if he hadn't, the Connachtmen would have taken the bull by force. Upon hearing this, Daire became indignant and announced, 'Under no circumstances will my bull be loaned to Connacht.'

"We all know Maeve well enough to guess her response. 'That bull will come to Connacht even if it takes all of Ireland to do it!' she shouted. She and Ailill gathered an army composed of forces from several of Ireland's provinces, including one from Leinster, and began marching towards Ulster on the Monday after the beginning of Samhain. As we all know, the Leinstermen had a reputation of being not only fierce fighters but also efficient soldiers."

The people erupt in a short cheer for their province.

"I'm certain they were renowned not only for their fierceness," suddenly shouts out one of the jesters, "but also for their humor!"

Irial smiles and continues, "As the army got under way, Maeve observed that the Leinstermen set up camp before any other soldiers, they ate before others had cooked their food and, by the time the others were eating, the Leinster harpers were playing. This efficiency disturbed Maeve. She believed the Leinster soldiers would get all the credit for the Connacht army's victory so she wished to have them sent back, but Ailill, who was originally from Leinster, had another idea. He suggested they divide the Leinstermen and scatter them among the rest of the army. This was done."

Connor, the tuath righ, looks past his young wife to the abbot beside her. "Are you getting all this?" he whispers.

The short bald monk turns and with an enchanted smile replies, "I'll probably need a brush up from Irial as I write down certain parts over the next few weeks. But I think I know most of it word for word."

The abbot isn't unusual. Everyone listening, excluding only the youngest, has heard this tale many times before and knows it well. Every file knows the thousands of lines by heart and, if he deviated far from the correct story, would reap the scorn of all those listening, possibly even losing his position as file. There is no fear that this royal file will forget his lines.

Irial continues with some background information. "The decision to go to war with Ulster might seem a dangerous one, because at that time the Ulster army was considered the most powerful in Ireland. The decision to attack them was not to be taken lightly. However, Maeve had special knowledge about the Ulster army. She was aware of the "pangs of Ulster," debilitating pains lasting five days and four nights or five nights and four days, from which all adult Ulster males periodically suffered because of a curse placed on them years ago. She timed her invasion for Samhain, when the Ulstermen would experience these pangs. Maeve believed her army could march through Ulster, seize the prize bull, and return back to Connacht before the Ulster warriors had recovered. What she had overlooked, however, were the few exceptions to those who experienced the pangs: women and boys under the age of 18. She would suffer for this oversight. An Ulster boy named Cuchulainn was only 17."

"Cuchulainn from his earliest years showed unusual prowess in all forms of fighting. He was an excellent swordsman, phenomenal with the spear and the best horseman in Ulster. He showed such promise at an early age that it was decided he should receive training from Scathac, the shadowy one, a woman whose prowess as a teacher of martial arts was legendary. When Cuchulainn was seven years old, he sought out Scathac, who dwelled on the islands off the coast of Scotland, and she agreed to instruct him along with another Gael, Ferdiad. When his training was finished, Cuchulainn returned to Ulster, now superior to any warrior in Ireland, England or indeed in all of Europe. Ferdiad returned to his own province, Connacht. The two were to become life-long friends with a bond as close as brothers."

Now that the main character, Cuchulainn, had entered the story, the listeners become more intent. Cuchulainn exemplifies honor, courage, independence, loyalty, truth and fairness, all qualities highly prized by the ancient Gaels.

"The Connacht force finally reached Ulster, where they came upon a message, 'Come no further!' This they ignored. The army was given another written warning, and Ailill sent two chariots to investigate the road up ahead. When the chariots did not return, a party was sent to search for them, only to discover that they had been killed. Cuchulainn was nearby. As the army moved along, stragglers or those sent out to plunder the countryside frequently didn't return. The number of missing Connacht soldiers grew so staggering that Maeve was forced to sue for peace with stipulations. She and Cuchulainn came to an agreement that, while the Connacht army could continue searching for Daire's brown bull, they would stop plundering Ulster. In return, Cuchulainn would take on any Connacht challengers in single combat, thus reducing the number of dead suffered by Connacht."

By this point in the story some of the younger children have grown restless. It was too long to expect them to remain quiet, especially with all the excitement generated by the feast. With regret, a few of the mothers walk them out of the assembly hall and into another house nearby where they play. Any child who makes noise during the telling of the tale is quickly silenced and removed.

"Every morning Cuchulainn woke and took on the Connacht challengers, one at a time. He fought in gorges, woodlands, meadows, among rocks and rushing rivers. He won against every foe, but eventually the brown bull was found. The army began its return trip to Connacht. The Ulstermen, still helpless from their pangs, put all their reliance on Cuchulainn, hoping he could slow the army just long enough for them to recover. When the Connacht army reached the border between Ulster and Connacht, Maeve couldn't resist trying one last strategy against the boy who had frustrated her so, the one she had grown to hate more than anyone else in the world, Cuchulainn.

She knew of Cuchulainn's boyhood friend, Ferdiad, whom he thought of as a brother. Maeve, by suggesting Ferdiad was a coward, forced the Connacht warrior to fight Cuchulainn.

"Ferdiad stepped into the ford to challenge Cuchulainn, who turned away. He had no wish to fight his great friend. Soon Cuchulainn pleaded for Ferdiad to step away." This is the climax of the story, where so many of the cultural traits loved by the Gaels were exhibited by both warriors: Ferdiad, unable to avoid his fate because of honor, and Cuchulainn, unable to avoid his fate because of loyalty to Ulster. As every Gael loved, it was to end in sadness.

"At a river ford between the provinces, the two close friends fought. The battle lasted several days and, with the coming of each dusk, the combatants retired

Cuchulainn and Ferdiad

to opposite sides of the ford. During the first evening they joyfully shared their meal before separating. During the second evening they shared their healing medicines. During the third evening they remained apart. On the fourth day Cuchulainn killed Ferdiad."

Irial pauses momentarily, just long enough for listeners to reflect. Pride and honor caused the demise of one and terrible guilt for the other.

He continues in a lighter tone. "While the battle lasted between the two champions, the pangs of Ulster ended, and the Ulstermen collected on Cuchulainn's side of the ford to watch the fight. To have stopped the fight would, of course, have besmirched the honor of both combatants. After Ferdiad breathed his last, the Ulster army fell on the Connachtmen. A savage battle resulted in which the Connacht army retreated into their homeland to which the brown bull had already been dispatched.

"The brown bull, days ahead of the army, finally met the white horned bull of Connacht. Both bulls charged and a ferocious fight ensued. It lasted all day and all night. When morning came, the army of Connacht saw the brown bull of Ulster coming towards them with the mangled remains of their white-horned bull hanging from his horns. He headed towards Ulster and, upon reaching it, died.

"A peace between Connacht and Ulster, which lasted seven years, followed this battle. But we know Maeve," continues Irial as he rolls his eyes. "Throughout those seven years she seethed over the humiliation her army had suffered, and she blamed the entire disaster on Cuchulainn. Maeve spent those years plotting revenge. When all her preparations were complete, she again led an army into Ulster. She resorted to magic to get Cuchulainn alone, and then she had several of her warriors attack him simultaneously. (She was not foolish enough to agree to single combat this time.) Cuchulainn held them off for a time, but eventually he was mortally wounded by a spear thrown by Lugaid of Munster.

"Sagging from the blow, Cuchulainn asked of Lugaid, 'I am thirsty, I would like a drink from the nearby lake.' Lugaid accepted this proposal as long as Cuchulainn promised to come back. 'I will promise this, but if I cannot come back myself,' Cuchulainn said, 'I shall call you.'

"Cuchulainn staggered over to the lake, fell down at its edge and drank deeply from it. Finally, too weak to return, he dragged himself over to a stone pillar standing close by to which he tied himself. He would meet his enemies on his feet as an Irish champion should. Motioning with his hand, he called them over before grasping the handle of his trusty sword, whispering, 'I have been the best I could be.'

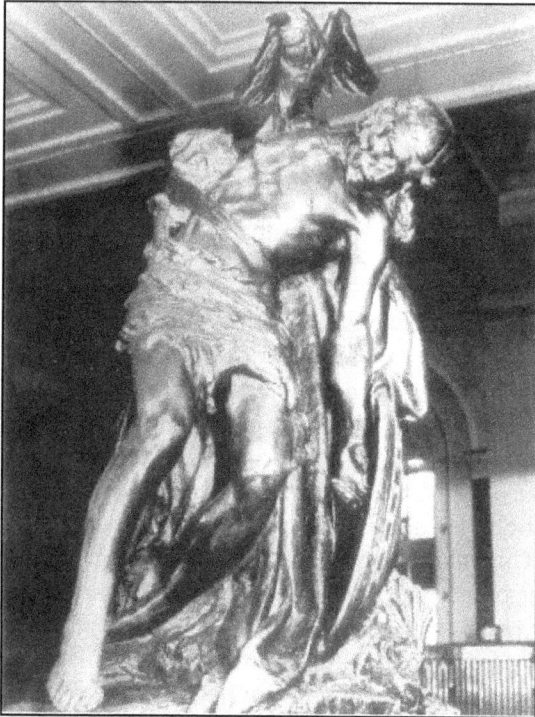

Cuchulainn Statue

"The Connacht soldiers crept nearby and formed a circle around the stone. They watched Cuchulainn closely, but even the bravest of them was afraid to step within reach of that terrible sword that had killed so many of their compatriots. Then they saw a raven flutter down and land on his shoulder. The Ulster champion was dead. At this point, Lugaid of Munster very cautiously approached the stone. Seizing Cuchulainn by the hair, he cut off his head. Simultaneously, Cuchulainn's sword hand jerked in a final spasm and cut off Lugaid's hand. Knowing that the Ulster army could not be far away, the Connacht soldiers swiftly fled toward home.

"Shortly afterwards, the Ulster righ and his warriors arrived at the scene and were devastated by the sight of their dead champion. Immediately setting off after the Connacht soldiers, they caught up with them near the River Liffey where they wreaked a terrible vengeance. Soon after, the walls of the Ulster righ's house sported many new trophies. Most prominent of all was the head of Lugaid of Munster."

Connor's hall erupts in clapping and cheering while many begin discussing the story, reliving its best moments.

Irial, showing signs of weariness, pauses for a sip of beer from a horn proffered to him. As a young file, Irial would go well into the night telling his tales, but age has crept up on him. The audience fears he is done for the night, so they begin calling out names of other stories to encourage him to continue. Irial looks to Connor. "Could we have just one more?" asks the righ. Irial smiles warmly at his friend and then turns suddenly.

"What's that?" asks Irial. "Did I hear someone say Cuchulainn was the bravest Irish warrior ever?" He pauses and the room quickly grows quiet again. No one wants to miss a word spoken by the royal file. "Perhaps. But perhaps there would be another soul out tonight who might dispute that claim."

"Finn mac Cool!" someone shouts.

"Exactly," smiles Irial in the direction of the shout. "Finn mac Cool, a Leinstermen himself a few hundred years after Cuchulainn. Perhaps I should tell about his death. It is the proper night to tell such tales, after all."

The audience shouts encouragement. Finn mac Cool, like Cuchulainn, was a supreme warrior, but he is preferred by the common people. His stories, which are legion, make up what is known as the

Fenian Cycle, named after his band of warriors, the Fianna, who lived in the 3rd century A.D.

"Before I begin," Irial says, "perhaps someone could refresh my memory." The audience laughs for they know his memory is unmarred like the finest gold. He looks to the younger ones, who need more stimulation, on the floor about him. "What was the name of the Ard Righ who ruled over the Fianna?"

One young brown-haired boy, not more than four, stands up and immediately recites, "Cormac mac Art would be his name. He ruled from Tara and was one of the best Ard Righs ever."

"Ah, yes, that's right," mumbles Irial as though to himself. "Now another, why was he the best righ ever?"

This time a girl with eyes of ocean blue and blonde hair braided with a blue ribbon jumps to her feet. She is almost six. "He made lots of new laws, good ones, and he also made the Fianna stronger."

"He did, he did," nods Irial. "Thank you. And Finn was their leader, as I remember. He was a good man, I suppose. Of course he must have been a good man for he was from Leinster." He scratches his head for a moment and then turns to another group of children, asking, "But who exactly were these Fianna?"

A boy of three starts to stand, but overcome by the expectant gaze of the audience sits back down while his five-year-old sister stands up instead. "The Fianna were warriors from many different clans all over Ireland," she proudly says. "They were the Ard Righ's army. They also had to protect Ireland from invaders across the sea, for which they had look-outs all along the coast. If any boats came, the lookouts lit fire signals and also sent word by runners." She sits down amid the beaming smiles of her parents and older siblings near her.

"They certainly sound important," suggests Irial. "The Ard Righ's royal troops were needed to protect the island from invasion. I suppose they were skilled. Could anyone join? Could, for example, a lazy farmer join for a month or two?" He fastens his gaze on the children of Connor, the tuath righ.

A boy of eight, pulling his red cloak embroidered with gold spiral designs away from his feet, stands up and immediately says,

"There were several conditions for entry into the Fianna." Obviously reciting from memory, he continues, "First, any entrant had to disown his clan so they could not be . . . compensated if the entrant were killed but also so that no one else could gain . . . compensation from the clan if the entrant were to damage anything or anyone. Second. . ." The boy falters for a moment. As Irial looks about for another to call on, the boy suddenly continues in a spate of words, "Second, the entrant had to have memorized the twelve books of poetry." The boy composes himself before resuming, "Third, the entrant had to be able to defend himself while standing in a hole up to his belly while nine Fianna threw their spears at him from a distance. He would have only his shield and a hazel rod to defend himself."

"That is very good," interrupts Irial, "but let us see if any of your siblings can finish off the list."

Immediately the boy's younger sister stands up. "Fourth, they must be able to jump a pole as high as their chest while running," she states in a high clear voice, "and then stoop under one at knee-level without breaking stride. Finally, and this last was a trial Finn made up himself . . .," she pauses to shyly look around at the audience, proud to have added this extra piece of information, "Finally, any new entrant had to race one of the Fianna for a distance of over a mile . . . with a two-inch thorn stuck in the bottom of their foot . . . and they had to retrieve the thorn before finishing . . . and win the race." Her face flushes with excitement as she sits down.

"Well, that does sound right to me," exclaims Irial. "Any entrant who could manage to do all this successfully was accepted into the Fianna. So the Fianna were the very best in Ireland, and they looked up to Finn as the best among them. Not only were his fighting skills sharply honed, but he also exemplified generosity." Irial recites from memory:

If the brown leaves had been gold that the wood let fall,
if the white waves had been silver,

Finn would have given them all away,
all away.[7]

"He was also the wisest of men. He had the unusual gift of a sage's knowledge. He obtained this as a child when he caught the Salmon of Knowledge. While cooking the fish for his teacher, a wise druid, he burned his thumb on the fish's side, and, when he put his thumb into his mouth, the knowledge of the salmon was imparted to him. Finn and his Fianna were extraordinary. It's too bad neither exists any longer. This is the story of their demise."

Pausing for a moment to remember the first lines of the tale, Irial begins quietly, "As Ireland's Ard Righ, Cormac mac Art, was dying (268 A.D.), he gave orders not to bury his body at Newgrange, where the righs of Tara had been buried until then. Some say Cormac had the gift of second sight, the ability to see the future. He knew Ireland would become a Christian nation, thanks to St. Patrick, and he did not want to be buried at a pagan gravesite. His officers ignored his order and took his body to Newgrange. As they attempted to cross the Boyne River, it rose so high that the burial party could not proceed. They tried three more times, and each time the raging waters turned them back. They made one final attempt, and this time as they entered the river the waters snatched the body from the bearers and carried it down river to Ros na Riogh[8] where he was then buried.

"Upon Cormac's death, his son Cairpre became Ard Righ of Ireland. Shortly after gaining the throne he decided to demand the Boruma tribute. The Leinster righ, Breasal Belach, refused to pay it, however." Irial uncharacteristically pauses slightly to catch his breath and take a sip of beer. With concern growing on the faces of both Connor and Mor, Irial continues.

"Cairpre asked Finn to prepare the Fianna for a battle in Leinster. But Finn was from Leinster, and to fight his own people was not an easy thing to do. He struggled over which was the more honorable cause, to follow his clan or to follow his Ard Righ. He collected his

---

[7] An anonymous 9th-century author.
[8] Today's Rosnaree, which lies just east of Newgrange.

men at the site of Garbhthamhnach,[9] and on the day before the battle Finn and his men joined the Leinstermen. The next day, in a hard-fought battle the Leinstermen, because of the addition of the Fianna, were victorious and did not have to pay tribute. It is said some 9,000 men were left dead on the field, including three sons of the Ard Righ himself. After this, Cairpre gave command of the Fianna to another."

At this point, a young boy, one of Connor's sons, runs from where his father sits to the center of the hall between the two beds of red, burning coals. He proudly holds out a gold armband for Irial. Irial takes the band from the boy, pats him on the head, and then looks up to Connor. "I appreciate your concern, my lord, but the tale is not through."[10]

"Many years later (in 283 A.D.) Cairpre feuded with the Munster righ. Realizing Cairpre could draw on a larger army given enough time, the Munster righ marched on Tara. He had with him Finn's now small contingent of 3,500 men, because Finn was his father-in-law. Finn proceeded to the battle site at Gowran (just east of Tara) to meet Cairpre who had 10,000."

Irial paused to address his audience. "Of course Finn knew he could not win against such impossible odds. Many of his own Fianna were opposing him, but he could expect them to hang back and fight only grudgingly. Honor drove Finn on.

"It was a terrible battle with many losses on both sides. On that day the most valiant fighter was Finn's grandson, Oscar. He slew dozens of men, until at last he came face to face with the Ard Righ, Cairpre himself. He cast his spear at Cairpre and it passed right through his body to the other side. Cairpre struck out at Oscar with his final gasp of strength and the blow to Oscar was also mortal. The dying Oscar saw Cairpre's men set the Ard Righ's helmet on a pillar to fool his army into believing Cairpre was still alive so, drawing

---

[9] Cruel Grave, where the two daughters of Tuathal were buried. Their misfortune was the cause of the original Boruma tribute.

[10] Connor had asked Irial for another story, for which he was obliged to pay. By paying now, he acknowledged Irial was done, allowing him to rest. Armbands of precious metal or rings were often used as payment.

upon his last bit of strength, Oscar threw a stone that struck the helmet and broke it to pieces. Oscar now fell to the earth, dead from the effort.

"Some of the Fianna carried Oscar to where Finn stood. There amid the tumult of battle Finn gave a great cry of anguish and raised the war cry of the Fianna. He said a few words over the body of his grandson before he again plunged into the thick of battle. He was still a strong man though his hair and beard were white as flax, and in his shining war coat and helmet of gold he was an awesome figure to all his enemies.

"He killed many warriors before at last coming upon the five sons of Urgriu, his mortal enemies. When Finn saw them he dropped his battered, broken shield and went to meet them with his great sword grasped in both hands. He perished that day at the battle of Gowran along with the might of the Fianna."

Irial finishes amidst thunderous applause and cheers. The tales of Finn had already multiplied since they were first told, but even Irial doesn't realize how many more stories of Finn's famous exploits are still to be born.

Unlike the Ulster Cycle, which was told only by trained filid, the Fenian Cycle was told frequently by local storytellers. Their untrained memories were imperfect, which led to distortions of the original tales. Unlike the filid, they also weren't above altering the original stories. Numerous versions of the same story resulted (in some, Finn never dies but goes to sleep to return again someday; in others, he's killed while hunting), and new ones sprang up from fertile imaginations. Over the centuries, the feats of Finn grew dramatically in the retelling of his exploits. In later stories he could hurl boulders of gigantic size and fought and subdued giants and dragons with ease. He was transformed from a man with exceptional physical skills to a giant possessing supernatural capabilities.

Connor's young son runs down again with another golden armband for Irial, but this time Irial waves him off. "I have already received my gift from you, bountiful Connor. Another is too much."

Connor stands now and quietly says, "I will not take back what I have freely given."

Irial pauses, looking at his righ, before responding. "Then your gift is mine to give." Slowly he takes the gold from the youth and passes it on to the cook, whose eyes light up like the embers before him. "You have served the clan well this night. Accept this from your righ as a token of his appreciation."

His old bones now tired, Irial raises his file branch and walks out into the night amid one final round of applause and cheering. For others, the night will continue with a professional harper, more tales from other storytellers and socializing. Only in the wee hours of the morning will things calm down enough for people to begin to sleep in the assembly hall. None dare leave the rath before the first light of dawn, when preparations will begin for the huge feast to be held on one of the nearby hills attended not only by those here tonight but also by those being housed at each of the nobles under Connor's rule. The entire clan will come together to celebrate Samhain.[11]

---

[11] The Irish day started at dusk rather than at midnight so Samhain stretched, as every day did, from one dusk to the next.

The Ui Cinnsealaigh Clan

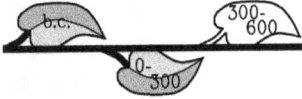

abraid Loingsech and his soldiers landed in Wexford and seized the throne of Leinster at Dinn Rig. However, the descendants of this army settled in many areas outside of Leinster, including Connacht and Munster. At one time they controlled parts of Meath that included Tara, and Leinster tradition states that their righs once ruled over that royal residence: "The king of Ui Cinnsealaigh [anglicized as Hy Kinsella] of the spoils has control of the house of Tara; this is the truth for all time, for it is the house of the king of Leinster."[1]

Around the 4th century, after the death of Cormac mac Art, the two groups that would come to dominate Leinster, the Hy Kinsella and the Hy Dunlaing, migrated from the west through the Gowran pass into Leinster. In a series of battles, they defeated the Hy Bairche, who had controlled South Leinster since the 1st century. The two new groups then peacefully agreed to divide Leinster, the Hy Dunlaing taking the northern half and the Hy Kinsella taking the southern half. The dividing line between the two territories was the present border of County Kildare and County Carlow. The Hy Dunlaing stronghold was at Naas, in north-central Kildare; the Hy Kinsella's was at Rathvilly, situated on the northern border of County Carlow. These two groups occupied the richest farmland in

---

[1] From the ancient Irish *Book of Rights*.

Leinster while the groups they subdued were removed to bog land and mountainous areas.

At this time another group was also expanding, the Hy Neill of Ulster. In a series of battles they took control of Ulster from the Ulaid, the people of Cuchulainn, and then expanded south into Meath. They became the most powerful clan in Ireland, eventually extending their control to include the royal site of Tara, previously ruled by Leinster. This set the stage for the bloody encounters between the Leinstermen and the Hy Neill, encounters that involved the illustrious family of Enna Kinsella.

In 365 the battle of Croghan Hill was fought between the Leinster righ, Enna, and Ireland's Ard Righ, Eochaidh Muighmheadhoin of the Hy Neill, a very successful campaigner. The annalists recorded only the broad outlines of this encounter, but based on other documented battles we can fill in the details.

In the spring of 365 a tuath righ under the control of Enna in the Leinster territory of Offaly refused to pay tribute to Enna. The Ard Righ Eochaidh, aware that several other tuatha in Leinster would refuse to pay the next installment of their tribute to Enna if the rebellious Offaly righ was supported by the Hy Neill, called a war council to do just that. Eochaidh needed little excuse to attack Enna, because he held Enna responsible for the death of one of his relatives years before.[2] All the tuath righs of Meath who paid tribute to Eochaidh

---

[2] An early Leinster dynast, Cuilenn of the Ui Labrada, slew a Hy Neill man Ciar Culdub, who was apparently under royal protection. Cuilenn was dispossessed of his lands as a result, and these were forfeit to the ard righ. Cuilenn, however, was granted land in recompense by Enna Kinsella, who later came to dominate south Leinster, which strongly suggests that Enna put Cuilenn up to the murder in the first place.

arrived at his fort and agreed to support the rebellious Offaly righ in Leinster. A battle between Eochaidh and Enna seemed inevitable. The discussion then turned to the number of warriors each Meath tuath could supply, where and when the force should come together, and how the army should proceed into Leinster. Meanwhile, Enna, unaware of the danger about to surface, began assembling a war party of his own to raid the lands of his rebellious Offaly under-righ.

The Meath tuath righs, upon returning home from Eochaidh's war council, sent out messengers to their nobles and assembled their allotment of fighting men and women.[3] Within a week they were marching to the agreed upon meeting point, a cairn in southern Meath. Eochaidh had not asked for all the fighters the province could muster because by Meath law he was able only to command each fighter for six weeks every three years.[4] He had to leave some of the warriors at home for use in the following years, so the number to call out was always a gamble. The attacking righ had no idea how many his opponent would muster. Eochaidh had decided that 100 horse riders (all nobility) and 500 foot soldiers (mainly from the free class) would be enough.

A week later Eochaidh, now in southern Meath by the border of Leinster, scanned with satisfaction the army waiting at the cairn. Almost 2,000 people were gathered; along with the 600 warriors were numerous servants escorting packhorses carrying tents, bedding and rations of bread, meal, dried meat and milk. Eochaidh gave marching orders and the force left the

---

[3] Not until 697 were women exempted from battle through the influence of St. Adamnan at the synod of Tara (before 697 women were chosen only if a family had no sons). While this synod granted them protection from battle, it also stripped women of the right to inherit land (except in special situations) because they no longer defended it.

[4] This agreement varied from province to province and from righ to righ depending on how powerful the leader was.

cairn, snaking its way over the border into Leinster towards the tuath of the rebellious Offaly righ. It was late June, with harvest still seven or eight weeks away, which worked well for Meath because the foot soldiers could not be kept in service during harvest time.

Long before the Meath army entered Leinster, Enna had learned of its intentions. He had already sent word that the province was under attack and that warriors should meet in the territory of Offaly. Constrained by time, he could count on collecting only 80 horse riders and 400 foot soldiers. While these forces were being assembled, Enna dispatched a messenger envoy to Eochaidh. The envoy, wearing traditional dress and carrying a white staff in one hand and a sword in the other (symbolic of the options, peace or war), leapt onto his barebacked horse and galloped off. He rode alone without fear of being harmed. (The code of chivalry romanticized by French writers in the 13th and 14th centuries comes from the Celts.) Days later, after meeting with the Meath righ at the rebellious Offaly righ's fort, he packed away his white staff and carried his sword aloft through the fortified Meath camp. The messenger, upon returning to Enna, related that Eochaidh was not about to forgo battle unless Enna submitted to him and paid tribute.

After a long march north from Hy Kinsella, the Leinster army encountered Eochaidh's army. Since it was late in the day both forces set up camp less than a mile apart, Enna on Croghan Hill and Eochaidh surrounding the Offaly righ's fort. In the following exchange of messengers, Eochaidh demanded that Enna submit to him while Enna demanded that Eochaidh vacate Leinster. Neither side was willing to capitulate, so both set up night pickets around their perimeter. Night battles were a last resort, however, since the confusion they engendered was too risky.

Croghan Hill where Enna's men camped

The next morning, before dawn, trumpets and horns blared from both encampments to signal wake-up, troop displacement, emblem bearers to the front, and numerous other orders. Nervously the men and women fell in behind their nobles, some drinking voraciously, all having packed enough food for that day in a satchel hung at their side. Through the dim early morning light, across an open field with a gentle upgrade in favor of the Leinster army, the nobles from the two provinces faced each other. Many pulled clothing tight around them to ward off the chill.

Each tuath's druid stood at the front of the battle line, next to the tuath righ, wearing a large cloak in the color of his clan. Before them stood their warriors armed with spears mounted on white hazel. The soldiers wore their long white shirts with splendid cloaks colored according to clans. In one hand most held their polished blue-green swords while the other was protected by the red bronze bosses in the center of the many-colored shields.

Since the Gaels believed that courage flowed down the generations, the druids' voices filled the air with heroic deeds done in the past by ancestors of the clan. They praised the warriors of today for their courage and prowess, and they lamented those who had been slain in the past. The clansmen remembered why they had come to fight: for their families, their history, and the land from which neither was divisible. They listened quietly with only their shields, weapons, and courage. Finally, they prayed with their druids for victory.

As the first rays of the sun streaked across the soft Irish grass, Enna's champion stepped into the path between the two forces and shouted, "Ho, I am Donagh, descended from Labraid Loingsech, renowned warrior of Leinster, and a match for any 100 Meath men. At the age of 16, having lost my shield, I stopped a sword thrust with my left arm and then took the said sword to kill my opponent." A cheer erupted from many of the Leinstermen, aware of their champion's history, as they pounded their shields with their spear shafts or swords. Standing in family groups, fathers with their sons (or perhaps daughters) behind them, uncles with their nephews at their shoulder, cousins side by side, they quieted quickly, knowing what was to come.

Running out a few steps from Meath's side, a huge man with a great sword hanging from his side, Meath's champion, returned, "I am Murtagh, descendant of Conn of the Hundred Battles, the most renowned warrior of all Ireland. When I was the age of 18, a noble of Munster cast a spear at me in battle. I caught it and threw it back, impaling both him and the Munster Champion." Meath, to encourage its champion, now raised its own fury of sound.

"In Leinster, we've heard of you and your assorted skills," shouted the Leinster champion again. "We hear you prefer to perfect your skills not on the battle field but in the cattle barn instead." (Milking the cattle was a woman's job.) Again a thunderous din erupted from Enna's men amid howls of laughter. They were forgetting the morning chill.

"In Meath, we hear more about your righ than about you. Enna's specialty, when he's not milking the cattle, is mounting them. We hear many a Leinsterman can apparently claim descent from such a coupling." With each successful gibe by their champion, the warriors in the ranks grew bolder, keener for battle. This was the enemy. They had reason to hate them. Finally, when Enna judged they were at battle pitch, the Leinster righ called his champion back.

Seeing this signal, every righ, including Enna, turned to his fighters. Raising his voice, he shouted, "Our people are under attack! If we lose here, nothing can stop Meath from ravaging Leinster, from pillaging your house, your children. We must stop them here." Enna paused for breath and looked across the field. Turning back, he continued, "If we win, you will be remembered forever for these deeds. Your children will listen endlessly to your heroics on this day, and their children, and their children. You will never die." As he turned to face the Meath army, his druid began shouting the clan war cry. The men and women grew heady amid the countless trumpet blasts, horn blasts, and war cries. The situation was mirrored at the bottom of the hill among Eochaidh's men.

Suddenly Enna's hereditary standard bearer raced out ahead of the throng through the still wet grass shouting "Abu Enna." He was followed immediately by Enna and the specially chosen band of warriors who surrounded him. The flag, with its golden sun, fluttered violently in the charge as the rest of the Leinster force rushed after it. Near the bottom of the hill, among the dozen or so Meath flags (one for each tuath righ), Enna could make out Eochaidh's, a righ sitting on a throne with a golden lily in his right hand. The flags served two purposes: warriors separated from their clan could quickly identify in which direction they needed to return, and druids, watching the battle from a distance, carefully noted all the deeds of valor, as well as cowardice, done by the nobles whom the flags identified. These exploits would be recited over and over at future fairs and assemblies.

From behind the Leinstermen a hail of stones erupted as the slingers let loose their missiles. Moments later the crash of stones on upraised shields could be heard along with screams and moans among the unfortunate who had been hit. The missiles from the Meath slingers also rained on the Leinster force. The slingers, not wanting to hit their own people racing towards the enemy, now drew their swords and proceeded into the melee. As the forces came within 100 paces of each other, they slowed to a trot. Taking careful aim at an enemy, those in the front ranks let loose their spears like a shower of whistling nails and then ran pell-mell across the final yards of green grass while shouting and brandishing their swords. The nobles, riding horses and surrounded by their clans, clashed into the enemy with swords swinging in great bloody arcs from side to side. Wheeling and charging again, they were protected by their clan, their brothers, sisters, and fathers. A white fog quickly cloaked the brilliant morning sun as the chalk and lime covering the shields was shaken free.

Some of the foot soldiers on both sides, moments before encountering the ferocious tide of humanity, coolly went down on one knee and braced their spears securely on the ground to impale the enemy, but most, especially those new to battle, simply charged ahead, unable to control their high-strung frenzy. Those foot soldiers not armed with swords were armed with javelins. Like ghosts in the chalky fog, they made rapid and irregular advances into the ranks of the enemy as they whirled the javelin rapidly around their head, appearing from nowhere to unleash their weapons with such force that they could penetrate through the body of an enemy and even into armor. Immediately after loosing this terror, they disappeared into the confusion of their own side and began pulling back the cord attached to the end of their javelin. Over and over they repeated this maneuver. Even soldiers who had lost their weapons were a danger for they were remarkably swift, able to leap up behind riders, pulling them off their horses and into the peril below.

From the beginning of the battle, many freemen from both sides chose to flee the confusion and observe from a safer vantage point. The Irish nobility, aware that their druids were watching, preferred glory. Enna, surrounded by his best fighters, hacked his way towards Eochaidh's fluttering banner while the fighting around him ebbed and flowed. The battle wasn't the ponderously slow mass of close contact fighting often portrayed today but instead a fluid dance with advances and retreats constantly weaving the two sides together. Only the druids, at a safe distance, could appreciate the macabre beauty of the event without suffering injury.

Finally Enna's core of fighters met Eochaidh's core and the intensity of the attacks increased dramatically. All knew that if either provincial righ was killed, the battle was won. One instant, the blade of Eochaidh's champion had snaked its way toward Enna only to be blocked by a well-timed shield thrust. The next instant, one of the Leinster nobles had somehow managed to force his way into the inner circle of Eochaidh only to be cut down as he prepared to deliver a killing thrust. Suddenly a javelin snuck past the defense of Eochaidh's guard and an instant too late his shield came up. The metal point entered the Ard Righ's chest and protruded grotesquely from the other side. Upon seeing Eochaidh crumple, Enna's men fell back and the fighting around this center point slowed, all looking to see if Eochaidh survived. The Meath righ's banner was allowed to fall as Eochaidh's entourage lashed their shields together to carry the body from the battlefield. As comprehension came to both sides, the Meath warriors rushed from the field with the Leinster warriors pursuing only for a short way. By mid-afternoon, Enna stood victorious on the hill.

The physicians, who had been working on those able to crawl to the outskirts of the battlefield throughout the morning, were now able to help the more seriously wounded who were arriving on sledges. They cleaned and sewed up wounds, applying poultices where necessary. When they finished working on one person, they quickly moved to the next closest wounded, regardless of which province they hailed from, the lack of uniforms making this difficult to discern anyway. Out of the 480 Leinstermen, fifteen were killed and another sixty wounded seriously enough to require a physician.

On the Leinster side, those not wounded stumbled over to the fluttering banners of their clans, sat down on the beaten grass, and slowly ate their rations while listening to mournful tunes from their righ's musicians. All the captured Meath soldiers, mainly the wounded, were kept as slaves. Prisoners not wounded were fettered with iron manacles but without causing pain.[5] All prisoners were treated with the utmost hospitality.

Enna returned to the top of the hill to watch the fleeing Meath army and to decide his next move. He would raid in Meath and take as many cattle as possible. While he was instructing his scouts to search for cattle across the border in Meath, Eochaidh's captured druid was brought before him.

"What say you now, druid, that the tables have turned?" Enna asked. "Only yesterday Meath thought to raid in Leinster!"

---

[5] Under Irish law a penalty existed if pain was inflicted.

Croghan in County Offaly

The historian of antiquity, Keating, has the druid respond, "Thou wouldst never conquer from this hill on which I am, if I were to live." Upon this, Enna laughed loudly and transfixed him with his spear. "Alas," said the druid, "that is a foul laugh and it is this that will be given as a name to thy posterity after thee for ever." Enna was therefore given the name Cinnsealaigh (Kinsella), meaning "foul laugh." Another meaning often given is "foul head."[6]

The battle, fought near the border of Meath in Northern Leinster, demonstrates Enna was powerful enough to lead his army across Hy Dunlaing territory and defeat the powerful Hy Neill forces in their own backyard. Enna went on to dominate

---

[6] Dennis King, a renowned expert in Gaelic languages, stated in a personal communication on the meaning of Kinsella: "The Kinsella surname is not derived from Old Irish cinn (head) and salach (foul or dirty). Rather, the Old Irish word cennselach is an adjective meaning dominating, ascendant, valorous, and strife from the noun cennsel (modern cinseal)." Dennis also noted that when Keating claimed the surname meant "foul laugh," he must have been thinking of "gean salach."

Ireland. He and his Leinstermen not only burnt Tara, the Hy Neill capitol, but they also destroyed the capitols of Ulster (Emhain) and Connacht (Cruachain).

> To the burning of Tara,
> With Enna the high renowned.
>
> Famous the march he went
> To the burning of Cruachain,
> After demolishing Emhain;
> It was a valiant, contentious deed.[7]

By the end of his reign he controlled not only Leinster but also Northern Ireland and Munster, as the following 1,500 year old ballad illustrates:

> The tribute which was given to Enna,
> From Leath Cuinn [Northern Ireland] of the feasts,
> Was a screaball[8] from each house,
> All of fionndruine.[9]
>
> The tribute which was given to Enna,
> From Mumba (Munster) with insults
> Was an ounce of gold from each lios [fort]
> In the ensuing year.[7]

With a major clan in Leinster taking its name from him, Enna Kinsella was one of the most powerful righs of Leinster during the 4th century. His descendants dominated South Leinster for subsequent centuries, indicating that his immediate family held onto that power. Happily, we can follow their

---

[7] An anonymous 9th-century author.
[8] Unit of monetary measure equal to 1/24 of a cow.
[9] White bronze metal.

fortunes because, according to the historian Alfred Smythe, more genealogical information has survived about Hy Kinsella than about any other Irish clan. From the 4th century on, Hy Kinsella controlled the fertile lands of the Slaney valley in Carlow and Wexford. As the number of Enna's descendants increased, Hy Kinsella split into six clans named after Enna's sons and two subsidiary clans descended from two of Enna's brothers.

The battle between Eochaidh of Hy Neill and Enna of Hy Kinsella was not unique, and conflict continued generation after generation, beginning with warfare between their sons, Niall of Hy Neill and Eochaid of Hy Kinsella. Enmity between Niall and Eochaid arose over who rightfully should reside at Tara as Ard Righ of Ireland. Eochaid felt it was his right and had a proclamation in the *Book of Rights* to back up his claim,[10] so he marched to Tara and took up residence. After he had been there for nine days, a learned druid convinced

Over 1500 years have taken their toll on the Eochaid holed stone, which no longer stands upright.

him that his presence violated Irish law, so he left. Niall then went to Tara and assumed the sovereignty of Ireland in 378, according to *The Four Masters.*

---

[10] "The king of Ui Chennselaig of the spoils has control of the house of Tara; this is the truth for all time, for it is the house of the king of Laigin."

As Eochaid was journeying back to Leinster, he stopped in the house of Niall's druid, where the druid's son insulted Eochaid's honor and died as a result. The druid went to Niall and asked him to avenge the death of his son. Niall agreed, marched on Leinster, and threatened to devastate the land. Eochaid tried to placate him with cattle and gifts, but the druid convinced Niall not to be satisfied until Eochaid was delivered to them. So Eochaid offered himself up, and the druid ordered him chained to a pillar stone "to be seen," Keating says, "to the west of the Slaney, between Cill Brighde and Tulach, and that stone is in a standing position; it is high and broad, and perforated near the very top."

After Eochaid had been chained to the stone, the druid sent nine warriors to kill him. At their approach, Eochaid with superhuman strength broke the chains that bound him, killed them, and fled to Alba (Scotland), where he was granted protection by Scotland's Ard Righ, Gabhran, son of Domhanghart.

Niall, ignorant of Eochaid's whereabouts, forgot the Leinsterman and attended to more pressing matters. In 383, Magnus Maximus withdrew his Roman legions and Niall undertook frequent raids on the practically defenseless England and Wales. The British came to fear Niall's forces much as the Irish feared the Vikings centuries later. On these raids, Niall often captured people and took them back to Ireland, where they served as slaves. One of these was a 16-year-old named Patrick, about whom we'll learn more later.

Niall, not content with ravaging England and Wales, decided to invade the Roman territories of modern-day France. He asked the Ard Righ of Scotland to assemble an army and follow him and when Gabhran arrived with his men, Eochaid was among them. When Eochaid later found Niall seated on the opposite side of a riverbank, he drew his bow and let an arrow fly. The arrow went through Niall's body and he immediately expired.   Eochaid's murderous deed is memorialized forever in the following ballad:

> Niall, Eochaidh's son great in fight –
> Erin and Scotland are in affliction
> He through whom a swift Saxon arrow was put
> By Eochaid, son of glorious Enna.[11]

---

[11] An anonymous 9th-century author.

Christianity

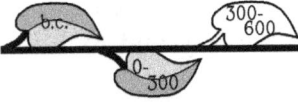

hile the Irish loved their battle stories, at assemblies and feasts they just as frequently called for tales of the saints. In these, St. Patrick featured prominently as the sole converter of Ireland to Christianity. Patrick first came to Ireland when he was 16 – a slave captured in Roman Britain by the pirate forces of the Irish Ard Righ, Niall of the Nine Hostages. He was sold to Miliucc, a tuath righ in Ulster, and for six years Patrick acted as shepherd to Miliucc's sheep. Ill-fed and ill-clad, exposed to snow, rain and animals such as the wolves and wild boars that roamed the forests, the slave boy was often frightened and always lonely. In his misery, he turned to the religion of his childhood and prayed a hundred times each day and night.

One night as Patrick lay asleep, he heard a voice in a dream telling him that he would soon return to his own country. A few nights later the same voice said, "Patrick, your ship is ready." Straightaway he abandoned Miliucc's flocks and escaped from Ulster. He made the perilous journey across the country and finally arrived safely at a harbor on the southeast coast of Ireland (perhaps in Hy Kinsella), two hundred miles from his master in Ulster. A poor man took pity on the fugitive, brought him to his hut, gave him food and shelter, and guarded him while he slept. When Patrick woke, there was indeed a ship ready to set sail. He asked permission to board the vessel, but the captain, recognizing a runaway slave, drove him away. Disconsolately, he turned back towards the poor man's cabin and as he did so he began to pray. Before his prayer was finished he heard the sailors calling him back to the ship. The captain had changed his mind and Patrick boarded the vessel. He entered a continental monastery and took the habit of a monk.

Historians have discovered that the Christianizing of Ireland began before Patrick. The annals state that in the year 431 the pope sent Palladius to Ireland to be bishop "to the Irish believing in Christ."[1] Historical documents show that he was quite successful in Leinster where he set up a number of churches.[2] Little else is known of him.

After St. Patrick was ordained bishop by Pope Celestine I, he requested a return to Ireland to baptize the people and to teach them the faith. His work in Ireland, covering a whole generation according to the annals, took place in the 5th century:[3] "St. Patrick came to Ireland and proceeded to baptize and bless the Irish, men and women, sons and daughters, except a few who did not consent to receive faith or baptism from him." He landed at Wicklow where he was opposed by the Leinstermen, one of whom struck a companion of Patrick on the mouth with a stone, knocking out four of his teeth. Patrick set off in his boats again and landed north of

St. Patrick

---

[1] *Monumenta Germaniae Historica*, ed. T. Mommsen (1892).
[2] *The Oxford Companion to Irish History* (Oxford, 1998).
[3] For the controversy on the date and identity of Patrick, see D. A. Binchy, "Patrick and his Biographers," *Studia Hibernica* ii (1962): 7-173.

present-day Dublin,[4] where he may have established his first settlement. His goal of converting as many of the Irish as possible called for an aggressive plan, something, with the knowledge he had gained of Ireland as a slave, he was uniquely suited to do.

In spring, as was the Irish custom, the Ard Righ's druid prepared to light the first fire of the year. Before he could light it, flames were noticed rising further east, on the hill of Slane. St. Patrick had lit a paschal fire to celebrate Easter.

Laoghaire, the Ard Righ, stared in outrage as the blaze on the neighboring hill grew stronger and stronger. "Who has dared to light this fire?" he demanded. No one was able to answer though the druids were greatly concerned about the profanity of the event upon their religion. The Ard Righ, with a large retinue, rode to the Hill of Slane to extinguish the fire and punish the offender.

Upon reaching the hill they found Patrick, holding his staff and standing before an altar outside his tent, surrounded by his tonsure-headed disciples. Immediately the druids recalled an ancient prophecy:

> One shall arrive here, having his head shaven in a circle, bearing a crooked staff, and his table shall be in the eastern part of his house, and his people shall stand behind him, and he shall sing forth from his table wickedness, and all his household shall answer – So be it! – and this man, when he cometh, shall destroy our gods, and overturn our altars . . . He will seduce the people and bring them after him . . . He will free the slaves . . . He will magnify kindreds of low degree . . . and he shall subdue unto himself the kings that resist him . . . and his doctrines shall reign

---

[4] During St. Patrick's time this would have simply been a bay. The town of Dublin wouldn't exist for many more centuries.

for ever and ever.[5]

With his druids and warriors around him, Laoghaire pronounced a sentence of death on Patrick, but the monk showed no fear. He began to preach his religion to the assembled host and even reproached the Ard Righ for worshiping the sun. Many of the Ard Righ's household who were listening became Christians and, though Laoghaire was not converted, he revoked the death sentence.

Patrick impressed Laoghaire so much that the Ard Righ persuaded Dubhtach, his chief file and a devout Christian convert, to expound to Patrick the whole of the Irish law, an awesome recital. Then Laoghaire, at Patrick's request, appointed a committee to revise the code. Three righs, three churchmen and three historians were gathered for the purpose and after three

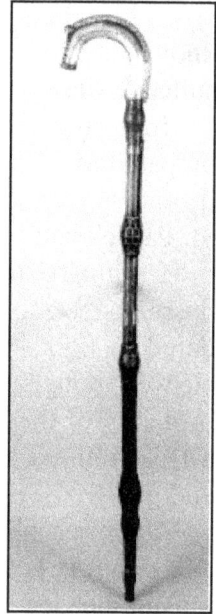

Kells staff

years they produced the civil code known as the *Senchus Mor* (the Great Tradition or the Brehon law). It contained no new laws but was a codification of the old, with the addition of some church canons and the deletion of measures that were cruel or arbitrary. Patrick, broad-minded and eminently sensible, saw to it that most of the common law was left untouched and the customs of the age respected. His only opposition was to open pagan worship and idolatrous rites, and in that he was fierce and fearless. The introduction to the *Senchus Mor* states that "what did not clash with the word of God . . . and

---

[5] *The Tripartite Life of Patrick,* ed. and trans. Whitley Stokes (London, 1887, 2007).

with the consciences of the believers was confirmed." Like all the old law, which was recited orally, the *Senchus Mor* is in verse. The file Dubhtach, who transcribed the *Senchus Mor*, "put a thread of poetry around it for Patrick."

With his handful of monks, Patrick carried his pastoral staff on a circuit of Ireland, going, as the Irish righs did when they collected their tribute, in a sunwise (clockwise) direction, preaching the gospel as he went. Though he was often in danger from hostile righs, he converted many men and women to the new religion and Christianity spread across the country.

By converting the Irish, the saint also turned them from conquest. As with the Vikings when they were converted centuries later, the Irish sea raiders became a thing of the past. After their conversion, Irish mariners brought trade goods instead of war. Although raiding foreign lands ended, raiding among the Irish themselves continued to be endemic.

The pastoral staff Patrick carried was special, according to tradition, coming from Jesus himself:

> St. Patrick acquired his famous pastoral staff while on a journey from Germanus to Rome.[6] In the midst of his travels, he stopped at a house on an island in the Tyrrhenian Sea. In this house lived a young married couple who, astonishingly enough, had children and grandchildren who were old and decrepit. The couple had been married at the time of Jesus, and He had visited their home. After partaking of their hospitality, Jesus blessed them, saying they would remain new and young until the Judgment Day. On departing He left His staff, with instructions that it be given to St. Patrick when he too passed that way.[7]

---

[6] St. Patrick went on this journey before arriving to convert Ireland.

[7] Mary Murray Delaney, *Of Irish Ways: A Complete Look at Ireland's History, Customs, Literature, Landscape, Traditions, and More* (Minneapolis, 1973).

St. Patrick brought this staff wherever he went. While he was preaching in Munster, Aengus, the Munster righ, became curious about the visitor and summoned him to Cashel. Patrick preached the gospel and the righ, believing in it, asked to be baptized. As Patrick blessed Aengus, the spike of his staff went through the king's foot, but Aengus did not flinch. When the ceremony was over and Patrick saw the wound he had inflicted, he was stricken with remorse. "I didn't cry out or protest," Aengus explained, "for I thought the piercing was part of the ritual that I had to endure."

As with other Irish heroes, esteemed cultural traits have been woven into and amplified among the stories of St. Patrick. One example is the ancient ritual of fasting that Patrick used for bargaining against one more powerful than he. In the ancient European world a person of low social status had no way to redress a wrong committed against him by one of much higher social status. The Celts, in an effort to correct this, practiced fasting. The person of low social status would sit outside the other's home and fast. The humiliation of having someone fasting outside his door forced the higher-ranking person to take action since turning a blind eye to the situation was not an option in his culture.[8]

In the following story,[9] Patrick spends Lent in seclusion while bargaining with God:

Patrick went to a mountain in Connacht (later to be named Croagh Patrick in honor of this tale) on the first Saturday of Imbolc (the Irish version of Spring, which began on February 1) to ask God

---

[8] In 1980-81, IRA prisoners in Northern Ireland used fasting against the British, the less powerful against the more powerful. The British, neglectful or ignorant of Celtic tradition, allowed them to starve.

[9] Mary Low, *Celtic Christianity and Nature: Early Irish and Hebridean Traditions* (Edinburgh, 1996).

to grant several requests.[10]   After a time an angel came to him and said, "God does not give you what you are demanding because it seems to him excessive and obstinate and great are the requests."

"Is that his pleasure?" said Patrick.

"It is," said the angel.

"Then this is my pleasure," said Patrick. "I will not go from this mountain till I am dead or till all the requests are granted to me."

Croagh Patrick

Then Patrick remained on the mountain in much displeasure, without drink, without food, from Ash Wednesday to Easter Sunday after the manner of Moses for they were alike in many things. To both God spoke out of the fire. Six-score years was the age of them both. The burial-place of each of them is uncertain.

Now at the end of those 40 days and 40 nights the mountain was filled with black birds so that Patrick could see neither heaven nor earth. He sang maledictory psalms at them, but they did not leave him. Then his anger grew against them. He struck his bell[11] at them so that the men of Ireland heard its voice, and then he flung it at the birds so that its gap [the metal striker inside] broke out of it and that is Brigid's Gapling. Then Patrick wept till his face and the chasuble

---

[10] Patrick's requests are never actually described.

[11] All Irish abbots had bells of their own to signal dinner time, prayer time, etc. in their monastery.

in front of him were wet. No demon came to the land of Ireland after that till the end of seven years and seven months and seven days.[12] Then the angel went to console Patrick and cleansed the chasuble and brought white birds around the mountain and they sang sweet melodies for him.

"You shall bring that same number of souls out of pain that can fill the space which your eye reaches over the sea," the angel said to Patrick.

"That is not a favor to me," said Patrick. "My eye does not reach over the sea very far."

"Then you shall have both sea and land," said the angel.

"Is there anything else that God grants me besides that?" said Patrick.

"There is," said the angel. "Seven people every Saturday from now till Doom are to be taken out of hell's pains."

"If he should give anything to me," said Patrick, "let him give me twelve men."

"You shall have them," said the angel, "and now get down from the mountain."

"I will not get down," said Patrick, "since I have been tormented, till I am blessed. Is there anything else that will be given to me?"

"There is," said the angel, "you shall have out of hell's pains, seven people every Thursday and twelve every Saturday; and now get down from the mountain."

"I will not get down," said Patrick, "since I have been tormented till I am blessed."

"Is there anything else that you would demand?" said the angel.

"There certainly is." Patrick continued with his demands, bargaining to get more and more people out of hell, till eventually he asked that he himself should be judge over Ireland on the last day. At this point, even the angel's patience came to an end.

"Assuredly," said the angel, "The Lord will not give you that."

"Unless He does," said Patrick, "departure from this mountain shall not be got from me, from today till Doom, and what is more, I

---

[12] The numbers 3, 5, 7, and 9 all had magical connotations to the Celts. The meeting of three rivers, for example, was always considered a sacred place.

shall leave a guardian here."

As the angel went to leave, Patrick went to mass. The angel came back at Nones.[13]

"What have you brought me?" said Patrick.

"This," said the angel. "All creatures, visible and invisible, including the twelve apostles, spoke to the Lord and they have obtained your request. The Lord said, 'There has not come, and there will not come, after the apostles, a man more admirable, were it not for your hardness.' What you have prayed for, you shall have. Strike your bell," says the angel, "and there will be a consecration of the people of Ireland, both living and dead."

So Patrick said, "A blessing on the bountiful King who has given this, and now I shall get down from the mountain."

Patrick died on March 17 around 493. He was 75 years old. Where he was buried is uncertain and hotly disputed.

The Christian religion spread throughout Ireland gradually rather than in one comprehensive conversion, as is popularly believed. St. Ibar, a disciple of Patrick,

Celtic cross

[13] The monastic day was split into six (or sometimes seven) time periods corresponding to biblical events. Nones occurred at 3 p.m. when Christ died on the cross.

successfully introduced Christianity to Hy Kinsella. Around 480, he founded a monastic settlement on Begerin Island in Wexford Bay.

Historians, puzzled by the fact that there was little opposition by the Irish people to conversion from paganism to Christianity, give reasons ranging from similarity between the two religions (the tripartite concept, already part of the Celtic religion, made the Trinity readily acceptable) to Patrick's great skill in grafting Christianity onto pagan superstitions. The Celtic cross was not only a symbol of Christ's passion but also a symbol for the sun and four seasons. Much of this half-pagan, half-Christian religion is found in the Irish stories of the middle ages and in the present-day superstitions of the common folk.

The death of St. Patrick roughly corresponded with the fall of Rome. The traditional view of the years following Rome's fall as "Dark Ages" of terror and chaos throughout Europe was not mirrored by events in Ireland. Although intertribal warfare was constant, the country enjoyed relative cultural and religious stability. Alongside this, well-established diplomatic and trading contact along the Atlantic seaboard encouraged the development of a strong missionary impulse in Irish Christianity. Between 500 and 800, the Irish Church spread the gospel widely across the Continent. Enthusiastic and dedicated Irish holy men flocked to the European Continent to preach the Gospel. They were the forerunners of the Irish renaissance on the Continent, which reached its height in the 8th and 9th centuries at the courts of Charlemagne and Charles the Bald.

The aim of these Irish monks was primarily conversion, but well educated in the fine monastic schools of Ireland, they brought their books and their high ideals of scholarship with them. Most of the monasteries they founded had schools and libraries connected with them. The Irish won renown for their high standards of education and scholarship. The aristocracy flocked to their schools and it became the fashion to have an Irish scholar or two in residence at European courts, to enhance the prestige of rulers rich in temporal power but poor in intellectual attainments. The most prominent of the many missionaries was St. Columban, a Leinsterman.

Born in Leinster around 530 and educated at Bangor, St. Columban left Ireland around 585 for France with twelve companions. He swept through the country like a whirlwind

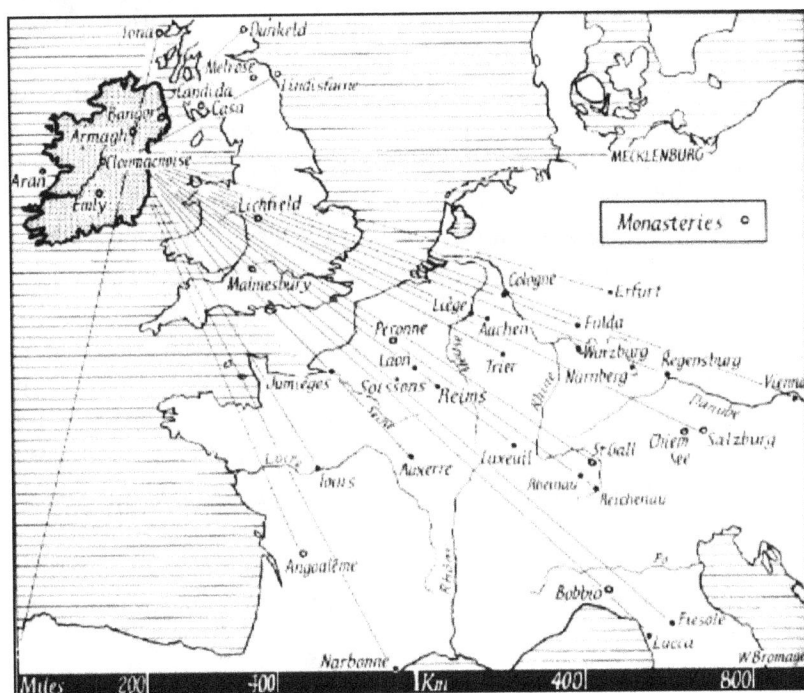

Irish monasteries founded on the Continent during Europe's Dark

converting all he came across. On the south-western slopes of the Vosges,[14] Columban founded the monastic communities of

---

[14] In modern day France.

Luxeuil and Fontaine, mother-foundations of the Benedictine movement; then he continued towards Switzerland. At Lake Constance, his companion Gallus fell ill, stayed behind and laid the foundation of the monastery named after him, St. Gallen, which even in 801 still had a pronounced Irish character. Columban himself crossed the Alps and set up his next and final monastery in Lombardy, at Bobbio near Pavia. There he died in 615. "A man more holy, more chaste, more self-denying, a man with loftier aims and purer heart than Columban was never born in the Island of the Saints," remarked Archbishop Healy in his eulogy.

If Columban's abbey in Italy became a citadel of faith and learning, his earlier foundation, Luxeuil in France, became the nursery of saints and apostles. From its walls went forth men who carried his rule, together with the Gospel, into France, Germany, Switzerland, and Italy. There are said to have been 63 such apostles. These disciples of Columban are credited with founding over one hundred different monasteries.

By the 9th century "the transmission of European civilization was assured. Wherever they went the Irish brought with them their books, many unseen in Europe for centuries and tied to their waists as signs of triumph, just as Irish heroes had once tied to their waists their enemies' heads. Wherever they went they brought their love of learning and their skills in bookmaking. In the bays and valleys of their exile, they reestablished literacy and breathed new life into the exhausted literary culture of Europe."[15]

---

[15] Thomas Cahill, *How the Irish Saved Civilization* (New York, 1995).

Saint Brigid to Crimthann

Saint Brigid

long with St. Patrick and St. Columcille, St. Brigid, who was born in 453, is one of the three patron saints of Ireland. Though not from Hy Kinsella, her works affect the territory greatly in future centuries, so a brief description of her life follows. Several locations claim the honor of being the birthplace of St. Brigid, including a town in Hy Kinsella during the reign of Crimthann, son of Enna Kinsella, but the most likely is near Dundalk in County Louth. According to legend, Brigid was an illegitimate daughter of a righ named Dubtach and his servant. Dubtach's wife demanded that he sell the pregnant servant. She was sold to a druid with the stipulation that the child must eventually be returned to the father. The druid took the mother and child back to his home in Connacht where Brigid spent her childhood. Miracles were attributed to her even as a baby. As an infant she restored life to a dead child when she touched the body.

Brigid was raised a Christian by her mother without any interference by the druid. She grew up to be a beautiful girl, meek, humble and sweet, who loved to retire into solitude and pray.

Dubtach kept track of his daughter as she grew. He heard so many miraculous things about her that eventually he demanded her back, as stipulated by the initial agreement. The druid grudgingly complied and Brigid returned to her father. Dubtach greeted her warmly, but her stepmother treated her with coldness and contempt.

Brigid, who always gave the poor anything she could, began giving away her father's valuables. When she returned to visit the druid and her mother, she gave away the druid's precious milk. When the druid became furious over losing his means of survival, she prayed to God and the milk was miraculously replaced. Dubtach could finally no longer stand this and resolved to sell his nine-year-old daughter to the Leinster righ, Crimthann, son of Enna Kinsella, as related in the following by Denis McCarthy (who refers to Dubtach by his anglicized name Duffy).

> Brighid, the daughter of Duffy, was brought to the court of the king,
> (Monarch of Leinster, MacEanna [Crimthann, son of Eanna], whose
>   praises the poets would sing.)
> "Hither, O Monarch," said Duffy, "I've come with a maiden to sell;
> Buy her and bind her to bondage – she's needing such discipline so
>   well!"
> Ah, but 'twas wise was the king. From the maid to the chieftain he
>   turned;
> Mildness he saw in her face, in the other 'twas anger that burned;
> "This is no bondmaid, I'll swear it, O chief, but a girl of your own.
> Why sells the father the flesh of his flesh and the bone of his bone?"
>
> Brighid, the daughter of Duffy, was mute while her father replied
> "Monarch, this maid has no place as the child of a chieftain of pride.
> Beggars and wretches whose wounds would the soul of a soldier affright,
> Sure, 'tis on these she is wasting my substance from morning to night!"
> Ah, but 'twas bitter with Duffy; he spoke like a man that was vext.
> Musing, the monarch was silent; he pondered the question perplexed.
> "Maiden," said he, "if 'tis true, as I've just from your father heard tell,
> Might it not be, as my bondmaid, you'd waste all my substance as well?"

Brighid, the daughter of Duffy, made answer. "O Monarch," she said,
"Had I the wealth of your coffers, and had I the crown from your head,
Yes, if the plentiful yield of the broad breasts of Erin were mine,
All would I give to the people of Christ who in poverty pine."
Ah, but 'twas then that the king felt the heart in his bosom leap,
"I am not worthy," he cried, "such a maiden in bondage to keep.
Here's a king's sword for her ransom, and here's a king's word to decree
Never to other than Christ and His poor let her servitude be!"

So Dubtach left to return home with his daughter. He soon had reason to become angry with her again. Brigid had removed the precious jewels from the sword the Leinster righ had given her father and given them to a passing beggar!

When Brigid was sixteen, having traveled with St. Patrick, she decided to become a nun of Leinster. She took her vows and established a community in northwest Leinster, County Offaly, but did not remain there long. She traveled throughout the country, establishing churches wherever she stopped, which is why so many places regard St. Brigid as their

St. Brigid's Cross

patron saint. At one stop, while explaining the mysteries of the Christian gospel to a dying pagan, she wove rushes together into a special type of cross, known as Brigid's cross, which is still made in Ireland and hung over doorways to protect those inside from illness or bad luck.

After she had traveled for seventeen years, the people of Leinster yearned for her return. To please them, she asked the Leinster righ (no longer Crimthann, son of Enna, but instead a righ from north Leinster) to give her a plot of land on which to build. The righ promised her land, but refused to identify its

111

location. Brigid kept asking and the righ kept stalling, until Brigid lost patience with him.

"Well, give me as much land as I can cover here with my cloak," she pleaded.

The righ readily agreed to this and Brigid took off her cloak. Four of her nuns each took a corner of the garment, as if to lay it flat on the ground, but instead turned to the four points of the compass and began to run as fast as they could, holding on to the corners of the cloak as they ran. As the nuns pulled, the cloak grew longer and broader until it covered a full square mile. The righ became alarmed.

"Stop!" he shouted. "Stop! What are you doing?"

"I'm taking the land you promised me," Brigid retorted, "and I'll take your whole province from you as punishment for your niggardliness."

"I'll give you the ground your cloak covers now if only your women will stop running!" the righ cried.

Brigid called for her nuns to stop, the righ kept his word, and Brigid received the land for her church. A huge oak, her favorite tree, grew on this site and was the origin of the name Kildare ("Cill-dara," church of the oak). The warmth of Brigid's personality and the animation of her leadership attracted so many to her convent that it became one of the showplaces of Ireland, containing, it is asserted, ten thousand nuns. Its abbess could no longer handle such a complex establishment alone. She invited a bishop, Conleth, to take up residence at Kildare to help her. He and Brigid, bishop and abbess, ran the double monastery as co-equals.

Ruins of the Cathedral of Kildare

Centuries later, a Welsh monk named Giraldus Cambrensis visited Kildare and wrote:

At Kildare, which the glorious Brigid renders illustrious, are many miracles worthy of notice, and the first that occurs is Brigid's fire, called the inextinguishable fire,[1] not that it cannot be put out, but because the nuns and religious women are so careful and diligent in supplying and recruiting it with fuel, that from the time of that virgin, it hath remained always unextinguished through so many succession of years, and though so vast

---

[1] The eternal fire tended by the nuns was extinguished by the English in the 16th century.

a quantity of wood hath been, in such a length of time, consumed, yet the ashes hath never increased.

The annals record the death of St. Brigid, Abbess of Cill-dara (Kildare), in 525. "It was to her Cill-dara was first granted, and by her it was founded. It was she who never turned her mind or attention from the Lord for the space of one hour, but was constantly meditating and thinking of him in her heart and mind. She resigned her spirit to heaven, the first day of the month of February." She was buried in her abbey church, but three centuries later when the Vikings arrived, her relics were removed to Downpatrick in Ulster. Seven centuries after this, during the Reformation, her relics were destroyed, with the exception of her head, which was brought to Neustadt in Austria and finally to the Jesuit church in Lisbon.

Like St. Patrick's church at Armagh, St. Brigid built Kildare on the site of an ancient pagan temple. Kildare was dedicated to the Celtic goddess Brigid, who was known as the soothsayer, the healer, the armorer, and the deliverer of fertility. In a conscious effort by clerics to ease the conversion of many Irish to Christianity, these attributes were transferred to St. Brigid herself. Many rituals performed on St. Brigid's day, February 1st, remain deeply pagan. Marking the end of winter and the beginning of spring, St. Brigid's Day required a feast but the gathering of food was especially significant. Stocks of food were running low at this time of year. Housewives took special pride in laying out a generous spread – fruitcakes, oatmeal cakes, rich milk and butter, bread, cheese, and any meat that could be caught – because an abundance of food was taken as an indication of the woman's thrift in managing the household larder throughout this lean part of the year. A cross of straw or rush was made in every home and hung inside the front door for protection while children ran from homestead to homestead singing and performing in return for food.

Crimthann

It was late August, and Crimthann had been inaugurated Hy Kinsella righ only a week ago, six months after the death of his famous father, Enna Kinsella. As expected of all new righs, he was preparing a raiding expedition into a neighboring tuath that had not submitted to him. Almost two-dozen nobles, mostly young sons looking for adventure, had elected to travel with him. Freemen were also needed but could not be forced to go because it was harvest time, so Crimthann offered to negate the fall tribute of any volunteer. After word of his offer spread, two score freemen stepped forward.

Dunchad, the royal file of the recently deceased Enna Kinsella, retained that position under Crimthann. He helped the new righ by hurrying preparations for the raid and pressuring all involved into getting an early start. Although surprise was a critical element of any raid, they left hours later than originally planned because of Crimthann's desire to wait for his cousin, who couldn't decide which horse to ride. They journeyed north on one of the well-managed dirt roads,[2] traveling only as fast as the men on foot could walk. Since this first raid of Crimthann's would be an indicator of his potential, they maintained the pace with few halts for rest. A defeat on a righ's first raid could end in the clan electing a replacement for him. Dunchad worried about the lateness of the day. Night would be coming on when they reached their destination, and one did not travel at night. The night belonged to the Sidh.[3]

---

[2] Everyone living by a road had a duty to keep it in good condition or a fine could be levied against him. Responsibility for maintaining sections of road along desolate stretches fell upon the tuath righ.

[3] The Sidh were the magical people the Gaels had defeated when they came to Ireland. They were believed to dwell underground in fairy forts and to come out at night.

Dunchad, who had been on numerous raids with Enna, steered them immediately toward some faraway hills, where the neighboring tuath grazed many of their cattle in the summer. To reach them would take most of the remaining daylight. When they entered the enemy tuath, marked by a huge stone alongside the edge of the road, Crimthann sent a few riders ahead to scout for any sign of enemy nobles. A few scouting riders could be mistaken for filid. Crimthann's main party of horsemen couldn't be mistaken for anything but what it was: a raiding party. An enemy seeing them would immediately alert the countryside. Within an hour they reached the hills. Crimthann ordered the horsemen to scatter in groups of about five and search for cattle. At any moment word of their arrival would spread and an opposing force begin to form. They had to find the cattle before the enemy was alerted and rushed them into hiding. So far Dunchad approved of the young righ's command, though Crimthann had asked him little and appeared to want to run this raid on his own.

Furiously forcing his horse up the hill, Crimthann scanned the surrounding forest for clearings, large fields where cattle would be grazing. Dusk was coming on. The four men with him could barely keep up with the young righ.

"Watch the branch!" cried out his cousin.

Another shouted, "Over here, an opening."

"No, we're still too low."

"Where are the damn cows?" cried a noble in exasperation.

Crimthann remained quiet as he intently drove his horse ever upwards. Breaking out from the woods into a huge clearing, Crimthann stopped as the four others caught up with him.

"Damn," said the exasperated noble again after scanning the field, "Nothing. The cattle must be higher up on the mountain."

As he turned to head back into the dark trees and climb higher, Crimthann whispered, "No!" Too softly for the first noble, who had already reentered the woods, to hear. The other three turned and stopped. Crimthann was pointing to a spot at the far end of the clearing where the dusk almost cloaked some people milling about and perhaps a cow or two being herded into the trees. "They're hiding them in the woods."

Crimthann let out a whoop and spurred on his horse while his friends blew their horns and followed. The time for surprise was over. Now the party must gather to claim the cattle. How many cows were they hiding? Twenty would be acceptable, but closer to forty would bring honor to the young righ, if he could get them home. The horses thundered across the field as others from their party met them, drawn by horn calls. As they had called Crimthann's nobles, the horns would call herders from the surrounding area. Word would take a while to get to the nobles who owned the cattle for they all lived in the valley below. Time was still critical, however. Dusk had fallen.

Within minutes a dozen horses entered the woods where the cattle path could plainly be seen, and a minute later they came upon the cattle. The herders whose duty it was to watch over them had scattered.

"A nice lot we have here, Crimthann," shouted his cousin as he forced his horse to the other end of the struggling herd.

"Aye, I'd say you've close to sixty penned up!" shouted another noble.

"If we can get them home," answered Crimthann testily, unwilling to accept congratulations yet.

By the time the herd was back at the other end of the field where Crimthann had originally spotted them, the Hy Kinsella freemen had caught up, guided by Dunchad, the royal file. He had realized that, in the excitement of looking for the cattle, the young nobles had forgotten about the freemen, an essential piece of getting the animals back to Hy Kinsella. The freemen took over driving the cattle, big beasts in fine condition from eating the lush mountain grass. A few nobles rode in front to call out an alarm if they were about to be ambushed, but most rode in the rear where an attack was more likely. It was now only a matter of time before the owners of the stolen cattle would be notified in the valley below. Rather than riding immediately after the raiding party in ones and twos, they would take an hour or more to collect a party of their own to give chase, providing Crimthann's party with some breathing room, Dunchad thought. But the owners would have little difficulty following the path left by sixty cattle. And they would all be traveling on horses, while Crimthann's men were forced to travel at the rate of a plodding cow.

"Can't we move these beasts faster?" shouted Crimthann as he looked over his shoulder.

Dunchad ambled his horse over to the Hy Kinsella righ and quietly said, "It's getting dark. If we keep going we'll surely lose most of the cattle either to injury or wandering. We wouldn't want to upset the Sidh either." He paused before saying, "We started too late today. I suggest we turn these cows loose. We can get an early start and raid another area come light."

The sounds of grunting drovers, heavy hoof beats striking through the underbrush and the excited lowing of cows were all that came to Dunchad's ears for a time. When he finally began to pull his horse away, he heard Crimthann's edgy reply, "The new day has just begun[4] and so have we. We'll use the moon's light. It's nearly full."

Luckily Crimthann's party didn't have much forest to travel through before returning to the valley below so they lost only

---

[4] The Irish day started and ended at nightfall rather than midnight.

nine cows among the trees. At any moment a cattle owner could appear out of the night, sound the alarm and reveal their location. Word not to sound horns for any reason was spread among Crimthann's men, and the drovers were encouraged to move along as fast as possible. The success of this raid depended on the cattle owners' having to pick up the trail all the way back on the hill where the cows had been grazing. A figure ran across their path ahead. A noble peeled off in chase but soon returned, having lost his quarry. Soon enough they were back on a small road.

Minutes turned into hours of anxious watching. The cattle plodded along while the Hy Kinsella freemen struggled to keep them together. To speed up the pace, Crimthann ordered some of the slowest cattle left behind. Many of the younger nobles rubbed their necks, strained from looking back at the imaginary sound of pursuers. Dunchad simply followed in the rear, almost appearing to sleep sitting up. Time passed. The raiders reached the major road and soon passed into Hy Kinsella. Some of the younger nobles breathed a sigh of relief.

Shortly after crossing the boundary of the two tuatha, the faint sound of galloping was heard behind them. This time the pursuit wasn't imaginary.

Dunchad immediately sat up on his horse and quietly alerted Crimthann. The approaching hoof beats were unmistakable now. The cattle were plodding across a large open plain. Were those glints of metal reflecting the moonlight behind them?

"Drovers," shouted Crimthann to the men herding the cattle, "continue on to the holding pen." Looking at those around him on horseback, he finished with, "Nobles, stand with me." All turned to face the threat, gripping the spears and shields they'd brought with them, and most made sure their swords were ready to be drawn if fighting came to close quarters. The horses stirred nervously, revealing the moods of their riders.

It all came down to this fight. The Hy Kinsella nobles began blowing their horns to alert the countryside. If Crimthann couldn't turn the cattle owners back, they would recapture most or all of the cattle.

Shouting out the clan war cry, Crimthann spurred his mount to meet the charge of his pursuers. His horse was twenty yards from the enemy. Fifteen yards. Ten yards. He let loose his spear and slowed his mount while drawing his sword and shield. Dunchad, watching from a distance, smiled appreciatively. The shield was Enna's famous war shield, which had seen many battles. Behind Crimthann came his men. The two groups crashed together in the darkness, resulting in great confusion but little serious damage to either party.

Even with the moonlight, it was difficult to tell who was enemy and who was friend. The only way to be sure was to go after anyone who broke from the milling group and made for the cattle. When this happened one or two of the Hy Kinsella nobles would immediately chase him down and force him back to the melee. If any of the cattle owners reached the herd, most or all of the drovers would abandon their task and the cows would stop. Neither Crimthann nor any of the other Hy Kinsella nobles wanted to fight the cattle owners to the death, which would be required if the herd stopped.

Crimthann had to buy the drovers enough time to reach the cattle enclosure, a circular wood fort not far away. The Hy Kinsella righ blocked a wild sword swing with his father's shield as his horse whirled away from the enemy. Alongside, a horse went down in agonizing squeals as the rider leapt free. Men savagely twisted their mounts first towards their enemy, then away. Crimthann's arm went up with his sword, then down, again and again. Glints of silver appeared and disappeared, moonlight playing off shields and bare swords. The righ's horse charged, turned, and charged again. What was taking the drovers so long? The first cattle were just entering into the enclosure.

The cattle owners pushed forward in a concerted effort to reach their herd and broke free from Crimthann's men. The Hy Kinsella nobles caught up barely in time to stop them. The fighting was close to the cattle now, and the drovers were getting worried. A few had already scattered to safety. The horses milled around each other like fish in a bucket. The cattle owners were frantic. The enclosure was now mere yards away. Finally horns echoed through the night. The cattle were behind the walls.

At first this spurred the cattle owners on to even greater efforts. Some jumped from their horses and hacked at the locked wooden entrance door behind which their cattle lowed. Dunchad, now inside the enclosure and looking down from its high walls, saw Crimthann's cousin ride alongside the door and scatter the enemy nobles while trying to grab the reins of their horses. Slowly the cattle owners realized they were beaten and began disentangling themselves from Crimthann's nobles. Amid shouted threats and insults they withdrew and regrouped a little distance from the enclosure. After a short, heated discussion, the cattle owners turned for home. Crimthann's nobles had won today, thought Dunchad, but the nobles of the enemy tuath would raid Crimthann's lands in a week, a month or a year. The cattle would change hands again and again.

As the cattle enclosure gate tentatively opened, Crimthann finally let out a victory whoop. He'd managed to pull in forty-five healthy cows. "At first light we'll bring them back to my fort," he shouted. "All must come and enjoy the feast!" The feast was to last for three full days with all the locals invited. When a check was made of those on the raid, every drover was present, several nobles were injured, and only one lay dead. Crimthann's cousin had gone down in close fighting at the end of the raid.

Crimthann, son of Enna Kinsella, was baptized by St. Patrick at Rathvilly and became the first Christian Leinster righ. Like the other early Leinster righs, the politics of his reign revolved around the ancient Boruma tribute. Ireland's Ard Righ, the Laoghaire who refused to convert to Christianity, tried to collect the tribute in 457 from Crimthann, and the battle of Ath Dara[5] resulted. In this battle Laoghaire was captured, and before he was allowed to go free Crimthann made him swear an oath that never again would he attempt to collect the tribute. He was released after swearing "by the Sun and the Wind that he would remit them the Boruma [tribute]."

Laoghaire didn't stand by his promise very long, for the next year he invaded Leinster again and attempted to collect the tribute. Unfortunately for him, he fared no better than his father, Niall of the Nine Hostages, against a son of Enna Kinsella. One source states that at Greallach Dabhaill beside the Liffey in 458 "the elements wreaked their vengeance upon him, that is, the Air forsook him, the Sun burned him, and the Earth swallowed him up because he had violated them."[6] Another says he was killed by Leinstermen at Carbury Hill in 463.

The Leinster and the Hy Neill righs remained locked in a power struggle. The annals state that years later, in 484, Crimthann was responsible for the killing of yet another Ard Righ, Ailill Molt of Connacht, in the battle of Ocha, when he attacked near Tara. While Crimthann was away fighting this battle, a subordinate clan of his in Hy Kinsella revolted and attempted

---

[5] The Ford of the Oak, on the River Barrow.
[6] *Keating's History of Ireland.*

122

to take the throne from him. He returned to subdue them and even force them off their lands, but the following year, in 485, he was killed by the leader of the displaced clan, his own nephew.[7]

From the scanty history we have of him, Crimthann seems to have been a strong leader for Hy Kinsella and Leinster in general. In the ancient ballads he's described as winning battles frequently in Munster but also in the other provinces, including the distant Ulster. Under his rule Leinster expanded.

The following ballad, in the *Book of Leinster*, was written in honor of Crimthann by Dubhthach Ua Lugair,[8] Ireland's chief file and brehon during Crimthann's time. We shall include most of it here as an example of a file's praise for his righ:

Crimthan, the famous king of [the] province of Erinn [Ireland],
The Hector of Elgga [Ireland];
The topping chief of a thousand laudations,
Of bristling mansions;

A righteous word, the grandson of Bresal Beolach,
Son of Fiacha;[9]
The vigilant chief on the border of Bregia;
The shielded hero.

The fame which is proclaimed by the boastful bards of Banba
    [Ireland]
Throughout the great world;
The puissant king, the battle-torch;
The [man of] deedful conflicts

---

[7] Oengus mac Maicc Erca.
[8] Dubhthach Ua Lugair was considered the leading file of his time. He became St. Patrick's first convert at the royal court of Tara.
[9] Meaning Bresal Beolach was the son of Fiacha.

The splendid countenance above the Leinstermen
Of the broad-bordered Liffey;
The munificent prevailer in every fair succour;
The mountain of red gold.

The tree which wards the Domnann [men of Meath] multitudes
Off the death-battle plain;
The defeat of Meath, mad, terrified;
The serpent's knot.

The intolerable strength that cannot be
Subdued or checked;
Hard his battle, Crimthann with victory
And with trophies.

The battle of the Samair [in Munster], at Samhain,
It was he that sustained,
When he gave the overthrow at Raith-Bresail [in Munster],
Upon Magh Mossaid.

The son of perfect Enna Cendselach,
Head of an original family;
The Suir [River Suir in Munster] flowed over the knees of his
    horses
Passing by Dun-Sighe [fort in Munster]

The conqueror of Erinn all;
The victor of Ane; [now Knockany in Munster]
The hero of Magh Fine was seen
Passing over Ess-Maighe. [now the waterfall of Caherass in
    Munster]

The great fair-man of Mesnech,[10] and of Masten [now

---

[10] Probably the name of a place that the poet received as reward for the
poem.

124

Mullaghmast in County Kildare],
And of Mughna;
For ever shall live, what he did
At Ath-Mic Lughna.

The Leinstermen around Crimthan son of Enna,
Strong and valiant,
Except the hosts of Heaven with their Creator,
There is none to equal.

[The file continues by mentioning several battles and describing
the land that Crimthann gave him in return for the poem.]

The nine orders of Heaven, and the tenth, the order[11]
Of the mountainous Earth;
They are the securities of the price vouchsafed
For Crimthann's poem.

Destruction of Meath, magnifying of Leinster,
Leap over Lulcach:
There came not a king so good into body
As Crimthann.

The area of northeast Hy Kinsella, later to be northeast
County Wexford, was given by Crimthann as a gift to Dubhthach Ua Lugair, considered the leading file of his time, for this
ballad. According to oral tradition, the land had previously
been owned by Finn mac Cool but the line had died out with
the death of Finn's son Oscar at the battle of Gowran. Those
with the Kinsella surname would eventually settle on this land
1,000 years after the death of Finn.

Shortly after Crimthann's death, an event of importance to
all Ireland occurred. In 498, Fearghus Mor moved with his

---

[11] The Church Militant on Earth.

brothers and clan to Alba, the northern part of the neighboring land mass separating Ireland from the continent. As a result of this migration, the Romans, who called the Irish Scoti, referred to that area as Scotland, meaning "the land of the Irish." The clan that moved into Scotland was known as the Dalriada. They would eventually take over Scotland and a close relationship would always be enjoyed by the two countries.

Brandubh and Saint Maedoc

F or the year 543 there is the following entry in the annals: "The fifth year of Diarmaid, son of Fearghus Ceirrbheoil in the sovereignty of Ireland. There was an extraordinary universal plague[1] throughout the world, which swept away the noblest third part of the human race."

This entry is an example of how the ancient annals can be used to verify facts being established today. Some extraordinary catastrophe is known to have occurred in the middle of the 6th century, as evidenced by major disruptions among people around the globe. Tree ring evidence compiled by cross-sectioning and analyzing ancient oaks discovered in Irish peat bogs shows a huge reduction in tree growth in the years 536 to 542. Normal growth did not recur until the 550s. Other old records from around the globe tell how the sun became dark for 18 months, resulting in crop failures followed by famine and disease. In Ireland, populations were decimated. Banditry and cattle raiding increased and small armies roamed the countryside. Farmers began to build stone defenses around their farms in order to protect themselves and their livestock.

This catastrophe even had a dramatic effect on Irish linguistic and literary culture. In the mid-6th century a very rapid linguistic change occurred. Many word endings were dropped,

---

[1] This plague, which was called "blefed" by the Irish, came from Africa into Europe.

middle syllables were lost in numerous words, the way words were pronounced changed and a new accent emerged. Grand-parents could no longer understand their grandchildren and vice versa.

David Keys recently investigated this momentous happening in the book *Catastrophe*. From numerous ancient sources he deduced that around 530-540 either a large comet struck the earth or a gigantic volcano erupted. Core samples taken from the Greenland ice cap helped him conclude that the cause was an eruption of the volcano Krakatau on Java in the year 535.

No records describe specifically how Hy Kinsella fared during this plague but after a decisive defeat by the Hy Neill in 516 Hy Kinsella lost their monopoly of the Leinster throne until the close of the century. Then a descendant of Feidlimid, son of Enna Kinsella, became righ. His name, Brandubh, meant "black crow," and his initial residence was at Tullow in northern County Carlow.

Brandubh

Brandubh is first mentioned in a tale that took place shortly before Aed, son of Ainmirech, became Ard Righ of Ireland in 572. Brandubh, the Leinster righ, on his way home from raiding east Meath and collecting a great deal of plunder, met a leper asking for alms. Brandubh gave him a cow captured from the Meathmen. When he pitched his tent on the banks of the River Slaney that evening and slept, he had a vision.

He was carried to hell where demons met him with open jaws. He saw one evil spirit greater and stronger than the rest waiting at the gates with his mouth open to devour Brandubh. At that moment a monk came forward and placed in the mouth of the evil spirit a cow like the one the Leinster righ had given to the leper. The demon continued to try to devour Brandubh, however, so the monk struck the monster's head with his staff and closed his fiery mouth.

Upon awakening, the Leinster Righ told his counselors what had occurred. The dream so distressed him that he began to waste away. Brandubh's counselors mentioned Maedoc, a famous local religious man, and described the many miracles attributed to him. They advised their righ to send for holy water blessed by this holy man, whom many already proclaimed a saint.

Brandubh replied, "By no means. I will instead go in person to this man of God." Mounting his chariot, the Leinster righ drove to Maedoc. When the monk heard Brandubh arrive, he went out to meet him, at which point the righ immediately recognized him and cried out, "This is the saint that rescued me from the demon's mouth and from the pains of Hell."

The righ prostrated himself at the saint's feet, saying, "I am truly contrite for having wrought so much evil, and whatsoever you shall prescribe for my soul's salvation, in the name of God, I will perform." Brandubh told Maedoc about his vision. The monk prayed over the Leinster righ and healed him of all his pain. In return Brandubh gave him rich offerings, including the land on which Ferns monastery was built in 570. Moreover, Brandubh promised that after his death his remains and those of his posterity would repose in St. Maedoc's cemetery.

While St. Patrick, St. Brigid, and St. Columcille are Ireland's most famous saints, the Irish usually prayed to local saints who were considered more likely to intercede for local folk. St. Maedoc became one of Hy Kinsella's most famous local saints. For generations, during feasts and gatherings, stories of Maedoc's holiness were told, like this story about the founding of Ferns on the land Brandubh had donated:

When founding the monastery at Ferns, Maedoc's fellow monks complained that they had no water supply of any kind. Pointing to an alder tree close by, Maedoc said, "Cut down that tree, my brothers, and a fountain will issue from its roots." Alder trees thrive in watery places and so they cheerfully carried out the pious abbot's directive.

Instantly a lively spring, which became known as St. Maedoc's well, surged forth.[2] Not long after, local women coming to the stream to wash their clothes upset Maedoc greatly. Approaching them he cried, "Go from hence, I beseech you, and come not here again."

But one, bolder than the rest, refused, saying, "We will not go away. This place belongs to all so the water is ours to use." She turned back to her task and continued washing, trampling on the clothes as she did so. Suddenly her feet stuck to the clothes, the clothes to the stones beneath, and the stones themselves to the earth, until she was utterly powerless and helpless, like a statue unable to move. After vainly struggling to free herself she gave up.

Her father, Beccus, a local landowner, ran to the pious Maedoc and asked him to please pardon his foolish daughter. Maedoc prayed fervently in silence until the protesting woman was set free. Beccus was truly grateful and humbly offered himself, his family, and his home to the saintly man.

Another captivating tale tells of a local herdsman whose mother was at the point of death.

A herdsmen appealed to Maedoc to let him have some holy water to bring to her in the hope that she would be cured. Maedoc readily agreed, but by the time the herdsman reached her she had already expired. He returned to Maedoc to relate the sad news. The saintly abbot uttered a fervent prayer and bade

---

[2] The well can still be reached by entering a tunnel underneath the current road through Ferns.

the herdsman, "Return at once to your dear mother and bid her come to this place."

Rushing to her bedside the herdsman exclaimed aloud, "Mother, dear. Bishop Maedoc has called you to his presence." She rose up instantly on hearing these words as if from a deep slumber and, having first thanked the Lord, she hastened to the holy man of God and thanked him profusely.

While Maedoc was busy founding the monastery at Ferns, Brandubh was becoming involved in politics outside of Leinster. In 572, Aed, son of Ainmirech, became Ard Righ of Ireland, and three years later he held a Convention in Drumceat (Daisy Hill in Ulster.)[3] Aed commanded Scotland (the Irish Dalriada clan who had settled there in 498) to give him a yearly tribute, but the Scottish Ard Righ, Aodhan, demanded complete freedom. Leinster lent its support to Scotland because the Scottish Ard Righ and the Leinster righ, Brandubh, were brothers. Keating tells of an event that happened when Brandubh was a young Leinster righ years before the convention of 572.

> Some say that the wife of Gabhran, who was called Ingheanach, and the wife of Eochaidh Feidhlim, daughter of Cobhtach son of Dathi, were both pregnant at the same time and were brought to bed on the same night. The two women were shut up in the same house, no one being with them, but both being together, while there was a guard placed on the outside by Gabhran. As to these women, Gabhran's wife gave birth to a daughter, and the wife of Eochaidh to twin sons. Now, Gabhran's wife never brought forth any children but daughters; and as the wife of Eochaidh had brought forth twin sons, she asked her to give her one of them, and Eochaidh's wife consent-

---

[3] Tara had been abandoned as a dwelling site by 565. Aed was a member of the northern Hy Neill, who ruled over most of Ulster.

ed to this. When the household, who were on guard, perceived that the women had been delivered, they asked the queen what offspring she had given birth to; she said that she had given birth to a son and daughter, and that the wife of Eochaidh had given birth to a son. All were delighted at this; and this son which the queen got from Eochaidh's wife had a name given him, and he was called Aodhan son of Gabhran; and Eochaidh's second son was called Brandubh son of Eochaidh.

And a long time after this, Gabhran, chief of Dalriada, who was king of Alba, died; and Aodhan assumed the sovereignty of Alba after him, and came to spoil and plunder Ireland, and endeavored to conquer it, as he was of the posterity of Cairbre Rioghfhada. A large company of the men of Anglia, Alba, and Wales came with him; and when they landed in Ireland, they set to plunder Leinster in the first instance. Brandubh son of Eochaidh at that time held the sovereignty of Leinster; and Aodhan sent envoys demanding hostages from him as securities for his paying tribute to him, saying that otherwise he would waste the whole territory of Leinster. While Brandubh was in trouble at this message, his mother told him to take courage, and that she would avert the attack of Aodhan from him. Upon this the mother went to the camp of Aodhan; and when she had reached it, she inquired of Aodhan why he had come to waste Leinster. "Thou hag," said he, "I am not obliged to give thee any information on that matter."

"If I be a hag," said she, "thy mother is a hag; and I have something to say to thee in secret." Thereupon he went with her apart. "Aodhan," said she, "I told thee that thy mother was a hag; and I tell thee now that I am she, and that accordingly Brandubh is thy brother. Therefore, send to Alba for thy supposed mother, and she will confess, in my presence, that I am thy mother; and until we meet, do thou refrain from spoiling Leinster."

He acted as the woman directed; and when the women came together, the queen of Alba admitted that it was Brandubh's mother who gave birth to Aodhan; and when he heard this, he bound the women to keep the matter a close secret lest he should lose the sovereignty of Alba at the hands of the Dalriada should they become aware of the affair. Thereupon, he sent for Brandubh; and they both formed a friendly alliance; and Aodhan left the country without inflicting injury on it.[4]

The Convention of Drumceat over tribute paid to Ireland's Ard Righ by Scotland was resolved by St. Columcille, a relation of both Ireland's Ard Righ and Scotland's Ard Righ, who declared Scotland should be forever absolved from paying tribute though a war contingent could be demanded.

Another interesting dispute at this convention concerned the filid of Ireland, of whom there were approximately 1,000. Aed, Ireland's Ard Righ, wanted to banish all of them for taking advantage of their position by demanding large fees for their work. Again Columcille made his decision known, and all lived by it. The filid should remain, but stricter regulations regarding payments for their services should be placed on them. Brandubh, the Leinster righ, had the same problem decades later. Without a St. Columcille to change his mind however, he banished all filid from his province. (They were such an integral part of Irish society that they were welcomed back immediately after his death.)

A further outcome of the convention was the establishment of a system of secular education. There was to be a chief college for each of the five provinces, and under their administration were to be minor colleges, one for each tuath. All were to provide free education. This education system, which would eventually transform into the hedge schools of later-day Ireland, lasted for 1,300 years.

---

[4] *Keating's History of Ireland.*

Brandubh was a very powerful provincial righ. He expanded the borders not only of Hy Kinsella but also of Leinster.[5] After a number of conquests he moved his residence to Rath Brandubh in west Wicklow. By 586 he had again defeated the Hy Neill in their territory.[6] Given his proven strength, the Hy Neill should have known not to provoke him.

In 597 Prince Cummascach, son of the Ard Righ, went through Leinster on his "free circuit of youth." By ancient tradition the son of the Ard Righ was allowed, once in his life, to enjoy the hospitality of all the other provincial righs. He could stay at each provincial righ's house for a period of his choosing with all the friends he desired, eating and drinking until he was satisfied. Before leaving his father's house, the prince had demanded one other privilege, the right to sleep with every provincial righ's wife. The prince's request preceded him, so, when he arrived at Brandubh's home with a huge entourage of rowdy friends, Brandubh greeted them disguised as a servant[7] and told them the righ was away in Britain raising tribute.[8] The entourage entered Brandubh's large feasting hall where a huge meal was waiting. As the guests immediately began to eat, Brandubh and his men closed the doors and began piling wood around the outside of the hall. Maedoc now arrived to deliver to Brandubh "The Sword of Crimthann,

---

[5] He took over part of Munster and formed the territory of Ossory.

[6] On the plain of Magh Ochtairr at the hill over Cluain Conaire in East Meath.

[7] According to Irish tradition, if Brandubh greeted them as himself and allowed them to eat, they were under his protection. Because a servant invited them to stay, they were technically under no one's protection until Brandubh himself returned.

[8] The colony of Irish that existed in Wales at this time was later driven out, many say by King Arthur.

[and] the Shield of Enna."[9] Brandubh gave the signal, his men set the wood ablaze, and soon the entire hall was on fire. The Leinstermen surrounded the house to prevent anyone from escaping. Glasdam, the prince's file, changed clothes with the prince while calling out, "I am of the filid class. It would be a great dishonor to you if I were hurt. Let me pass."[10]

Brandubh answered, "Let it be so. Climb up to the ridge-pole[11] and leap out over the flames to the ground. We will let you pass."

Prince Cummascach, disguised in his file's clothes, leapt out and was allowed to pass, while Glasdam remained behind and was burned to death with the rest. The file's plan failed however when Cummascach stopped at a monastery on his way home where he was identified and killed. A reprisal by the prince's father, the Ard Righ, was inevitable.

Aed, the Ard Righ, took a year to collect enough forces to challenge Brandubh, a testimony to the Leinster righ's power. By the year 598, Aed felt confident and marched on Leinster to collect the Boruma tribute and seek revenge for his son. He left a swath of devastation on his way south to confront Brandubh at Dunbolg[12] in Leinster. Brandubh sent Bishop Maedoc of Ferns, the Ard Righ's own half-brother, to sue for an armistice, because the Leinster righ needed more time to muster his forces.[13] Aed refused the armistice and addressed his half-brother with such insulting language that Bishop Maedoc predicted Aed's doom.

---

[9] These famous weapons, the shield from Enna Kinsella and the sword from his son, Crimthann, were passed down for generations.

[10] The filid, considered almost sacred, were not to be injured for any reason.

[11] The support beam on which the two sides of a roof meet at the top.

[12] Now Dunboyke near Hollywood in County Wicklow.

[13] Brandubh would have collected not only men but also women for the battle. After 697 women were exempted from battle through the influence of St. Adamnan at the synod of Tara.

To gain time for his army to assemble, Brandubh rode up to the Hy Neill line alone, and in the tradition of Cuchulainn challenged the best of them to single combat. Blathach, the chief marshal of the Ard Righ came out on Aed's favorite horse and took up the challenge. Blathach was a great warrior, praised for his skill with the spear, but he was no match for the famous Brandubh, who soon overthrew him, cut off his head, and returned in triumph to his own people with Blathach's head and the Ard Righ's favorite steed. Brandubh had bought a day, but he needed more time. Since his army was much smaller than the Ard Righ's with no hope of success in open battle, he devised another plan, which required knowledge of the enemy's encampment.

Ron Kerr, one of Brandubh's warriors, smeared calf's blood mixed with rye dough over himself until he looked like a leper. He fixed his knee in the socket of a wooden leg, which he borrowed from a cripple, and put on an ample cloak, under which he concealed a sword. To complete the deception he carried a begging wallet. In this wardrobe he hobbled to the royal camp and presented himself at the door of the Ard Righ's pavilion to make a complaint.

Asked for tidings, Ron Kerr replied, "I came from Kilbelat this morning. I went to the camp of the Leinstermen, and in my absence some persons, certainly not Leinstermen, came. They destroyed my cottage and my church, they broke my quern[14] and my spade."

The Ard Righ said that if he survived the upcoming battle, he would give the leper twenty cows as reparation for this injury. Inviting the leper into his pavilion, Aed asked him what the Leinstermen were doing.

---

[14] A hand-powered grindstone used to grind grain into flour.

Disguising as well as possible his manly voice and martial bearing, the leper said that they were preparing victuals for Brandubh and his army.

Suspecting from his expression that Ron Kerr was not a leper but a spy, Aed dispatched one of his territorial under-righs to stand guard with sufficient forces to prevent the Leinstermen from surprising his camp.

While Kerr spied out the Ard Righ's encampment, Brandubh met secretly on the side of a mountain at some distance from both camps with a righ from Ulster[15] who was supporting the Ard Righ. The Leinster righ induced the righ from Ulster to abandon Aed. The righ from Ulster said, "A blood-covenant and an agreement shall be made between us." Whereupon "they seated themselves on the mountain and made a bond of fellowship that should never be broken."[16]

Once the Ard Righ's forces were depleted by the loss of the Ulstermen, Brandubh collected 3,600 oxen carrying great hampers and concealed in them armed men covered with provisions. Together with a herd of 150 untamed horses, they set out by night towards the Ard Righ's camp. The advance guard around the camp, hearing the trampling and din, started to arms and questioned the party. They replied that they were a friendly contingent bringing a stock of provisions for the Ard Righ. When the guards examined the sacks and saw the provisions, they let them pass. Brandubh's men entered the royal enclosure, tied bags filled with pebbles to the tails of the wild horses and let them loose among the tents, causing terrible confusion. In the chaos, the men leapt from the hampers at a signal, formed into ranks and attacked the camp.

---

[15] The Ulidian righ, a major righ under Hy Neill power.

[16] They erected a commemorative cairn on the mountain and changed its name from Sliabh Neachtain to Sliabh Cadaigh, "the Mountain of the Covenant."

Upon hearing the uproar, Aed called for the cowl that St. Columcille had given him years before, promising that it would preserve him from death in any battle. "That cowl," replied the attendant, "we left behind us in the palace of Ailech in the North."

"Alas," said the Ard Righ, "then it is all the more likely I shall be slain by the Leinstermen."

The Ard Righ's forces were completely surprised and after a dreadful fight in the darkness, were routed. The Ard Righ fled from the field but was overtaken and beheaded by Ron Kerr. For this feat, Brandubh granted Ron Kerr "the privilege of dining at the royal table, and his paternal inheritance free of tribute to him and his representatives for ever."[17] After this great victory Brandubh moved his clan, the Hy Felimy,[18] to the more fertile lands around Ferns. He also moved the principal see of Leinster from Sletty to Ferns and named Maedoc bishop of Leinster.

After this great victory Brandubh took advantage of Hy Neill's weakness. He attacked them in their own territory of east Meath later that year and won. He attacked again in 601 but lost. In 605 he was defeated by the Hy Neill at Slaebre and soon after was assassinated by Saran, the administrator of a monastery in Hy Kinsella.

> Saran Soebhdhearc (of the evil Eye), a guide indeed;
> Airchinneach [manager] of Seanboith Sine,[19]
> Was he, it is no falsehood without bright judgment,
> Who killed Brandubh, son of Eochaidh.[20]

---

[17] Irish annals.
[18] One of the six clans descended from Enna Kinsella.
[19] The name of the monastery located east of Mount Leinster in Wexford.
[20] An anonymous 9th-century author.

A tributary righ, unhappy with his position under Brandubh, planned the murder while the Leinster righ's power was at an ebb after losing the previous battle to the Hy Neill. The assassination took place in Brandubh's own house, and the Leinster righ, totally surprised by an attack from a religious man, fell without making his confession or receiving the holy sacrament. The following tale embellishes the incident to honor both Brandubh and St. Maedoc.

On hearing this, the pious Bishop Maedoc was greatly grieved. Bursting into tears he passionately said, in reference to the slayer, "I wish that his hand should fall from his side, having murdered our Church's and our country's defender; for he was the protector of widows and of the poor." Then coming to the place where the righ's body lay, St. Maedoc offered up a prayer. Suddenly Brandubh arose in the presence of all.

The Leinster righ then said, "I beseech thee, Father, if thou promise me God's Kingdom that I may now go to Heaven. I have sufficiently fulfilled my course of life, and the Lord will grant you another righ."

This desire pleased the bishop. Having offered up his prayers and having given absolution and the holy sacrament to Brandubh, the latter passed out of this life to one of eternal glory. He was buried with much honor in Ferns cemetery and here his posterity, who belonged to the royal family of Leinster, subsequently reposed. Maedoc himself, who was to die on January 31, 624, was also buried at Ferns.

Saran, Brandubh's murderer, filled with remorse for his deed, went to the Leinster righ's tomb. Here he engaged in a course of rigorous penance. He remained there day and night, almost in a state of nudity, and subjected himself to prolonged fasts. When he had continued for some time in this state, Saran heard Brandubh's voice issuing from the tomb, "Thou art forgiven thy crimes, O Saran Buite." Immediately St. Maedoc's curse is said to have fallen upon him, for his hand then dropped from his side. Some pious persons, cognizant of this circumstance, led Saran away from the tomb. Afterwards he led a most religious life and died, it is hoped, a true penitent.[21]

After Brandubh's reign, control of the throne of Leinster began to slip from the hands of Enna Kinsella's descendants and they had to be content with ruling only south Leinster (Hy Kinsella). For several centuries Hy Kinsella rarely ruled Leinster, while the three clans of north Leinster began to claim the throne. Previously, when the Leinster righ went into battle, usually against the Hy Neill, he commanded both north and south Leinster men. With Hy Kinsella too weak to claim the throne of Leinster but still strong enough to resist submitting to north Leinster, the Leinster righ often commanded only the men of north Leinster; those of Hy Kinsella didn't answer his summons. The province of Leinster was split in half and the Hy Neill profited from its weakened condition. They cultivated an alliance with north Leinster and helped fight off any contenders to the throne of Leinster from Hy Kinsella. Leinster began to lose more than its share of battles and therefore its land. Not until the 11th century did a strong Leinster righ appear to regain the lost territory. That man, Dermot Mac-MaelnamBo, was again from Hy Kinsella, a descendant of Enna Kinsella.

---

[21] John O'Hanlon, *Lives of the Irish Saints* (Dublin, 1875).

The 7th and 8th Centuries

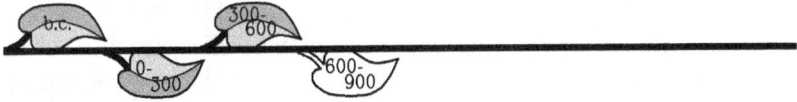

From the 7th to the 9th century, the province of Leinster was largely controlled by righs from north Leinster, although the territories submitting to them varied. The territories of Offaly, Leix, and Hy Kinsella were rarely controlled by the Leinster righ for any length of time, and rebellion and revolt were common among the territories of every province. The Leinster righ might gain the submission of Hy Kinsella for a few years but lose it suddenly when the Hy Kinsella righ felt strong enough to challenge his overlord. Ossory, a buffer state between Leinster and Munster, was controlled by only the strongest of Leinster or Munster righs. Often it was not under the control of either province.[1] During these centuries the other provinces frequently intruded in Leinster, as Irish politics became more complicated and Hy Kinsella was mired in internal disputes.

End of the Boruma Tribute

Finnactha Fleadhach (the festive), Ard Righ of Ireland, "bore away the Tribute twice without opposition," but the third time he demanded it in 674 the Leinstermen rose up against him. Extensive preparations were made on both sides. Before the battle of Logore in Meath the religious class hoped to gain

---

[1] The Ossory righ might even turn the tables and become Leinster righ.

141

a peace agreement. An assembly was held to which south Leinster sent their holiest man of the time, Moling.

Moling, born in Hy Kinsella at the beginning of the 7th century, was a descendant of Enna Kinsella. His father was a brugaid (inn keeper).[2] He embraced the religious life at a young age and founded the monastery of Tigh Moling or "House of Moling" on the Barrow River.[3] He built a mill and as a penance to God spent eight years and seven days digging a watercourse with his own hands. This devoted monk who had many miracles attributed to him was the man who arrived at the assembly presided over by the Leinster righ, Bran Ua Faelain (from a north Leinster clan).

Moling received a joyous welcome and was seated at the Leinster righ's side. After deliberation it was determined that Moling should be the province's delegate to argue for peace with the Hy Neill. He left immediately and proceeded northwards to the Faire of Teltown[4] (in Meath) where the Ard Righ, Finnactha Fleadhach, was presiding. Aware of his mission, the Hy Neill paid no heed to Moling. Suddenly the heavens opened up with a downpour of heavy rain and hail that called the games to a halt yet no rain or hail fell where Moling stood; the grass was perfectly dry. Seeing this miracle, the Hy Neill requested Moling to drive away the rain in the name of the Lord so the games might continue, promising in return to satisfy Moling after the games concluded.

Moling prayed to the Lord, blessed the heavens and the rain instantly ceased while the sun made its appearance. The games

---

[2] Moling's ancestors must have slipped from the nobility to the top rung of the common man's class. Brugaid was an extremely well-respected position in Irish society.

[3] Now St. Mullins, one of the two most important monasteries of Hy Kinsella, the other being Ferns.

[4] The longest running sporting event in the world, it was similar to the Greek Olympics but also had story, music and poetry competitions.

continued but when they were done the Hy Neill refused to keep their promise to Moling and remit the Boruma tribute. One righ began arguing so vociferously against Moling that the holy man made the sign of the cross on his breast. The righ instantly became pacified and even began to entreat the others to agree with Moling and forgive the tribute. Many nobles were still opposed, so Moling said to the Ard Righ, "Grant me at least, oh Righ, until Luan." (Luan means Monday but can also mean the Day of Judgment.) The Ard Righ thought he meant until the following Monday and granted his request. But Moling meant the Day of Judgment, and the Ard Righ could not take back his word.

Moling was eventually made bishop of Ferns in 691 near the end of his life. (He died on May 13th, 696.) The reason such a holy man wasn't made bishop of Ferns sooner was because the throne of Leinster was controlled by north Leinster, who understood the political expediency of building up the power and prestige of their own Kildare monastery at the expense of Ferns.

Hy Kinsella did attempt to regain the throne of Leinster during these centuries. In 707 the Hy Kinsella righ, Bran, attacked the Leinster righ, Ceallach Cualann, at Selgge (near Glendalough in County Wicklow), but the battle was a draw largely because British mercenaries hired by the Leinster righ proved quite effective. If Bran of Hy Kinsella had also employed mercenaries, he would probably have won and become Leinster righ. When a later Hy Kinsella righ employed such mercenaries centuries later, the consequences for Ireland were lasting and devastating.

In 718 another Hy Kinsella righ, Aed Mend, fought in a battle alongside the men of north Leinster when the Hy Neill were again demanding the Boruma tribute. Marching with 21,000 men to collect the tribute, the Ard Righ Fergall met the

Leinster righ (from a north Leinster clan), who had only 9,000 men, at the Hill of Allen in Kildare, which was the Leinster righ's stronghold. Fighting for their capital, the mainly north Leinster army miraculously won and killed the Ard Righ in the ensuing battle.

Aed Mend was the great-great-grandson of Crumdmael, who had been Hy Kinsella and then Leinster righ, as had Ronan, his father before him. Because of this heritage, Aed Mend had high ambitions. After the battle at the Hill of Allen in 718, he spent years consolidating his power in Hy Kinsella and waiting for an opportunity to regain the throne of Leinster. In 726, as Hy Kinsella righ, he attacked and defeated Munster and was recognized as Leinster righ. His defense of Leinster against the Ard Righ in 718 came back to haunt him years later though.

The son of the Ard Righ killed attempting to take the Boruma tribute in 718 attacked Leinster in 733 to avenge the death of his father and to claim the Boruma tribute again. In the battle fought at Ballyshannon in Kildare, Aed Mend was killed by this Ard Righ in single combat. The Ard Righ left the field "sore hurt, and lived after; the other, by a deadly blow, lost his head from the shoulders." The Boruma tribute was claimed for the last time.

Hy Kinsella's attempt to keep the throne of Leinster was thwarted when Aed's brother, Faelan, died "unexpectedly and at an early age." Hy Kinsella was left without a strong leader and became torn by internal disputes as clans descending from Enna Kinsella fought over the right to rule the territory. Such disputes, signals of weakness to other provinces, allowed Ossory to raid the prosperous lands of south Leinster in 749. Seven years later the Hy Kinsella righ attempted to retaliate and marched into Ossory but was soundly defeated. South Leinster was fracturing along clan lines and would long await a strong leader to consolidate the power of its people. The annals for the next few decades describe more internal disputes from which no solid contender emerged. North Leinster's claim to the throne of Leinster remained unchallenged by south Leinster.

The province as a whole reflected the degradation of south Leinster. Ever since Crimthann Kinsella, the Hy Neill had been encroaching on Leinster. In his time Hy Neill raided Leinster, and Leinster raided Hy Neill. The situation was a stalemate. By the 7th century it had deteriorated, with many battles going against Leinster. By the end of the 8th century Leinster had grown so weak that the Hy Neill neglected to attack it with major armies and actually defended it from raids such as Munster's in 789. The glory days of Leinster seemed to be behind them, but the power of an Irish province ebbed and flowed.

Viking Ship

The year 795 brought a new twist to Irish politics: the first recorded Viking raid occurred on the west coast of Ireland. It was only a matter of time before Hy Kinsella felt the Vikings' greed. Cairbre, son of Cathal, was the Hy Kinsella righ when they first struck in 826. Cairbre defeated them in this initial encounter, but when they returned eight years later Ferns was plundered and Cairbre himself was captured. Before his death in 842 Ferns was plundered and burned again. Some of the Vikings who arrived in south Leinster remained to settle. In Wexford a defensive armed Viking camp evolved into a thriving trading town. A Viking camp was also recorded along the

River Liffey in 841 that would eventually become Dublin.

In 868 another important political event occurred. In a routine raid, the Ard Righ of Ireland plundered south through Leinster and attacked Ossory with the help of the Leinster righ who had submitted. Ossory, a weak territory up until then, responded by raiding in Leinster all the way north to Dunbolg. The incensed Leinster righ

Viking raid on a monastery

was defeated when he brought the fight back to the fort of the Ossory righ. The Ossory righ, now bursting with confidence, went on to attack and defeat the Viking town of Waterford. Ossory, Hy Kinsella's neighbor to the west, realized after defeating the Leinster righ that it could play a more prominent role in Irish politics.

The 10th century proved just as depressing for south Leinster as the 9th had been. More dynastic disputes among the six clans of Enna Kinsella's descendants within Hy Kinsella provoked successful raids from outside. South Leinster's power was at its ebb. A dramatic change would occur during the next century when the clan descending from Crimthann was accepted as the dominant one.

Ireland from the 9th to 12th Centuries

Ireland's Place in Europe

efore delving into the history of medieval Ireland, it's important to understand the history and beliefs of Ireland's neighbors. Modern thinking places Ireland at the edge of Europe and on the periphery of the civilized world, but early medieval people saw things differently. In a society where travel by water was preferred and quicker, Paris was closer to Ireland than to Italy or Germany. Ireland and England were major trading posts between the Scandinavian north and the Mediterranean south.

In Spain and Portugal the "noble Irish" obtained more valuable privileges than the English. The great Italian financial houses, the bankers of Lucca, the Ricardi, the Friscobaldi, and the Mozzi, were active agents in medieval Ireland. Bordeaux in France had a colony of Irish merchants as did St. Omar, Marseilles, Bayonne, St. Malo and Nantes. They imported Irish wool, skins, hides, fish, woolen cloth, fine linen, leather and grain. Throughout medieval Europe, Irish leather was as highly regarded as Italian leather is today. In relation to medieval Europe, Ireland was closer to the center than the edge.

European Feudalism

Early medieval Europe was barbaric by today's standards. By their own standards, each culture considered itself advanced and every foreign culture barbaric. To appreciate the level of culture in Ireland, comparison with the surrounding cultures is helpful. Feudalism developed in continental Europe and was

147

introduced into England by the Normans in 1066. Feudalism became the customary rule of life for most nobles of Europe, but not for nobles of Ireland.

European feudalism was fairly well established by the end of the 12th century. Previously, primogeniture,[1] for example, was practiced but not universally accepted. When a king died, his relatives fought over the throne. Late in the 12th century Henry II of England had to fight off numerous threats to his throne from three of his own sons. On his deathbed he demonstrated the advantages of primogeniture by ceding his crown to his eldest son, Richard the Lion Hearted. Primogeniture reduced but did not eliminate bloodshed among relatives.

Feudalism, including primogeniture, was a collection of customs that described the duties of every person in a society with respect to each other. It outlined what each person's responsibilities were and how far their power extended, including a noble's ability to wage war. In the wars of early medieval Europe, armies were small and battles rare. Skirmishes and raids were the rule; few engagements involved thousands. Decisive action was avoided as too risky. The strategies of war centered on doing the greatest possible harm to the adversary by setting his villages on fire and massacring the peasants, who were his property and source of income. The citizen, the monk, and especially the peasant bore the brunt of feudal warfare.

To the non-Celtic feudal noble, war was an exciting game in which fame and money could be won without great risk of personal injury. Nobles captured and ransomed each other much more often than they killed each other. After a battle, noble prisoners were kept for ransom. Since no profit could be made from prisoners of an inferior class, such as archers,

---

[1] The oldest son inheriting the throne.

arbalesters and servants of the army, they were massacred or mutilated to prevent them from fighting again.

Victory to the leader of a feudal expedition during early medieval times meant:

> He does not leave a good knight alive . . . , nor treasure, nor monastery, nor church, nor shrine, nor censer, nor cross, nor sacred vase; everything that he seizes he gives to his compan-ions. He makes so cruel a war that he does not lay hands on a man without killing, hanging, or mutilating him.[2]

Raiding was common but not constant, which presented a problem to the feudal noble whose only function was fighting. Unlike an Irish noble, he did not oversee his peasants, involve himself in law, or perform any other duty. He needed plunder to satiate his appetite for power and wealth. To get through the boredom of peaceful times, many a noble came up with cun-ning ways to gain wealth. He stole by robbing merchants and travelers and by levying illegal taxes and tithes on the peasants and citizens of his land. Universal exploitation made the prop-erty and life of the feudal peasant hardly safer in peace than in war. The following example indicates how far a noble would go to satisfy his greed:

> One day, a bailiff, the officer of a certain count, wishing to please his master, said to him: "Seignior, if you will listen to me, I will tell you a way to make a good sum of money each year."
>
> "With pleasure," replied the count.
>
> "Allow me then, seignior, to sell the sun on all your land."
>
> "How," asked the count, "can one sell God's sun?"
>
> "Very simply: many of your men wash their clothes and dry them in the sun. If they give you no more than twelve deniers

---

[2] From a lay of Girart de Roussillon.

for each piece of cloth, you will make much money." And this is how that bad officer led his seignior to sell the sun's rays.[3]

The life of a noble was rich and varied; the life of a non-Celtic peasant, at the other end of the social spectrum, was not. The conditions of the peasant's tenancy were only slightly better than slavery. His lord could tax him, sell him, evict him at will, fine him if his daughter married, force him to use the lord's mill and oven, and take the peasant's best cow when the peasant died. The peasant was not allowed to carry weapons in his own defense. His lot was unremitting labor, toiling for a meager livelihood from his holding when not working long hours on the soil of his landlord. He was obliged to accept his lord's tasks without argument and was forced to do them at a moment's bidding ("nor shall he know in the evening what he shall do on the morrow"). Irish society was different because it was ruled by the clan, a group of mixed social rankings totally different from the nobility under feudalism.

The Roman Catholic Church

Even the church was victimized in European feudalism, but unlike the peasant, it had the power to fight back. To the nobles, the church was an inexhaustible supply of wealth but also a competitor for power.

The concept of the Roman Catholic Church as an institution independent of civil authority with only spiritual and moral functions is a modern one. Today the church is a powerful international organization, centralized under a supreme head whose authority none of the faithful question. The church has renounced all secular rule while imposing an absolute unity of faith and doctrine. In the 12th century the church was alto-

---

[3] Achille Luchaire, *Social France at the Time of Philip Augustus* (New York, 1967).

gether different. Dogma and morality were fundamentally the same as today, but many people lived on the vast tracts of land that the church owned. The church's power was as much temporal as spiritual, and secular society and the church profoundly influenced one another.

The murderous politics that took place among the feudal nobles were mirrored, albeit to a lesser extent, in the Church. In Italy the marquis Borrell of Barcelona, in an attempt to strengthen his position, reestablished an archbishopric that hadn't existed for years. He then placed the bishopric of Gerona, held by an enemy, under the control of his friend, the newly ordained archbishop. This created a power struggle between the bishop and archbishop resulting shortly afterwards in the new archbishop's murder.[4] Just as the feudal nobility interfered in the political life of the church, so the church interfered with the political life of the nobility. Ireland's history provides only one of many examples during this time.

Irish Law

According to the historian Nicholas Mansergh, Ireland had developed "a distinctive, though brittle, civilization, which equaled, and probably surpassed anything that contemporary Europe produced." Ireland remained outside the sphere of feudalism because it had never been a part of the Roman empire. Its own legal system, called Brehon law, governed society. Irish nobles were far less likely to damage property of commoners or burn their towns, because Brehon law required indemnification, and no one was above Brehon law. A basic understanding of this law, since it regulated the operation of Irish society, will help clarify the historical events to follow.

The Brehon laws, obeyed but not created by the nobles, acted as a check and balance to a righ's power. An Irish righ

---

[4] Heinrich Fichtenau, *Living in the Tenth Century* (Chicago, 1991).

was unable to create laws in order to pay back his debts, a huge source of money and corruption in feudal Europe. Tales of bandits and dangerous journeys were common in Europe, but rare in Ireland before the arrival of the Normans. The Brehon laws bound society together. Living outside the law resulted in banishment, which in a clan-based society often meant death.

Of prime importance to the Irish, whose climate favored cattle raising over agriculture, was their ancient "Law of Daire," which stated that cows could be taken during a raid but not maimed or killed. Irish diet accounted for the logic behind this law and its critical importance to Irish society. Dairy products were a major part of Irish diet all year long, but milk, butter and cheese were almost all that sustained them from the end of winter until the first crops in early summer. Stolen cows were often returned as a gift in exchange for a righ's submission. Killing the cows of an area condemned the people to a slow death. Their food supply would be meager in summer, fall and winter, and in spring, if they lasted that long, they would starve. This benefited no one: the raiding righ could not gain tribute from a wasteland and could not farm conquered land without an excess population.

Another group of laws with far-reaching implications described honor price and eric fee. The measure of a person's social status was his honor price, and punishments were based on this price. For example, injuring someone required payment of a designated fraction of his honor price, so that injuring a righ cost the offender much more than injuring a slave.

In Ireland murder was the most serious crime one could commit. Throughout history many systems of justice redressed the taking of life by taking the murderer's life. For example, Exodus 21:24 states, "Thou shalt give life for life, eye for eye, tooth for tooth." Even causing another's death through negligence might entail the death penalty; Exodus 21:29 sentences ox and owner to death if an ox of known viciousness kills someone. The Brehon laws allowed a killer to atone for his crime by making a double payment. The first payment, the eric fee, was 21 cows given to the victim's kin, regardless of the victim's social status (measured by their honor price). The second payment was based on the victim's honor price and the kin's relation to the victim. A son or daughter received more than a niece or nephew, for example. This concept applied to other cases as well. A man who abducted the wife of another man paid the wife's full honor price (a considerable sum) to her husband and kin. The punishment for abduction proved extremely important in the history of the 12th century.

Supplying collateral for a loan was also practiced in various ways. An important item was pledged when borrowing oxen, for example. The same concept applied to righs when submitting to another righ. They handed over collateral in the form of hostages, who were close family members, in return for protection. If they rebelled against their benefactor, the hostages could be killed. Enforcing loyalty in this way was a common practice in Ireland and throughout Europe.

Irish law was pragmatic: laws were to be obeyed but victims were to use common sense. Someone stung by bees while carelessly watching the hives at swarming time had no claim against the beehive owner. Similarly, someone who lost something precious that was found in a likely rather than unlikely place was granted a smaller portion for not having looked very hard. The Brehon laws were unlike the laws of European countries influenced by Roman law.

The Irish adopted some European customs, however, particularly those practiced by the Vikings. For example, the Vikings expanded the use of slaves in Ireland. Before their arrival in Ireland captives taken during a raid or people banished by their clan might be slaves, but they were not bought and sold. The slave trade, common in ancient Rome, flourish-ed in Europe. The Irish adopted the practice but restricted it to "an act of defiance and humiliation" visited only on Viking prisoners of war.

Feudal King vs. Irish King

The powers of a feudal king differed dramatically from those of an Irish righ. After the 12th century the Irish political system, already influenced by Europe's, was to compete directly with feudalism. The following is a summary of both leaders' sphere of power, using England as the example for a feudal king.

<u>**English Feudal King**</u>   <u>**Irish Righ**</u>

Control over Land

The kings of England were the supreme landlords who ruled over their nobles. When the king summoned them to war, those who didn't respond forfeited their lands and thus their power. The king gave the land of rebel-lious lords to his supporters as reward.

In Ireland land was owned by the individual or the clan. A righ, like any Irishman, con-trolled only his own acreage, which could be less than that of some nobles he ruled over. When a righ, such as a prov-incial righ, summoned all to war, only those in his tuath needed to respond. Righs who had submitted to him were allied with but not ruled by him and could always break the alliance.[5] A rebel-lious Irish righ could not lose his land and, even if he were

---

[5] Attempts by over-righs to regain the submission of rebellious righs accounted for a great deal of the small-scale warfare in Ireland.

killed, his successor had to be someone from that tuath rather than a puppet from another tuath chosen by the provincial righ.

Influence over Laws

The king of England could create his own laws and alter the power of any segment of society. To raise money for his army he could (and frequently did) impose extra taxes.

The Irish righ could not create laws or limit the power of any segment of society. His only means of raising revenue[6] was raiding.

Influence over the Church

In England, the Church had a well-established hierarchy of power, which the king had great influence over, since he could veto assignments to religious positions made by the pope. The church brokered truces and sanctified battles and invasions, and a leader who had the ear of the church could use these powerful prerogatives to his advantage. William the Conqueror, for example, didn't invade England until he had the pope's support, which encouraged the monasteries of England to aid him.

The church in Ireland, until it began forming a hierarchy in the 12th century, was as fragmented as the politics of the island and thus had little power. An Irish righ would aim to control local monasteries so that riches brought in to it could be funneled his way.

---

[6] The Irish didn't use money during these centuries.

The Law of Royal Succession

The eldest son of the English king succeeded his father.[7]	The Irish righ was elected by the clan from among the relatives of the previous righ. The elections were often contested, which led to dynastic feuds.

The Right of Rebellion

In England, rebellion against the invested king was an attack on God's chosen one and was not undertaken lightly, because the populace would side with the king.	In Ireland, rebellion was every noble's right.

The powers of an Irish righ were clearly quite limited in comparison with those of a king of England. Forming alliances was the most effective way to increase power. A common method was marriage to a powerful righ's daughter. The nobles of Ireland practiced polygamy, allowing several alliances through marriage. In the 11th century, the Church began condemning polygamy to little effect.

Another common method of forming alliances was fosterage. Nobles fostered out their children to other nobles for their upbringing, seeing them only periodically during the year. Irish history rarely records foster-sons attacking foster-fathers or vice versa; instead, stories abound where they went to each other's aid. The bonds fosterage created between child and

---

[7] Primogeniture didn't become common until the 12th century. Before then, when a king died, a strong relative of the king seized the throne or the king's sons divided the kingdom and then each fought to the death trying to reclaim all.

foster parent were perhaps stronger than those between child and natural parent.

Irish Politics in the 9th-12th Centuries

Because monasteries housed the greatest concentrations of wealth, they played a key political role in each province during these centuries. They had their own grazing and farming land and served as safe-havens for skilled workers. Nobles traded for precious rings, armbands and pins at monasteries. Monasteries were targets for raids by competing righs, who required the wealth they controlled to increase personal power.

By the end of the 11th century, the Norse and then Danish invasions, loosely referred to as "Viking" invasions, created more concentrations of wealth in the trading towns of Limerick, Waterford, Wexford and Dublin (the major center). Leinster benefited greatly from having three of these towns along its border.

During the 11th and 12th centuries, an Irish righ who wished to rise in power followed certain steps. After inauguration in his territory, the righ had to secure the control of the province's most important monastery, such as Kildare in Leinster. Funds brought into the monastery could then be funneled into the righ's hands for distribution as bribes or as income for military expenditures. At this point or before, he must attain the position of provincial righ by forcing all other territorial righs to owe him tribute. Next the Danish towns had to be controlled so funds gained from trade could be added to his resources. Rising to Ard Righ required the submission of all the other provinces. All Irish nobles knew these steps, but dangerous pitfalls lay along the way. We will follow this process through the career of our ancestor Dermot MacMurrough in a later chapter.

Because of cultural differences, the Gaelic feudalism that developed in Ireland from the 9th to the 12th century, with the Ard Righ position its pinnacle, was different from that which developed in the rest of Europe. "The history of Ireland in the eleventh and twelfth centuries is the history of a race evolving its monarchy, and is therefore likely to prove a valuable contribution to European history."[8]

Ard Righ

The position of Ard Righ belonged in theory to the strongest provincial righ. By the 11th century two titles existed: Ard Righ with Opposition, which meant more than half the provincial righs had submitted, and Ard Righ without Opposition. Upon attaining the ultimate political position in Ireland, the Ard Righ without Opposition went on a "circuit," a sunwise (clockwise) tour of all the provinces where he was met by the provincial righs and given hostages. The Ard Righ gained recognition as the strongest ruler in Ireland but was given no other rights.

At no stage in Irish history was the position of Ard Righ equivalent to a monarchy, though it was moving in that direction. The Hy Neill, the most powerful clan in early Ireland, distorted history by describing themselves as the sole Ard Righs of Ireland until Brien Boruma, but a cursory reading of the annals reveals that this position was honorary only. No Ard Righ before Brien Boruma commanded all of Ireland's provinces, and even Brien Boruma lacked governmental authority over the whole island. The Ard Righ's rule was very different from the totalitarian rule enjoyed by the later English or German monarchs.[9]

---

[8] Standish Hayes O'Grady.

[9] Similar to the Irish Ard Righ, the French monarch had little power during this time and was constantly being attacked by his own nobles.

Brien Boruma

Munster, one of Ireland's five provinces, had been ruled by the powerful Eoganacht clan for centuries, but by the 10th century their power had begun to wane while that of a relatively minor clan in northern Munster, the Dal Cais, had begun to increase. By the middle of the century the Dal Cais, who had never held the throne of Munster, challenged the traditional Munster ruling clan and initiated changes that would forever alter politics in Ireland.

In 976 the Dal Cais elected a new leader of their territory, Brien Boruma.[1] Brien aimed at the Munster righ position, even though no one in his clan had ever held the position. After a series of attacks against his enemies spanning two years, Irishmen and Dane alike, he was acknowledged as the Munster righ.

While it was not unprecedented for the traditional ruling clan of a province or territory to lose power (the leader of Hy Kinsella was not always a descendant of Enna Kinsella), it was unusual. Already Brien Boruma was exceptional.

He spent the next few years building up his power base in Munster, curbing revolts, eliminating challengers to his power and building alliances. Then he began expanding his power

---

[1] Some history books confuse Brien's nickname, Boruma, with the Boruma tribute anciently levied against Leinster. He gained the nickname Boruma because "he belonged to the division of the Dal Cais known as Dal Cais Borumha" (from Rev. T. Olden's *Church History*). Although he did eventually gain Leinster's submission, he never exacted the ancient tribute from them.

through a series of offensive forays. He concentrated on Leinster first, because it had no effective leader. The claimant for the position of Leinster righ was from north Leinster, but south Leinster, the land of Hy Kinsella, wouldn't acknowledge him.

By 996, Brien had forced Leinster to give him hostages and pay tribute, proof that they had submitted to him and viewed him as their overlord. This was a challenge to the Ard Righ of Ireland, Maelseachlainn from the southern Hy Neill clan of Meath. Maelseachlainn tested Brien's power through a series of attacks and finally decided to negotiate. Witnessed by the church, the two signed an agreement stating that Maelseachlainn would rule the northern half of Ireland and Brien the southern half.

Very satisfied with this agreement, Brien used peace as an opportunity to complete his subjugation of Leinster by crushing anyone who refused to submit hostages and pay tribute. Most of the destruction was confined to north Leinster, the home of the Leinster righ, because Hy Kinsella supported Brien. (They would have supported anyone who destabilized north Leinster thus allowing them the opportunity to take the throne of Leinster for themselves, which they eventually did.) A revolt of north Leinster, in alliance with the Dublin Danes, was crushed by Brien Boruma at the battle of Glenn Mama in 999. The Leinster righ, Maelmorda, was found hiding in a yew tree at the end of the battle, and his resulting shame figured prominently in the years to come.

In 1001 Brien finally demanded the submission of the Ard Righ, Maelseachlainn of the Hy Neill. According to Keating, Maelseachlainn told Brien's ambassadors to convey his request for a respite of one month, which would allow him to summon the army of Northern Ireland. At the end of a month he would either give battle or send hostages to Brien. But when the Ulster righ, of the Northern Hy Neill, refused to support the

Ard Righ, Maelseachlainn journeyed to Brien and told him that he would give hostages and submit.

Brien, instead of accepting, asked Maelseachlainn to take a respite of one year to see if he could gain the Ulster righ's support. Maelseachlainn refused this offer, declaring that he would not fight against Brien. Celtic chivalry in war contrasted sharply with European military tactics of the time.

A few years after signing the peace agreement with Maelseachlainn, Brien gained the submission of not only Meath but also Connacht. He now held hostages from every province except Ulster. From 1002 to 1011, the country was peaceful except for inveterate raiding. The annals state that "a lone woman came from Tory in the North of Ireland (Donegal) to Cliodhna in the South (near Cork), carrying a ring of gold, and she was neither robbed nor insulted." Robbery was prevalent in other European countries; few if any could boast of a culture as safe as Ireland's for the common person.

Not content with defeating most of the provinces in Ireland, Brien Boruma raised an army and struck in Ulster. After a number of victories and setbacks, by 1011 he was recognized as Ard Righ of Ireland since every provincial righ had submitted hostages and was paying tribute. As often happened in Ireland, this triumph was short-lived. Within a year Leinster refused to pay tribute because of an insult to its righ, Maelmorda, and war was imminent. That an insult could trigger a major battle between provinces highlights the paramount importance of honor in Irish culture.

It all began when Maelmorda, the Leinster righ, arrived at Brien's royal residence, Kincora, bringing part of the tribute he paid as Brien's vassal, three large pine trees to make masts for shipping. The trees had been cut in the great forest that extended into the three north Leinster territories. Each territory furnished one of the three masts, and each territory sent a party of its men to carry its tree. During the ascent of a boggy mountain, a dispute occurred among the men concerning which group had the right to go first and therefore be considered the most honored. Maelmorda resolved the dispute by personally assisting in carrying the tree from his territory. He wore a tunic of silk with "a border of gold around it and silver buttons," which Brien had given him. While he was lifting the tree, one of his buttons came off. When he arrived at Kincora, he asked his sister Gormflaith, who was one of Brien's wives, to replace it. Taking the tunic and casting it into the fire, she reproached him in bitter and insulting language for his weakness in submitting to Brien and added that never would their father or grandfather have suffered such indignity. By accepting the silk tunic from Brien, Maelmorda had acknowledged Brien as his superior.

Her words naturally irritated Maelmorda and put him in a foul mood. Leaving his sister, he walked through Kincora until he came upon Brien's eldest son, Murrogh, playing a game of chess with his cousin. Looking on, Maelmorda suggested to the Ard Righ's son a move that caused him to lose the game. Angered at this, Murrogh said to Maelmorda, "That was like the advice you gave to the Norse, which caused both of you to lose the battle of Glenn Mama." The Leinster righ answered, "I will give them advice now and they shall not be again defeated." Murrogh replied, "Then you had better remind them to have a yew tree on the battle site so you can climb into it again when you lose." This insult infuriated Maelmorda who, early the next morning, left Brien's house "without permission and without taking leave."

Hearing of this, Brien immediately sent a messenger to ask Maelmorda to return and listen to an explanation. The messenger overtook him, but the Leinster righ's irritation had not yet subsided. He struck the ill-fated messenger a violent blow on the skull with his horse stick and "broke all the bones of his head." Maelmorda lost no time in returning to his own territory and making known to his clan the great insult he had received. He used all his influence to excite them to avenge his wrongs, which set the stage for the battle of Clontarf in 1014.

Munster's description of this battle[2] is a wonderful piece of political propaganda that has the Irish rising up and casting off the yoke of Viking domination once and for all, literally pushing their oppressors into the sea. The annals written in Munster exaggerate how powerful Brien was and how threatening the Vikings were. The annals written in the other provinces tell a different story. They portray a Brien Boruma who could barely control the other provincial righs and show the Viking threat to have long since passed. By 1014, the Vikings had settled at several sites, Dublin being the major one, where they carried out trade beneficial to themselves and Ireland.

Battle of Clontarf

Maelmorda, the Leinster righ, had managed to assemble the men of north Leinster (Hy Kinsella would not support him) and the Danes of Dublin. Opposing them were Brien's Munstermen and two small

---

[2] *Cogadh Gaedhel re Gallaibh. The War of the Gaedhil with the Gaill, or, the Invasions of Ireland by the Danes and other Norsemen*, ed. James Henthorn Todd (London, 1867).

groups from Connacht. Maelseachlainn, previously Ard Righ and now just Meath righ, decided to watch the battle from an overlooking hill.

In the battle of Clontarf, Brien and his Munstermen were surprised at dawn and severely beaten back by the Leinster forces, which began raiding the Munstermen's camps around midday. The Meath righ, seeing a chance for easy victory, drove his forces into the Leinster forces, catching them completely by surprise and pushing them into the sea. Thus a defeat for Munster was turned into victory, but one that came at a great price. Both Brien Boruma and his capable son Murrogh were killed that day.

As his major accomplishment, which had repercussions for centuries, Brien demonstrated that the Ard Righ position could be won. Any righ smart enough, lucky enough, and strong enough could seize it, including one outside the traditional clans of southern or northern Hy Neill. The next two centuries saw a series of contests for the over-lordship of all Ireland. The Gaels were creating their own type of feudalism at the same time France and England were experimenting with a Roman version.

Brien was also responsible for the custom of using surnames. His descendants, starting with his grandson, were so proud of their heritage that they added to their name the term O'Brien, meaning "descendant of Brien." During the 11th century the custom spread throughout the country. Families naming themselves after their fathers adopted "Mac" (the first MacCarthy was the son of a man named Carthy), and those naming themselves after more distant ancestors adopted "O" (the first O'Rourke was a descendant of a man named Rourke). Not until the next century did the rest of northern Europe adopt surnames.

Dermot MacMaelnamBo

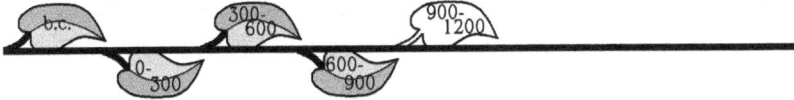

he passing of Brien Boruma left Ireland in political turmoil, as minor righs jockeyed against each other for
provincial thrones and provincial righs contested for the position of Ard Righ. While he was in power, Brien had favored
Hy Kinsella for their help in reducing the power of north
Leinster. During his tenure, a major power shift occurred in
Hy Kinsella. Brandubh's clan, the Hy Felimy, had lived in the
fertile area around Ferns since his demise in 605 but hadn't
produced another leader of note. The Sil nOnchon clan, descended from Enna Kinsella through his son Crimthann, had
again become the strongest branch of Hy Kinsella, but their
royal residence was located in less fertile parts of north Hy
Kinsella. Envious of the Hy Felimy lands, the Sil nOnchon
proceeded down the Slaney valley[1] into Wexford until they
reached Ferns, where they displaced the Hy Felimy.[2] (The
process was apparently a peaceful one, because no dispute is
mentioned in the annals). The surname Kinsella, first used as a
descriptor for a territory, originated within this group. A list of
the Hy Kinsella righs of Leinster and the clans they came from

---

[1] Between the Blackstairs and Wicklow mountains through a pass that runs
between Clonegall and Bunclody.
[2] The Hy Felimy were pushed east where they settled along the coast of
Wexford.

indicates how successful this branch of Enna Kinsella's
descendants was:

Leinster Righs from Hy Kinsella	Clan descended from Enna Kinsella	Death Date
Enna Cinnsealaigh	-	?
Crimthann	Sil nOnchon	485
Brandubh	Hy Felimy	605
Ronan	Sil Chormaic	624?
Aed Mend	Sil Chormaic	733
Dermot MacMaelnamBo	Sil nOchon	1072
Murrough	Sil nOchon	1070
Domnall	Sil nOchon	1075
Enna	Sil nOchon	1092
Dairmaid	Sil nOchon	1098
Donnchad	Sil nOchon	1115
Diarmaid	Sil nOchon	1117
Enna	Sil nOchon	1126
Dermot MacMurrough	Sil nOchon	1171[3]

In 1036 Dermot MacMaelnamBo of the Sil nOchon clan
emerged as Hy Kinsella righ. Dermot's early history is uncertain. Acts of kindness exchanged between him and the nobles
of Ulster are evidence of a connection between them, indicating perhaps that his mother was from Ulster or that he was
fostered there. His father, Donnchad MaelnamBo, a previous
Hy Kinsella righ, was well known for his ability to raid cattle
from enemy tuatha. (MaelnamBo means "devotee of the
cows.") Dermot aimed higher because he grasped the importance of what Brien Boruma had done. He set his sights on
becoming Ard Righ of Ireland. Early in his career he sought

---

[3] From Edward Culleton, *Celtic and Early Christian Wexford: AD 400 to
1166* (Dublin, 1999).

allies and found a dependable one in Donagh MacGillpatrick, the Leinster righ from Ossory.

With Donagh's blessing, Dermot successfully attacked the Waterford Danes to the south in 1037. At the instigation of Turlough O'Brien, Dermot's foster son and potential heir to the Munster throne, he also attacked the Danes of Limerick deep in the heart of Munster, demonstrating his growing power.

Recognizing the threat to the throne of Leinster that Dermot posed, the north Leinster clans combined with Munster to attack Hy Kinsella in 1041. Their forces penetrated all the way to Ferns, and the capitol of Hy Kinsella was burned to the ground. The north Leinster clans thereby made a dangerous enemy of Dermot MacMaelnamBo, whom the annals describe as Dermot "of the white teeth, laughing in danger." Dermot turned to the Leinster righ, Donagh MacGillpatrick, his ally and protector, but Donagh was ill and died that year. Needing the aid of additional forces, Dermot waited until Donagh's son, the new Ossory righ[4] was able to assist him in a two-pronged attack the following year. While Dermot raided and plundered in Munster, the Ossory righ invaded north Leinster. Both attacks were successful, and Dermot, now the most powerful righ in Leinster, became Leinster righ by receiving hostages and tribute from all the tuath righs.

Dermot had married Dervorghal, a granddaughter of Brien Boruma. Normally marriage brought families closer together, fostering peace and perhaps making them allies. Dermot and his father-in-law, Donogh O'Brien, the Munster righ, were exceptions to this rule; they fought constantly.

In Irish politics, raids and small scale attacks occurred sporadically as righs tried to gain power over other righs, collecting hostages and tribute as their reward. Leinster and Munster, like

---

[4] Even though his father had been the Leinster righ, the new Ossory righ had to win that distinction for himself.

two dogs, circled each other and attacked at any opportunity. In 1049 Dermot, tired of this stalemate, battled Meath instead, and quickly gained their submission. Fearing the support Leinster would gain from Meath, Munster was forced also to attack Meath.

As this tug-of-war over Meath developed, in 1051 England's leading noble family, the Godwins (including a young boy named Harold),[5] were forced out of England by their king, Edward the Confessor. Dermot MacMaelnamBo took them in and even gave them Leinstermen and arms to continue their battle against England's king. They were victorious and regained their extensive land-holdings back in England. Edward remained king of England but had little power, and it was only a matter of time before Harold would take the throne from him. Harold's family gave Dermot the battle standard of the king of the Saxons as a token of thanks. If Harold had been able to drive William the Conqueror back into the sea fifteen years later, the history of Hy Kinsella might have been quite different.

Dermot, still in a stalemate with Munster but with the added complication of Meath, changed tactics and concentrated on building up his power in Leinster. In 1052 he attacked the Dublin Danes and placed his son Murrough in charge of the town. But even within Leinster, Munster would give him no peace. In an alliance with Meath, Munster soon swooped down, attacked the area around Dublin and somehow managed to capture Mor O'Connor, the wife of the Ossory righ. The Meath righ took a fancy to her and, having no idea how headstrong she was, refused to give her up; she apparently acquiesced. After some months of living together in the Meath righ's home at Cro Inis on Loch Ennell, Mor O'Connor

---

[5] Fifteen yeas later, Harold would lose his kingdom and life to William the Conqueror at the Battle of Hastings (1066).

demanded that the Meath righ seize, as a private residence for herself, the fort of Carrick on the opposite shore of the lake, the royal residence of one of his most important righs. The Meath righ, to his disadvantage, complied and ever afterwards the fort remained the personal property of each bannrigh (queen) of Meath.

Persistence and longevity were important factors in an Irish monarch's rise to power. Though recently defeated outside Dublin, Dermot persevered in his battle against Munster and now Meath. At this time Turlough O'Brien, Dermot's foster son who had called on Dermot's aid before in attacking Limerick, began to battle against his uncle and Dermot's enemy, the Munster righ.[6] Meanwhile, the Ossory righ, grief-stricken over the loss of his wife, joined with Dermot for a major offensive in Meath. They plundered and took away many cows but were unable to regain Mor O'Connor; the Ossory righ died of grief early the next year.

For several years Dermot concentrated on helping Turlough O'Brien by seeking to devastate Munster. He finally succeeded in 1061 when the Munster righ gave Dermot hostages and tribute. Full of confidence, Dermot sent a naval force to invade the Isle of Man and then attack Bristol, one of England's largest ports. The force succeeded on the Isle of Man but failed against Bristol and Dermot became the last Irish righ to lead a mercenary force against England. His son Murrough, already in charge of Dublin, was also given responsibility for the Isle of Man. Dermot once more turned to face his old nemesis, the Munster righ. In 1063 he defeated him again and the Munstermen, at Dermot's strong urging, elected Turlough O'Brien as their new righ.

---

[6] Turlough certainly felt no pangs about attacking his uncle, who had killed his own brother, Turlough's father, to gain the throne of Munster.

In England, Edward the Confessor died in 1066. Harold Godwin became king, but his reign was short-lived. He successfully repelled a major invasion by the Danes, but days later the Normans, led by William the Conqueror, landed near Hastings. Harold was killed in the battle and William, with his Normans, took over England, turning vast tracts into wasteland in the process. A new power had taken hold in England, but for decades its contact with Irish society would be minimal.

Dermot MacMaelnamBo, now firmly in control of the southern half of Ireland, felt confident enough to test Connacht. He assembled forces from Munster and Leinster and marched on Connacht, but the province's righ refused to submit. Within a few months, this Connacht righ was killed by a rival and the newly elected righ offered Dermot the province's submission. In 1067, Dermot was acknowledged Ard Righ with Opposition, meaning he controlled more than half of Ireland. In appreciation for Munster's help, Dermot offered Turlough O'Brien the sword of Brien Boruma and the battle standard of the king of the Saxons. Dermot's luck, however, did not last. Within two years his son Murrough, ruler of Dublin and the Isle of Man, was killed in a raid by Meathmen and buried in Dublin with the epitaph, "Empty is the fortress without him." A year later, Meath killed another of Dermot's sons.

After settling a revolt within Hy Kinsella, Dermot set about gaining vengeance on Meath. He marched on the province in 1072 but was killed by his perennial rivals, the north Leinster clans. The first to be known as "King of Leinster and the Foreigners," Dermot was described as "the best and most worthy prince that ever reigned in Ireland." An interesting line in one annal calls him "King of Ireland, Wales, Hebrides, [and the] Danes of Dublin," though no record of his extending control into Wales survives.

Dermot MacMaelnamBo achieved almost as much as Brien Boruma, but longevity wasn't given him. The position of Ard Righ was again open to any taker and Turlough O'Brien, Hy Kinsella's stalwart ally, became the main contender. His first move was to devastate Hy Kinsella because it had grown too powerful under Dermot MacMaelnamBo.

Dermot MacMurrough

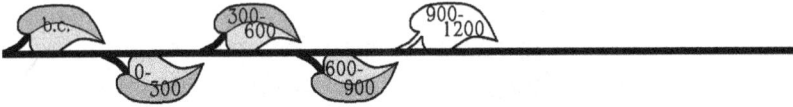

he years following Dermot MacMaelnamBo's death saw dissension throughout Leinster. In the previous century Leinster righs had come from north Leinster, south Leinster, and Ossory. Each territory believed it had a right to the throne but none was strong enough to obtain submission from the other territories. The situation in Munster was much clearer. Rivals to the throne were few, since all the clans had lived under O'Brien rule for generations. The O'Briens ruled as Munster righs and, after Dermot MacMaelnambo's death, their strategy in Leinster was to exacerbate the province's lack of cohesion by playing its territories against each other – always supporting in battle the weaker territory to diminish the power of the stronger. This strategy proved very effective until Munster had to deal with larger problems.

The Munster righ had been intruding in Meath and Connacht as well. He became powerful enough in 1106 to depose the Connacht righ, Donnogh O'Connor, whom he considered a threat. The Munster righ appointed Donnogh's brother, Turlough O'Connor, a mere lad of 18, to serve as puppet on the throne of Connacht. The Munster righ would rue this choice.

By 1120 the upstart Turlough O'Connor had already come close to being acknowledged as Ard Righ of Ireland with Opposition. In the process he had befriended the Leinster righ,

Enna MacMurrough.[1]   Enna had managed to unite Leinster, though north Leinster and Ossory accepted his rule only grudgingly and rebelled at every opportunity.   In the summer of 1126, his promising career unexpectedly ended when he died at Wexford. Taking advantage of the power vacuum, the Connacht righ, Turlough O'Connor, swept into Leinster and installed his son Connor as king of Dublin. Unwittingly, Turlough then made the same mistake the Munster righ had made years before with him.   He marched south and recognized Enna's 16-year-old brother, Dermot MacMurrough, as not only Hy Kinsella righ but also Leinster righ.

Turlough chose Dermot MacMurrough as Leinster righ to placate the powerful Hy Kinsella territory while he rode off to raid Munster and Ossory, forcing them both into submission. Ossory's submission proved easy to obtain, Munster's much harder. His solution to the Munster problem was ingenious: separate the province north and south and have the sections ruled by rivals, the O'Briens and the MacCarthys.[2]   After taking a full year to gain Munster's submission, Turlough O'Connor returned to Leinster in 1127 and deposed Dermot MacMurrough.   He had no intention of letting a powerful territory like Hy Kinsella remain in the control of Leinster. Turlough instead promoted his son Connor O'Connor from king of Dublin to Leinster righ, even though Connor was from Connacht and not Leinster.

Placing a "foreigner" in control of a province was unprecedented, because Brehon law stated that a clan was ruled by one of its own. A clan might, and often did, submit to another clan,

---

[1] The name MacMurrough comes from Mac "son of" Murrough, the son of Dermot MacMaelnambo who had ruled Dublin and the Isle of Man. Enna was actually a grandson of Murrough; MacMurrough was being used by this time as a surname.
[2] The MacCarthys were a branch of Eoganacht, the old Munster ruling clan.

but this only meant paying tribute and giving up hostages. To be led by someone from another clan meant something altogether different. Turlough O'Connor was making his own rules. He had gained submission from all the provinces of Ireland except Ulster and was now considered the Ard Righ of Ireland with Opposition. This was the political situation in which Dermot MacMurrough found himself.

Dermot, well aware of the history of his great-grandfather, Dermot MacMaelnambo, faced a number of obstacles. First he had to consolidate his power in Hy Kinsella by eliminating other members of his extended family who were contending for the throne. Turlough O'Connor's selection of the young Mac-Murrough meant nothing to these other claimants.

Luckily for Hy Kinsella, Turlough was immediately distracted by Munster. Even though divided, it was still not willing to submit to Turlough. For months the Connacht righ ravaged the province by land and sea until Ireland's archbishop intervened and established a truce between the two provinces for the rest of the year. Leinster took advantage of O'Connor's distraction and expelled their "foreign" Leinster righ, Connor O'Connor, from his residence in Dublin. The leader of this revolt is not recorded but, judging from Turlough's subsequent actions, he must have blamed Dermot MacMurrough, the puppet he had chosen to rule Hy Kinsella. With the year almost over (the Irish, like other Europeans, rarely fought during the winter), Turlough quickly marched to Leinster and recognized Donal O'Faelain from north Leinster as Leinster righ and king of Dublin. He was employing the well-respected strategy of supporting a weaker clan against a stronger clan, Hy Kinsella.

The abbess of Kildare, head of Leinster's richest and most important monastery, died in 1127. The O'Faelain Leinster righ jumped at the opportunity to name his niece as the new abbess, thereby ensuring a steady flow of money from Kildare into his own coffers. The Leinster territory to which the previous abbess belonged was privately outraged over the loss of riches this would entail. Publicly they claimed that O'Faelain had no right to appoint his niece, because they hadn't recognized him as Leinster righ. A battle ensued at the monastery between the two territories and the Leinster righ lost. The significance of this loss would become apparent in just a few years.

Barbaric events like this, which occurred throughout Europe and on the grandest scale in Italy, must be viewed in the perspective of the times. When the pope died three years after the power struggle in Kildare's monastery, the noble families of Germany, Italy, and France immediately chose his successor[3] and elected two popes. One of them, Anacletus II, backed by the strength of the Duke of Sicily, defeated the other, Innocent II, in battle and forced him to flee from Rome. Both acted as pope, Anacletus II from Rome and Innocent II from France, until 1138 when Anacletus II died. Each pope called the other the "anti-pope." The same sequence of events would be played out in Rome several more times during the century.

As the year 1128 began, Munster continued its protracted struggle against Connacht, but soon Ireland's archbishop established another truce between the provinces for the rest of the year. The truce may have been set up at Turlough O'Connor's request, so he could concentrate on just one opponent, Leinster. He intended to achieve more than just submission from Leinster and sent a huge force to invade and cripple the province. Surprisingly, Turlough did not lead the force himself. Instead he chose one of his subordinate righs, Tiernan

---

[3] Although the cardinals chose the pope, they were told how to vote by the European nobility, to which many of them belonged anyway.

O'Rourke, and he chose well. Leaving much of the rest of Leinster untouched, Tiernan swept into Hy Kinsella in a hot year of drought.

Unlike the leader of almost any other raiding party in Ireland's history, Tiernan was set on annihilation. He immediately broke the Law of Daire by maiming and killing cows, which he didn't even bother to take with him. He killed thousands of cows and left them to rot while burning houses and crops on his way through Hy Kinsella, to ensure that the people would starve to death. Unlike typical Irish raiding, this was European-style warfare aimed at destroying the common farmer.[4]

Hy Kinsella fought using guerilla tactics against the mass of invaders from Connacht, but disputes over who should be Hy Kinsella righ hampered their resistance. The foreign army penetrated the heart of south Leinster and reached Wexford. Dermot's fighting men did manage to save the coast of Hy Kinsella. Tiernan who had initially intended to march his men up the coast from Wexford to Dublin instead forced the Wexford Danes to convey him by sail. Hy Kinsella had imposed more losses on him than he had expected so he took the safer route.

Dermot MacMurrough was now fighting not only competitors for the throne of Hy Kinsella but also starvation among his people. He was able to concentrate on this for the next few years without fearing the heavy hand of The O'Connor,[5] who was busy battling not only Munster but also Meath, Ulster and even his supposed ally, Tiernan O'Rourke. By 1132, although

---

[4] There is evidence Turlough O'Connor spent some of his youth being educated in foreign countries.

[5] Any righ was referred to as "The" together with his surname. So Dermot MacMurrough, when he was proclaimed Hy Kinsella righ, also became The MacMurrough, meaning he was the head of his clan.

he still wasn't sole contender for the Hy Kinsella throne, Dermot felt confident enough to attack Kildare and install his own aunt as abbess. Now the funds from this monastery, the richest in Leinster, were funneled to Hy Kinsella.

By 1133, thanks to the influx of money from Kildare, Hy Kinsella had recovered from the devastation of the Connacht attack five years earlier only to be devastated again. Nature was the enemy this time: a serious cow infection proved fatal to much of the Hy Kinsella herd. Instead of waiting patiently for his lands to recover, as he had after Tiernan O'Rourke's invasion, The MacMurrough went on the offensive. He no longer had years to wait for the few remaining calves to multiply and replenish his herds. Cows were out there for his people; he just had to take them.

Dermot began by eliminating his one remaining rival in Hy Kinsella and then attacking north Leinster. He subdued Donal O'Faelain, the man Turlough O'Connor had proclaimed Leinster righ years before, took many cows, and finally seized the throne of Leinster. In one summer he had replaced the cows lost that spring by infection and rose from Hy Kinsella righ with Opposition to Leinster righ. But, at 23 years of age, could he hold onto the Leinster throne?

Dermot was well versed in the politics of his time and knew not to relax. The next year he attacked the territory of Ossory, failed and tried again successfully. He attacked the O'Briens of Munster and gained their submission, and he then sacked Waterford for its riches. To retain submission from the rest of Leinster, Dermot was trying to prove he could expand the power of the province by gaining tribute from outside. Perhaps while on this excursion, Dermot fathered a son, Donal, from whom the Kavanagh line would spring.[6] Dermot had the luxury of subduing his rivals without interference from O'Connor because the Connacht righ was under siege from Munster, Meath and at times Ulster. Around this time Dermot married and his wife bore him a son, Enna, from whom the Kinsella surname would spring.

As Dermot gained power, the world around him was changing. In 1135, King Henry I of England died. His nephew Stephen, Earl of Blois, took the throne by force and succeeded him. Henry I's daughter, Matilda, asserted her right to the English throne, however, creating continual complications for Stephen. After years of warfare, during which the countryside was ravaged and peasants massacred, Matilda's son Henry II succeeded Stephen. He was to have a tremendous impact on Irish history.

More significantly for Dermot, in the 12th century the Irish church had begun restructuring itself based on the hierarchical model of the Roman church. Not all abbots in the Irish church wanted to unify under one archbishop, for that meant relinquishing their power. By 1134, however, the reformers had won, led by Malachy O'Morgair, and the archbishop of Armagh was recognized as head of the Irish church. The reformers wanted to submit to Rome and looked to the pope to bless their changes. They had a larger dream, however. They wanted a monarchy in Ireland with one ruler whom they could support and who in return would support them, rather than the current multitude of rulers who separately influenced their monasteries. A new power was emerging in Ireland, a fact that went unrecognized by most of the provincial righs.

---

[6] For unknown reasons Dermot fostered out only this child. He sent him to the monastery of St. Caomhan in Hy Kinsella. (Kavanagh means "belonging to Caomhan.")

The first true test of Dermot's provincial power came when north Leinster revolted in 1137. Always rivals of south Leinster, the nobles of north Leinster had gained the backing of the Meath righ. Dermot marched north to attack Meath but was met by an overwhelming force, the combined armies of Meath, part of Ulster, and part of Connacht. Exercising discretion, Dermot signed a treaty with the Meath righ declaring that he would aid the Meath righ "against anyone with as great an army" and the Meath righ would not support north Leinster again.

This treaty set the stage for an encounter between Dermot MacMurrough and his most hated enemy, Tiernan O'Rourke. Within a year Tiernan, who hoped to expand his territory into Meath, had gained Turlough O'Connor's help, and together they marched a large army into Meath and plundered. True to the treaty, Dermot immediately brought up a Leinster army to join the Meath righ's army. The combined armies of Meath and Leinster camped alongside the armies of the Ard Righ for a week with only a small pass through woods separating them. O'Connor and O'Rourke finally withdrew. Dermot had stood face to face with the Ard Righ and stared him into a standoff. Perhaps at this point Dermot MacMurrough, like his great-grandfather before him, set his sights on becoming Ard Righ of Ireland.

North Leinster revolted again in 1141, and by this time Dermot had run out of patience. He realized that gaining submissions from other provinces did not impress north Leinster. They had recently held the throne of Leinster and felt entitled to it. Hesitant to leave Leinster for fear north Leinster would rebel, Dermot was hamstrung. (Another revolt had occurred in 1138 on Dermot's return from Meath.) Since diplomacy had failed, he tried a different approach. In one stroke Dermot crushed all challengers to his rule by killing or blinding seventeen of them, demonstrating just how much power he controlled. Many righs in Irish history who displeased their subjects were deposed for lesser outrages. That did not happen to Dermot. Rebellions within Leinster ceased for years. But Dermot's act revealed to the rest of Ireland that Leinster was fragmented. Like ravens noticing weak prey, the other provincial righs circled.

The O'Brien of north Munster arrived first. He marched into Leinster, took over Dublin and then proceeded to raid Hy Kinsella. The O'Connor came next. He raided mostly north of Hy Kinsella, thereby obtaining the submission of Dermot MacMurrough. Like a master chess player, The O'Connor used this submission to force the Leinster righ to help him attack first Munster then the Meath righ, Dermot's ally. Dermot could no longer honor his commitment to support the Meath righ, because he'd submitted to Turlough O'Connor. The Connacht righ deposed the Meath righ and again attempted to set his favorite son, Connor O'Connor, on another province's throne, which met with even less success than his attempt in Leinster. Six months after occupying the throne of Meath, Connor was assassinated by the nobles of that province.[7] Not surprisingly Meath was next to feel the wrath of Turlough O'Connor.

Meanwhile, the Irish church continued its policy of reform under the leadership of Malachy O'Morgair. In 1141 he helped found the Cistercian monastery of Mellifont, the first monastery in Ireland based on continental European tradition rather than Irish. The invasion of Ireland had begun quietly.

After the assassination of Turlough O'Connor's son, warfare among the provinces became even more intense. The new archbishop of Armagh intervened, but to no avail. The annal-

---

[7] When asked why he had killed Connor O'Connor, the assassin remarked, "I considered him as a stranger in sovereignty over the men of Meath."

ists describe "great war, so that Ireland was a trembling sod." Dermot, alone among the provincial righs, remained aloof from this warfare. At this point in his life he had risen as high politically as he could go. The ard righ position was unattainable for The MacMurrough because north Leinster could be counted on to revolt. Instead Dermot entrenched his position in Leinster and immersed himself in the Irish church. Perhaps, now in his thirties, he had found religion. Perhaps he realized the church was becoming a powerful political contender, one that would be a far more trustworthy ally than either O'Brien or O'Connor.

In 1145, Dermot promoted one of his foster brothers to the bishopric of Leighlin, a diocese in Hy Kinsella. In 1146 he built St. Mary de Hogges, a nunnery in Dublin.[8] A few years later Dermot began construction on the Abbey de Valle Salutis near Ferns in Baltinglass. The fame of Dermot's kindness to the church spread so far that he received from the eminent French Abbot Bernard of Clairvaux[9] a letter addressing Dermot as "King of Ireland" and a certificate of confraternity.

In 1148, Malachy O'Morgair set out to ask the pope to bless the Irish reforms but never arrived. He died at Clairvaux in the arms of Abbot Bernard soon after the midnight of Samhain. Upon hearing the news, the pope finally sent an envoy to recognize the Irish efforts at reform. The envoy would take years to reach Ireland, however, because of the civil war in England.

Abbot Bernard, distraught at the death of his friend, wrote the life of St. Malachy, in which he exaggerated the paganism of Ireland and emphasized the need for continental Europe to

---

[8] Located near College Green and St. Andrew's church, it is now a tourist office.
[9] Bernard was considered the leading cleric in Europe. As a close personal friend of the pope, he exercised enormous influence.

come to its aid. Since he was very influential, all Europe listened, most importantly Rome. The excuse needed to justify an invasion of Ireland was born.

While fighting still ravaged Munster, Connacht and Meath, a formidable new competitor appeared on the Irish political scene. Ulster, which had for many years been absent from the warfare in southern Ireland because of internal dissension, reemerged under the leadership of one man, Murtagh MacLoughlan. He began by attacking the Ard Righ with Opposition, Turlough O'Connor, in 1147, and raiding between O'Connor and MacLoughlan continued for years.

In 1151, the north Munster righ, an O'Brien, was close to defeating the south Munster righ, a MacCarthy. The MacCarthy sent messengers to Turlough O'Connor asking for help. The O'Connor immediately prepared to help MacCarthy, again using the strategy of aiding the weaker opponent in order to reduce the stronger one. He requested the aid of Leinster, since Dermot had previously submitted to him. Dermot and his Leinstermen met Turlough and the Connacht forces at a site known as Moinmhor in south Munster. They woke early one morning to heavy mists in the gap between the Boggeragh and Nagles Mountains and awaited orders.

At almost the same time, O'Brien was returning to north Munster with one of MacCarthy's bands chasing close behind. The O'Brien had chosen to fight on his own land, which he had almost reached. He just had to pass through the gap between the Boggeragh and Nagles Mountains known as Moinmhor, which was unusually misty that morning . . . .

The seven battalions of north Munstermen under O'Brien were annihilated in the largest battle on Irish soil since the Battle of Clontarf more than a century before. Only one shattered battalion, including O'Brien himself, escaped through the mist. Pursued by his enemies, O'Brien soon found he wasn't welcome even in his own lands, where other members of his family had opportunely seized power. Looking for a noble to take him in, he continued north until he finally reached Murtagh MacLoughlan in Ulster.

Turlough O'Connor, flushed with victory and possessing hostages from Munster and Leinster, returned home only to find Murtagh MacLoughlan waiting for him. His army spent, Turlough immediately turned over not only the Munster and Leinster hostages but also those from Connacht. Murtagh MacLoughlan was now the undisputed Ard Righ of Ireland.

Ossory, a buffer state between Munster and Leinster, had been on the losing side of the battle of Moinmhor. Ever since his initial successful attack against Ossory almost thirty years before, Dermot had controlled it, but always against the will of the Ossory righ. To curry favor, the Ossory righ had been with O'Brien at the battle of Moinmhor and was taken prisoner by Dermot's son, Enna. The Ossory righ was brought back to Ferns as a hostage, and Dermot placed another noble from Ossory on that territory's throne. Perhaps at this time Dermot gave Enna a new last name to impress on his clan that Enna was his chosen successor. He was to be known as Enna Kinsella, after his most illustrious ancestor. Enna unfortunately had taken a fancy to the wife of the Ossory righ he had captured, and they had an affair,[10] which was not unusual in 12th-century Ireland but which had lasting repercussions for him.

For Dermot's help in the battle, Turlough O'Connor granted the Leinster righ some land in Munster along with Terryglass monastery. The abbot had died, and Dermot replaced him with Aedh MacCrimthainn, whom he had already asked to compile what was to become an invaluable resource

---

[10] Thomas A. Brennan, Jr., *A History of the Brennans of Idough, County Kilkenny* (Lebanon, N.H., 1979).

on early Irish history and life, the *Book of Leinster*. Dermot continued his courtship of the church by founding two more convents, Kilculliheen near Waterford and Aghade north of Ferns.

After years of waiting, the Irish church reformers finally received the pope's blessing. The pope's envoy, Cardinal Paparo, reached Ireland in 1152 and a synod was held at Kells. The cardinal brought news that the pope agreed with the reform. Urging additional reforms, he accepted their submission to Rome. The Irish church had voluntarily accepted Rome's rule. Only in later generations would the full implications of this development be understood.

An Englishman[11] was elected pope Adrian IV in 1154. At the request of the English establishment, the pope issued the papal bull *Laudabiliter,* giving England the right to conquer Ireland. Before 1066, William the Conqueror used a similar proclamation to justify the Norman invasion of England.

Few Irish nobles realized that the clergy had turned against them. The newly-appointed papal legate advocated reforms to Brehon laws to bring them more in line with the laws of Rome and pushed for a monarchy in Ireland. To the church, even a foreign monarchy was preferable to the chaotic political situation in Ireland.

While the synod of Kells was a crowning achievement for the Irish churchmen, the Irish nobles showed little interest. O'Connor had renewed the battle with MacLoughlan over who would should be Ard Righ. In 1152 they met at Moy[12] and agreed upon a treaty whereby MacLoughlan was again recognized as Ard Righ without Opposition. Dermot, a strong ally of MacLoughlan, may have negotiated the peace between the two provincial righs. With Turlough's acquiescence, Meath

---

[11] Nicholas Cardinal Breakspear.

[12] A plain between the rivers Erne and Drowes near Ballyshannon.

185

was split in half and lands previously belonging to Tiernan O'Rourke were taken back.

Tiernan O'Rourke, furious at losing this land and totally disregarding the treaty, immediately attacked Meath. Given an excuse to reduce his subordinate righ's growing power, O'Connor again requested the Leinster righ's aid. Remembering vividly O'Rourke's devastation in Hy Kinsella many years ago, Dermot was only too glad to accept the invitation. Together they razed to the ground O'Rourke's castle in Drumahaire[13] and raided throughout his lands. Turlough then divided Tiernan O'Rourke's territory in half and gave the more fertile southern portion to another O'Rourke, leaving the north for Tiernan.

Realizing his total defeat, Tiernan O'Rourke tried to placate O'Connor by going on a pilgrimage to St. Patrick's Purgatory[14] as penance. Meanwhile, on his march home Dermot MacMurrough stopped for the night at the royal residence of the new ruler of east Meath. O'Rourke's wife, Dervorghal, sent the Leinster righ a message saying that she had repudiated her husband "because of some abuses done before to her" and that she wished Dermot would save her. According to Brehon law, a woman had the right to repudiate her husband for many reasons. If O'Rourke had hit her, she had just cause. The east Meath righ, Dervorghal's brother, gave Dermot his blessing to fetch his sister.

---

[13] At Dangan, parish of Kilmore, east of County Roscommon.

[14] A story relates that St. Patrick preached to the Irish about purgatory, but they would not believe him unless they saw it for themselves. St. Patrick miraculously caused the earth on an island in Lough Derg to open and reveal the flaming entrance of the place of punishment. Thus the pagans were converted to Christianity. The location of this ancient shrine is shrouded in mystery.

Dermot returned to O'Rourke's stronghold and picked up Dervorghal along with her furniture and vast number of cattle. Together they rode back to Ferns. Dervorghal was 44 and Dermot was 42, so they were no star-crossed lovers acting out of youthful impetuousness, as some later sources claim.

Dermot MacMurrough's scheme to shame O'Rourke worked far better than he had hoped. When O'Rourke returned, he rushed to O'Connor, paid tribute and hostages to the Connacht righ and pleaded for help. To save face, he recast the story as an abduction during which Dervorghal had kicked and screamed the whole way to Ferns. The next spring, in 1153, O'Connor marched to bring back Dervorghal. Under pain of excommunication, Dermot returned her with all her possessions. He did not, however, pay the honor price O'Rourke demanded because he contended that she had not been abducted but had come willingly. O'Connor apparently agreed with Dermot.

In 1155, the forty-five year old Dermot married for a third time. To forge another alliance, he chose Mor O'Toole, daughter of the Hy Murray righ, one of the north Leinster clans. Dermot's family had grown to include sons Enna and Donal and daughters Urlacam and Dervorghal. From Mor he would have two more children, Aoife and Connor, both of who would prove pivotal in Ireland's history.

Early the next year, Turlough O'Connor achieved immense success

Dermot

by gaining the submission of all southern Ireland and creating peace within its provinces. Before he could reap the benefits of this achievement, he died. The succession of Turlough's son Rory illustrates how the Irish political situation was evolving. Rory was immediately accepted as Connacht righ by the province. He was not forced to undergo the severe challenges Dermot MacMurrough had faced in his climb to provincial righ. Standard rules for succession were being accepted by the Irish. Most remarkably, he was immediately considered a contender for Ard Righ against Murtagh MacLoughlan.

On Easter day of 1157, the Meath righ killed one of his lesser nobles. This was not in itself a significant event, but the Meath righ had sworn, in the presence of the church, that he would not harm this noble. In the past few decades, this type of oath had been broken many times and no harm had come to the offending party (other than paying the steep fines required by Brehon law). The Irish church, now a unified political hierarchy, tested their new-found power at the synod of Mellifont. As Ireland's first continental European monastery, Mellifont was an appropriate site for such an uncharacteristic encroachment by the Irish church into political affairs. First the monastery, which had just reached completion, was consecrated by the archbishop of Armagh. Then the clergy and righs who were present agreed to excommunicate the Meath righ and dethrone him. The nobles of Ireland and the people of Meath accepted the synod's ruling and a new Meath righ was named. The church had intervened successfully in Irish politics on a provincial level.

During the next several years, Dermot MacMurrough and the Ard Righ Murtagh MacLoughlan came to depend on each other. Rory O'Connor, unwilling to accept MacLoughlan as Ard Righ of Ireland, allied with Tiernan O'Rourke and intruded in the politics of Munster or Meath, but they were always turned aside by the combined forces of Leinster and the Ard Righ in Ulster. While Dermot was away in Meath countering one of these expeditions, the Wexford Norse in Dermot's own Hy Kinsella revolted. Donal Kavanagh, Dermot MacMurrough's son, took command of an expedition and defeated them decisively.[15]

In the winter of 1161, Dermot fell so ill that everyone, including himself, thought that he would not see spring. If he recovered, Dermot promised to build a monastery in honor of all the saints. His condition worsened. Finally, as though by a miracle, he began to recover. Dermot did live to see the spring, so he granted lands outside the city walls of Dublin to the All Saints monastery.[16] He believed God must have spared him for a reason.

The archbishop of Dublin died unexpectedly the following year and Lorcan O'Toole, Dermot's brother-in-law, succeeded him as archbishop, probably with Dermot MacMurrough's help. God was smiling on the Leinster righ. Lorcan was a fervent reformer who transplanted many European church practices to Dublin. Only later in life would Lorcan understand the perils these European practices introduced to Irish tradition.

In the summer of 1162, for the first time, Dermot sponsored, attended, and protected the synod of Clane. Ireland's archbishop presided, and more reforms to the Irish church were passed. The Irish clergy would have approved if a man like Dermot were to establish a monarchy in Ireland, their long-sought goal. He must have been aware of their potential

---

[15] It's odd that Dermot's son, Enna Kinsella, was not in command of this force. He might have been with Dermot in Meath, or Dermot, assuming he would inherit the throne, might have sent him to England to be educated and build alliances.

[16] Now Trinity College.

support. At fifty-two, Dermot had left behind the rashness of youth, replacing it with wisdom.

During the next few years, Dermot concentrated almost exclusively on religious affairs while the rest of Ireland continued to engage in political raids. Tiernan O'Rourke was especially active raiding in other provinces and stamping out revolts in his own territory. Years had passed since Dermot committed his Leinstermen to a battle of any significance. He appeared to be content to settle down to a religious life and on his death allow his son Enna to assume the throne.

Like Leinster, Ulster had squabbles of its own. Most of these were raids by tuath righs into each other's lands and were of little consequence, but on rare occasions they had far-reaching effects. One of the territorial righs in east Ulster raided in MacLoughlan's lands in 1165 and not only took many cows but also killed many people. For centuries, east and west Ulster had been bitter enemies, perhaps even more so than north and south Leinster. MacLoughlan soundly chastised the east Ulster righ that year, but the dispute wasn't over.

Dermot chose not to become involved in the affairs of Ulster but instead made a new ally. Henry II of England had asked Dermot for aid against the Welsh, who had invaded and pillaged part of England. Henry was amassing an army of men from England, France, Flanders, Ireland and Bretagne. Dermot sent some Dublin Danes and Leinstermen for six months. Henry II was unsuccessful in his efforts, mostly due to heavy rains that made penetration of the dense forests of Wales too dangerous. Finding his forces inadequate, he sent them back with gifts. Unlike Irish methods, English warfare involved drawing huge forces from several countries. Dermot received his men back and continued his work for the church. In 1166, he ordered a new cathedral to be built for Ferns.

On Easter, Dermot's ally, Ireland's Ard Righ, went on an unprovoked raid in Ulster. He captured the east Ulster righ, whom he had chastised the year before, while he was in his Easter house[17] and blinded him, thus ending his ability to be righ. MacLoughlan then killed all of the east Ulster righ's hostages. Such an atrocious deed had occurred before without punishment, but the Irish church had never before been able to speak out against it with one voice. The archbishop of Armagh, considering it an affront to the church, excommunicated MacLoughlan and sanctioned military action. The east Ulster nobles, each having lost a son, were furious and willing to fight. They persuaded other Ulster territories to support them. These territories in turn persuaded Rory O'Connor, who needed little persuasion, which meant Tiernan O'Rourke would also support them.

So certain was he of victory that Rory O'Connor went on a circuit of Ireland, a ritual reserved only for the Ard Righ, while the rest of the forces attacked MacLoughlan. Rory arrived first in Leinster and asked north Leinster for their submission, which they eagerly gave in hopes that O'Connor would support them against Dermot MacMurrough.

Rory next turned to south Leinster. Dermot was crippled but still a formidable adversary, so Rory prepared carefully for their encounter. Hy Kinsella was relatively inaccessible because of the surrounding mountains, with only a few passes allowing entry for an army, but the passes themselves were filled with nearly impenetrable woods. Rather than following the existing road through one of these passes, Rory's army cut down trees and created their own road in order to avoid being ambushed. The O'Connor defeated the men of Hy Kinsella north of Ferns and, during the frenzied retreat, Dermot ordered

---

[17] Irish righs would build giant feasting halls for special occasions such as provincial fairs or religious celebrations.

Ferns to be burnt, probably to discourage Rory from plundering it and taking away cows and crops. Rory forced the defeated Dermot to give up the throne of Leinster. The MacMurrough was back where he started forty years before, mere Hy Kinsella righ.

Rory O Connor completed his circuit of Ireland by collecting hostages from the rest of the provinces. While he had been on the march, his allies tracked down and killed MacLoughlan. With the Irish church against the Ard Righ, even many of his own people had forsaken his cause. O'Connor convened all of Ireland's leading righs and was declared Ard Righ without Opposition.

Even before the convention ended, O'Rourke assembled his own men, along with the men of Meath, Ossory, north Leinster, and Dublin, and marched to destroy Hy Kinsella. Tiernan would finally wreak revenge on his most hated enemy, Dermot MacMurrough.

Dermot was now left with two examples from Irish history to consider: he could fight to the death as MacLoughlan had just done, or he could run from province to province in search of a benefactor as O'Brien had done after the massive battle of Moinmhor. Dermot characteristically did neither. He took a novel tack, perhaps inspired by the story of his ancient ancestor Labraid Loingsech described in his own *Book of Leinster*. On August 1, 1166, he left for England to seek the aid of Henry II. Dermot hoped with the help of God to return to Ireland and, like Labraid, claim the title Ard Righ. He dreamed Ireland would see its first monarchy, the MacMurroughs. An entry in the *Book of Leinster* reads:

> Mary, great is the deed which was done in Ireland today, that is, Dermot, son of Donagh MacMurrough, Righ of Leinster and the Foreigners was expelled across the sea by the Men of Ireland. Alas, alas, O Lord, what will I do?

The Normans

ermot, with his wife Mor and daughter Aoife, landed at Bristol, England where he began to search for Henry II in late autumn, 1166.

Meanwhile, O'Rourke's force reached Ferns and, furious at MacMurrough's disappearance, destroyed Dermot's castle.[1] Tiernan first divided Hy Kinsella into east and west, giving west Hy Kinsella to the Ossory righ (the same man captured during the battle of Moinmhor) along with a hostage, Enna Kinsella. He gave east Hy Kinsella to Murrough Mac-Murrough, Dermot's brother. Before leaving, O'Rourke collected hostages from Hy Kinsella for Rory O'Connor and also 100 gold pieces, the price he demanded as his wife's honor price for being abducted. Dermot was paying heavily for having answered the call of Dervorghal.

In the fall of 1167, Dermot traveled to Normandy to find Henry II, spent months following the king's trail (Henry II was constantly on the move), and finally caught up with him in early spring in his court at Aquitaine.[2] Henry greeted Dermot warmly and heard his suit, but he had no men to spare since he

---

[1] The Irish did not have castles like those being developed in England or France, so Dermot's castle is considered the first like them in Ireland. Dermot would exhibit more of his innovativeness in the coming years.

[2] Dermot travelled to modern day France to find Henry II because, at this time, France was Henry II's major kingdom with England considered only secondary.

was putting down numerous revolts himself. Instead he gave Dermot gifts and a parchment stating that the king of England gave any of his subjects the right to come to Dermot's aid.

Dermot left within a fortnight to return to England where, after much searching, he approached an English noble who had fallen on hard times. This was Richard FitzGilbert, the Earl of Pembroke, but more commonly known as Strongbow.

Negotiations proceeded between Strongbow and Dermot until the red-haired earl agreed to help the Irish righ, with the following stipulations: upon arriving in Ireland Strongbow would marry Dermot's beautiful, golden-haired daughter Aoife, and upon Dermot's death Strongbow would inherit the throne of Leinster. Dermot had no right under Irish law to grant Strongbow the succession, but Dermot was no longer considering only Irish law. If God willed it, Dermot was going to create a new monarchy, patterned after the English monarchy, in which the oldest son inherited the kingdom. In Europe, kingdoms could also be handed down through a daughter, which had just

Strongbow

happened when Henry II was allowed to rule in England. Strongbow would similarly inherit Leinster through a daughter's rule, while Dermot and his line ruled over him as kings of Ireland. Unfortunately, Strongbow could not leave right away. He had to gain the permission of Henry II, since he felt the parchment was not enough.

Dermot, excited that his plan for invasion seemed possible, immediately prepared to return to Ireland himself. He traveled to the tip of Wales closest to Ireland and waited for good winds at St. David's monastery, but the weather was poor. Over the ensuing days the bishop of St. David's listened with interest to Dermot's tale and remarked that his half-brother, a prisoner of the Welsh king, could be of assistance if he were freed.

The meeting between the Welsh king and Dermot went so well that the prisoner, Robert FitzStephen, was ushered in. The Welsh king told FitzStephen that, if he agreed to help Dermot and leave Wales forever, he could go free. FitzStephen accepted and, if they were successful, Dermot promised him the town of Wexford and the adjoining lands. The Welsh king volunteered his son for the adventure and told Dermot he should seek more help from the Flemish of Pembrokeshire.[3] After staying for only a few days with the Welsh king, Dermot departed for Pembrokeshire. The Flemmings listened to his story, agreed to participate and wanted to sail immediately. Dermot saw the hand of God in all these events.

The evening before Dermot departed for Ireland he was "sniffing from the Welsh coast the air of Ireland, wafted on the western breezes and, as it was, inhaling the scent of his beloved country. He had no small consolation feasting his eyes on the sight of his land, though the distance was such that it was difficult to distinguish between the mountains and clouds."[4] The first landmark Dermot would have seen when he set sail was Croghan Kinsella.

The next day Dermot, the Welsh king's son, and a Flemish platoon of archers and sergeants arrived in Hy Kinsella at Glass

---

[3] The Flemish had come over with William the Conqueror.
[4] Giraldus Cambrensis.

Carrig.[5] They secretly made their way back to Ferns, where Dermot's brother, Murrough, immediately gave up the throne. Dermot, who wanted to remain anonymous until reinforcements came, lived in a small cell at the abbey he had built in Ferns.

Within a month, Rory O'Connor heard that Dermot had returned with foreigners, so he and O'Rourke assembled an army and thundered into Hy Kinsella. Dermot met them and treated for peace, pleading that he was an old man who simply wanted to fish, not fight. While negotiations were going on, O'Rourke predictably stole out of camp and attacked the Hy Kinsella men.[6] Rory O'Connor believed a force was coming to relieve Dermot and ordered an attack. Dermot and his men were put to flight in which 100 Leinstermen and two knights were killed. One of the knights was the son of the king of Wales, whose death would recruit more Welsh fighters to Dermot's side.

When the confusion ended, Rory allowed Dermot to remain Hy Kinsella righ with the understanding that Dermot had again to pay O'Rourke 100 ounces of gold as the honor price for abducting Dervorghal, had to hand over to Rory seven more hostages, had to forswear his claim to the throne of Leinster and had to send the foreigners back home. Dermot agreed to everything and the enemy force left.

The following spring, in 1168, as Dermot impatiently waited for the arrival of FitzStephen, Ossory finally set Enna Kinsella free. He was found wandering slowly toward Hy Kinsella – blinded. Dermot's hopes for passing on the throne

---

[5] A small creek and promontory on the coast of Wexford about 12 miles south of Arklow Head and the same distance from Ferns.

[6] They were probably expecting an attack, because no nobles from Hy Kinsella were killed in this initial sortie (although six Connaught nobles were).

of Hy Kinsella to Enna, now unfit to be righ, were dashed. He had only two more sons, Connor and Donal. Where were the Norman-Welsh forces? At 58, when the average lifespan for a male was less than 40, time was running out.

A year later, on May 1, 1169, the Norman-Welsh army, under the command of FitzStephen, landed at Bannow Bay in southern Hy Kinsella and camped along the creek called Baginbun. FitzStephen sent word to Dermot, dug in, and waited impatiently for reinforcements.

At the creek of Baginbun
Ireland was lost and won.[7]

The next day they were reinforced by about 200 Flemmings,[8] who came in two ships. Donal Kavanagh soon brought word that Dermot was on his way with a force of 500 Hy Kinsella men. A number of the local Irish also joined.

When Dermot arrived, the Normans confirmed their agreement with him, assembled their forces and started for Wexford with banners unfurled. Approaching Wexford, they saw arrayed against them 2000 Danes standing outside the walls. The Norman-Irish force was out-manned almost two to one, but upon seeing the Normans in chainmail the Danes retreated behind the walls. A battle raged all day around the walls of Wexford town. At dusk the Normans gathered on the neighboring strand and set fire to all the Danish ships.

The next morning, after Mass had been celebrated,[9] Dermot paraded his men in front of Wexford while they carefully considered how to attack the walls, which turned out not to be necessary. The Danes suddenly opened their gates and surren-

---

[7] From a folk poem.
[8] Ten men at arms and 190 archers.
[9] Mass traditionally occurred at dawn.

dered. Days ago, upon hearing of the arrival of FitzStephen, Dermot had urged the bishop of Ferns to ride to Wexford. During the night the bishop had convinced the Danes to submit to their former righ.

The army marched back to Ferns and feasted for three weeks, resting and recuperating, while Dermot conferred with Robert FitzStephen. Dermot's first goal was of course Ossory; it was strategically important, and the Ossory righ had blinded his son Enna Kinsella. During the next three weeks, some of the surrounding tuath righs arrived to submit to Dermot. Dermot spent the rest of the spring and summer consolidating control of Leinster by gaining submission from all the righs in the province. Often he was forced to go into Ossory and regain its submission. The last time, he took a combined force of Normans, Welsh, Flemmings, Wexford Danes and Irish. One night they camped among the ruins of Dinn Rig, the site where Dermot's ancestor Labraid Loingsech and his foreigners captured the throne of Ireland under similar circumstances. Stories of this ancient battle, complete with fairies and spirits still seen to that day, were told with relish by the Irish to any foreigner who would listen. After dinner that night guards were placed around the entire encampment.

Deep in the black of night, one of the foreign guards, already on edge because of the ghost stories told during the day, believed he saw an approaching army. Suddenly he began shouting, "St. David! Barons, knights!" and pulled out his sword. One of the guard's companions, nervous from the evening's stories and mistaking the guard for an enemy, struck him on the helmet and drove him to his knees. Confusion ensued as the Irish and Normans thought the Danes were attacking in the night and vice versa. The result was very little sleep for anyone. The foreigners were greatly relieved to march out the next morning to attack Ossory, which soon submitted for the last time. Dermot was now firmly in control of all of Leinster except for its most important town, Dublin.

Rory O'Connor, no longer able to ignore Dermot's challenge, assembled his forces and, together with O'Rourke, once more marched on Hy Kinsella. Now supported by his foreigners and many more Irish, Dermot prepared the dense woods and bogs around Ferns for battle. FitzStephen, an expert in this type of warfare due to years of campaigning in Wales, dug pits near entrances to thick woods, cut down trees to place over attack routes and rendered the area impregnable. Rory arrived and asked to meet first with FitzStephen alone in an attempt to bribe him into repudiating Dermot. FitzStephen refused to be bought; his loyalty to Dermot was already firm. Rory then met with Dermot and offered to restore him to the throne of Leinster if he would help Rory kill all the foreigners. Dermot emphatically refused.

Frustrated, but apprehensive about attacking Dermot in his homeland, Rory sent a scouting party into the prepared area around Ferns. The force was destroyed. He again attempted to negotiate, this time with the bishop of Ferns acting as arbitrator. A truce was agreed upon whereby Rory O'Connor recognized Dermot as Leinster righ and Dermot recognized O'Connor as Ard Righ. Secretly the two righs agreed that Dermot would permit no more foreigners and, once he'd strengthened his position in Leinster, Dermot would send these foreigners home. In recognizing Rory as Ard Righ, Dermot handed over three hostages: the son of his foster brother, the son of Donal Kavanagh, and his own youngest son, twelve-year-old Connor MacMurrough. Rory promised that, if Dermot remained faithful, he would allow one of his daughters to marry Connor MacMurrough.

Back in England in August of 1170, after years of asking Henry II for his permission to leave and having finally received it, Strongbow, at the age of 39, was making final preparations on the docks of Wales. Suddenly a messenger from Henry II arrived to announce that the king had changed his mind and forbade Strongbow to set sail. Strongbow sailed the next day anyway with 200 knights and 1,000 mixed fighting men. He arrived in Waterford, but the town had thrown a chain across the harbor to keep him out. Strongbow landed nearby and two days later attacked the town. Sticking to traditional Norman tactics, he made no attempt to negotiate the surrender of Waterford.

The walls of Waterford were stone and clay with round towers at strategic points. The Danes repelled the first attack and then another. The Normans retreated to study the walls more closely. Soon another attack was undertaken and, while the defenders of Waterford were kept busy at one end of the town, a handful of Norman knights pulled down a weak section of the wall at the other end. The Norman force stormed into the town, killing only those with weapons.[10] When Dermot first received word that Strongbow had arrived in Ireland, he also learned Waterford was taken. God had sent Dermot an avenging angel.

Dermot and FitzStephen marched with Dermot's daughter Aoife to meet the Norman earl. Upon their arrival, Strongbow turned over the leaders of the town for execution but Dermot pardoned them all. Strongbow and Aoife were immediately married in the Waterford church, where Dermot publicly pronounced his daughter and Strongbow heirs to Leinster's throne, which was Aoife's dowry[11] along with a fortress in Leinster.

---

[10] 700 were killed.

[11] The custom of the bride's family giving a dowry to the husband was foreign to Ireland, where a dowry was expected from the husband. Dermot was once again willing to modify Irish culture and accept English concepts.

A war council was held and all agreed that Dublin, the most important town in Leinster and of all Ireland, must fall. Leaving a small garrison behind in Waterford, Strongbow's force marched toward Dublin while Dermot quickly returned to Ferns and assembled an army. From Ferns he marched toward Dublin with over 5,000 Norman, Welsh, Flemish and Irish, a mixture of cultures never seen before in an army on Irish soil.

When word reached Dublin of their imminent doom, they pleaded for Rory O'Connor's help. He marched with an army of 10,000 to Dublin and placed the men along the three principal southern routes into Dublin. Along the two forested routes, trees were felled to block access while the third route was entrenched.

Dublin was in Leinster and, even more in Dermot's favor, his mother's clan lived in the town's outskirts. These relatives kept Dermot informed about all of O'Connor's activities and took the Leinster righ's army through little-known passes in the Wicklow Mountains, past Glendalough and down the hills to Dublin. The Leinster army outflanked O'Connor's army and arrived at the gates of Dublin.

Negotiations between Dermot and Dublin began on September 21. When Rory O'Connor discovered this, he chose to depart rather than attack. Lorcan O'Toole, Dermot's brother-in-law and archbishop of Dublin, urged the citizens of the town to accept Dermot's demand of 30 hostages. Dublin's king acquiesced, but a squabble broke out as to who the hostages should be. As the disagreement among the Danes continued, a storm started, casting lightning down on the town and burning part of it, a sure portent of doom.

When the disagreement over Dublin hostages dragged on for three days, the Norman forces began to grow restive. They wanted plunder, not an easy surrender, so a group of them attacked the town. Most of the Danes, perhaps ready for this attack, immediately boarded their ships and sailed for the Isle of Man and the Orkney Islands. Any Danes who remained were banished to Dublin's outskirts on the other side of the River Liffey. Historians agree that the Normans attacked without either Dermot's or Strongbow's approval. In fact, Dublin fell before either Dermot or Strongbow knew it had been attacked.

By October 1, Dermot and Strongbow felt confident enough to leave Dublin and solidify their position in Leinster. They began by raiding north Leinster and banishing the righs who had so willingly submitted to Rory O'Connor four years earlier. Next they revisited Ossory and split it in half, leaving a garrison of Flemmings in charge of the southern half. With Leinster firmly under control, Dermot pursued his ultimate goal, becoming Ard Righ of Ireland.

Norman knight

Together Dermot and Strongbow entered East Meath on the pretext of helping the dispossessed Meath righ, one of Dermot's earlier supporters. They restored him to the throne of Meath and he supplied hostages. Some of the Ulster territorial righs also offered hostages and north Munster, now under the leadership of Dermot's son-in-law, even sent a force to aid the

Leinster righ. Dermot and the foreigners next entered the territory of Tiernan O'Rourke in Connacht, but as his lands were raided, O'Rourke escaped to Rory O'Connor's fort. Dermot MacMurrough had gained the submission of Leinster, Munster, Meath and part of Ulster. He already could be considered Ard Righ with Opposition. Only Connacht and the other battered territories of Ulster hadn't submitted.

Rory O'Connor sent a message to Dermot, who was now marching his army deep into Connacht:

> Contrary to the conditions of our treaty of peace, you have invited a host of foreigners into this island, and yet as long as you kept within the bounds of Leinster we bore it patiently. But now, forasmuch as, regardless of your solemn oaths, and having no concern for the fate of the hostages you gave, you have broken the bounds agreed on, and insolently crossed the frontiers of your own territory. Either restrain in future the irruptions of your foreign bands or we will certainly have your son's head cut off and we will send it to you.[12]

Dermot, supremely confident in God's will, replied:

> We will not desist from the enterprise we have undertaken until we have reduced Connacht to subjection, which we claim as our ancient inheritance, and until we have obtained with it the monarchy of the whole of Ireland.[12]

Upon receiving this response, O'Connor decided to submit and wait for a better day, because he could not beat the forces arrayed against him. Upon hearing of this decision, Tiernan O'Rourke exploded with anger. If O'Connor did not kill Dermot MacMurrough's hostages then Tiernan "pledged his

---

[12] From Giraldus Cambrensis.

conscience that Rory O'Connor would not remain Ard Righ of Ireland."[12]

The Shannon river meanders through Athlone [a town on the border of Connaught and Leinster] . . . . The surrounding countryside is pleasant, calm, not heroic. There are reeds, watercress, bog cotton, rushes and the hoofmarks cattle make in soft soil; and the low green banks of the lazy river reduce the mean haste in men's minds.

To this pleasant spot were led the three fright-faced hostages of Dermot MacMurrough. As they gazed with unbelieving senses towards their Leinster across the river for the last time they may well have shrieked that their executioners would pay a heavy price. But that was all they could do. Shriek. A year of pleasant idleness in the O Connor household was reduced to the obscenity of the execution mound.

The heads of the three princes were slashed off, and their gashed bodies were sent to Dermot MacMurrough, father of one, grandfather of another, foster uncle of the third.[13]

O'Rourke had called Dermot's bluff. Rather than ravage Connacht, Dermot and the foreigners returned to Dublin. By winter, the crushed Dermot had traveled back to Ferns with his hopes and plans unfulfilled.

In May of 1171, Dermot died after a 46-year reign. His dream of founding a monarchy, sustained by his belief that he was doing God's will, died with his son Connor.[14] Dermot requested to be buried "near the shrines of St. Maedoc and St. Moling" in Ferns. The shaft of a now broken Celtic cross marks his final resting place in the graveyard.

---

[13] Nicholas Furlong, *Dermot King of Leinster and the Foreigners* (Tralee, 1973).

[14] With the death of Connor, Dermot knew the succession of his throne would pass to his nephew, Murtough MacMurrough, who would be elected as the next Hy Kinsella righ.

On May 16, while Strongbow was visiting the dying Mac-Murrough at Ferns, the former king of Dublin led an assault to retake the town. The Norsemen came from Norway, the Hebrides, and the Isle of Man in a fleet of 60 ships carrying, some claim, 1,000 men. After failing to retake the town, the former king of Dublin was captured, tried by his Norman enemies in his own hall, and beheaded right then and there.

Strongbow arrived in Dublin shortly after the battle and prepared to defend the town again, this time from the Irish. As Ard Righ, Rory O'Connor summoned all the provinces for a combined attack on Dublin, but he was not a creative or skilled righ. He laid siege to Dublin, waited a few weeks outside the town's walls, and through boredom grew careless. Rory allowed his men to wander and raid the surrounding lands indiscriminately. Having waited for such a chance, the Normans rode out and completely surprised Rory, who was bathing in the River Liffey. He barely escaped with his life, and the siege ended.

Strongbow had hardly regrouped the Dublin forces before he received word that Robert FitzStephen was under siege at Wexford. After Dermot's death, Strongbow had elevated Donal Kavanagh to the throne of Hy Kinsella, but the men of Hy Kinsella revolted against Donal and chose Dermot's nephew, Murtough, as Hy Kinsella righ instead. Murtough's first act as Hy Kinsella righ was to take Wexford from Robert FitzStephen.

While marching down to relieve Robert FitzStephen, Strongbow came under attack in Hy Kinsella and his only son, a youth of about seventeen, ran away from the battle. After learning that his father had turned the tide and defeated the force in front of them, the boy came back to congratulate him. Strongbow first reproached his son for cowardice and then took out a sword and sliced him in half.[15]   Such was the Norman culture that conquered England, most of France, and Italy.

The grave of Strongbow and half his son

Strongbow then stopped at Ferns, and while he was there Donal Kavanagh captured Dalbach O'Breen and his son. Decades before, Dermot had made O'Breen a Hy Kinsella noble and awarded him land, but when Dermot needed help before fleeing to England in 1166, O'Breen had refused to return the favor. Strongbow had both him and his son decapitated for their defection from Dermot. Their bodies were then fed to the dogs and their lands taken. The Irish soon realized

---

[15] John O'Hart, *Irish Pedigrees: or, The Origin and Stem of the Irish Nation* (Baltimore, 1976, 1892).

that rebellions, customary under an Irish righ, would be handled differently by a Norman ruler.

On October 17, King Henry II landed in Ireland and proceeded to Cashel where the Irish church immediately took an oath of obedience to him. Henry held, as legal pretext, the papal bull *Laudabiliter*, authorizing him to take over Ireland "to proclaim the truths of the Christian religion to a rude and ignorant people, and to root out the growth of vice from the field of the Lord."[16] The pope himself congratulated the Irish bishops on their good fortune in a letter saying:

> Our dearest son in Christ, Henry, noble king of the English, prompted by God, has with his assembled forces subjected to his rule that barbarous and uncivilized people ignorant of the divine . . . and we are overjoyed.

After also obtaining submission from all the Irish righs but Rory O'Connor, Henry traveled to Dublin and remained there for the winter before returning to England.

Tiernan O'Rourke, Dermot's old enemy, continued raiding. After submitting to Henry II, he plundered in Meath, burnt a tower full of clergy and then went to a parley with the Normans at the Hill of Ward. When Tiernan arrived under a flag of truce, the Normans shot him through with arrows.[17] His head was cut off and placed on a spike, while his body was dragged

---

[16] E. Curtis and R. B. McDowell, *Irish Historical Documents 1172-1922* (London, 1943).

[17] This is one of the many incidents reported differently by Irish and English sources. English sources state that Tiernan attacked the English under a flag of truce but also reveal (without giving the reason why) that Tiernan's cousin was shortly after rewarded with land. This cousin had rebelled against Tiernan a few years before and had tried to kill him. This cousin probably lured Tiernan to the English knowing full well they would deal with him treacherously.

behind a horse all the way to Dublin where it was hung feet upwards.

That summer Strongbow called the accepted leader of Hy Kinsella, Murtough MacMurrough, to Ferns. They agreed to make peace and Strongbow recognized Murtough as Hy Kinsella righ. Strongbow also set up Donal Kavanagh as righ of a territory just north of Hy Kinsella, but the next year Donal's own son revolted against him and attacked the Normans, killing many of them. In 1175, Donal Kavanagh himself was killed by the Irish of Hy Kinsella.[18]

The Irish church was also beginning to realize its mistake. In 1178, the Normans, whom the pope had chosen to bring religion to the "Island of the Saints," attacked the monastery of Armagh, burned it to the ground and took the sacred staff of St. Patrick. Dermot MacMurrough's plans had gone awry. He had followed the formula used by King David of Scotland decades before: bring in Normans to fight the enemy, stabilize the country, and found a solid royal establishment. Time was against Dermot, however, and his work was left unfinished. Many now judge him by subsequent events, of which he had no foreknowledge. Perhaps that's unfair.

Had he been successful the name of Diarmaid na nGall (Dermot MacMurrough of the Foreigners) might yet be revered as that of the true founder of the national monarchy.[19]

---

[18] He was killed by the O'Foirtchern and O'Nolan of Hy Kinsella. One annal calls him Leinster righ upon his death but this title must have been honorary for Donal could not even control the Irish of Hy Kinsella, much less those of all Leinster.

[19] Francis John Byrne, *Irish Kings and High-Kings* (New York, 1973).

A 12th-Century Commoner

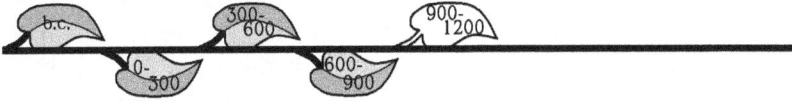

ust as the Anglo-Saxon-Danish culture of England underwent severe changes after the Norman invasion of 1066, so did the Gaelic culture of Ireland after the Normans arrived in 1172. Still, the influence of Gaelic culture can be seen in Ireland today, especially if one is familiar with earlier Irish society. This chapter describes a typical day in the life of an Irish farmer just before the arrival of the Normans in Ireland.

What made the Irish common man, the freeman, different from his English or continental European counterpart was not so much his diet or climate but his society. While the English or continental European common man was subservient to one class, the nobility, as defined by the rules of feudalism, the Irish freeman was subservient to his clan, a group that embraced the spectrum of classes from slave to righ, which made all the difference in allowing for his much greater freedoms, as we shall see. The typical 12th-century Irishman was not a noble but a freeman, called a "boaire" or strong farmer. Here is a description of the day of a boaire named Donagh living near Ferns in 1165.

Shortly before sunrise Donagh awoke to the dim candlelight in his house. The head of his couch, like the other six in the twenty-foot circular house, rested against the wall with the foot pointing toward the central fire. He slipped from the couch and methodically began to dress, as beside him his wife, Sive, rolled out to light another candle and do the same. Today would be his last plowing day so he picked out his yellow linen tunic from the seat-chest at the end of his couch. He wrapped this over his woolen underclothes and around his waist, to be cinched finally with his large black leather belt. Next he took down from the hook on the wall his red and blue woolen cloak fringed with fox-fur and fastened it at his shoulder with a plain brass brooch. Finally, sitting down, he tugged on his leather boots and pulled on his gloves. Only a few yellow strands of embroidery remained on the gloves to remind him of his daughter Mor's early attempts at needlework.

Without saying a word he walked over to the fire his wife had just stoked and slipped the cord of his lunch sack around his neck. Picking up a few oatcakes and a skin of milk his wife had prepared for him the night before, he slipped those into the sack resting on his hip and kissed his wife goodbye. With a knowing smile she handed him the bag of oats he'd almost forgotten to bring with him. All was done quietly for neither wanted to disturb Donagh's aged mother, who was failing. As Lorcan, the youngest, was still rubbing sleep from his eyes, Sive put out the candle that had been burning in the center of the house all night (so any passersby would know they were welcome).

Stepping over the threshold of the wattle house,[1] which kept the floor reeds in, Donagh followed the flagstones to the sluggish spring nearby. The round house was situated by several other round houses, some serving as barns for various animals, others as storage sheds, outhouses and even a sunroom. All were surrounded by a low but stout wooden wattle fence that the kindred had helped Donagh make years before to protect the family and animals from wolves and other wild beasts. Upon reaching the well, a small shallow depression outlined with rocks but full of cool crystal-clear water, Donagh dropped the bag of oats on the ground and scooped up handfuls of water to drench his face. The water ran down his finely trimmed mustache as well as through his long brown hair. Shaking his head vigorously, he set about washing his hands with the soap that lay in a small bucket

---

[1] The walls of houses were made of sticks woven together. They would last seven or so years.

nearby. Refreshed and ready for the plowing ahead of him, he picked up the bag and walked towards the barn. As he passed the pigsty a few squeals erupted. "You'll be fed soon enough," intoned Donagh.

He pushed aside the barn door and the strong odor of fresh manure hit his nostrils. Quietly he called out, "Aire. Righ. Come." From the gloom two large oxen plodded forward. Grabbing their harness and yokes from the nearby wall, he walked them outside, quickly closing the door behind him so none of the other cattle could escape. The remaining cattle, eager to graze, began lowing. Meanwhile, the oxen immediately wandered towards the wooden enclosure's gate and patiently waited for Donagh to open it.

"C'mon Dub," Donagh called to his large black guard dog. Already at the man's side, the animal ran up to the gate and waited with

Inside a boaire farmer's enclosure

the oxen. The farmer lifted the withe that kept the wooden gate closed, stepped outside and chained Dub to a post. The surrounding sheep, which dotted the open pasture like tufts of grass in a bog, were used to his morning appearance and continued their grazing.

"That's a good boy," he said while rubbing the guard dog's head. "I'll be back mid-afternoon. You keep everyone safe, you hear?" The dog cocked his head toward Donagh as if in agreement. Turning to the oxen, the farmer yoked them together and then, holding their rope in his hand, he followed the path to the nearby servant's white-washed house.

The sun was just beginning to peek over the tree-tops, bathing the meadow and its farmstead in golden light, as Donagh knocked on his servant's door.

"Wake up, Aedh," he shouted before continuing on down the path that led into the surrounding forest of alders, beech and oak. Donagh had a fair distance to walk today. The plot he meant to plow was the most distant one he owned, so he had little time to talk. The servant, Aedh, was to take Donagh's pigs and the pigs of two other farmers into the woods where they would fatten themselves on the plentiful supply of acorns that had fallen in the kindred's woodland last fall.

While he entered the dark woods, Donagh began whistling a tune as thoughts about his servant drifted through his mind. Aedh can talk from morn to night without even pausing to breathe. He's not the smartest, which is why he's a servant in the first place. Keeping the oxen moving at a decent pace, Donagh remembered the time two years before when Aedh killed three of Donagh's cows. Aedh's kindred head,[2] the man legally responsible for all relatives in the male line of descent for three generations (starting with a great-grandfather) had decided not to have his kindred pay the fine. (If a member of the kindred could not pay a fine, the entire kindred had to pay it, unless they disinherited the member.) The kindred head chose instead to have Aedh work it off. Therefore, Aedh was Donagh's

---

[2] The kindred head was responsible for all the relatives in the "derbfine," an Irish term meaning all males who had the same great-grandfather (that is, up to and including second cousins) together with their families. The kindred head was the legal spokesman for the entire derbfine and acted on their behalf whenever one of them required legal help. He could act as a substitute father for any of the derbfine's orphans and also could banish a member from the derbfine if the others in the kindred agreed (normally because the person was too great a legal liability and couldn't be kept in check by the derbfine). The kindred head couldn't pass his position on to his son but had to pass it on to a son in another branch of the derbfine.

servant until the three cows could be replaced, and then he would be free again to rejoin his kindred.

Soon the small, well-beaten footpath emerged from the forest and cut close to another enclosed group of houses with fewer buildings inside the circular wooden fence. It belonged to Conor, his twenty-year-old son, who had married only last year and with the help of the kindred had built this farm next to his father's. Conor waited with his one ox at the intersection of the footpath and the main road. As an "ocaire" (small farmer), one ox was all he could afford. Together they walked to the distant barley field they shared with Donagh's brother, Padraig. Most of their crops were oats and flax, which fed and clothed them, but barley[3] brought far more profit and could one day allow Donagh to increase his rank above boaire.

"This should be one of our last plowing days, Da," said Conor amiably as they met. "I suppose you'll be stopping by the mill to grind what's in the bag?" Unable to afford a nice cloak like his father, he pulled his bright-green jacket closer around him to ward off the morning dampness. His brown and black trousers, which were tight-fitting and reached all the way to his moccasins, were held down by a strap that passed below the instep.

"It's a bag of oats I'll be grinding," responded Donagh. "Since the mill isn't on the way home, do you mind bringing my two oxen back at the end of the day?" Conor and his ox swung in to pace alongside as they turned onto the wide main road.

"Consider it done," replied the younger man.

"You'll need to be mending that," Donagh mentioned as he pointed to a deep rut in the road.

"It'll wait," nonchalantly answered Conor.

Donagh stopped, causing the oxen to bump into and almost knock him over. Surprised, Conor turned around to see the mounting frustration on his father's face. "It will *not* wait," he said sharply. "Don't you understand? At any time you can be fined for that rut.

---

[3] Donagh doesn't plant barley in all his fields, because if for any reason it didn't make it to harvest, he and his family would starve. Growing a range of crops is safer; if any one crop failed, the others could support him through the resulting lean year.

It's on the road in front of your property. Fill it in tonight, after the plowing."

Surprised by the severity of the speech, Conor mutely nodded his head and they continued on.

Finally Donagh, walking in stride, broke the silence, "Sorry lad but it's wee things like that which keep my older brother, Padraig, in the position he's in now, still an ocaire (small farmer) like you, and yet he's older than I. He works at relaxation harder than most men work at their fields, so fines and penalties keep coming his way. I don't want to see you become like him. It's those that lack responsibility, that are a tad lazy, that end up going nowhere in this world. 'The Lord helps those that help themselves.'"

Shortly they stopped at one of the many fields surrounded by a ditch and a low pile of branches, firewood that hadn't been consumed that winter. The low pile would grow taller as the warm weather continued and refuse branches were added to it, until winter would again require its use.

"Waiting on Padraig again," mumbled Donagh as he dropped the bag he'd been carrying and hunkered down at the edge of the road, careful to keep the fringe of his cloak on the deep green grass rather than in the road's dirt.

"Maybe you shouldn't be so tough on him, Da," suggested Conor. "Last time he did have an excuse."

"I'll agree to that. His dog shit in the neighbor's lawn, so he had to pick it up and pay the neighbor an equal amount of butter." Donagh snorted, "If he'd chained up his dog in the first place, he wouldn't have had to pay, which in turn made him late for our plowing that day!"

A man whose face looked remarkably like Donagh's appeared around the corner of the forest pulling an ox, a harness and a yoke. His clothes, more similar to Conor's than to Donagh's, revealed his social station. From a distance, Donagh's brother Padraig waved.

Donagh rose with a smile and unfastened the brooch at his shoulder, allowing his marvelous red and blue cloak to slip to the ground. When his brother was close enough he asked, "You ready to start plowing the barley field, brother?"

"I'd rather be plowing my wife's field but that wouldn't help us feed the mouths we already have," Padraig laughed. "It would only create another which, in turn, would provoke the Kindred Head against me."[4]

They yoked up the two ocaires' oxen and Donagh's two oxen, attached the harness, made the sign of the cross over the plow they had left here yesterday and began on the largest plot, Donagh's. Grabbing the handles of the plow, Donagh signaled the oxen to start up, while Conor led them forward in a sunwise direction and Padraig dropped in the seed. The ground opened easily beneath the heavy plow and the smell of fresh earth rose to mingle with that of sweat. When the oxen slowed down, Donagh hit them from behind with his sharp goad. It was a beautiful morning to be plowing, thought Donagh. He started singing a plowing song, and they quickly joined in.

By midmorning Sive was enjoying the wan March sun as she sat with her mother-in-law, Brigit, on a small bench just outside their sunroom, a small circular house with a window cut in its golden thatched roof to allow light in. In her lap she absent-mindedly pet

---

[4] Because of societal pressure, Ireland didn't suffer from overpopulation as many other European countries did. Two factors kept families small except for those of the highest-ranking nobles. First, in Ireland, every few years the land within a kindred was redistributed equally. When a father died, the sons inherited his land equally, but at a time determined by the clan the land was redistributed. A family with twenty sons was forced to live on small portions of land until the land was redistributed, when they earned a larger share of land at the expense of their relatives. However, their relatives put a great deal of pressure on the family *not* to have twenty sons but to stop after four or five, so this situation would not occur. Perhaps the other sons would be sent to monasteries, trained as scholars, or become craftsmen. Second, the amount of wealth one held determined one's social rank. In the case of a family with 20 sons, each son would inherit only a few items from his father, so each son's social rank would be much lower than his father's. A family with only a few sons would allow each son to inherit more, leading to a higher social rank.

Devil's Paw, their cat. The morning chores had been successfully completed. After she had milked the sheep, her eleven-year-old son Murrough had taken them with the herding dog, cows, and the bull to a neighbor's for grazing. One of the neighbors whose pigs were being looked after by Aedh in return looked after Donagh's live-stock. Her seventeen-year-old daughter Mor had milked their two cows, one of which was rented from a noble to replace one of those Aedh had killed, and fed the fowl.

At the feet of the two women, the youngest children, Lorcan and Cacht, pretended to be cooking with leaves and pieces of wood.

"Mother," said Mor, Sive's oldest daughter, as she hung one of her brother's orange linen bed blankets over the enclosure fence to air out, "can I swim down at the River Slaney after I'm done here?" She picked up a blue wool blanket also used for sleeping and threw it over the fence as well, causing the chickens pecking next to it to scatter away in confusion.

"Now what would you be wanting a swim for today?" asked her mother with a smile. She had noticed her daughter spending an unduly long time plaiting her hair and rouging her cheeks in front of their burnished brass mirror that morning. The brightly-colored red fingernails had not been missed either. "It's not very warm in the River," she continued, "and we've hot water here in the tub."

"It's not swimming she's about," croaked Brigit at her side, her eyes gleaming brightly at her granddaughter, "it's young Turlough." The old woman went back to mending the pile of clothes she had beside her. The cock chose this time to belt out a cock-a-doodle-do as he strutted by.

The blush that rose in Mor's face could be seen only momentarily for quickly she turned back to hanging more sleeping blankets over the fence, a chore she did daily. "And would that be wrong?" she softly asked.

"Oh no, child," laughed her mother as she pushed Devil's Paw from her lap and adjusted the yellow hood that covered her hair, a sign she was married. "Turlough's a good lad with a decent future. I suppose I'd rather see you pursued by Dermot MacMurrough's son Connor but you're a bit old for him."

A cackle burst from Brigit, the grandmother, which brought on a coughing spell, forcing her to lay down her mending needle. Quickly Sive produced a cup of water over which she made the sign of the cross and handed it to the older woman. Drinking deeply, she looked kindly on Sive as her attack ceased. Taking a deep breath, Brigit spoke weakly, "She's saying of course you can go, lass, but since Turlough is too young to take up farming implements, she'd prefer it if no wild oats were sown." Brigit loved to embarrass her granddaughter. The old woman pulled her dark blue cloak tighter around herself, pausing in her mending while she composed herself.

A mischievous expression developed on Mor's face as she asked, "May I take Barley?" She motioned to their horse, really only a work pony, which had been set free to roam in the enclosure hours ago.

"Next you'll be asking us to move out so you and Turlough may move in!" chided Sive. Realizing Mor wasn't sure what her mother's answer had been, Sive quickly said, "Of course you may, lass."

Moments later, Mor finished hanging all the linen and woolen blankets, turned towards her mother and grandmother, and said, "Bye, then. I'll be home in time for dinner." She scampered off through the enclosure gate with a bridle and their brown pony, Barley, following closely behind. Neither woman noticed that on her way out she'd bent down to pick up a sack similar to the one in which Donagh had carried his lunch.

"That's a good one we have," mentioned Brigit as she picked up her mending again. "She'll make a fine wife. Oh, and you will too," the old woman suddenly added as Cacht, Sive's eight-year-old daughter, stood up and leaned against her withered arms.

"I want to go, too," said the child, obviously bored with her cooking game.

"Ah, no you don't," quietly answered Sive, "your older brother Murrough should be returning from delivering the sheep and cattle any minute." Cacht turned a glum expression towards her mother, who continued, "and he said he was bringing back Enna, Ashling, Donchad and Dervorghal."

Cacht's eyes widened and she jumped from her grandmother's side. "Yes," she shouted, "is it surely true?"

"As true as the yellow eye in the blue face you see above you now," answered Sive. "Now help your grandmother stand as I shoo both of you out of the enclosure with young Lorcan here. I need to do some weeding in the garden." She grabbed Lorcan's hand, her youngest of only four years, and together they leisurely walked the short distance through the gate. Just outside the gate was another bench, positioned alongside the fenced-in garden. The meadow that surrounded their farm had a large solitary oak tree, which the grazing sheep collected under during storms. During the day, only the breeze disturbed the long winter grass.

A typical herb garden

Sive wandered over to the earth Donagh had hoed a few weeks earlier and began pulling weeds from among the herbs, garlic, carrots, onions and celery. A small part of the garden had also been set aside for medicinal plants, and here Sive weeded very carefully while softly singing a sweet planting melody. Meanwhile, Brigit pushed aside the clothes she'd brought that needed mending, patted the worn wooden bench on either side of her and invited Lorcan and

Cacht to take a seat. "I have a tale about your ancestors," was how she began. That was enough to attract her grandchildren's attention. They both scrambled into their accustomed positions.

As Brigit began telling her story, Sive continued singing and mechanically picking away, always throwing the weeds with her right hand rather than her left so as not to displease the fairies. She found this relaxing, and soon her thoughts drifted back to Brigit's arrival at their house. It was almost fifteen years ago when Brigit and Conor, Donagh's parents, had asked if they could live with them. It was a great honor to Donagh, for his parents had three boys from which to choose, and, though Donagh's oldest brother hadn't done well, Donagh's youngest brother was a boaire like them. Not that Sive, or Donagh for that matter, had much choice in the matter. If they had declined taking care of his parents they would have been cast out of the kindred.[5] Sive remembered her trepidation at sharing the house with another woman, but from the first day Brigit arrived the older woman made it clear she was not interested in being the matron of the house; she was a guest. It had become a blessing rather than a burden. All remembered the passing of Donagh's father, Conor, with sadness rather than relief. Until the end he had managed to help in small ways, not least with his merry wit and love of song. Sive stopped for a moment to look at her two children, mesmerized by their grandmother, who connected them with a past that stretched back thousands of years. That's a good one we have, thought Sive.

---

[5] A son who disobeyed his father and refused to maintain his father in old age was called a "cold son." The father could prohibit everyone from giving the cold son hospitality or a dwelling place. Anyone who flouted his prohibition was liable to pay for offences committed by the cold son. The cold son lost all legal standing and rank and became a nonentity. Upon the death of the father, 1/3 of the cold son's inheritance went to whichever member of the kindred took care of the father, since it now fell on the kindred to support the aged man. If a father had several sons, those he did not choose to live with were not considered cold sons. This rule did not apply to daughters because once a daughter married she belonged to her husband's kindred.

At midday, Donagh, Padraig and Conor stopped to eat their lunches. Before drinking from their skins of milk, each spilled a small portion on the ground for the fairies. "We were given the butt end of the kindred lands last time it was partitioned," mentioned Padraig.

Donagh rolled his eyes, for he'd heard this more than once from his brother. "I've said it before but I'll say it again, Padraig. You chose this piece of land, you could have chosen others, and therefore you would have done your cooperative farming with another such as our younger brother. In any event, the kindred head will call for a repartition of land in another year or two, what with some of the older kindred having passed away. Their kids don't own a fair portion now."[6]

"I must say, I'm looking forward to that," observed Conor. "Not that I don't like having my land affixed to yours, Da, but of course I'll receive a larger portion now that I'm an ocaire."

"That you will, son, though you'll also . . . ," Donagh's voice traveled off as his eyes drifted to the road. The Leinster righ himself was riding by with his family and a small entourage. Normally he would have had an escort of thirty, but because it was the sowing season he was only allowed three in his escort, so as not to divert his people from their work. It was easy to pick out the Leinster righ, firstly because he had a beard, something grown by all the nobility but by few of the commoners, and secondly he was huge. It was said that at age fourteen he already looked like a full-grown man. Conor waved as they rode past and received an acknowledgment in return.

---

[6] Every few years, as determined by local custom and the number of deaths, land would be redistributed among kindred in a process called gaveling. When a tenant who owned part of kindred land died, gaveling redistributed the land of the whole kindred among all the adult male members. Only the land of one kindred, not all of the clan land, was affected. The land seems to have been redistributed piecemeal, so not all of one person's land would be connected. Often people walked miles to reach other tracts of their land, which allowed them to keep the same house, so the best land could be redistributed fairly and not always belong to the same family.

"How's the land seem?" boomed The MacMurrough's deep voice.

"Wonderful fresh and fertile," answered Donagh, knowing it would make Dermot happy. The MacMurrough was joined to the land, as all righs were upon their inauguration, and therefore the fertility of the land responded to the rule of the righ. If the rule was right and just, the land was fertile; an unjust rule brought plague and years of leanness.

Padraig stood up and shouted to one of those riding in Dermot's escort, "So you've finished yer fields have you Ugaire?" while managing to spew forth half of the oatcake in his mouth.

"Aye, just did the last two days ago," replied a short man riding alongside The MacMurrough's son, Conor. Ugaire of the long arms was from their own kindred. "Thought it a ripe time to take a vacation," he threw out with a grin.

"Don't drink too much of the good people's wine or you won't be asked again!" Padraig warned. The royal party continued on and Padraig sat down again. "I wish The MacMurrough had asked me to be in his escort. I could use a week of good food and wine at some noble's house."

"Yer not done with your plowing yet," Donagh reminded him.

"Aoife, now she's a fine-looking lass if I ever did see one," sighed Conor.

"And she's just one more reason I wish The MacMurrough had invited me instead of Ugaire," Padraig added.

"And he may invite you next time," shot back Donagh, "but instead of being needed for an escort it could be a war party!"

"Oh, he's not one for fighting in recent years," answered Padraig, "though of course I'd go. I wouldn't want to lose the right to plow my land for a year."

"It's passing strange to me that you'd worry about that, Padraig, seeing as you do so little of it," commented Donagh. "Now I suppose we should take care of Conor's field next, to ensure you'll stay around, Padraig."

Conor and Padraig's fields were each half the size of Donagh's and, being right alongside, they did not take very long to plow and sow.

As they finished and were unharnessing the oxen, Padraig un-characteristically grew awkward. Stumbling over his words, he finally managed to ask Donagh, "May I have a favor, brother?"

Donagh waited for Padraig to continue, but after a long silence Donagh said, "What would you be asking me?"

Padraig hesitated yet again and finally burst out with, "I'd like you to rent three cows from a noble. For my use." He looked away before adding, "I'd pay you back. You know I would."

Donagh brushed his hand through his long brown hair while fighting back the impulse to shout at his brother. He understood his brother's predicament. A farmer had two choices in how to rent cows from a noble: he could become a free client, who had to pay a great deal up front but then little at the end of the rental term, or he could become a base client, who had little to pay up front but then a great deal at the end of the rental term. Padraig couldn't afford to be a free client himself because the initial fee was too high, but he was smart enough to realize that becoming a base client was very risky. "I want to help you . . . ," began Donagh before looking over at Conor.

Donagh coughed and started over, "Padraig, I have my sons to look after. You shouldn't be asking me this anyway, and you know it. You should be asking the kindred head. That's what he's there for. He helps out those in the kindred, not me."

"You know yourself," quickly responded Padraig in a sharper tone, "that he's already had to support me more times than he cares. I'll get no more help from him." Pausing to curb his emotions, Padraig added, "I know I haven't been the best worker up to now. I know you may think you're taking a risk by accepting this, but I don't want to be an ocaire the rest of my life. I want to pass something on to my children, as you've done to Conor here. Give them a step up in life." Finally, he took his brother's hand and added in a whisper, "I don't want them to lose their freedom because of me."

Donagh roughly shook Padraig's hand away. "You know you could take us both down!" Padraig looked listlessly at the ground.

He had no one else to ask. "Give me time to think," grumbled Donagh.

Padraig raised his head hopefully and then remarked, "May the Lord aid you in your decision. You'll see a changed man in me, you will."

Donagh reached down and grabbed his cloak, which he managed to clasp together with his brooch without looking at his brother. Since he still had to stop by the kindred's mill and grind the bag of oats, he decided to leave his plow in the field until tomorrow when he would retrieve it. Conor took his father's two oxen, and the three men said their goodbyes. Donagh, continuing up the main road toward the River Slaney, soon came across a leper who was probably coming from begging at either The MacMurrough's castle or the Ferns monastery.[7]

"Say a prayer for me," asked the leper.

"And you for me," responded Donagh in greeting.

At the next footpath Donagh turned off and entered the forest again. The undergrowth at this point was so dense that it was all but impenetrable, allowing visibility of only a dozen or so feet. The path Donagh now followed had been hacked through the forest generations ago to allow access to the river beyond.

Upon reaching the mill he found one of his other kindred members, Brien Dark Eye, just finishing his own grinding. "Is that the last of your oats?" asked Donagh.

"Aye it is," answered Brien. "'Tis late enough in the year that we'll get through Lent fine though."

"Surely you will," replied Donagh. "Lent's always a lean time."

"Speaking of lean times, have you heard the kindred head's called for all to man the weir in three days time?" He didn't wait for a reply but continued, "to help out those who could use more. Fish for dinner would be a nice change from porridge." Brien brushed the last of the flour from the grinding stones into his bag, heaved it over his back and started for home.

---

[7] A heavy fine was levied on anyone who mocked the disability of an epileptic, a leper, a lame man, a blind man or a deaf man.

"It would at that," remarked Donagh, "it would at that." He climbed the ladder to the upper story with his bag of oats. Once up top, he began pouring his oats into the hopper so they dropped between the grinding stones below. After his bag was empty, he returned to the bottom floor, dropped the bag on a nearby bench and sat just outside in the afternoon sun, waiting for his oats to be ground into flour.

An Irish grinding mill with a horizontal waterwheel underneath

It was late in the day as Donagh came out of the forest and caught sight of his home. The wickerwork fence that enclosed the various structures was now almost four years old, but it still had almost as many more to go before it needed replacement. Inside, his white-washed houses and animal barns, topped with their golden-thatched roofs, looked trim and well-managed. Over by the great oak he saw his son Murrough playing with their herding dog among the cropping sheep. Most of the sheep were black with patches of white, but he did own a few prize dun-colored ones. Striding up the path to the boy, the father said, "Have you been a good farmer today, lad?" He tousled the boy's long blonde hair.

"Aye, I have, Da," he responded. "All the cattle are in their barn, including the oxen Conor brought back." Then with a twinkle in his eye he added, "Mrs. Gormlaith gave me a bit of her sheep curds today for being good. I helped bring her back some of the cows who'd been scared off by a wolf."

"Did she, now?" asked Donagh with a raised brow. "Wish she'd thought enough to send along some for me." He chuckled as he kept walking toward the gate. The family's huge guard dog, Dub, walked up to lick the man's hand. "Hello, Dub. I suppose we might have a job for you soon. Would you like to go hunting a wolf with the rest of the kindred?" Dub wagged his tail excitedly as Donagh unchained him. The dog immediately began scratching against the enclosure gate to get in.

Donagh leaned against the large wooden pole by the gate as he lifted up the withe. Inside the family enclosure, Brigit, now sitting back on a bench outside the sunroom, put down the clothes she'd been mending and smiled warmly at her approaching son. "I see you remembered the flour."

"Aye, and I have welcome news. The kindred will be fishing in three days time so we can have a respite from cakes and oatmeal." Suddenly he added, "But how are you feeling today, Mother?"

Shaking her head slowly in the lingering evening sun, she answered, "I've done something to anger the fairies, I'm afraid. I think I feel another fairy dart in my ankle." She bent down and rubbed her ankle joint ineffectively. "I don't think I'll make it to the upper pastures this summer."

"Don't talk that way, Mother," admonished her son. "I'll have Sive mix up an ointment for you which will take care of that ache. Then we can . . . ."

"Well, hello, husband," came Sive's voice abruptly as she stepped out from the nearby thatched house into the cool March air. Sweat beads had formed on her forehead from bending over the fire as she prepared the meal. She walked up to him and, with hands full of flour, hugged him before delivering a kiss. "I'll take that," she said, while loosening his fingers from the bag of flour and disappearing back inside.

Looking down at his mother's small pinched face, Donagh said, "You're cold, Mother." He took off his cloak and carefully wrapped it around the one she already wore. Sitting down next to her on the bench, he drew the ladle from the bucket of water beside them, relaxed for a moment and then began discussing the day in an effort to take his mother's mind off her pains. As they sat in the sun, wonderful odors of baking cakes and cooking oatmeal wafted past.

Before too long, Aedh entered the enclosure, driving all the pigs he'd been watching towards their sty. Donagh edged closer to his mother as the screaming and stampeding little beasts of gray, black and reddish-brown swarmed into their waiting mud. They were dangerous animals when provoked but an important source of meat since they reproduced so quickly. The big sow, having just given birth to eight new piglets, came in last.

"Dinner's almost ready," called Sive from inside. "Has anyone seen Mor?"

Brigit smiled broadly but said nothing as Donagh asked, "Isn't she inside with you?"

As Aedh sat down alongside Donagh and Brigit, a stranger knocked on the enclosure's doorpost and patiently waited to enter. Dressed in tight blue pants and wearing a large gold and green cloak pinned at the shoulder with a simple brooch, he seemed to be a farmer. Dub began barking and jumping at the gate, trying to keep the stranger out.

"Hello, sir," called out Donagh in a friendly tone as he stood up and walked over, grabbing Dub by the neck and telling him to stay down. "My name's Donagh. What can we do for you?"

Pushing his long black hair away from his brilliant green eyes, the stranger replied, "I'm called Brandubh. I was hoping I could have a bite of supper and a stay."[8]

---

[8] Every free landowner above the rank of ocaire was expected to welcome guests. A righ was expected to have a torch burning near his fort so strangers could find it more easily. The host was not to inquire who the guest was or where he came from until after a meal was eaten. The amount of food

"One more for supper, Sive!" Donagh shouted as he opened the gate, kissed the stranger three times on the cheeks and gestured towards the empty space on the bench beside his mother and Aedh. Before the stranger moved to take the spot, he handed over a small knife he'd been carrying.

"Aedh, you'd best be taking Murrough's spot now that we have company," mentioned Donagh. Morosely, Aedh stood and slowly walked back out through the gate. Murrough's entrance quickly followed on Aedh's departure, since the servant had taken over the boy's duty of watching the sheep outside the enclosure.

Donagh handed the stranger's knife to Murrough and said, "Put this away and fetch the basin for Brandubh's feet. It appears he's walked some miles today."

As Murrough raced inside, Mor opened the gate and walked the pony, Barley, inside. Her long brown hair, so nicely plaited that morning, looked to have been redone much more quickly that afternoon.

"My, but yer a bit late," observed Donagh. "The cattle are already in, and dinner's almost ready. You'll have to milk those two cows after."

"I suppose she's won the honor of washing our guest's feet," chuckled Brigit.

Mor's face, still flushed from the day's activities, radiated only contentment. When Murrough arrived with the basin of water and a

---

was regulated, so a guest could not overindulge. A guest who had eaten food in a house was considered under the protection of everyone belonging to the house. Since every guest was considered to be Christ, he came when he liked, stayed as long as he liked, and left when he liked. No matter how many guests, or how long their stay, under no circumstances could the host ask them to leave without losing honor. The costs were expected to be recovered eventually since generosity was reciprocal. If, on the arrival of guests, an Irishman discovered he had no food or drink, he suffered great disgrace. (This applied to all ranks, including royalty.) If the disgrace occurred not through the negligence of the host but through the fault of someone contracted to supply the provisions, the contractor was liable by law to pay the fine for the disgraced host.

cloth, she knelt down, carefully removed Brandubh's common sandals, and began cleaning the grime from his feet with a colorful linen towel. Her eyes revealed she was still on the banks of the River Slaney with her Turlough.

"Dinner is ready," cried Sive from inside the house.

Upon entering the house, all stepped from the stone walkway onto the brightly colored rug Brigit had made years before. In the center of the circular room burned the fire with the nearby kneading trough, griddle (still holding a few oatcakes) and a great pot suspended over the flames. This contained a bubbling porridge, the source of the wonderful smells that had been wafting their way. To the right of the hearth stood the dinner table, while all around the edges of the room, pointing towards the hearth, were couches for sleeping and sitting. At their ends were movable padded chests containing each person's clothes and blankets. These chests were now pulled up to the table; one of the extra chairs was pulled up for Brandubh.

The stranger sat and looked around. Hanging from the rafters were several burning candles, though plenty of light still came in from the open windows and door. Also hanging from the rafters, and appropriately separated far away from the candles, were sacks that probably contained flour, malt for the beer and salt. A few smoked fish hung in groups also. The rest of the smoked meat had been consumed before Lent began. The walls were cheerily decorated with embroidered cloths and woven tapestries. By the entrance was the wash barrel that they would all use after the meal.

"Sit by me," Cacht said to the stranger.

Brandubh pulled up the chair Donagh had proffered to him just as Sive placed a bowl of porridge and an oatcake before him.

"And here's your beer," Donagh said warmly, setting a wooden mug down before him. The children shared a square, two-handled wooden cup filled with drinking water.

"What did you find for the porridge today?" asked Brigit of Sive, who was just settling down herself.

"I put fish in it, of course," remarked Sive, "but because of our company I also added a few eggs and the last of our dried beans."

Suddenly all grew quiet. Donagh led the prayer for their meal, after which all made the sign of the cross over their food. Immediately the conversation resumed. Brandubh slathered butter[9] onto his oatcake from the tub in front of him, while Mor reached over to grab some of the hazel nuts sitting in a common bowl.

"It tastes wonderful," remarked Brandubh. "You still seem to have plenty in such a lean time."

"My wife is very good with our food supply," proudly acknowledged Donagh while cutting himself a piece of hard cheese with his knife.

"And we must credit The MacMurrough as well," added Sive. "The land smiles warmly on him."

"It does indeed," agreed Brandubh.

"There's more here when you have a need," said Donagh, pointing to the beer cask by his leg. "Or there's the pitcher of water on the table."

Sive, having finished putting together a plate for Aedh, pushed it over toward Murrough, who ran out to deliver it. Conversation flowed easily as the food was consumed, but the stranger revealed little about himself.

After all had finished, Mor cleaned up while Sive dropped the rocks from the cooking fire into the bath barrel, a large oak tub bound with willow hoops standing near the doorway and filled with water. Donagh tested the temperature with his hand, and when it was right he pulled the wicker door in front of the bath, disrobed and settled in to wash himself.

"Time you put the fowl back in their pen, Cacht," said Donagh as he scrubbed his arms with the soap Sive had given him. "And Murrough, you should be tying Barley to her stake." Brandubh, still sitting at the table, was talking with Sive.

"But I want to hear Brandubh," whined Cacht.

---

[9] Fresh butter, lightly salted was a favorite food but did not age well. Butter to be aged was either heavily salted, reducing its appeal, or placed in a basket and buried in a bog. Often 30-40 pounds of butter were buried to weather the long winter, resulting in a substance like cream cheese.

"And so do I," cried Murrough.

"There'll be more time for that the sooner you both finish your chores."

Sive kept the conversation flowing as she simultaneously packed Donagh's cakes and filled up a flask with more goats' milk for tomorrow's lunch. All were curious about why Brandubh was traveling, an unusual thing for a commoner, but asking was considered too rude. Instead, the family subtly tried to find out where he might be from, since any prying into the stranger's life would be considered impolite. Brandubh appeared disinterested in local talk and instead offered to tell a few tales. By this time Donagh had finished his bath, so Sive handed him a towel. Normally she would bathe next, but the guest took precedence. Brandubh now removed all his clothing and sat in the bath. By this time Cacht and Murrough had returned from their chores, so they lay down on their couches along with Mor and Lorcan.

From the barrel of water, Brandubh began to tell tales of Finn and the Fianna. He embellished the stories, which each person in the house knew by heart, with subtle humor. A small degree of embellishment was acceptable, even desirable in a good storyteller, but any audience severely frowned on significant deviations from the traditional story. Brandubh knew this and using tone, patience, and body motions told superb tales. Part way through a story, he climbed out, dried off and pulled a chair closer to the hearth, where he continued with a mug of ale now in his hands. The entire family took turns in the tub, and by the time Brandubh began slowing down, dusk was settling in. Aedh, the last to take a bath, was just climbing out.

"Time to take care of the cows, Mor," said her father quietly. Donagh quickly set about emptying the bathtub before nightfall. He had to work fast because it was unlucky to leave the used bath water indoors overnight, but if it were emptied during nightfall the fairies would be upset. Dragging it outside and away from the house, he tipped the water out and then returned the tub to its place. Because of the lateness, it would have to be refilled tomorrow. When he returned, he noticed Sive had stoked up the fire for the night as a precaution to help Brigit through her sickness. Once his mother recovered, they'd go back to smooring[10] the fire at night instead. Standing just outside the doorway, he watched as his wife helped little four-year-old Lorcan light the candle that would burn all night in the center of the house. Mor returned shortly and almost bumped into her father.

"Just making sure you were back quickly. We don't want to offend the fairies." He followed her inside where they took to their accustomed beds. The new day had just begun.[11]

---

[10] Covering it with ashes. Many of the fires would have burned for centuries.

[11] The Celts believed the new day started at nightfall, not sunrise. They followed a lunar rather than a solar calendar.

The Norman Incursion

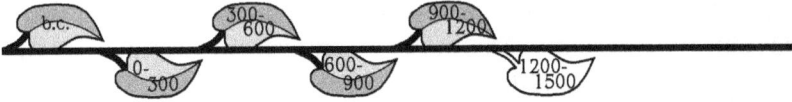

Strongbow died only four years after Dermot MacMurrough but lived long enough to have a far-reaching impact. He allowed Dermot MacMurrough's nephew, Murtough, to remain Hy Kinsella righ while at the same time rewarding the heirs of Dermot MacMurrough's son, Donal Kavanagh, with rule over a section of northern Hy Kinsella (now County Carlow). Enna Kinsella received nothing because of his blindness. According to Irish law, he could not rule. The rest of Leinster, Strongbow gave to several Norman families, who ruled under him as lieutenants.

After Strongbow's death in 1176, his lieutenants began to seize more land from the Irish and build castles throughout Leinster, including Hy Kinsella. Their descendants protected the land they had seized and, in most cases, took more from the native Irish nobles, who were forced to either serve the Norman lords or move into the mountains and bog lands. The kings of England, in an effort to help these Norman nobles in Ireland, encouraged settlers from England to form colonies around the castles. Few of the English resettled, however, so the Norman lords were forced to use the Irish as their cultivators. Being accustomed to French feudalism, the Norman lords tried reducing the free Irish tenants to serfdom.[1] The ancestors of the Normans had done this very effectively to the Anglo-Saxons a century before, but this did not work with the Irish, and a mixture of French and Irish feudalism resulted. Near the close of the 13th century, English settlements with a large Irish peasant population were quite extensive in counties Louth, Dublin, Meath and Kildare, in what was called The Pale (Norman controlled Ireland). The Norman culture predominated in the Pale with its administrative center in Dublin. In Leinster, the hardest-hit province, only a few Gaelic clans survived with their culture intact by retreating to the woods, hills and bogs.

The Norman culture imposed on those living in the Pale was a dramatic shift from the Gaelic culture they were accustomed to, particularly in terms of law. According to Brehon law, the land belonged to the clan of which the righ was a member. According to feudal rules, the land belonged to the king who could award or remove it from any individual at his whim. When the lord ruling over them, calling himself a baron or an earl, broke the ancient Brehon laws, the Irish were left with no recourse, since the lord himself didn't acknowledge these laws. In these situations the Irish peasants began demanding English law to protect themselves from their greedy Norman lords without understanding what English law was. The Irish experiment with English law was a dismal failure and, when after a century they were able to shake it off, the majority gladly reverted to their ancient Brehon laws.

From the earliest days of the lordship, the English king was represented in Ireland by a deputy, usually known as the Chief Governor of Ireland. As his name implies, he was the crown's supreme judge, head of the civil administration, and chief

---

[1] For example, the second earl of Clanrickard kept one of his peasants in prison until he surrendered his lands, which would have been impossible under Brehon law.

military commander. He could declare war, call on the king's nobles to help him, and had an army at his disposal. His office was itinerant; he asserted his authority by traveling around The Pale, administering justice as he went. A council made up of the great Normans of Ireland advised him.

In 1216 the Chief Governor of Ireland was William Marshal, the lord of Leinster and a descendant of Strongbow and Aoife. Marshal attempted to expand the area within The Pale by taking land from the diocese of Ferns. The bishop of Ferns, Ailbhe O Mael Muaid (O'Mulloy), was an Irishman at a time when most Irish clerics had been replaced by Norman. Initially he sought to discredit Marshal's claim through the English judicial system, but realizing quickly that he would not succeed, used the only other pressure he had available against Marshal; the bishop excommunicated him. He also is said to have placed a curse on Marshal that resulted in the death without children of Marshal's five sons and caused the division of Leinster into small sections among heiresses. After this confrontation with the bishop of Ferns, Marshal forced through a law that excluded Irishmen from the bishoprics of Ireland. The Irish church was Normanized. Under Marshal, the process of territorial conquest and colonization continued and land was taken from the Irish and populated with peasant settlers from England, Wales and southern Scotland.

The descendants of Dermot and his brother, Murrough MacMurrough, were forced to settle on their lands as favored tenants under the rule of the Normans. Murrough's descendants, the MacDavy Mors,[2] lived in the midlands of Hy Kinsella, while Dermot's lived in northern Hy Kinsella. They intermarried with the families of their Norman lords and

---

[2] Murrough's descendants were to change their surname several times over the next few centuries. They will be referred to as the MacDavy Mors, though many have taken the name Davis.

enjoyed favored positions as stewards (rent collectors) of the Normans' tenants. Though the MacMurroughs had lost some of the power of their previous position, they were satisfied with their favored role as stewards over the Irish in Hy Kinsella. This pragmatic political example by the MacMurroughs molded the attitudes of their vassals. Those who wouldn't accept the life of a farmer, especially the aristocracy of each clan, moved into the mountains of Wicklow and Wexford, out of the reach of the Normans. Peace reigned in Hy Kinsella during the beginning of the 13th century. A hybrid society of sorts emerged. This mutual toleration promoted mutual indulgence, resulting in a long-lived peace. Calm was doubly insured by the relative insulation of the Irish dynasties of East Leinster from the rest of Ireland by a strong belt of Norman settlement.

The reduction in power forced on the Gaelic aristocracy occurred because the Norman method of conducting war was superior to the Irish, not because of better weapons (virtually the same were available to both).[3] The ruthless tactics of the Normans were deplored by Gaelic culture and therefore only slowly adopted by the Irish. The Normans often funded warfare by imposing crushing taxes on the peasants. The Irish righs, unable to respond in kind because the Brehon laws protected commoners from such abuses of power, could not compete in hiring mercenaries. Scottish fighters, the mercenaries of choice, became so common that the name "galloglass," meaning foreign warrior, was coined for them. Norman tactics also included assassination and deception under a flag of truce

---

[3] Some argue that the Normans, with their chain mail and terrifying couched lance charges, had better weaponry. The Danes' use of chain mail since before the Battle of Clontarf hadn't secured them any advantages, though, and a cavalry charge was impossible in the majority of Ireland's hilly, boggy, or heavily forested lands.

(the method used against Tiernan O'Rourke). In the early years of the Norman incursion these tactics were not adopted by the Gaels because they would cause a righ to lose honor and therefore his throne. A Norman, living under a different set of cultural rules, had no such fears. His sole purpose in warfare was to eradicate his enemy; he didn't have to worry about honor.

The Norman warrior

This fundamentally different conception about honor in war, along with the support of the English crown in the form of men and money, helps explain how the Irish gradually lost more and more land to the Normans as the 13th century progressed. The Normans had grown accustomed to victory. Descended from Vikings who had settled in French Normandy centuries before, the Normans were cousins to the Vikings who had been defeated by the Irish army at the Battle of Clontarf in 1014 and had ceased to be a political force in Ireland. The

Norman Vikings had fared much better than their Viking cousins in Ireland for they had conquered England in 1066. English historians downplay the notion that it was a French conquest, as something distasteful to their national pride, but the political machinery the Normans brought with them was purely French, and they were in manner and speech French.

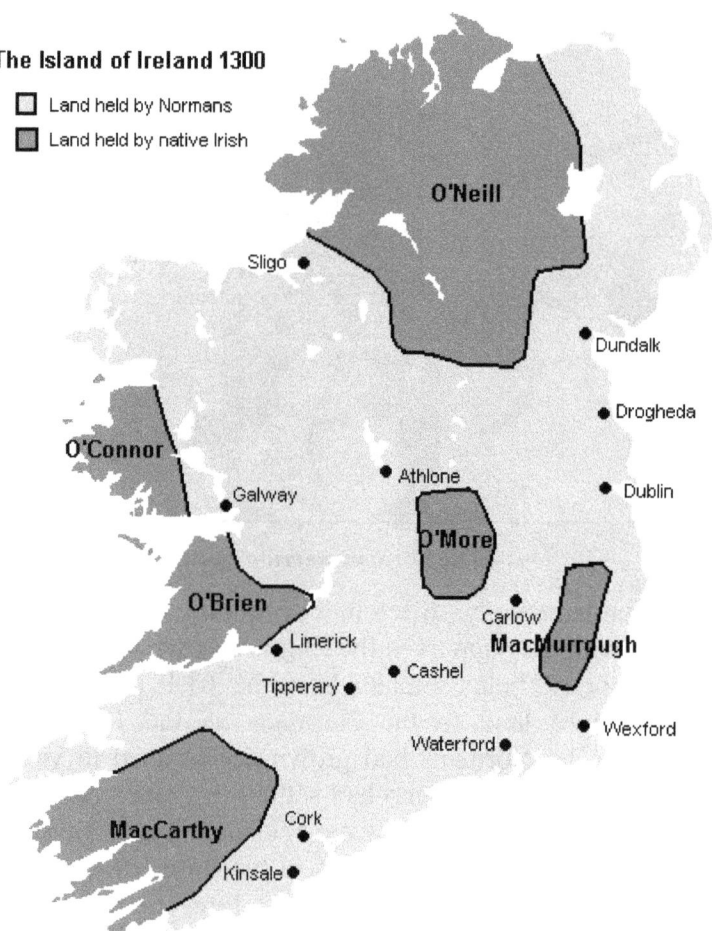

The Island of Ireland 1300

☐ Land held by Normans
■ Land held by native Irish

O'Neill

Sligo ●

● Dundalk

● Drogheda

O'Connor

● Athlone

● Dublin

Galway

O'More

O'Brien

Carlow ●

MacMurrough

● Limerick

Tipperary ●   ● Cashel

● Wexford

Waterford ●

MacCarthy   Cork ●

Kinsale ●

At the beginning of the 13th century, while the colony of The Pale expanded, the rebels in the Wicklow and Wexford mountains seemed destined to fade away, as the Anglo-Saxons had under similar circumstances in England centuries earlier. This did not happen, however; not only outlaws, but entire clans survived for generations. Celtic culture and the landscape that nurtured it accounts for the resiliency of the Gaels.

What became of the people of Hy Kinsella during the 13th century? Early on, history tells us that Enna Kinsella, who appeared to be Dermot's certain successor before he was blinded, was no longer eligible for the throne, according to Irish law.[4] The descendants of Donal Kavanagh were rulers of a tuath or two in northern Hy Kinsella, today's County Carlow, according to Strongbow's wishes. The descendants of Murrough MacMurrough, the MacDavy Mors, were elected to rule Hy Kinsella after Dermot's death.

Then, like a field reaped of its golden wheat by the sickle, the recorded history of the Irish in the territory of Hy Kinsella is cut short. More research into this period would help greatly, but some conjectures can be made based on later events and an understanding of Irish culture. The three families, the Kinsellas, the Kavanaghs, and the MacDavy Mors, were all eligible for the throne, according to Brehon law. After one of these clans achieved the position of Hy Kinsella righ, as the MacDavy Mors had initially done, they would fight for the successor also to be from their clan. If they succeeded for a few generations, the wealth gained from being righ, distributed throughout their clan, would allow them to dominate all the other clans and suppress future resistance to their rule.[5]

---

[4] No Irish righ with a blemish was able to rule.

[5] The nobles of any tuath, coming almost exclusively from the ruling clan, gained 1/3 of the inheritance of any of their clients who died without a male heir (through an ancient law known as "dibad"). This didn't suddenly

Exactly what events occurred during this period of dynastic feuding is unknown, but how the events played out is certain.

The last of William Marshal's sons died in 1245; the kingdom of Leinster was divided[6] among his five daughters in 1247. From then on, the descendants of Strongbow were mainly absentee landlords and this change in lordship sparked an uprising among the Irish of Leinster in 1249. The Chief Governor of Ireland was forced to devastate large areas of Leinster in an attempt to put down an insurrection headed by "the sons of kings."[7]

The north Leinster clans went into rebellion in 1269. The hard-edged attitudes of officials towards the Irish destroyed any possibility of a return to the previous lasting peace. Their insensitivity brought the crisis to fever pitch in 1270 when a devastating disaster struck the Irish – a combination of heavy snow, plague, and rainstorms destroyed their remaining food-stuffs and livestock. Their economic base now destroyed, the Irish burnt Norman settlements from the mountains to the sea in order to gain food.

The MacMurroughs' initial response was both hesitant and pragmatic. Between 1269 and 1273, Muircheartach MacMurrough, traditional overlord of the north Leinster clans, remained aloof from war. At the crux of MacMurrough indecision was their duality. The MacMurrough leaders were fully incorporated within the feudal settlement, but yet they retained their leadership of the Irish of east Leinster. Muircheartach's entry into the war during 1274 was not because of a deterio-

---

transfer the wealth of the tuath to the ruling clan, but over generations made the ruling clan richer at the expense of the other kindreds.

[6] The five new lordships created were Carlow, Kilkenny, Kildare, Leix and Wexford. The new owners were now Bigod, Mortimer, de Clare, Mortimer and Valance, respectively.

[7] Who these sons were is intriguing but unknown.

rating relationship with his cousins, the Norman lords. His main concern had to do with the growth of north Leinster's power. His assumption of the leadership of the war against the English probably represented a combined decision to protect his traditional position and to short-circuit north Leinster's ambition from regaining the title Leinster righ. Significantly, only when he moved to war did east Leinster become widely disturbed. His victory over the Normans at Glenmalure that year affirmed his leadership of the Irish of east Leinster. The MacMurrough-Kavanaghs, as they began to call themselves, had become the victors in the dynastic struggle over the throne of Hy Kinsella. The Kinsellas and MacDavy Mors remained prominent clans but never again played the leading role taken over by the Kavanaghs.

The Normans quelled the rebellion within a few years and coaxed the MacMurroughs back to their favored position as stewards of the Irish for them. In 1282 the Welsh were rebelling, less than 60 miles across the Irish Sea, and the Normans were worried the Irish would rise up in support of their Celtic cousins. In an effort to avoid this, Muircheartach MacMurrough and his brother were summoned to the Norman town of Arklow under a safe conduct and then assassinated. This crime delayed war with the MacMurroughs for years.

The north Leinster clans were not so easily cowed. They broke out in rebellion again with the O'Nolans, vassals of the MacMurroughs, and wreaked havoc in County Carlow and County Wicklow. The MacMurrough response was instructive; they, with Norman forces, crushed the north Leinster alliance. Swift action such as this, aimed at helping their Norman overlords, preserved the MacMurrough rulership.

Warfare in Ireland became endemic by the 14th century. The fusion of Irish and Norman tactics resulted in longer fighting seasons with larger and bloodier battles. Mercenaries, once unusual, were now the norm. The Normans, referred to as Anglo-Irish by those still in England, began to side occasionally with the Irish against their own government.

The Norman incursion slowed; less and less Irish territory was taken, and in many cases, was lost.

> For the Normans could not rule the country themselves, but they were strong enough to prevent anyone else from ruling it, so that it was more disunited than it had ever been under tribal rule. The stalemate could have been ended by the extension of English rule to the Irish . . . but this would also have stopped the further extension of the invasion, which from the invaders' point of view was unthinkable. That they themselves could be exploited in the same way by later waves of invaders of course did not occur to them. It is the tragedy of colonialism that it is self-perpetuating, and that each generation of exploiters considers the previous one fair game.[8]

---

[8] F. O'Connor, *The Backward Look* (London, 1967).

The Gaelic Resurgence

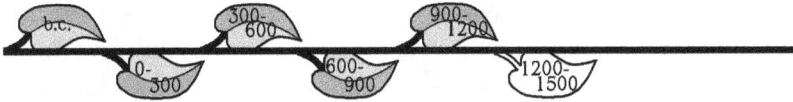

he Gaels of Scotland, under Robert de Bruce, won a major victory against England at the beginning of the 14th century and secured freedom for Scotland. In 1315, Robert's brother, Edward de Bruce, landed with an army of Scottish veterans on the coast of northeastern Ulster. The reasons for this Irish invasion remain uncertain: perhaps Robert was creating a Celtic Alliance;[1] perhaps he was diverting England's attention from Scotland; or perhaps Robert's brother Edward needed a throne also. Edward de Bruce arrived, quickly adopted the title King of Ireland, and was supported by several of the more important Irish righs such as the Ulster righ, Domnall O'Neill. Edward set up his own administration in Ulster in opposition to England's center of Dublin.

During his first year, Edward tested the strength of the Normans in Ireland's Pale by marching south into Meath. Running out of food, he was forced to return to Ulster while pursued by an Anglo-Irish army which, when it encountered him, was soundly defeated. Emboldened, the next year Edward went further south, criss-crossing Meath and entering north Leinster. Again his forces were opposed by the Anglo-Irish

---

[1] Letters were sent from Robert de Bruce to leading men in both Ireland and Wales asking them to join Scotland in its resistance to England. They spoke of their people "who proceed from a common root, who share the same race, ancestors, and country of origin."

and again a victory was won by the combined Scots and Irish force. More Irish flocked to Edward's banner but again hunger drove his forces back to Ulster.

Finally, in 1317, Edward marched his forces further south than they had ever gone. They harassed Dublin, whose defenses were too strong, then continued into Hy Kinsella where the MacMurrough-Kavanaghs finally cast off their favored role as stewards of the Normans and rose in favor of the Scots. They joined the Ulstermen and the army of Edward as it traveled south through Leinster into Hy Kinsella towards Wexford. Ferns, lying directly in the army's path from Carlow, became the scene of some of the bloodiest battles. With the addition of the O'Byrnes and O'Tooles of the Wicklow Mountains, Edward attacked the castle of Ferns and routed the Norman bishop of Ferns who defended it. Ferns, after being in Norman control for a century, was back in Irish control. In a few more years, however, it would be recovered by the Norman bishop.

For three and a half years, Edward de Bruce tried to make his new kingdom in Ireland a reality and bring England's control to an end. Then he was killed in the battle at Fochart, just north of Dundalk, in October 1318. Edward's conquest suffered from poor timing due to one of the worst famines to afflict Europe in the later middle ages. Edward's

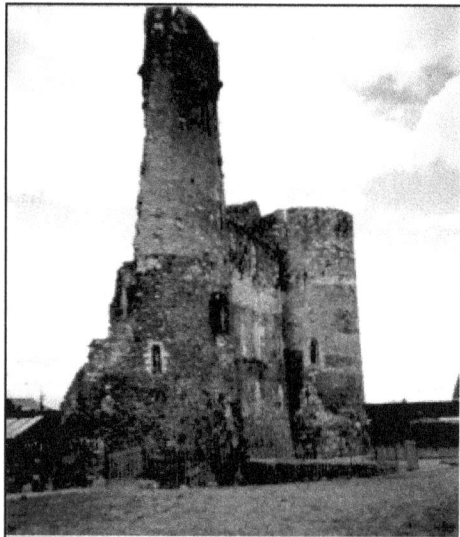

The ruins of Ferns Castle

force was hamstrung by lack of food, and the Irish, barely able to survive themselves, were unable to aid this huge army of Scotsmen. As the army marched across Ireland, most of the Anglo-Irish chose to remain true to England. For Edward's plan to succeed, he needed not only to defeat the Normans, which he did in several battles and skirmishes, but also to convince the Anglo-Irish to renounce their fealty to England's king. This they weren't yet prepared to do.

Even before the defeat of Edward de Bruce, the Irish had approached England's king for a cessation of hostilities. He disregarded their advances, so they turned to the church. Domnall O'Neill of Ulster and numerous other Irish righs in 1317 sent to the pope, John XXII, their Remonstrance against England's oppression. They charged the kings of England with violating the spirit of the original grant of Ireland to England by Pope Adrian in the 12th century, especially in terms of the native church. They charged the colonists in The Pale with constant cruelties against the native Irish, robbing them of their land and reducing them to slavery, "so bringing into servitude the blood that has flowed in freedom from of old." They quoted a Norman cleric, a leader forced on them in their own Irish church who had said that to kill an Irishman was no more than to kill a dog. The pope, siding with England's more powerful king, did nothing.

Although Edward de Bruce's invasion was successfully repelled, the power of the Normans in Ireland was on the wane. The fighting had left The Pale very weak. The colonists had lost a great number of men in battle, and the ravages of Edward had turned the country into a desert. The Gaels, now including the MacMurrough-Kavanaghs and therefore the Kinsellas, took to raiding in earnest. By 1320, Irish co-operation and collusion between north and south Leinster was an established fact.[2] In 1328, Domhnall mac Airt MacMurrough was inaugurated as Leinster righ and this may represent the re-establishment of the title with all its traditional responsibilities and vassals of Leinster. After the election he went on the traditional circuit of Leinster, including through the north Leinster clans' territory, before planting his banner less than two leagues from Dublin.

The Gaelic resurgence just beginning was helped along by its strong culture. Although the most powerful families of this period were all Anglo-Irish – the de Burghs of Connacht, the Butlers of Kilkenny and the Fitzgeralds of Kildare and South Munster – they were all eventually seduced by Irish culture, beginning with the de Burghs. In 1328 the Anglo-Irish lord of Connacht, Richard de Burgh, died, and his grandson, William, succeeded him. Raised in England, William was murdered five years after taking over his Irish lands, not by the Gaels, but by his own kinsmen, who resented his external authority. They had become fully immersed in Gaelic culture by now and would not accept any foreign authority, even from their kinsmen who owned their lands.[3] After this incident, the de Burghs sundered their ties with England, changed their name to Burke and joined the Irish.

As Norman generation succeeded Norman generation, Irish clans had formed ties of blood with them. The Normans began wearing traditional Irish clothes, speaking Gaelic and wearing their hair long.[4] They began encouraging Irish literature and music. They even began adopting Brehon laws, which relaxed their harsh treatment of the Irish peasants, though not completely, since the increased wealth created by the oppression of

---

[2] West Leinster – Offaly, Leix, and Ossory – no longer considered themselves ruled by the Leinster righ.
[3] Sean Duffy, *Ireland in the Middle Ages* (New York, 1977).
[4] Normans wore their hair short so that it could not be grasped in battle.

their old system was too desirable to give up. They essentially became Irish and won the devotion and fidelity of the people. Many even discarded their Norman names in favor of Irish names:

> After a few generations the Anglo-Normans had completely forgotten Norman-French, and as they never, with few exceptions, learned English, they identified themselves completely with the Irish past, so that among the Irish poets we find numbers of Nugents, Englishes, Condons, Cusacks, Keatings, Comyns and other names.[5]

The great Norman family of the de Burghs was transformed first into Burkes and then over generations into MacWilliams. The de Birminghams became MacYoris; the Dexecesters, MacJordans; the de Angulos, MacCostellos. As long as the Irish retained their native culture and language, their power of infusing what was best into the lives of other resident races was marvelous. The Normans became "more Irish than the Irish themselves." The French culture of the Normans, which supposedly stood at the apex of European civilization, succumbed to the Gaelic.

The exchange of Norman culture by good Anglo-Irish families for the Irish culture they had set out to conquer, reoccurring over and over, so angered England's crown that totally eradicating all things Irish, including the language, became of paramount importance.

Another factor in the Gaelic resurgence was subtler. Many Anglo-Irish families came to inherit a relatively small landholding in Ireland, which was frequently too small to retain their interest and too insignificant to bother defending or investing in. This was especially true in Hy Kinsella and it

---

[5] Douglas Hyde, *A Literary History of Ireland* (New York, 1899).

happened within a close span of years. When the Marshal lordship of Leinster was divided into five shares in the mid-13th century, the de Clares inherited one-fifth in Kilkenny. With the death of the last de Clare in 1314, this fifth was now further divided among his three sisters. Another fifth in Wexford County had gone to the de Valence family, but the last de Valence died in 1324, so this fifth was also split in three. The Bigod family received another fifth share in Carlow County, but in 1338 the last male heir died and it was split between two heiresses.[6]

Those who inherited the splinters of the great Irish estates also owned vast domains in England. Defending a small parcel of land in Ireland was not a worthwhile proposition compared to managing peaceful English properties. One by one, these small estates became vulnerable to the attacks of the Irish. In many cases the original Irish occupants of these lands were still there, lurking in the nearby hills and bogs, waiting for an opportunity to recover their inheritance. The historian Hore writes:

> Donal McArt Kavanagh, who was The McMurrough[7] at the epoch of the Bruce invasion, seized the opportunity of this shattering blow to English power in Ireland to extend the territory of his ancient race, by recovering for them the greater part of the

---

[6] The English realized too late the damage that had been done. They created new titles for the Anglo-Irish still loyal to them in Ireland with the stipulation that these grants could not be inherited by heiresses. If an earl died without sons, his estate was not divided but instead passed to his closest surviving male heir. John fitz Thomas, the baron of Offaly, was made earl of Kildare in 1316; James Butler was made earl of Ormond in 1328; and Maurice fitz Thomas, the head of the Munster Geraldines, was made earl of Desmond in 1329. These families would dominate Ireland because their vast estates remained intact.

[7] The Kavanaghs continued using the title The MacMurrough as a sobriquet for righ in honor of Dermot MacMurrough.

county of Carlow, and three parts of County Wexford. He assumed his ancestor's title of King of Leinster [in 1327] and caused the bordering Englishry to render him blackmail for the consideration of protecting them from being plundered, and it was deemed politic to pay him eighty marks yearly, which was continued to his successors for two hundred years under the name of McMurrough's Black Penny [black rent]. This is the sole recorded instance of "cios dubh" [black rent] being paid by the Crown to a line of Irish kings. As the clan increased they ejected the colonists descended from and planted by Strongbow's barons, banishing Lord Carew from Idrone, and uprooting Lord Neville from Baron's Court near Gorey, in order to extend a main line of their family, the Sliocht Cinnseallaigh (Kinsella clan), in that direction.

When the Kavanaghs began to recover their ancestral lands in the 14th century, they rewarded those clans closest to them, those instrumental in their rise to power, the Kinsellas and MacDavy Mors. The Kinsellas were given land in and around Gorey. The MacDavy Mors settled around today's Askamore in the hills a few miles west of Gorey.[8]

By the middle of the 14th century, England's king, Edward III, began to fear that The Pale, the colony in Ireland, was close to extinction. The majority of the descendants of the Norman lords had become indistinguishable from the enemy Irish, and many of the English settlers on their estates were following their example. In addition, many of the native Irish righs were attacking the Norman settlements and taking back the lands they had previously owned. Edward sent a huge army to Ireland in 1361 and moved the center of The Pale's government

---

[8] Art Kavanagh, *In the Shadow of Mount Leinster: a History of Ui Cinnsealaigh from the Earliest Times up to 1650, with Special Emphasis on the Kavanaghs* (1993).

from Dublin to the castle at Carlow,[9] because Carlow was equidistant from the two main centers of effective lordship, the area around Dublin and the south Leinster-east Munster region. Carlow town was also located on the River Barrow, which was an important navigable artery of the colony. The great castle of Carlow and the town walls were repaired, but the move soon proved disastrous as Irish raids increased and Anglo-Irish lords feared to travel to Carlow. Frustrated, England's king ordered the issuance of the statutes of Kilkenny[10] in 1367, which became the main cause of MacMurrough-Kavanagh resurgence.

The purpose of the statutes of Kilkenny was to prevent, by legal and religious penalties, further assimilation. The statutes declared marriage, intimacy or even commerce with the Irish to be high treason and punishable by death. Forfeiture of land and imprisonment were the penalties for using Irish dress, language or customs, or even for adopting an Irish name. The Brehon laws were obviously banned, but so was the payment of Irish minstrels, poets or storytellers. Even playing the Irish game of hurling exacted a punishment. No Englishmen was to sell horses or armor to the Irish or, in time of war, food. The Irish were excluded from cathedrals, abbeys, and benefices among the Normans. Every "chieftain of English lineage," politely called Anglo-Irish to his face and Irish dog behind his back, was required to arrest any of his people who broke these statutes. Only on the boundaries of The Pale (Norman-controlled Ireland) could hired soldiers be maintained. In case the material punishments were not enough, the archbishops and bishops were to excommunicate any who disobeyed the statute.

---

[9] Sean Duffy, *Ireland in the Middle Ages* (New York, 1977).

[10] These statutes, contrary to popular belief, did not enact anything new but merely codified prior law. Nevertheless, this codification challenged the honor of all Irishman.

The statutes of Kilkenny mark the acceptance by the Normans of their failure to conquer Ireland. They expected to enforce these statutes only in The Pale (about 1/3 of Ireland), but even here the measures were a failure. The statutes of Kilkenny were disregarded almost from the very date of their issuance. Within 20 years the Chief Governor of Ireland, the highest official in all Ireland, Gerald Fitzgerald, asked for and received the royal license to send his son in fosterage to the native Irishman, Conor O'Brien.

Art MacMurrough-Kavanagh

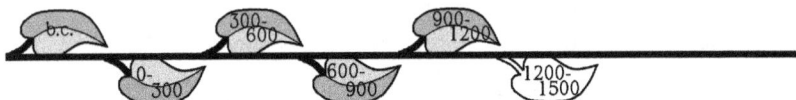

he Kavanaghs had developed into a clan to be reckoned with by the Normans in the 14th century. From 1354 to 1375, six leaders of the MacMurrough-Kavanagh family were killed directly or indirectly by the government of The Pale,[1] demonstrating their anxiety over the revival of the ancient title Leinster righ. When they weren't able to kill them, they paid "black rent."

Art MacMurrough-Kavanagh led the Leinster Irish to war in 1358. He reached out and began aiding the Irish of Leix (O'Mores) and they in turn aided him, resulting in a major O'More victory that year. The Normans became nervous, and after a few setbacks, invited Art to a parley in 1361. Here he and his likely successor were captured and confined in the castle of Trim. There they were either murdered or died naturally less than a year later. Only later, with a new MacMurrough-Kavanagh leader, would the Normans realize what a disastrous mistake they had made.

In 1376, at the age of twenty, Art's son, also Art MacMurrough-Kavanagh, succeeded to the throne of Leinster. Since the MacMurroughs' capitol of Ferns was still under Norman control, the ancient inauguration hill of Knockavoca could not be used. The hill Art may have used was at Loggan, near

---

[1] Sean Duffy, *Ireland in the Middle Ages* (New York, 1977).

Gorey.[2] The inauguration ceremony had been much the same for more than a thousand years:

> As the cool predawn mist of mid-October saps the warmth from Conor Kinsella's body, he stares out across the lands ruled by the MacMurrough-Kavanaghs from his vantage point on the inauguration hill. Turning slowly to survey the scene, he passes his gaze over the heads of those standing outside the ring of alder trees near him until it rests on Art, a tall handsome man with a stern countenance but wonderfully fit. The young MacMurrough-Kavanagh stands alone within the circle of alder trees atop a small mound, known as the righ's mound, at the highest point of the inauguration hill. Dressed in a white cloak (signifying his purity) fastened at his shoulder with a magnificent gold brooch, Art awaits the inauguration rite, calmly looking into the distance. Waiting with Conor are the other nobles of Hy Kinsella, abbots of local monasteries, assorted servants, and the righ of the O'Nolan clan, Gavin, the protector of the inauguration site.
>
> A few more nobles arrive, and Gavin, a large man who looks as though he has spent too much time feasting, mentions they now wait only for Ronan MacKeogh, the MacMurroughs' royal file. Moments later, when Ronan rides up, all eyes turn to Art. Slowly dismounting, Ronan walks over to Gavin, who opens a gate leading through the stand of alders. Pushing a small branch away, Ronan walks slowly between the trees and up to Art.
>
> Not looking at anyone but Art, the sage begins the ancient ceremonial rite of the Celts, "Art, son of Art, son of Murtogh, son of . . . ." He continues for generations, connecting Art with the first Irish to settle Ireland. When he reaches Heremon, the first Irish righ of Art's line, he stops. "Know this, Art MacMurrough-Kavanagh, you will reign alone as Leinster righ, yet must think of the many. You must seek peace, yet command war when necessary. You will arbitrate as judge, yet obey the law of the brehons."

---

[2] Art Kavanagh, *In the Shadow of Mount Leinster* (1993).

Ronan explains to Art that he is responsible for his people and that, since his strength resides in them, it's in his interest to look after them.[3] "You are the father of your people: gracious, condescending, and beloved. You cannot allow yourself to be ruled by caprice. Even the lowliest member of your clan is a kinsman and friend, whom you are born to protect and bound to regard. You must venerate old age, respect genius and listen to the counsels of the elders of your clan.[4] The land itself will bear testimony to your abilities, rewarding good rule with prosperity, poor rule with famine and pestilence." Ronan finishes by explaining the laws that will regulate Art MacMurrough's conduct.

Art looks upon all those assembled outside the ring of alder trees and calls forth in a loud, clear voice, "I swear to uphold these laws and always abide by them."

Ronan extends his hands, which hold a thin golden crown, and Art bends down to allow the ollamh to place it on his head. As Art raises his head, Ronan hands the new king the white rod of rulership.[5] Effortlessly the sun breaks above the horizon of hills like a huge gleaming eye. Standing on the rock, Art turns around slowly three times in a sun-wise direction, surveying all his lands from his hilltop position.

Two servants standing on either side of the gate to the alder grove raise large copper trumpets to their lips and announce the birth of a new righ. Gavin O'Nolan pushes forward and shouts in a loud, clear voice, "The MacMurrough." The abbots follow with the call and then the other nobles.

Stepping down from the righ's mound, Art removes his cloak and carries it with him. When he reaches one of the clerics, he says, "Maeleoin, abbot of Baltinglass, I present to you my inauguration clothes."

---

[3] A righ would postpone or even cancel rent in times of scarcity and attend to the needs of the poor.
[4] Michael Steven Newton, *A Handbook of the Scottish Gaelic World* (Dublin, 2000).
[5] Signifying how his rule should be straight and without sin.

Turning to Gavin, Art unbuckles his sword.[6] "Gavin, keeper of the inauguration hill, I give you my weapons and horse." Gavin in turn hands his own weapons to Ronan. Finally, Art addresses all of those watching. "I shall strive to return Leinster to her former greatness. Though our enemies encircle us, they will not encroach on our ancient lands. Through negotiation, and war if necessary, we shall free the land and our people. I promise it." A cheer springs up amidst slaps on the new righ's back. As the group quiets down, Art continues, "There is a feast waiting for us. Let's not tarry overlong." He begins dispensing gifts to each of the nobles and clerics present from a nearby wagon which contains:

> 6 gold-hilted swords, 6 exquisite shields, 6 scarlet cloaks
> 8 coats of mail, 8 shields, 8 swords, 8 horses, and 8 cups
> 6 shields, 6 richly ornamented swords, 6 horses with gold bits, etc.

The group immediately returns to the feast that is being prepared at The MacMurrough's house, and after a few days the new righ leads a cattle raid. The captured cattle, probably coming from the Butlers of Ossory, are given to his subjects.

Art MacMurrough-Kavanagh soon rode out of the Wicklow hills where his main strength lay and began attacking the Normans in County Carlow, the key to communication within The Pale. Unlike any MacMurrough-Kavanagh before him, he was able to recruit mercenaries from other Leinster clans.[7] Within a few years only Carlow town remained outside his control. Having severed the major access route between Dublin in the north and the southern Anglo-Norman outposts at Kilkenny, Waterford and Wexford, Art forced The Pale to negotiate with

---

[6] A proverbial sword inscription read, "Do not draw me without a reason, and do not return me without honor."

[7] His mother was an O'Byrne, one of the north Leinster clans, and his father had already created strong ties with the O'Mores of Leix.

him at Moone in southern Kildare in 1379. During this meeting they handed over to him the supervision of the roads between Carlow and Kilkenny in exchange for "black rent."

Art MacMurrough-Kavanagh had only begun. He and his followers attacked the English settlements in ancient Hy Kinsella, the area his ancestors ruled for more than 1,000 years. The settlers fled in panic to the safety of the nearest coastal towns. The land vacated by the settlers was then occupied by Art's followers. In 1386, the town of Ferns, which had been under Norman control for more than two hundred years, was retaken.

Although the Normans of The Pale respected Art's power, they did not consider him an equal. In 1390 when he married a FitzGerald, a daughter of the Earl of Kildare whose family had turned Irish generations before, Art was exasperated to find that the Norman authorities would not let him claim her dowry, which was an estate in County Kildare. The Normans refused Art's request because English law did not admit that a "mere Irishman" could hold English land. To demonstrate what a mere Irishman could do, Art led a great host and burned the town of Naas, then went on a rampage and left ruin in his wake among the Normans of counties Kildare, Wexford and Carlow. He even burnt Carlow town, still the seat of The Pale's government. The town submitted a petition to the king's council in Ireland in 1392 describing the ruinous state of houses, the widespread pillage and arson, and more ominously the dwindling number of English who were willing to live there for fear of Art MacMurrough-Kavanagh.[8] At the end of the year the ancient flag of the Leinster righ floated over more than 30 castles in the counties of Carlow, Kildare and Wexford. In addition, The Pale had shrunk to a mere sliver of land along the

---

[8] The situation deteriorated so much that Richard II had the administrative center of the Pale moved back to Dublin when he came to Ireland in 1394.

eastern coast. The Normans rued their decision to keep a dowry from this mere Irishman.

By 1394, many Norman nobles had packed up and returned to England, while those who remained had to pay "black rent" to avoid Irish attacks. In the Irish reports to Richard II, England's king who ascended the throne in 1377 (a year after Art had ascended to his throne of Leinster), the name of Art MacMurrough-Kavanagh kept cropping up. Richard saw that Ireland was becoming a drain on England's treasury, The Pale was near collapse, and the Irish, especially this Art MacMurrough-Kavanagh, were getting bolder by the year. Richard decided that there was only one answer, to go to Ireland himself and straighten out this wild band of untamed savages.

On October 2, 1394, England's young king landed at Waterford and, like others in later times, decided that he would adopt a strategy of "shock and awe" to frighten the Irish into capitulating. According to contemporary accounts he brought with him the greatest army Ireland had ever seen: five hundred ships carrying 8,000 to 10,000 troops, including archers, men at arms, horses and artillery. In the 12th century an expedition of one-tenth the size would have overawed the Irish; by the 14th century the natives were too used to mailed soldiers to be easily dismayed.

Hy Kinsella was the King's first target. In preparation for his attack he sent small, well-armed detachments to fortified towns such as Carlow, Ross and Wexford. Then Richard and his army marched north from Waterford towards New Ross along the Barrow. Art MacMurrough-Kavanagh attacked the town, which was defended by 104 crossbowmen, 1,200 long bow men, 1,200 pike men, and 104 horsemen, all fighting from behind battlemented walls and entrenched positions. The Leinster righ burned the town to the ground before retreating back to the woodland fastness at the foot of Mount Leinster.

England's king continued on to Kilkenny. From here Richard II sent out the Earl Marshal of England to ask Art MacMurrough for his submission. The Marshal brought a large force to Carlow and proclaimed to the Irish "that they before the first Sunday of Lent would surrender to the king the full possession of all their lands, tenements, castles, woods, and forts, which by them and all other of the Kinsellas, their companions, men, or adherents, later were occupied within the province of Leinster." Art refused to treat with any but the king of England and so the parley broke up.

Upon hearing this, King Richard II flew into a rage. He brought his whole army into County Carlow and gave orders that they were to sweep the entire MacMurrough territory. Nothing was to be missed and no one spared.

His soldiers carried out his orders to the letter: they slaughtered all before them, burned villages and carried off herds of cattle. One of his commanders tells how he had "several fine encounters with them [the Irish], in one of which he

Seal of MacMurrough-Kavanagh

slew many of the people of the said MacMurrough and how he burned nine villages, capturing 8,000 of his cattle in the process."[9] Art MacMurrough-Kavanagh was almost caught on one such raid, when he and his wife barely fled their bed before the soldiers were upon them. They escaped but lost the great seal of the MacMurroughs to the English.

As his army continued to pillage Hy Kinsella, Richard proceeded to Dublin, which he reached early in November, and spent Christmas at the castle. In a letter to his uncle he revealed his plan: the Irish were to be forced into an honorable submission and recognized as vassals of the crown, with the exception of Art MacMurrough-Kavanagh, the chief Irish enemy. Four objectives were to be met: (1) The Irish righs, except the MacMurrough people, were to surrender the lands they had "usurped" from the Normans and promise a double obedience in the future to the king as liege-lord and homage to the Anglo-Irish earls. In return they were to be confirmed in their "Irish lands," namely those territories which they had held from the time of the conquest. (2) The "rebel English" were to be pardoned and restored to their due allegiance. (Only eight, from Munster and Connacht, appeared to claim their pardon.) (3) The Norman Pale was to be strengthened by planting a new colony in it and by grants made to new Englishmen. (4) To carry out the third objective, the warlike Art MacMurrough-Kavanagh and his vassals must be compelled to quit the lands of Leinster.[10]

The Irish in the rest of Ireland were spoiling for a fight, and several righs urged Niall More O'Neill, the Ulster righ, to lead a general resistance against Richard. O'Neill hesitated, due to the diplomacy of Norman Archbishop Colton, while awaiting the fate of Art MacMurrough-Kavanagh.

Richard finally induced Art to submit by surrounding his fastness in the Wicklow Mountains with a chain of fortified

---

[9] Art Kavanagh, *In the Shadow of Mount Leinster* (1993).
[10] Edmund Curtis, *A History of Ireland* (London, 1968).

garrisons and using small bodies of mounted archers to scour and devastate the area within the encirclement. In January of 1395, Art MacMurrough-Kavanagh, seeing he could not hope to win against Richard, surrendered at Tullow in Carlow. He promised to leave Leinster with all his clan by the first Sunday of Lent and conquer lands occupied by other "rebel" Irish. In return, Richard finally granted Art the estate of his wife's dowry and, for the remainder of his life, the annual fee (80 marks) he had been collecting as "black rent." Art MacMurrough-Kavanagh's capitulation, and the sheer size of Richard II's army, convinced nearly all the other Irish righs to submit in January in exchange for full pardon and confirmation of their ownership of lands held since the Norman incursion. To commemorate Richard's diplomatic victory a great ceremony was held in Dublin's Christ Church Cathedral, where The O'Neill of Ulster, The MacMurrough of Leinster, The O'Brien of Munster, and The O'Connor of Connacht, the four leading native righs of Ireland, were knighted by England's king.[11]

An anecdote describing one evening during which Richard II entertained these righs in Dublin captures the great differences between the Norman and the Irish culture of the time:

> When Art MacMurrough and three other Irish kings visited Richard II in Dublin the English were horrified to see the royal guests sitting down to table with their ministers and whole retinue. "They told me this was a praiseworthy custom of their country," records the official English scribe, but such democratic

---

[11] During the submission of the Irish lords, many of their sub-lords submitted also. Feidlim O'Toole, from a north Leinster clan, wrote to Richard asking to be his direct subject and not the subject of the men of Hy Kinsella, because his ancestors had always resented the over-lordship of the MacMurroughs. The ancient hostilities between north and south Leinster were still smoldering. Sean Duffy, *Ireland in the Middle Ages* (New York, 1977).

conduct would not be allowed by this feudal master of ceremonies. So they were separated – the kings were segregated at one table, the retinue at another. "The [Irish] kings looked at each other and refused to eat, saying I had deprived them of their old custom in which they had been brought up." But the boorish "allotted tutor in manners" informed them that it was not decent or suitable to their rank, "for now they must conform to the manners of the English." They yielded "with the dignity of courteous guests."[12]

Before leaving Ireland, Richard added to the Leinster righ's rancor by granting to John de Beaumont the lands of Hy Kinsella. Leaving in May of 1395, Richard was congratulated in England on his spectacular triumph.

The king had left 25-year-old Roger Mortimer, his heir, to enforce the terms and keep the peace. Mortimer was an odd choice because of his conflict of interest: his family claimed title to much of Ulster, land which The O'Neill had taken over. The annals state that in 1396 Mortimer, with the earl of Ormond and Kildare, launched an assault on Ulster and plundered and burned Armagh.[13] The peace was already broken.

Presumably, Richard had felt that Mortimer's appointment would at least be agreeable to the Leinster Irish, because Mortimer was not an outsider but a descendant of Dermot MacMurrough's daughter Aoife and Strongbow.[14] When Mortimer inquired as to why Art MacMurrough-Kavanagh wasn't preparing his clan to leave Leinster, a reply from Art was quick in coming. It stated, "I and all of the Leinster clans have sworn that they would never rest as long as a hostile power existed on these shores. In no way will we lie down at

---

[12] Martin McMahon, *I Cry for My People* (Sandgate, Qld., 1996).

[13] Sean Duffy, *Ireland in the Middle Ages* (New York, 1977).

[14] Roger's great-great-great-great-grandfather had married one of Aoife and Strongbow's granddaughters.

the feet of a boyish viceroy and lick the hand of a descendant of Strongbow! The brave memories of our ancestors forbid it!" Mortimer responded to this stinging insult by laying plans to put an end to this insolent Irishman. He asked one of the Anglo-Irish families to invite Art to a feast at their castle:

The king came, attended only by his inseparable minstrel. All without the castle spoke peace – all within, cordiality. The flower of the Saxon chivalry were there – and he who had beaten their hosts in the field, was resolved not to be vanquished in the courtesies of the banquet. The table was laid upon the dais – fresh rushes were spread upon the hall – the "dresser" blazoned with plate shone at the back of the host. The flesh of deer and swine, of wild geese and cranes, favorite dishes of the country, crowded the board. Foreign wine with the hue of the roseate eastern sun abounded, and usquebaugh (liquor) tempered with fennel-seeds and honey, stood in flagons on every hand. The ornamental ship laden with spices perfumed the hall. Now, the king's harper was famous throughout all Leinster for his powers, and the Saxon lords were anxious to hear his melodious performance. His master requested him to play them some strain of love or mirth, suited to the hour. He prepared to comply, but whether in reaching for his harp or in changing his attitude, he saw from a window of the castle that it was being gradually surrounded by armed men. He seized the instrument and struck the thrilling notes of the Rosg Catha, or Battle Song. The unsuspecting king chided him for his breach of propriety, and he feigned to change the air, but again sterner and wilder than before the battle song swept over the strings. Suspicion, like an electric blaze broke upon the mind of Art; he walked to the window and beheld his peril. His whole form and countenance changed. That terrible fierceness which struck so forcibly the attention of one whose authority we will by and by have to quote, came over him. He seized his trusty sword, his shield and his casque. His treacherous guests stood appalled at the premature discovery of their plot, and in their confusion he passed unopposed from the banquet room. They called aloud on the armed men without to seize him, but "by the strength of his hand and his bravery" he escaped from them, bringing safely away with him his faithful harper.[15]

Rather than deter Art, this treachery made him even more impetuous. Just as his surrender to King Richard had convinced the Irish to follow his example, now his aggression encouraged them. By the summer of 1398 Mortimer could no longer overlook Art's numerous raids. He marched with an army of about 10,000 soldiers to battle the O'Byrnes and the O'Tooles in an open field near Kellistown of County Carlow in July. The battle was long and bloody but in the end the Irish forces were victorious and Mortimer was killed.[16] One chronicle report stated, "The consternation which the result of this battle spread through The Pale was unbounded. The scattered remains of the army cowered under the walls of Dublin like sheep that a storm had suddenly blown from a bare hill."[15]

The news of this disaster filled King Richard with fury and despair (Mortimer had been the King's only heir). He revoked the grant of the dowry estate to Art's wife and landed at Waterford in June of 1399 with a large army, vowing to burn The MacMurrough out of his woods.

Art was ready with 3,000 hardy men who "did not appear to be much afraid of the English."[17] Preparing for battle, Art removed the women, corn, cattle and other food to the interior of the forests while he and his followers awaited the approach of Richard. Rather than sending his archers into the woods this

---

[15] Thomas D'Arcy M'Gee, *Art MacMurrough* (Dublin, 1847).

[16] Instead of armor he was said to have rashly worn only the linen dress of an Irish righ.

[17] As recorded by Jean Creton, King Richard's French chronicler.

time Richard ordered the woods to be cut down. The Norman army traveled along a great highway of dead wood.

As Richard advanced, Art retreated, taking all the food of the area with him, surprising and killing foragers and filling Richard's camp nightly with alarm and blood. Richard continued his march to the sea, finding nothing but a few green oats for the horses, which perished in great numbers. For weeks, food was so scarce that a single loaf of bread had to make do for five or six men. "Even gentlemen, knights, and squires, fasted for days in succession."[18] As the death toll mounted, morale fell among Richard's army.

At last, this great army came to the sea coast where several vessels full of food were waiting. Richard had brought a scribe with him "in order to faithfully record the king's glorious achievements." The scribe wrote, "The famished men rushed into the sea and poured money into the hands of the merchants; some of them even fought in the water over a morsel of food. In their thirst, they drank all the wine they could lay their hands on. I saw a full thousand men drunk on wine that day."[19]

King Richard, no longer bursting with confidence, tried diplomacy, which the French chronicler, Jean Creton describes:

> Between two woods, at some distance from the sea, I beheld MacMurrough and a body of his men. He was riding a horse without saddle or housing, which was so fine and good, that it cost him, they said, four hundred cows. In coming down, it galloped so hard I had never seen another animal, I declare for a certainty, run with such speed. In his right hand he bore a great long dart, which he cast with much skill.

---

[18] Thomas D'Arcy M'Gee, *Art MacMurrough* (Dublin, 1847).

[19] It is thought that the scene of this extraordinary incident occurred on the beach of Arklow.

The meeting was short. Jean Creton goes on to report that Art MacMurrough-Kavanagh "called himself lord and king of Ireland" and that he swore he would never submit to Richard "for all the treasure of the sea."

Richard, upset at his failures in both war and diplomacy, swore in a loud voice that he would never depart from Ireland until he had Art MacMurrough-Kavanagh in his power, dead or alive. His report to England on this expedition, however, was one of glowing success. Richard marched to Dublin with what remained of his army, where they ate sumptuously and were well housed. On the king's arrival, he laid a price of 100 gold marks on MacMurrough's head.

Shortly after arriving in Dublin, Richard received the disturbing news that his cousin, Henry Bolingbroke (the future King Henry IV), had returned from exile and had usurped England's throne. Less than two months after arriving in Ireland, Richard hurried back to England but was almost immediately taken prisoner and deposed.[20] No other hostile army ventured into the fastness of Hy Kinsella for 150 years.

On September 30, 1399, Henry IV became the new king of England. The doggedness of Art MacMurrough-Kavanagh, which caused the death of Mortimer and Richard II's distraction with Ireland, led to far more than just the expansion of the MacMurrough-Kavanagh lands. The new dynasty begun by Henry IV, one that could finally be called English,[21] led to the War of the Roses, a civil war that wracked England for many years and left Ireland to its own devices throughout most of the 15th century. County Carlow, the center of MacMurrough power, remained a totally Gaelic enclave until the close of the 17th century.

---

[20] He was literally starved to death in prison.
[21] Until Henry's take-over, the English kings had spoken only French and continued their Norman traditions.

With his greatest enemy gone, Art MacMurrough-Kavanagh continued to reclaim his ancient patrimony. In 1406 he overwhelmed the castle at Ferns, which had been retaken by Richard II, and repossessed it. He then marched down the River Slaney and captured the strong castle at Enniscorthy followed by the town of Wexford. In 1408, accompanied by the O'Brynes and O'Nolans, he marched to the outskirts of Dublin after routing the English forces that had assembled there. Deciding his men were not prepared for a siege of the strong-walled city of Dublin, Art instead demolished some castles in the area. He was in control of all east Leinster.

On January 1, 1417, Leinster's royal residence went into deep mourning. Art MacMurrough-Kavanagh had died in New Ross. The entry in the annals reads:

> Art Cavenagh, King of Leinster, the son of Art, son of Murtogh, son of Maurice, a man who defended his province against the English and the Irish, from the age of sixteen to his 60th year; a founder of churches and monasteries by his bounty and contributions, died, after having been forty two years in the government of Leinster, on the 7th day after Christmas.

Contemporaries felt Art was murdered by means of a poisonous potion a woman gave him to drink. No evidence was ever produced, but O'Doran, the brehon of Leinster, died the same hour, and in Gaelic culture, the Chief Brehon sat next to the righ and shared his plate and cup. Art's funeral procession was said to have extended for six miles as it followed the body to St. Mullins, where he was buried.

The FitzGeralds of Kildare

fter the failure of Richard II's attempt to restore England's rule in Ireland, The Pale dwindled further. The common English and the clerics left, unable to endure the Irish menace or the Anglo-Irish lords' heavy taxes. The "first conquest" begun by Henry II was an obvious failure. The 15th century was far too tumultuous for England to attempt to reign in Ireland, so the Anglo-Irish and the Irish were left to themselves. What emerged was the growing conception of a new culture and civilization with almost complete racial unity. The "foreigners" had disappeared.

While the Gaelic resurgence continued, after the death of Art MacMurrough the Kavanaghs' influence began to decrease for a number of reasons: Art's son Donnchadh did not have the charisma of his father; the north Leinster clans wanted the position of Leinster righ themselves; and the Normans played the Irish clans against each other.

One of the great Anglo-Irish families who settled in County Kildare of north Leinster was the Fitzgeralds. Maurice Fitzgerald was one of the original Normans recruited by Dermot MacMurrough in 1168, and as a reward for his assistance his sons were granted land in north Leinster. Maurice's great-great-grandson, John, was named the first Earl of Kildare in 1316 and established his family at Maynooth. The Fitzgeralds steadily increased their wealth and influence through political savvy, including the use of expedient marriages with the lead-

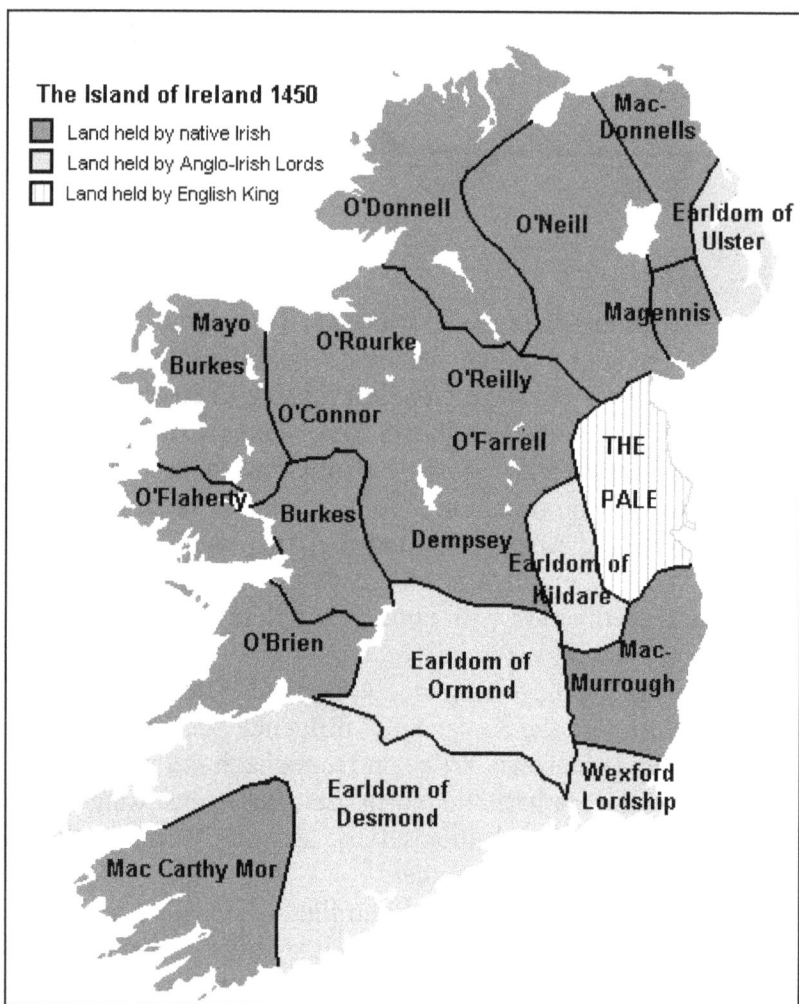

The Island of Ireland 1450

- ☐ Land held by native Irish
- ☐ Land held by Anglo-Irish Lords
- ☐ Land held by English King

Mac-Donnells

O'Donnell

O'Neill

Earldom of Ulster

Mayo

O'Rourke

Magennis

Burkes

O'Reilly

O'Connor

O'Farrell

THE

PALE

O'Flaherty

Burkes

Dempsey

Earldom of Kildare

O'Brien

Mac-Murrough

Earldom of Ormond

Wexford Lordship

Earldom of Desmond

Mac Carthy Mor

ing Irish families. By the end of the 15th century they would become the most powerful clan in all of Ireland.

In 1461, King Edward IV of England came to the throne and appointed the Anglo-Irish Earl of Desmond as Chief

Governor of Ireland. The Norman families of Ireland were referred to as Anglo-Irish, in contrast to the "pure" English who were frequently coming to Ireland and, just as frequently, leaving. In 1467, worried about the power of the Anglo-Irish lords of Ireland, King Edward sent over an English noble, the Earl of Worcester, to look into the situation. The English feared the Anglo-Irish lords wanted Home Rule[1] for Ireland: to be free from England's demands. In 1468, the Earl of Worcester arrested the Earl of Kildare, Thomas Fitzgerald, on charges he had helped the local Irish and even made alliances with them. More importantly, the Earl of Worcester had the Chief Governor, the Anglo-Irish Earl of Desmond, beheaded for "horrible treasons and felonies as well as in alliance, fosterage, and alterage with the Irish enemies of the King as in giving to them horses, harnesses, and arm."[2] These actions infuriated the Anglo-Irish aristocracy. The message was clear, the Anglo-Irish were to remain completely separate from the Irish. The fatal result for the English crown was the souring of its relations with the other Anglo-Irish families while turning the powerful Anglo-Irish Desmond family to open rebellion.

In 1470, left with no other great Irish lord to choose from, England's king chose the Earl of Kildare as Chief Governor of Ireland. In 1471 the Earl of Kildare created a standing army of 80 archers, paid for by the crown. Three years later he was able to force through an act calling for a larger force, 160 archers and 63 spearmen.

The Earl of Kildare died in 1478 so his son, Garret Mor Fitzgerald, was elected to take his place as Chief Governor. This seamless passage of government office from father to son

---

[1] Home Rule meant that Ireland would manage her internal affairs while still allowing England supreme control over trade, the army and navy, foreign policy and all imperial matters.

[2] Edmund Curtis, *A History of Ireland* (London, 1968).

worried the English king, always afraid of a competing throne arising in Ireland. He sent over the English noble Lord Grey to replace Fitzgerald as Chief Governor. Sensing the mood of his fellow Anglo-Irish families, in defiance of the crown, Garret Mor Fitzgerald called a parliament which confirmed his previous election as Chief Governor of Ireland. The king, worried about inciting his few Anglo-Irish supporters into revolt, withdrew the appointment of Lord Grey. The position of Chief Governor of Ireland brought with it control of the Irish government and, therefore, the ability to increase personal land holdings. By passing laws, Garret Mor could occupy the lands of absentee landlords, use their rents and profits for his own ends and possess what lands he could recover from Irish "rebels." The enemies of Garret Mor, as the Chief Governor, became the government's enemies, and government revenues were used to prosecute them. The Fitzgeralds of Kildare soon dominated Ireland. The real king of Ireland from 1478 until his death in 1513, Garret Mor Fitzgerald even went to the extent of coining his own money, normally considered a prerogative of the sovereign, using his crest instead of England's. The Irish at this time were closer to Home Rule than they would again be for 450 years.

Garret Mor continued to strengthen his position by building alliances (Offaly accepted his lordship by receiving black rent) and castles. He built several castles in the MacMurrough area into which he tentatively expanded. When he didn't fight the Irish himself, he set them against each other, as he did with the north Leinster clans of the O'Tooles, loyal to him, against the O'Byrnes, who weren't.

In 1495, with a new dynasty ruling England, led by Henry VII of the Tudor family, decisive action was again taken in Ireland. The Earl of Kildare was removed from power and summoned to England where he was kept in the Tower of

London. By this time the use of the Irish language was becoming universal even in The Pale. Henry VII met with Garret Mor, heard his view of the situation in Ireland, and declared, "Since all Ireland cannot rule this man, this man must rule all Ireland." The Earl of Kildare was restored as Chief Governor of Ireland the next year.

Upon returning from England, Kildare continued his policy of expansion and immediately set out to attack Antrim in Ulster with a body of Leinster Irish. This angered The MacMurrough because Kildare was usurping his traditional power. Joining a confederation of Kildare's enemies, The MacMurrough was severely defeated. Never again would the clan challenge Kildare, who had been accepted by the Irish as their new Leinster righ.

Garret Mor marched over more of Ireland than any other had for generations, bringing local righs under his power, determining who would succeed to the throne of The O'Neill or The O'Kelly and blowing up with royal artillery the castles of his enemies. Ireland had found in him an "uncrowned king." While he was an able man, a cunning man, and a popular man both with the English and the Irish, he was not a man willing to risk the prize offered him. At no other time since the coming of Strongbow could one person have made himself head of a new and independent Ireland so easily. Instead he remained comfortable as the Chief Governor and allowed the monarchy that might have been his to slip forever from the grasp of his family.

Garret Mor's life ended in 1513 in an unimportant skirmish with the O'Mores of Leix. He was experimenting with one of the king's newest muskets when one of the O'Mores picked him off with one of their own.

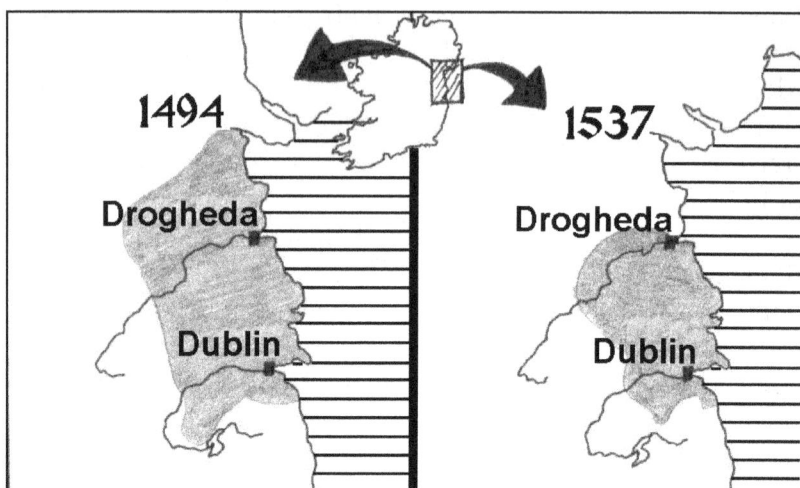

The Pale dwindles in size

Garrett Og succeeded his father as Earl of Kildare and Chief Governor in 1513. Like Irish righs of old, he distributed gifts upon his ascension, the acceptance of which signified acknowledgment of Kildare's lordship. He continued to rule as his father had done before him while the new King of England, Henry VIII, succeeded to the throne. Henry VIII received alarming reports in 1515 of the dwindling limits of The Pale. Even more alarming were reports that this haven of English settlers was becoming more and more Irish. Outside the Pale, the land was ruled by Anglo-Irish lords and Irish chiefs, all independent and each maintaining a personal army. Henry's advisors recommended he send an army to Ireland and once more try to conquer it. Henry calculated that the Irish chiefs alone could muster 22,000 men and rejected the idea as too hazardous to undertake. He adopted a more cautious approach, which required the removal of the major power in Ireland, the Fitzgeralds of Kildare.

In 1534 Garret Og was called to the Tower of London. Before leaving he appointed his eldest son, Thomas, as Chief Governor in his stead. Thomas, known to the Irish as "Silken Thomas" because of the silken garments he and his bodyguard wore, was only 21. The wise Earl realized the danger to Kildare supremacy and adjured his son to be guided by the advice of Dublin's council. The small pro-English faction, the Butlers, who hoped Garret Og would not return, spread a report that Garret Og was dead in the Tower, the victim of a cruel English king. In a dramatic moment on June 11, Silken Thomas, in the Dublin council chamber, surrendered the sword of state and declared himself the English king's enemy. Although the son of an English mother, Thomas understood Irish well and was moved to this dramatic action by the chanting of his Irish file, O'Keenan.

The FitzGerald's Castle of Maynooth

The Kavanaghs and Kinsellas rose in support of Thomas. Edmond Duff of the Kinsellas, as a joint leader of 1,000 men, successfully attacked the town of Ballymagir in County Wexford. This rebellion led by Thomas ended quickly, however, after Fitzgerald's men murdered a Catholic archbishop during another raid, which forced the church to excommunicate Thomas. The Irish, heavily influenced by the church, dropped their support. After failing to take Dublin castle, Thomas retired to the strong Fitzgerald castle of Maynooth. In 1535 the walls were breached with the first cannon used in Ireland, the garrison was slaughtered, and Silken Thomas surrendered unconditionally. He was sent to London where he was executed in 1537 along with five of his uncles (his father having died while being held in England three years previously). Henry VIII was determined to exterminate the whole Fitzgerald male line. Ireland was shocked at this ending of the great house of Kildare, an example of what could happen to anyone who dared to oppose the new Tudor dynasty of England.

The End of the Gaelic Nobility

b.c. 300-600 900-1200 1500-1800 0-300 600-900 1200-1500

ngland, which had dreamt of conquering France for generations, saw this hope stifled forever during the 15th century. In a reversal of fortune, England began to fear an invasion from France or perhaps from the growing power in Spain. For either one, Ireland would be a useful back door into England. This fear of invasion was to grow into paranoia and shape the history of the two countries, and the only way to combat this fear, England felt, was to transform Ireland into a little England along the same model as the Normans had transformed the Anglo-Saxons. Ireland had to be made one with England in politics, religion and culture.

With the power of the Fitzgeralds in Ireland extinguished, Henry VIII directed parliament to pass a series of laws aimed at destroying the Irish culture, laws similar to the statutes of Kilkenny, which had proved so ineffective. The laws condemned "black rent" as illegal and forbade intermarriage between English and Irish along with the use of Irish dress and language. Next, Henry ordered the closing of the abbeys and the transfer of their property to England. (Henry had become Protestant and required all his subjects to do the same.) An order that declared the king as the supreme head of the church of Ireland followed. The final step taken by Henry was to declare himself king of Ireland.[1]   This change of title signified a commitment to total rule in Ireland.

After all these "paper" changes, Ireland was still barely under the control of the English. In 1536 the English king received the following report from Ireland:

> Your highness must understand that the English blood of the English conquest is in manner worn out of this land, and at all seasons in manner, without any restoration is diminished and enfeebled . . . . And, contrarywise, the Irish blood ever more and more, without such decay, increaseth.[2]

Unable to mount a costly invasion, Henry resorted to a cunning policy known as "surrender and regrant." The Irish chiefs, along with some Gaelicized Anglo-Irish, were encouraged to surrender their territories, abandon their Irish titles, disown the pope, and acknowledge Henry as their king. In return they received their lands back from him by feudal grant, and English titles of nobility were bestowed on them. They were to be supplied with title, office, and property, all neatly within a framework of English law. The real purpose was to assert unquestionably the crown's claim to ultimate control over all of Ireland's land. Henry VIII's daughter, Elizabeth I, was to make this control a reality and apply it with ruthless severity.

To the Anglo-Irish the change in land tenure theoretically meant nothing new, just a reaffirmation of the relationship with their overlord, the king, which was supposed to have existed all along. For the Irish righs the change was enormous, both in

---

[1] Previous to this Henry was entitled King of England and Lord of Ireland. When the bill that proclaimed Henry VIII king of Ireland was presented to the Dublin parliament, it had to be reread in Gaelic since only one of the Anglo-Irish governors understood English!

[2] S. P. Hen. VIII, II.iii.338.

theory and in practice. They now no longer held their lands according to ancient Brehon law but by the king's law and by the king's goodwill, which required their good behavior in return. The Irish went along with this surrender and regrant policy because they felt it would prove as ineffective as the previous statutes of Kilkenny. How wrong they were. The new Tudor dynasty was intent on conquering Ireland to quell their fears of foreign invasion.

The Irish and Anglo-Irish began to serve the same monarch in civil and church affairs. In theory, all were entitled to the protection of the law. All were deemed capable of holding land in a precise, legal manner in Ireland. The right of access to the king's courts was implicit in the new agreement, and the following decades witnessed the extension of English law to all "free" Irish, who held their lands from the crown legally. A regular system of courts began to function, and justices of the peace assumed a quasi-military role in 16th-century Ireland as they pushed further and further into Irish domains. Finally, in 1539, the monasteries were closed and the occupants informed that they had to surrender their lands to the crown.[3] The Kavanaghs, who owned vast tracts of lands through their monasteries, rebelled but were quickly brought to heel.

Life in Hy Kinsella went on much the same as before. People resided on the same land, served the same lords, and continued to be governed by Brehon law and Gaelic custom. This situation would not last, however, and an incident in 1547 may have opened the eyes of some of the Kavanaghs. Crimthainn Kavanagh, the grandson of a Leinster righ, was killed by Enna

[3] It was the year before, in 1538, that the "fanatics of the 'Reformation,'" led by Archbishop Brown of Christchurch, had burned the thousand year-old staff of St. Patrick in Dublin.

Kinsella,[4] probably over a land claim. Rather than being hanged for murder, Enna received a royal pardon. By rewarding Enna, the crown was hoping to provoke others into attacking the Kavanaghs. But it wasn't other clans that would weaken the Kavanaghs; it was their own dynastic feuding that crippled them in the years to come.

In the autumn of 1550, Cahir MacMurrough-Kavanagh, the Leinster righ, signed a surrender and regrant treaty, renounced his position as The MacMurrough, and promised that "in the future no one should be elected chief but that they would obey the King's law and hold their lands in knight-service and accept such rules as the King should appoint." So the last Gaelic title to be officially recognized by the crown, Leinster righ, ended.

Things were going to get worse. In 1568 Sir Peter Carew from Devon claimed to be a descendant of the original Norman family who had owned land in County Carlow after Strongbow's arrival, and he wanted his ancestral land back. The original Carews, having died out in the 14th century, had lost their lands to the MacMurrough-Kavanaghs. Peter Carew's claims were put before the Dublin council, and with very little evidence, the Council agreed that the land should revert to the Englishman. The MacMurrough-Kavanaghs were left with the choice of revolting or accepting Peter Carew as their lord and farming the land that was now considered his.

The choice they made and the new order that the English eventually required all Irish to accept is summed up nicely by Richard Berleth in *The Twilight Lords.*

> The clan Kavanaugh was the first to bear the yoke of this new order, and they, by an accident of history, were the least able to

---

[4] Enna was a son of Edmond Duff Kinsella, who had rebelled with Thomas Fitzgerald decades before.

resist it . . . By Elizabeth's day some of the clans were more feudal than tribal and had in large measure abandoned the practice of communal land tenure and an elected chieftaincy. Now [under the surrender and regrant policy] the flaiths [nobles] were made barons; their families, vassals. And perhaps more than others the Kavanaughs epitomized this transition. For while the MacMurrough-Kavanaughs traced descent from one of the five lines of Irish kings, they had long ago surrendered their native prerogatives. They were reared and educated in England; they were welcome at the English court; and it is little wonder that, being civil men, they attempted to fight Carew with his own weapons. Resorting to law, they took their case first to the Dublin Council, then to the Queen. Both suits were lost before begun. Their claim to Idrone and Carlow had been recognized by the Crown since the mid-12th century, but pressed to prove their ownership, they could produce no deeds, no patents, no pedigrees or rolls. For the lack of a parchment, the Kavanaughs lost their lands and way of life. They awoke to find themselves trapped between their English friends and their Irish countrymen. No longer warriors, most of the Kavanaughs had neither the means nor the inclination to resist Carew, and they relinquished their lands grudgingly, becoming subjects where they had once ruled. Their subjugation was not uniform. But the code of *cin comhfhocuis*[5] now worked against them. Solidarity was the law of the *fine* (clan), and disobedience by some meant that all would suffer. Consequently where some Kavanagauhs rose against the English intruders, fighting for their homesteads, they were suppressed and driven off by their own kinsmen fearing reprisals. The dilemma was not theirs alone . . . .[6]

In 1553, Mary became queen of England. Since she was a Catholic, the people of Ireland expected quick redress to the

---

[5] This meant loyalty to the clan. If a decision was made by the clan leader, all must follow it. Any who didn't had to be punished by the clan itself.
[6] Richard Berleth, *The Twilight Lords* (Maryland, 2002).

unjust laws previous monarchs had enacted against them; such was not the case. Under her reign confiscation of lands owned by Irish chieftains increased dramatically. The O'Mores of County Leix and the O'Connors of County Offaly had long been a source of terror to English settlements in The Pale. Both were found by English juries to have committed treasonous acts, and their lands were forfeited to the crown. The next step was to populate these areas with English settlers, the area then being referred to as a plantation. The confiscated areas were renamed King's County and Queen's County, names they retained until Ireland became a republic in the 20th century. In 1557 an uprising in this plantation was dealt with immediately and severely – one righ was hung and another crucified.

When Elizabeth succeeded Mary in 1558, she faced severe discontent by the Irish over the plantations enacted by Mary. There were six separate rebellions by the Anglo-Irish, with and without Irish allies. Elizabeth saw the domination of Ireland as critical to England's safety. Especially subversive, according to her and her advisors, were the Irish filid, now called bards.[7] The bards infuriated the English because they kept alive the traditions, history and identity of the Gaelic culture. Penalties against them were stern: O'Brien, the Earl of Thomond, was forced to hang three distinguished Irish filid. Elizabeth was not satisfied with just controlling the Irish people; their culture had to be eradicated.

English society, grounded in numerous strict rules and a love of unbendable regulations, abhorred the fluidity of Irish society where fosterage allowed the family to be extended in deliberate but uncertain directions; where tenants could change landlords at will; chiefs lived by levies and impositions;

---

[7] With the deterioration of Gaelic society, support for filid schools had dwindled, so the distinction between the trained filid and untrained bards had grown vague.

pasture-farming was mobile;[8] and ownership of farmable land shifted along with its bewilderingly movable fences. The English saw the Irish as feuding, whiskey-drinking, oatcake-eating musicians, bards, brehons, and righs, with women who wrapped themselves in shaggy Irish mantles. All seemed independent of good order and discipline; Irish flexibility was viewed as anarchy and lawlessness.

"These were the attitudes that presented English observers with a constant conundrum. How could the Irish be both savage and subtle? Both warlike and lazy? At once evidently 'inferior,' yet possessed of an ungovernable pride? Cowardly, yet of legendary fortitude in the face of death? Socially primitive, but capable of complex litigation? . . . They were dirty, lazy, dishonest and violent. Their laws were unethical and inequitable. Yet these 'corrupt customs' had invariably fascinated and drawn in the English who settled in Ireland, 'degenerating' them."[9] While the English thought of the Irish as inferior, the Irish believed it was self-evident that their culture was superior.

Strict rules to curb the Irish culture were again put in place and enforced when possible. If a traveler was seen riding in the Irish fashion, dressed in Irish clothes, or not wearing "a civil English cap," it was "advisable and lawful" to murder the offender. Even wearing a moustache after the Irish custom was denounced as meriting death, and the delinquent's estate was forfeited to the crown. The prospect of being hanged, drawn and quartered or disemboweled, however, did not deter either the Irish or the Anglo-Irish from retaining Gaelic culture. No wonder English hatred of the Gaelic culture, a challenge to their authority and superiority, grew year by year.

---

[8] "Booleying," or transhumance, was when the young people moved to hills or bogs for the summer months with the cattle.

[9] R. F. Foster, *Modern Ireland 1600-1972* (London, 1989).

An oral story survives from these troubled times involving Grainne O'Malley of Connacht, a famous female righ.[10] The story illustrates how the ancient Gaelic cultural values of hospitality and pride were still alive and well. When Grainne was returning from a state visit with Queen Elizabeth of England, she landed at Howth near Dublin. Upon finding the Anglo-Irish Lord Howth's castle gate closed because the family was at dinner, she became so upset at their Saxon rudeness that she took Lord Howth's child away from a nurse walking outside the gate and carried it off with her to Connacht. The Howth family had to pay a considerable ransom for their child, and they also learned a lesson in Irish hospitality. Ever after, when the Howths went to dinner, their gates and doors were left wide open.

Elizabeth's government continued the policies her father, Henry VIII, had put in place. After the English government felt the Kavanagh clan was under control, they put pressure on the Kinsellas and their nearby cousin clan, the MacDavy Mors. The lands of the Kinsella clan included most of northeast County Wexford around the town of Gorey,[11] where they can still be found. This part of Wexford had never been conquered, unlike southern Wexford. Throughout the turmoil of the 16th century they had pursued their native law and culture while remaining unobtrusive. Between 1571 and 1581, the Kinsella clan finally surrendered their lands to the queen.

The change they made was not for the better. In 1592, the Kinsellas and MacDavy Mors were so impoverished by raids and disturbances between the Irish and English that they owed

---

[10] Although Irish women had many rights, becoming righ was not one of them according to Brehon law. Grainne was allowed this unusual distinction because warfare had made the times so chaotic that the laws could not always be strictly followed.

[11] This district was formerly called "the Kinsellaghs."

£1,300 to the crown. In 1594, the leader of the Kinsellas, Art McDermot Duff, went to London to request the queen and privy council forgive his clan's payments. He also asked for several entitlements for the towns his clan lived in, including courts and the right to hold fairs. Interestingly, he also presented a letter from a major O'Byrne family begging pardon for their people. The Kinsellas were acting as intermediaries between the Irish and the English.

The English, under the Tudors, were very successful during the 16th century at divesting the Irish of their power, except in one province, Ulster. In 1594 Ulster decided it could no longer hope that this latest English tide would recede. A group of Ulster righs, led by Hugh O'Neill,[12] declared war on the English and defeated them in several engagements; what is called the Great Rebellion had begun. Flushed with this early success, The O'Neill contacted the king of Spain, Philip II, asking for troops, and Philip promised to help. Hugh O'Neill was a brilliant leader who wasn't solely hoping for foreign assistance. As discussions continued with Spain, the Gaels of Ireland organized into a loose confederation, with Hugh O'Neill as Ireland's presumptive Ard Righ. England's greatest fear, invasion through the back door of a hostile Ireland, was about to be realized.

Sir John Harrington, an Englishman of Elizabeth's court who visited O'Neill, found him seated in the open, surrounded by his clansmen. In this position O'Neill asserted he would rather be "The O'Neill than the King of Spain." Harrington marveled at the love and admiration the Gaels exhibited toward their lord. "With what charm such a master makes them love

---

[12] O'Neill needed English support to become Ulster righ so he played the loyalist for thirty years. Once he was firmly established as the Ulster righ in 1589, he began creating a network of support throughout Ireland and abroad, all the while working through a visage of loyalty to the English.

him I know not: but if he bid come they came; if go, they do go; if he say do this they do it."[13]

At The O'Neill's prompting, the Kavanaghs attempted to revive the forbidden position of Leinster righ in 1598. They began with cattle raids around Enniscorthy, which prompted a battle between the combined clans of the Kavanaghs and O'Mores against the royal forces. The Gaels won decisively, killing about 300 English while losing only 80 of their own.

The battles spread throughout Ireland as the Irish rose to arms. In 1599, County Carlow was laid waste by the rebels until only its castles and the towns of Carlow and Leighlin-bridge remained under the control of the queen's forces. England responded with the largest army ever, 20,000 men, 2,000 horse and 7,000 picked soldiers. Leinster was set aflame. Essex, the Lord Deputy, fought through "a country called the Kinseles" in north Wexford before he reached Arklow where he met and defeated his Irish adversaries. Part of this English force was later attacked by the Kavanaghs and the north Leinster clans of the O'Byrnes and the O'Mores in County Leix at a place subsequently called "the Pass of the Plumes" because so many English plumed helmets were left behind. It was the last major victory for the Leinster Irish during the Great Rebellion.

In 1598 and 1599, several more engagements occurred, even larger than those fought in Leinster, involving The O'Neill's forces and the English. In most of these the Irish were the victors.

Four thousand Spanish troops finally landed at Kinsale in 1601. The O'Neill, the leader of the Gaels in Ireland, risked marching across all Ireland with his entire force to meet them while an English force approached. One of The O'Neill's under-righs, O'Donnell, raided some cattle along the march through Munster. Shortly afterwards a file named Maolin Og

---

[13] Martin McMahon, *I Cry for My People* (Sandgate, Qld., 1996).

visited the camp, proved his rank by reciting stories, and flattered O'Donnell with a poem. Only then did he reveal some of the stolen cattle were his; "recompense for his cattle and flocks was given to the poet [file] with an increase and he took leave of O'Donnell and left him his blessing."[14] The filid were still highly respected. All Ireland waited with anticipation the outcome of the encounter between the Spanish, Irish, and English. On December 24, 1601, the battle of Kinsale was fought. The English army's superior organization led to the total defeat of the Irish.

Hugh O'Neill

---

[14] Lughaidh O'Clery, *The Life of Hugh Roe O'Donnell, Prince of Tirconnell (1586-1602)* (Dublin, 1895).

The O'Neill retreated back to the wilds of Ulster, where he continued to resist. The English marched to Tullahoge, County Tyrone, where the O'Neills had been inaugurated for centuries, and destroyed their famous inauguration stone. They regarded this act as representing the end of Gaelic independence. In 1603, the aging warrior O'Neill accepted the fact the Great Rebellion was over and laid down his arms before making submission to Queen Elizabeth.[15] He renounced his title of The O'Neill, forsook dependence on any foreign power, especially Spain, and surrendered his lands for regrant. The last unconquered province was now under English law and government.

A few yeas later, in 1607, The O'Neill was warned that he was to be charged with conspiracy against the crown, punishable by death. Although he had done nothing wrong since his submission in 1603, he recognized the charge as a ploy by the English to take all his lands. A few months later a Spanish ship arrived in Lough Swilly in which The O'Neill and ninety-nine of the ruling Gaels from Ulster departed to find asylum in Spain at last. This exodus, known as "The Flight of the Earls," brought to an end the Milesian aristocracy that had ruled over Ireland since the dawn of history.

For the next decade most of not only the Irish but also the Anglo-Irish, who regretted not having aided The O'Neill more, hoped that he would return to set Ireland free. In 1616, when news came of his blindness and then of his death, they abandoned hope "and trooped in in hundreds to get their patents from the crown."[16]

---

[15] He didn't know that the queen had died a few days previously.

[16] Edmund Curtis, *A History of Ireland* (London, 1968).

Gaelic nobles submit to England

The Planting of Ireland

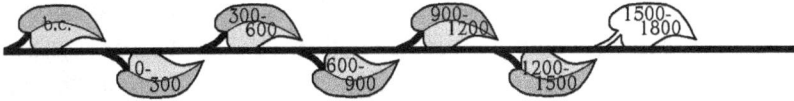

ngland took advantage of the Gaelic hopelessness following the death of Hugh O'Neill in 1616. The 17th century witnessed the submergence of Gaelic Ireland, a feat accomplished by England's intentional and concentrated assault on Ireland's society, culture and religion. England suppressed those things on which Irish society was based – their lands, names, and language. They adopted the strategy of establishing a plantation, eliminating the native Irish, and repopulating the country with more trustworthy English, on a scale never before seen in Ireland. They began with Ulster.

Five hundred thousand acres in Ulster were thrown open to settlers in 1609. Preference was given to English and lowland Scots. A second rank of grantees were highland Scots, primarily Presbyterian, and the third rank were "natives." The colony was not an immediate success and grew slowly over the years until 1660, when approximately 90% of the landowners in the six counties of present-day Ulster were Protestant. Even with such a large percentage of Protestant landowners, a large Irish Catholic minority remained. Retaining their culture and religion, they lived mostly in the mountainous and poorer lands. When local protests broke out, the instigators were transported to the new colony of Virginia.

Ulster wasn't alone in being populated with foreigners. In 1610 the English built a castle near Gorey called Fortchester to effectively conquer land that had always belonged to the Irish.

This still didn't pacify the Irish of northern Wexford (where the majority of Kinsellas settled), so in 1611 a writ was issued approving the seizure of 76,800 acres in that area for "good and sufficient English." By devious means, and despite considerable opposition, the lands were seized from 1610 to 1618 under the official name of the Plantation of Wexford. English nobles received 61% of the land, while 9% was divided among four Irish lords, Morgan McBrian, Donal Kavanagh, Dowling McBrian and Art McDermot Duff Kinsella. One hundred and twenty smaller landholders received patents for the last 30% of the land. The peasants were no worse off, but the small landowning clansmen were reduced to common laborers.

This change in land ownership throughout Ireland sparked a drive for surnames among the common Irish, only the nobility having adopted them previously. Because the commoners often adopted the surnames of their local landowners, the names Kavanagh, Carew and Fitzgerald are very common today. The names of smaller landowners, such as the Kinsellas and MacDavy Mors, are less common. The positive consequence is that a Kinsella is much more likely to be truly descended from Dermot MacMurrough than a Kavanagh.[1]

During the next twenty years the Irish landowners throughout all of Hy Kinsella, which included the Anglo-Irish since they remained Catholic, made desperate attempts to hold onto their land, while the English tried to wrest it from them. Over time landowners in the territory were reduced from 667 to 150. The only effective way the Irish had to halt the rapacious Eng-

---

[1] To complicate matters further for the Kavanaghs, "in the early years of the seventeenth century the surname Kavanagh was adopted by the ruling sept [clan] of Kinsellagh – descendants of Enna Cionsealach – while their collateral clansmen took that of Kinsellagh." The MacDavy Mor clan did the same. From K. W. Nicholls, "The Kavanaghs, 1400 - 1700," *Irish Genealogist* (1974-9): v, 435.

lish was to convert to the Church of England, but very few chose that route. The Borris Kavanaghs did and they went on to become the largest Gaelic landowners in Hy Kinsella. They also weathered future rebellions extremely well because to the Irish they were Gaels and to the English they were Protestant. Northern Wexford represents an extreme example of land takeovers at this time though. In the whole of Ireland as late as

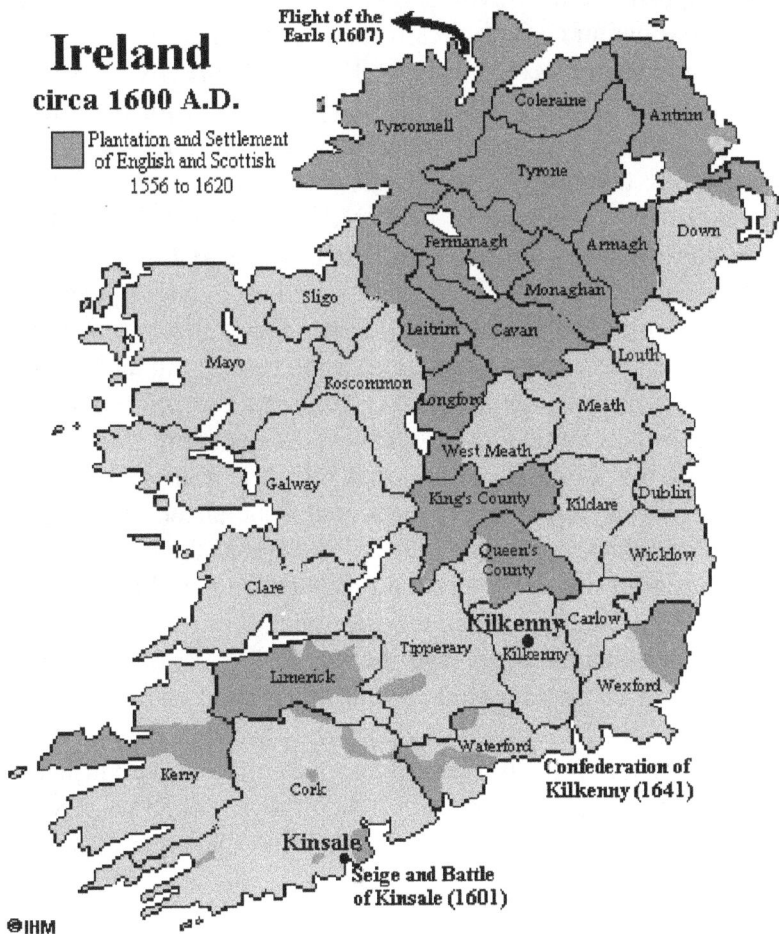

Ireland

circa 1600 A.D.

Plantation and Settlement of English and Scottish 1556 to 1620

Flight of the Earls (1607)

Tyrconnell
Coleraine
Antrim
Tyrone
Fermanagh
Armagh
Down
Sligo
Monaghan
Leitrim
Cavan
Louth
Mayo
Roscommon
Longford
Meath
West Meath
Galway
King's County
Kildare
Dublin
Queen's County
Wicklow
Clare
Kilkenny
Carlow
Tipperary
Kilkenny
Wexford
Limerick
Waterford
Kerry
Confederation of Kilkenny (1641)
Cork
Kinsale
Seige and Battle of Kinsale (1601)

©IHM

293

1640 Catholic landowners still held two-thirds of the land. This would change dramatically in the ensuing years.

By 1641 the grievances of the Irish nation, now a blend of native Irish and Anglo-Irish who had retained their strong Catholic faith, reached crisis proportions, and there was a general uprising. The rebellion was caused by several factors: the vast confiscations of lands, the unjust treatment of the Irish and Anglo-Irish, the favor shown the new English colonists, and the exclusion of Catholics from office and civil rights. The rebellion was masterminded by Rory O'More from County Leix and began on October 23, 1641. It met with immediate military success only in Ulster under Sir Phelim O'Neill, but was quickly taken up by the Anglo-Irish and spread to the rest of the country. The castle of Fortchester, in the heart of the Kinsella lands, was quickly taken over by the Irish.

In England the rebellion was reported as a general massacre of English men, women and children. No evidence exists that a deliberate massacre, as such, ever took place,[2] but anti-Catholic feelings were easily aroused in England and the report of a massacre was assumed to be true without question. Some estimates of the number of deaths inflicted ran higher than 200,000. In all these falsified accounts, the sheer barbarity of the crimes struck a genuine chord of horror in the hearts of the English: could a people who had roasted men and eaten them alive, sent women out to sea in leaky boats to drown, murdered children in a disgusting manner before their parents' eyes, held competitions as to who could hack deepest into a living body, really hold any pretensions towards civilization? Behind it all, it was alleged, were the treacherous and evil machinations of the Catholic clergy. Years later, when the evidence was examined more dispassionately, the number who died was estimated

---

[2] Walter D. Love, "Civil War in Ireland: Appearances in Three Centuries of Historical Writing," *Emory University Quarterly* 22.1 (Spring 1966): 57-72.

to be 4,000, though a figure of 2,000 may be nearer. Retaliatory attacks on Catholics soon added many more fatalities.

This normally would have prompted swift action from the English king, Charles I, but civil war had broken out again in England. By 1649 King Charles had lost the war along with his head, clearing the way for a fervent Protestant zealot, Oliver Cromwell, who was appointed Commander-General for Ireland by the English parliament. He believed implicitly in the exaggerated massacre of 1641, and it provided the moral basis for fresh English colonization that he was planning. Before leaving for Ireland Cromwell told his troops they were Israelites about to extirpate the idolatrous inhabitants of Canaan. He and his men landed near Dublin in 1649.

A combination of prejudice and hard political realities dictated what Cromwell and his troops did. The prevailing English view of the Irish stressed their ignorance, crudity, superstition and barbarity. Edmund Spenser, writing a century before, offered this English solution to the Irish problem: "the corrupt branches and unwholesome boughs are first to be pruned, and the foul moss cleansed and scraped away before the tree can bring forth any good fruit." Added to this prejudice were the powerful myths that had grown about the 1641 uprising, which created an overwhelming desire for revenge in England. Cromwell, the man leading the invasion, the one responsible for controlling the pent-up hatred of the English troops, was convinced that he was embarked on a godly crusade against the Catholics. He felt the Irish expedition had to be speedy, conclusive and cheap. An unsubdued Ireland was again seen as a back-door threat from England's enemies that needed to be shut tightly.

Ulster, totally under the control of the Irish again, was Cromwell's first destination, and the key to Ulster was a town known as Drogheda. On September 11 the town was sacked and a massacre transpired. According to Cromwell, "the slaughter of women and children is allowed to have impunity, as comprehended in right of war and the 137th Psalm, 'Happy shall he be that taketh and dasheth thy children against the storm.'" The town's garrison troops, almost to a man, and all priests, were killed. Those who fled to hide in St. Peter's church were easily dispatched – clustered in the steeple, they were burned to death. The voice of a miserable human torch was heard to cry out: "God damn me, God confound me; I burn, I burn." Cromwell repeated the words without emotion in his battle report to parliament. Defending himself concerning the estimated 3,000 slain, Cromwell said, "I am persuaded that this is a righteous judgment of God upon these barbarous wretches, who have imbued their hands in so much innocent blood."

The reaction to the news in England was one of delight and rejoicing. The ministers gave out the happy tidings from the pulpits. September 11 (9/11) was set aside as a day of public thanksgiving. The heinous Irish rebels had received their just rewards.

The lesson was repeated on October 11 in the town of Wexford in southern Hy Kinsella. Once again the Irish refused to surrender, and after eight days the town fell and was sacked. At Drogheda, Cromwell had chosen a policy of slaughter in the heat of battle; at Wexford his normally well-disciplined troops ran amok, and no effort was made to control them. Nearly 2,000 troops, priests and civilians were killed. Heath, in his biography of 1663, painted a poignant picture of 200 women, many of them of high rank, asking for mercy "with the command of their charming eyes and those melting tears," but it was denied to them as they were massacred. Cromwell again wouldn't accept blame, for it was God who had "brought a righteous judgment upon them [the inhabitants of Wexford] causing them to become a prey to the soldier."

This military policy of extreme violence had positive short-term results. The towns of Dundalk and Trim, faced with the example of Drogheda, surrendered tamely. The long-term results, a lasting and seething hostility to the English, proved devastating. Cromwell continued his attacks and, after a few setbacks, regained control of Ireland. Among his special targets during the campaign were the Gaelic filid, which the English had never managed to stamp out. Revered by the Irish, these bards were detested by the English authorities, who saw them as architects of Gaelic resistance.[3] Unable to find and kill them all, Cromwell sought out and destroyed their few remaining schools.

The war was finally over in May of 1652 when Ireland's army, both Irish and Anglo-Irish, surrendered to Cromwell's forces. It's estimated that of the 1.5 million inhabitants of Ireland before the rebellion, over 600,000 were killed or died from famine or disease.[4] Cromwell wrote:

> And if ever men were engaged in a righteous cause in the world, this will be scarce a second to it. We are come to ask an account of the innocent blood that hath been shed . . . . We come to break the power of a company of lawless rebels . . . . We come (by the assistance of God) to hold forth and maintain the luster and glory of English liberty in a nation where we have an undoubted right to do it . . . .

With the war over, England felt it could begin again with Ireland, but first they had to remove the estimated 30,000 rebel

---

[3] Caesar had reached the same conclusion over 1,600 years earlier during the Gallic Wars, when he was conquering the Celts of the area now called France.

[4] Fiachra O'Lionain, *Croghan to the Sea* (Enniscorthy).

soldiers still in Ireland. Parliament decided these soldiers could emigrate to any country at peace with England but not with their wives or children. Because of their reputation as excellent soldiers, representatives from France, Spain, Austria and Poland flocked to Ireland, signing up as many as possible.[5] Now the Irish "tree" could be pruned.

The Burren is where many dispossessed were sent

In 1653, Cromwell issued his famous "to hell or Connacht" edict, which read, "under penalty of death, no Irish man, woman or child is to be found East of the River Shannon." By this edict, all native Irish landowners in eastern Ireland were ordered to vacate their land and move to Clare and Connacht, a treeless, rockbound land. Of those forced to move, only about one in five received any land while their property was confiscated as pay for the English soldiers. Ireland had to pay for its own conquest. Eanna, Griffin and Edmond Kinsella, extensive

---

[5] Many returned illegally and began fresh insurrections. They were hunted down with dogs by the new Protestant landowners.

landowners around Gorey in northern County Wexford, were among those dispossessed of their lands.

The turmoil and pain this dispossession caused can hardly be properly understood today; it was far more than an economic downturn. To those within the Gaelic culture, Irish and Anglo-Irish alike, losing their land meant losing their identity. The landscape they had grown up with was teeming with memories and tales of ancestral deeds and names of previous inhabitants. The people took pride in understanding their environment in terms of this place-lore, and for this reason Gaelic families remained in the same location for thousands of years.

> A man who loves his own hearthstone, and all it stands for, always carries into every conflict a principle of more sacred steadfastness than the homeless, nameless, characterless and hopeless outcast who has no anchorage for his soul . . . . When I was young we learned at our fireside the native names of our towns, rivers, clan and family names – our genealogy, the story of our people and the ideals which ought to be ours.[6]

The area of land confiscated was estimated to be 11,000,000 acres out of the 20,000,000 acres of Ireland. Cromwell, hoping to fill this land with loyal Englishmen, made generous grants to his soldiers, but his dream remained unfulfilled. Many of the soldiers disliked the land they were given and returned to England, others were cheated out of it by their officers, and those who did settle often broke the law and married an Irish girl. Many former soldiers accepted the Gaelic culture so readily that by the end of the century an English observer was reporting indignantly that the descendants of Cromwell's army could speak no English.

---

[6] Lauchlan MacLean Watt (1937).

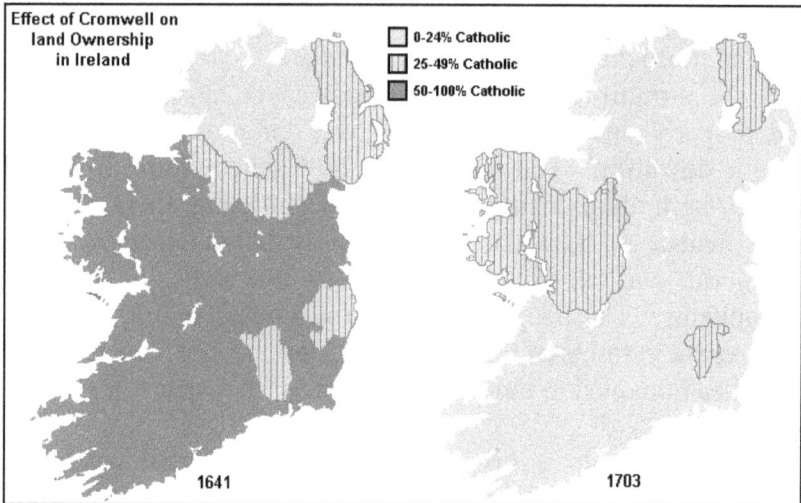

The English treasury was low on money, so when Cromwell learned that the English landowners of Montserrat in the Caribbean were willing to pay for laborers, he ordered "violators," Irish found east of the Shannon River, to be rounded up. Thousands of these unfortunate Irish, many the wives and children of the soldiers who had been deported, were then exported to Montserrat to work as slaves. In succeeding decades, the blood of Africans and Irish intermixed, resulting in today's Irish-African islanders. Few of the descendants of the original exported Irish have any concept of their Irish background. However, of the 1,600 families listed in the telephone directory, 30% have Irish surnames.

Cromwell, still the religious zealot, also began a more methodical persecution of Roman Catholicism. While there were fewer executions of Catholic clergy, there were more deportations of them. (Barbados, another English possession in the West Indies, was a common destination.) Priests were outlawed and priest-hunting encouraged with rewards. P. J. Corish describes "the ministry of the catholic clergy as intermittent and extremely furtive. They could not turn to the laity for shelter and support, for this would have exposed their hosts to too much risk. They lived in huts in the bogs, in the woods, or on the mountains. They were probably safest in towns, where some are known to have carried on a rather daring ministry under one disguise or another."[7]

The Catholic religion not only survived but began to thrive: over 95% of Ireland's population belonged to it. Catholicism lived on in the hearts of the poorer people, as a secret and sacred fire whose flames could be banked down for the sake of hiding but whose burning heat would never be totally extinguished. Priests, now disguised as shepherds and ploughmen, traveled the country.

Upon the death of Cromwell in 1658 much of the drive for resettlement eased, along with the hunt for Catholic priests. The result of Cromwell's settlement, imperfectly carried out as it was, was that 6,000 Catholic landowners, Irish and Anglo-Irish alike, were deprived of their holdings.[8] The Irish peasantry mostly exchanged old masters for new ones. What Cromwell's settlement really boiled down to was "that Protestants were left holding the bulk of Irish lands and had gathered into their hands extensive power over trade, local politics, and national government."[9] A basic distinction arose between landed and landless in Ireland, exacerbated by religious differences, which accounted for so many of its later troubles. This new ruling class was to be known as the Protestant Ascendancy. It was said, "an Irish nation still existed – separate, numerous and hostile."

---

[7] P. J. Corish, *The Catholic Community in the Seventeenth and Eighteenth Centuries* (Dublin, 1981).
[8] The wealthiest landowners, even though they were Catholic, were able to pay a substantial fine to retain at least part of their estate.
[9] Roger Howell, *Cromwell* (Boston, 1977).

Because of the savagery of Cromwell's retribution in Ireland, the English authorities refused to acknowledge this threat.
They chose instead to believe that Irish revolts were a thing of
the past, and for a few decades, they were. The English felt
free to continue their policy of stamping out Gaelic culture,
especially as represented by the filid.

The MacFirbis of Lecan represented one of the most
illustrious Irish filid families. From the 12th to the 17th centuries this family's school flourished. They alone were responsible for compiling three famous books containing a great deal
of information regarding Gaelic culture and history – the *Great
Book of Lecan*, the *Yellow Book of Lecan*, and the *Book of
Genealogies*. Even without these towering achievements, their
law reports and other historical compilations had secured for
them an exalted position in Gaelic literature and scholarship.

The most eminent member of this literary family was
Duald MacFirbis, the last of the hereditary filid of Ireland.
Born in 1585, he was properly instructed in the Brehon laws.
He devoted his life to compiling and saving all he could of his
Irish culture. In 1670, at the age of eighty-five, he was on his
way to Dublin to share historical information with a friend
when he stopped overnight at a small store which had rooms
for lodging. While he was resting in a chair in a little room off
the shop a young Protestant man came in and began taking
some liberties with the girl who worked there. To stop his
advances, the girl told the man that he would be seen by the old
gentleman in the next room. Growing upset, the young man
snatched up a knife from the counter, rushed into the room, and
plunged it into the heart of MacFirbis. The life of the last of
the regularly educated and most accomplished masters of Irish
history, antiquities, laws, and language was ended.[10] Once it

---

[10] Adapted from Eugene O'Curry, *Lectures on the Manuscript Materials of
Ancient Irish History* (New York, 1965, 1861).

was discovered MacFirbis had been a filid, the case was closed – nothing illegal had been done.

The English misjudged the seething hatred the Irish had developed since Cromwell, and by the time a new generation of Irishmen reached manhood trouble started anew. James II, the new king of England in 1685, was crowned a Catholic. The powerful nobles in England wanted no part of a Catholic monarch, however, so in 1688 the Protestant William of Orange, the new king's son-in-law, arrived in England and succeeded in deposing King James.

King James, unwilling to give up his throne so easily, sought help in Scotland, then in Ireland,[11] where an army quickly arose to support him. England's new Protestant king, William III, arrived to lead his own army in person. They took up a position on the River Boyne, twenty miles north of Dublin, and an English drama was played out on Irish soil. Although a national myth was later founded on it, the battle of the Boyne was itself indecisive. The myth was fueled by the image of brave King William astride a gray horse in the thick of the fighting, which starkly contrasted with the cowardly behavior of King James, who fled the field at the first sign of difficulties.

The following year King William's army engaged and defeated King James' army at the far more decisive battle of Aughrim in County Galway. This time the slaughter was very great, with 7,000 fleeing Irish cut down in the aftermath. The terms of surrender included a stipulation that all rebels be given safe passage to France. Since it concluded the war and exported the potential for future trouble, the arrangement was readily acceptable to the English government. Sixteen thousand soldiers left Ireland forever, ultimately forming the Irish

---

[11] There is a record of a Bonaventure Kinselagh who was an officer under Kavanagh's infantry regiment in King James II's army in Ireland.

Brigade in the French army that soon became known as the Wild Geese. Even when they fought on foreign soil for a foreign employer, the Irish Brigade was most fired-up when they engaged the English army.[12]

The English authorities, frustrated by these constant rebellions, decided they must so strip the Irish of power that they would never again be a threat. The Penal Laws were their solution.

---

[12] "At the battle of Fontenoy in 1745 the Duke of Cumberland's forces [English] overpowered the French center, but in a ferocious and headlong charge they were thrown back by the Irish Brigade, under the command of Charles O'Brien, the disinherited Viscount Clare. Fontenoy has always been seen by Irish nationalists as a proxy victory over the English." Alistair Moffat, *The Sea Kingdoms* (London, 2002).

The Enslavement of the Irish

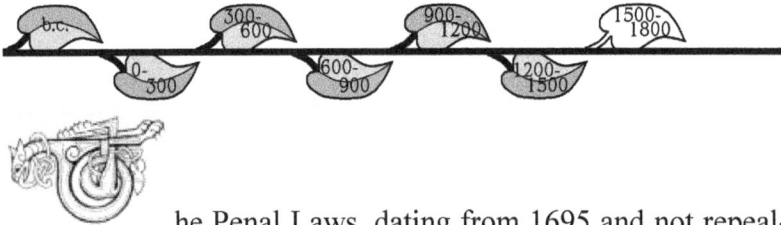

he Penal Laws, dating from 1695 and not repealed in their entirety until Catholic emancipation in 1829, aimed at the destruction of Irish culture and Catholicism in Ireland by a series of ferocious enactments. The threat to England of King James' rebel army had been alarming, and vengeance followed. The Irish were, in the words of a contemporary, to become "insignificant slaves, fit for nothing but to hew wood and draw water." To achieve this objective the Penal Laws were devised.

In broad outline, they barred Catholics from the army and navy, the law, commerce, and from every civic activity, including all professional vocations. No Catholic could own a horse worth more than £5.[1] Education was almost eliminated since Catholics could not attend schools or send their children to be educated abroad. No Catholic could vote, hold office, purchase land or practice their faith. Catholic estates were dismembered by an enactment directing that when a Catholic owner died his land was to be divided among all his sons, unless one of them became a Protestant in order to inherit the whole. Informing was encouraged as "an honorable service" and priest-hunting treated as a sport. A poem referring to the last two items states:

---

[1] If a Catholic was offered £5 for his horse, he had to sell it. This restriction provoked numerous deaths.

They bribed the flock, they bribed the son,
To sell the priest and rob the sire;
Their dogs were taught alike to run
Upon the scent of wolf and friar.

Rather than weakening faith, the measures forged a strong bond between priests and the majority of the Catholic population in Ireland as they colluded with one another to evade the law. As Lecky remarked, "Priests were an illegal class compelled to associate with smugglers, robbers, privateers, to whose assistance they were often obliged to resort in order to escape the ministers of justice."[2] Priests carried out their religious obligations by responding bravely and imaginatively to the challenges that faced them. Mass was celebrated "in secret rock-clefts, with sentries posted on the hilltops," and in "sand-pits, barns, the upper rooms of public houses . . . the ruins of ancient churches."

One of the most hated provisions of these laws was the one that obligated all Catholics, but not Protestants, to tithe the protestant church of Ireland. Since Ireland was 95% Catholic, the Protestant ministers received the bulk of their income from people who never came to their church. As a result of this forced giving, the annual income of ministers in Ireland was usually three times that of their counterparts in England. To enforce this hated law, the names of the heads of households that paid these tithes were duly recorded, and ironically these lists provide an excellent source of genealogical information for people tracing their Irish Catholic roots.

"The purpose of the penal laws was to ensure the Protestant Ascendancy by destroying or debasing the catholic upper

---

[2] W. E. H. Lecky, *A History of Ireland in the Eighteenth Century* (London, 1972).

classes rather than by eliminating Catholicism."[3] Protestantism defined the elite and dilution by converts was not wholly welcome. These laws destroyed what remained of the Catholic landowning and ruling class, leaving ultimately only a comparatively inconsequential remnant. Some of the landowning Catholics were absorbed into the Protestant Ascendancy through conversion. Many sank to a lower level in society, through subdivision of estates, to create a stratum of middling farmers whose tradition was a mixture of radical discontent and tenacious conservative memory; some drifted into exile.

Such were the main provisions of the penal code, "a machine as well fitted for the oppression, impoverishment and degradation of a people, and the debasement in them of human nature itself, as ever proceeded from the perverted ingenuity of man."[4] The Penal Laws produced terrible results of widespread ruin and omnipresent poverty, but the moral effects were worse, because the Penal Laws made it impossible to live within the law. The poor Catholic laborer, the Kinsella, Kavanagh, or MacDavy Mor bore the full hardship. His tribulations were insurmountable: his religion alone made him an outlaw, and in the Irish House of Commons he was described as "the common enemy." He had no one to help him. His landlord was almost invariably an alien conqueror, and the courts were of no assistance when every person connected with the law, from judge to jailer, was English.

> In these conditions suspicion of the law, of the ministers of the law and of all established authority worked into the very genes of the Irish Catholic and, since the law did not give them justice, they set up their own law. Cattle were 'clifted,' driven over the edge of a cliff, horses hamstrung, dogs clubbed to death, stables

---

[3] F. G. James, *Ireland in the Empire 1688-1770* (Cambridge, Mass., 1973).
[4] Edmund Burke.

fired and the animals within, burned alive. Nor were lawlessness, cruelty and revenge the only consequences. During the
long Penal period, dissimulation became a moral necessity and
evasion of the law the duty of every god-fearing Catholic. To
worship according to his faith, the Catholic must attend illegal
meetings; to protect his priest, he must be secret, cunning, and a
concealer of the truth. These were dangerous lessons for any
government to compel its subjects to learn, and a dangerous
habit of mind for any nation to acquire.[5]

The Penal Laws accomplished many of their anticipated
results. Within a few generations, the Irish Catholic population
was reduced to abject poverty and was almost 100% illiterate.[6]
Rebellions, with the emigration of Irish leaders, ceased. As
late as 1773, the effects of the Penal Laws were still obvious.
In that year Art O'Leary, who was serving as an officer in the
Hungarian army, returned to see his wife and children in Ireland. While home he entered his horse in a local race and won.
The Englishman whose horse had been beaten turned defeat
into grim victory by offering O'Leary £5 for the winning horse.
O'Leary refused. His wife learned of the tragic result when she
saw the winning horse, neck covered in her husband's blood,
return without its rider. This deed provoked her to write a
"Lament for Art O'Leary." The murder, never brought to
court, was perfectly legal.

---

[5] Cecil Woodham-Smith, *The Great Hunger* (New York, 1962).
[6] Apparently the illiteracy rate did not reach 100%. A story is told of a
town in Ulster, considered to be a hotbed of Protestantism, that had the
following neatly lettered sign prominently displayed at the town's entrance,
"All Creeds Are Welcome Here . . . But Papists." One morning the city
fathers were outraged to find that during the night their prized sign had been
defaced. Scrawled beneath the printed words was the message: "Whoever
wrote it, wrote it well. The same appears on the gates of hell."

In response to the Penal Laws, the filid of ancient times transformed into hedge school teachers. At the beginning of the 18th century, Protestant schoolmasters colluded with their Catholic counterparts by allowing them to take up positions as ushers, under-masters, and assistants in Protestant schools so they could earn a living while teaching their Catholic students. When this was discovered, however, laws were passed forbidding Catholics to work in schools. The Catholic teachers moved out to the countryside.

The purpose of the Penal Laws, which forbade Catholics an education, was not so much to reduce them to a state of ignorance and servitude as to force their children to take advantage of the Anglican schools available, which would train them to be loyal English Protestant subjects. This didn't happen. Instead, among the Catholics, teaching was done surreptitiously and schools were hidden away from public gaze. The safest area was considered to be beneath the sunny side of a hedge, and from this location they derived the name hedge schools. A pupil was usually placed on sentry duty to warn the master if a suspicious-looking stranger was approaching.

A wide variety of activities could be taking place in the classroom at any given time because all age groups were catered to. In a typical classroom scene Seamus would study his Greek as Bridget practiced her headlines and Maire learned her math tables while Sarah received speech therapy from the master's son. It would appear that enlightened chaos often ensued where the schoolmaster, like the head of any one-room school, had to be ringmaster of a myriad of intellectual animals. In general, discipline wasn't too severe. These hedge schools served as preparatory schools for students entering the priesthood, for service in foreign armies, and for trading on the continent or for employment at home.

The hedge schools offered an impressive range of subjects, including religion, history, arithmetic, book-keeping, science, surveying and land measuring, astronomy, geography, Latin, Greek, Hebrew, English, Irish and dancing. The livelihood of a hedge schoolmaster was largely dependent on his mathematical expertise as "the ordinary people of Ireland would set no store by a school in which arithmetic did not figure prominently."[7]

One prominent student of Trinity College in Dublin, Edmund Burke, claimed to have learned more Latin and Greek from an obscure schoolmaster on the banks of the River Nore in County Kilkenny than he afterwards acquired at the more celebrated places of education, including the university itself.

The hedge schoolmaster, a position only slightly less esteemed than that of priest among the common folk, had to survive in a very competitive academic market. Consequently student teachers had to undergo a long and arduous training under schoolmasters of repute. When the student teacher had learned all that was possible from the local hedge school-master, he issued a challenge to him. "This challenge was generally couched in rhyme, and either sent by the hands of a common friend, or posted upon the chapel-door."[8] The public viewed these contests with intense interest. If the student was defeated, he continued learning from his school master, but if he succeeded, he would seek out another teacher, often a great distance away, for this would be merely the first "of a series of challenges" which the pupil would have to undertake "before he eventually settled himself in the exercise of his profession."[8]

Many of these men saw teaching as their vocation. For some of them it was a hereditary position. The people dis-

---

[7] Martin Brenan, *Schools of Kildare and Leighlin A.D. 1775-1835* (Dublin, 1935).

[8] Antonia McManus, *The Irish Hedge School and Its Books, 1695-1831* (Dublin, 2002).

played their appreciation by conferring honorary titles on their best scholars and poets, "The bright star in mathematical learning," "The great Kinsella" and "The great O'Brien par excellence." One can understand why the hedge schoolmasters possessed such a high degree of professional pride.

The hedge schoolmaster was a central figure in the life of the community, serving his people in a multiplicity of roles, sometimes out of a sense of civic duty but more often out of economic necessity. He was the master of ceremonies at all wakes and funerals. He was the village scribe employed by the unlettered. He was also the cheap attorney of the neighborhood, who carried out an immense amount of legal work. Many were forced to work as part time laborers for subsistence. He was also the village surveyor. The people feared the satire of the hedge schoolmaster just as much as the priest's tirade from the pulpit. Nevertheless, most of these educators were destined to die in utter poverty.

Shaw Mason conducted a small experiment to test the accuracy of the hedge schoolmasters while they recited "poems attributed to Ossian, and other Bardic remains." He asked one to write down eight Ossianic poems. Later Shaw Mason compared their accuracy against those published in a volume entitled *Transactions of the Gaelic Society*, "and strange as it may seem, they were found to agree together word for word," with a few minor exceptions. The reason was the professional approach adopted by the schoolmasters themselves. They frequently met to recite their traditional stories and if anyone repeated a passage, which appeared to another to be incorrect, he was immediately stopped, the matter was then debated, and the dispute was "referred to a vote of the meeting. The decision of the majority" then became "imperative on the subject for the future."[9]

From the 16th to the 18th century, the percentage of land owned by Catholics in Ireland shrank dramatically. At the time of the Great Rebellion (1594-1603) Catholics owned 59%; after Cromwell's land settlement this fell to a mere 22%; after the Penal Laws of 1695 it fell even further to 14%; and finally in 1714 Catholics owned a stark 7% of Irish land.[10]

The Penal Laws affected not only land distribution but also tenure. By the 18th century the Irish had become a nation of tenant farmers ruled by the Protestant Ascendancy, and their life was one of desperation and deprivation. Nearly half of the rural population lived in small single-room, windowless mud cabins much worse than those lived in by their peasant ancestors 500 years previously. Some cabins contained a bed and chairs, but very few had such luxuries. Farm animals such as pigs and chickens normally lived in the cabin with the people. However, the cabins were warm in winter due to readily available peat. For food the Irish began consuming the new arrival from North America, which could be grown easily on small plots of land, the potato.

Greedy landowners increased their rental income by subdividing their lands again and again, until most families lived on less than an acre of land, paying rents double those in England. Since potatoes were such an efficient crop, landowners encouraged them as a source of food for their tenants. By the late 18th century it was practically the only crop grown on the tenants' small plots.[11] Many in their lifetime never tasted meat or bread: their every meal consisted of potatoes, and sometimes

---

[9] Antonia McManus, *The Irish Hedge School and Its Books, 1695-1831* (Dublin, 2002).

[10] Robert Kee, *Ireland a History* (London, 2003).

[11] Wheat, oats, barley, and rye continued to be grown on their lord's estates.

buttermilk. One visitor from France in the late 1700s noted that nowhere else in Europe had he seen such poverty as he saw in Ireland. "The Irish peasant is poorer than the lowest serfs in Poland and Germany."

In 1770, frustrated by violence breaking out between the English and the American colonies, Ben Franklin asked a British member of parliament how more stable relations could be obtained. The Englishman replied, "As you know, England has had numerous problems with the Irish. However, after applying a bit of influence, Ireland is now a peaceful addition to the king's empire. The same will be true with America." When Franklin visited Ireland the next year, he was treated to a round of extravagant parties and lavish dinners at several large estates around Dublin. One day he told his driver he wished to see some of the local farms, and after traveling several miles over almost impassable roads they came in sight of a large field where stacks of hay had been gathered. On one side of the road was a row of low, dark mounds, and as they got nearer Franklin saw that the mounds were made of mud. Then, to his surprise, people began emerging from these mounds: men, women, and children clothed in nothing but rags and all as thin as skeletons. Franklin, realizing these mud mounds were homes, asked his driver, "Who are these people?"

The driver replied, "They're Irish people, sir." Franklin was furious. It became all too apparent what was meant by "applying a bit of influence" on Ireland.

George Cooper, a British lawyer traveling in rural Ireland in 1799, described the interior of a typical mud hut:

> The hut was carved out of a bog. The wall of the bog formed 3 sides of the hut, and sod taken from the adjoining surface formed the remaining side and the roof. There were no windows nor was there a chimney. There is an opening in front, approximately 4 feet in height which served as door, window

and chimney. Light, smoke, pigs, and people all pass in and out of this aperture.

To enter, I had to go on all fours. The darkness and stifling turf smoke for awhile prevented me from seeing anything. The inhabitants then lit small rushes for more light and I was able to discern the size of this human burrow. In a space of seven to ten feet square there was a family of eight people, men, women and children, in this filthy stinking hole, squatting round the peat fire or lying on the damp ground. As for furniture, one or two broken stools and a "boiling pot" in which they cooked their potatoes. In a slightly raised space was spread straw upon which they all slept. As for clothes, all were wearing nothing but tattered rags.

I cannot conceive of any country where the situation is as miserable as that of the Irish peasantry. The condition of the Negro slaves in the West Indies is a paradise compared to it. The slave in our colonies has meat to eat and distilled spirits to drink, while the life of the Irish peasant is that of a savage who feeds upon milk and roots.

The fact that the vast majority of native Irish were desperately poor and illiterate from the 17th century on makes it very difficult for any descendants to trace their roots. Ancestors are not listed in deeds, wills or probate records, and there are no family letters or journals. Family history, if it was to be communicated, was oral. An example comes from an acquaintance of the authors, Kitty (Kinsella) Coffey, who told a story about a direct ancestor of hers, Thady Kinsella, living in the early 18th century on the estate of the Earl of Kildare in the town of Rathvilly in County Carlow. Home to the Kinsellas for over 1,000 years, this area was where Crimthann, the son of "glorious Enna," became the first Christian Leinster righ in the 5th century. Kitty recounted that one May day in 1732 the earl stopped Thady and told him that he wanted his daughter to report for work at the mansion the next day. Thady, knowing that the earl had a reputation for "having an eye for pretty young girls," looked the earl straight in the eye and said, "She will not be going to work in the mansion." Knowing the consequences of such a refusal, he quickly added, "so I'll be moving my family off this land tomorrow." The red-faced earl angrily replied, "Not only your family, but I want every person with that accursed name of Kinsella off my land forever."

The influence of the Protestant Ascendancy in Ireland reached its political peak in the 18th century owing to the loss of voting and office-holding privileges by the Catholic majority. The constant injustices suffered by the Catholic peasants led to local insurgencies, such as murdering local landlords, which became common. These insurgencies in turn became the precursors of more organized political movements in later years. In 1761 the Whiteboy movement began in the south. The Oakboys started in the north in 1763. In 1769 the Steelboy disturbances began in Antrim, and in 1785 the Rightboy movement started in Munster.

In the next century Revans, the secretary of the British Royal Commission of 1832-40, attributed the cause of Ireland's poverty:

> To a landlord system that profits from the intense competition of labourers [for land] to exact from the farmers an excessive rent. From the moment a farmer begins to make a profit, the landlord raises the price of the lease. The result is that the farmer is afraid to make improvements, for fear of being taxed by his master for a much higher sum than his improvement would be worth to him, and he confines himself strictly to subsisting.[12]

The extremely harsh treatment meted out to Irish Catholics did not meet the approval of all the English officials, many of

---

[12] Tim Pat Coogan, *Ireland in the 20th Century* (New York, 2006).

whom favored a relaxation of the Penal Laws. Some of the English, developing their own country through the introduction of new canals and roads, wished to similarly improve Ireland to gain wealth, but the Protestant aristocracy of Ireland fought such measures fiercely for fear their power might be reduced. They were content with slothful exploitation of their privilege and lived dissolute and useless lives. A few in the English government reasoned that unjust laws such as the Penal Laws would only lead to resentment followed by rebellion. After much prodding, in 1750 the English allowed Irish Catholics to join the army, but only as privates. In 1771 the Bogland Act was passed, allowing them to take leases on not more than 50 acres of unprofitable land (bogland). In 1778, the Gavelkind Act was repealed so that Catholics could inherit land on the same terms as Protestants.[13] As the penal laws were relaxed after 1782, the hedge schools moved indoors. Such partial measures were "too little, too late." When a body of several thousand people marched through the streets of Dublin in 1779, one of the English members of parliament commented, "England has sown her laws like dragons teeth and they have sprung up armed men."

The outbreak of the French Revolution in 1789 encouraged some in the Protestant and Presbyterian middle-class to campaign in the mid-1790s for reform of the representative system under the banner of the United Irishmen. Theobald Wolfe Tone, one of its notable leaders, published a pamphlet entitled "An argument on behalf of the Catholics of Ireland." The United Irishmen tried to unite Protestants and Catholics against English rule. Northern Wexford, home to the Kinsellas, was known to be a hotbed of support for the United Irishmen.

---

[13] Catholics no longer had to divide their land among all family members upon the death of the father, which diminished the land for each succeeding generation to such an extent that it was too small to live on.

Among the few records remaining from that time is one of a Terence Kinsella of Coolabullen who had been sworn into the organization.

This political action worried the English enough to have them pass the Act for the Relief of 1793. Although not granting full civil rights, the act lifted restrictions on Catholics to buy and sell land and to educate their children. The act also granted the right to practice at the bar, to marry Protestants, and to vote (if they owned land worth £2 or more), although only Protestant candidates could win election.

In response to such concessions, the Protestants of Ulster formed the militant Orange Order in 1795. They took their title from William of Orange, who had defeated the Catholic forces under James II at the Battle of the Boyne in 1690, and who had established the Protestant Ascendancy of Ireland. The goal of the Order was to prevent the union of Protestant and Catholic, which the United Irishmen were trying to promote. They would become far more powerful during the next century.

While some in the Protestant Ascendancy felt England had gone too far to benefit the Irish Catholics, Wolfe Tone and his United Irishmen felt they had not done enough. In 1796, Tone convinced the French to sail a military force to Ireland. Making it all the way to the Irish coast, they were turned back in Bantry Bay by terrible weather. Some in the Irish parliament made a last appeal to the government in 1797 to calm and conciliate the country by accepting a reform of the Irish parliament and a final removal of religious disabilities. But in England from the king on down it was clear that such measures were not to be hoped for, and all proposals to help Ireland were defeated. Finally, in May 1798, rebellion broke out.

The only formidable uprising took place in a quarter where no one would have expected it. County Wexford had experienced foreign rule longer than any other part of Ireland. On

May 26, a rebellion that was not suppressed until June 30 began in Wexford, led by Father John Murphy, who proved himself a very able leader. Northeast Wexford, led by a Protestant from near Gorey named Anthony Perry, would play a vital role. He was seized on May 23rd of 1798 by the British militia, comprised of men from County Cork, and tortured for 48 hours in Gorey. Edward Hay, in his *History of the Irish Insurrection of 1798*, gives the following account of Perry's torture:

> The noted sergeant nicknamed Tom the Devil – gave him woeful experience of his ingenuity and adroitness at devising torment. As a specimen of his savoir faire, he cut off the hair of his head very closely, cut the sign of the cross from the front to the back, and transversely from ear to ear, still closer; and probably a pitched cap[14] not being in readiness, gunpowder was mixed through the hair, which was then set on fire, and the shocking process repeated, until every atom of hair that remained could be easily pulled out by the roots; and still a burning candle was continually applied, until the entire was completely singed away, and the head left totally and miserably blistered.[15]

Under this torture Anthony Perry revealed the names of those he had been in contact with, including a John Kinnshela of Inch. Perry was not condemned by his fellow Irishmen for

---

[14] The term refers to the torture where pitch was poured on top of a head and lit on fire.

[15] The Irish memory is long. A hundred years after this event, in 1890, when Wexford was playing against Cork in a hurly match, the Wexfordmen were deemed too rough and Cork was awarded the victory. A ballad commemorating the game had the following lines: "Tom Murphy and Will Neville / Began to lay them level, / When they thought of Tom the Devil / With his pitch-cap and shears." From Fiachra O'Lionain, *Croghan to the Sea* (Enniscorthy).

his confession, and when he later escaped, he went on to show the greatest bravery in the coming month's engagements.

In various engagements, the Wexford men, who were generally armed only with pikes but had a few hundred musketeers, defeated small bodies of English troops, acquired confidence and increased in numbers, until they occupied the town of Wexford and held most of County Wexford. To maintain their cause, they needed to cut their way out to the surrounding counties, but several determined battles failed to give them the opening they needed.

By this time thousands of English militia were on their way to Ireland.[16] The Wexford rebels made Vinegar Hill at Enniscorthy their headquarters. On June 21, General Lake stormed it with an army of 13,000 men adequately supplied with muskets and cannon. As they moved their cannon expertly up the slopes, raking the hill with devastating volleys, one eyewitness account relates that "the Irish fell as though cut down with a giant scythe." Armed only with 12-foot pikes, the Irish launched desperate downhill charges at the cannon and lines of redcoats. Women and children fought alongside their men, but their undoubted physical courage could make little impression on the advance of the disciplined troops below them. After two hours of slaughter, Father Murphy directed a retreat. The rebels poured through a gap, leaving more than 500 dead on the hill.

---

[16] By the end of the year the English would have an army of 100,000 men in Ireland. In comparison, they sent 30,000 men to America in response to the Declaration of Independence of 1776. The English took every Irish revolt very seriously.

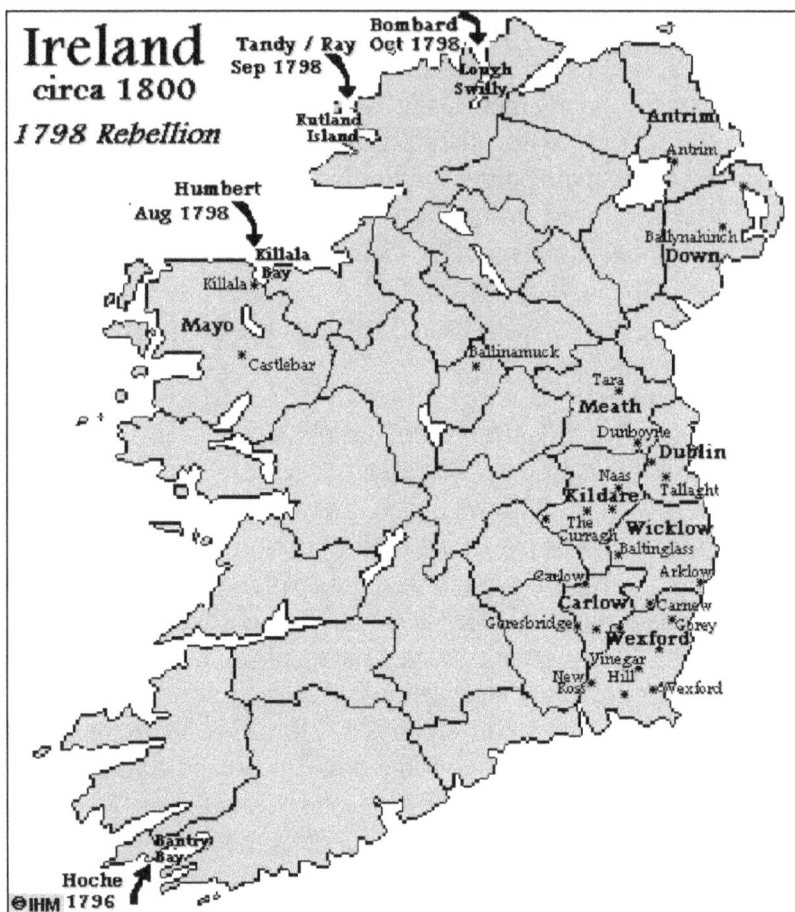

General Lake, the British Commander-in-Chief during 1798, ordered his troops after Vinegar Hill to hunt down and kill any rebels, wounded or not. In addition he issued an order to burn to the ground the hospital in Enniscorthy that was caring for hundreds of wounded Irish soldiers.

The English recovered Wexford town, and the rebellion in the county came to an end with 30,000 killed. Executions followed. One remnant of the Wexford army under Father John

Murphy penetrated into County Kilkenny hoping to raise the people, but after a defeat the remnant made their way home and dispersed. Father John Murphy was captured and in the market square in Tullow, County Carlow, he was tied to a triangle, the shirt was ripped off his back, and he was lashed repeatedly as officers interrogated him. Father Murphy refused to say anything and was taken from the whipping frame and hanged on a mobile gallows. When his body was taken down, his head was hacked off. Some soldiers set it on a spike outside the courthouse and then stuffed his torso in a tar barrel, which they set alight. One of the houses in Tullow market square was occupied by a prosperous Catholic family, the Callaghans. The soldiers set the blazing barrel outside their house and, pushing past the children, went inside. "There could be no objection in this house to the incense of a priest," they shouted as they forced open all the windows to let in "the holy smoke."[17]

Another remnant of the Wexford army, under Anthony Perry, marched north through Gorey. The English of northern Wexford had heard of the defeat at Vinegar Hill and began celebrating by ransacking the local countryside. Miles Byrne, one of the men in the Wexford army, said:

> They [the English] began to murder all they met, crossed and scoured the country in every direction, entered the houses, killing those even who lay sick, plundering and robbing the people of everything they thought worth taking away. . . . These cowards were at their work of extermination on Friday, the 22nd of June, when a division of our army, on its way to the Wicklow mountains came up. They saw several women lying with their bowels ripped up, and young children grasped in their arms; they became furious at the sight of such horrors, and a general cry for vengeance ran through the column. The route was changed and

[17] Alistair Moffat, *The Sea Kingdoms* (London, 2002).

orders given to scour the country on each side of the road to Gorey; those savages were found in various houses committing all kinds of crimes; they were beaten and driven back upon Gorey where they attempted to rally and give battle, but here again they were defeated, and pursued on the road to Arklow with great loss.

The Irish didn't follow up their success, instead turning back to reach the Wicklow mountains where they kept up the insurrection for a few more months.

Martin Kinsella, whose family was originally from the Wexford town, remembers hearing about three Kinsella brothers who fought in the 1798 uprising: "Two of the brothers were killed at Graige Bridge, the other escaped to Ballyfin in County Laois."

Written history does not remember the Irish peasant during these hard times; only the ancient Gaelic repository, oral history, can be relied on.[18] "A priest from Portlaoise recalled a story told to him when he was young by an old man who was himself a boy in 1798":

> A man called to his father's house asking for some food and a place to rest. The man was taken inside the house but, before entering, he left a sack, containing something, outside the door. The boy's curiosity got the better of him and he peeped inside the sack where he found the body of a boy.
>
> The man was a Wexfordman and had fought at the battle of Clonard together with his 14-year-old son. The boy had been killed there and the father said that he was carrying the body

---

[18] If you want to provide such oral history, please email the information to www.kinsella.org, and we will include it along with your name in future updates to this book.

back to Wexford so that he could bury it with his own people. The man was traveling by night and resting by day.[19]

---

[19] Alistair Moffat, *The Sea Kingdoms* (London, 2002).

Depravity and Death

Ireland no sooner saw the dawn of the 19th century than it found itself integrated with Britain by the Act of Union, which became effective in 1801. Years earlier Dr. Samuel Johnson, the famous English writer, had prophetically declared to the Irish, "Do not make an union with us [Britain], Sir. We should unite with you, only to rob you."[1] The 1798 rebellion had changed the minds of the Protestant Ascendancy from anti-union to pro-union while the vast majority of the country, the Catholic Irish, remained firmly anti-union. Ireland now faced another century in which its Gaelic identity would be increasingly de-emphasized. Britain, continuing the policy of eradicating Irish culture, which it had begun at least 300 years previously under the Tudors, now clung to the belief that the Irish could be converted to British ways through education. In pursuit of this goal they created charter schools. Predictably this attempt at rescuing the Irish from being Irish not only failed, but increased the support both Catholics and Presbyterians gave to the non-denominational fee-paying hedge schools.

The Irish were fervent about two things, religion and education. Lord Palmerston acknowledged the great sacrifices

---

[1] James Boswell, *Boswell's Life of Johnson,* ed. G. B. Hill, rev. L. F. Powell (Oxford, 1934-64): iii, 410. Johnson followed this remark with the comment, "We should have robbed the Scotch, if they had had anything of which we could have robbed them." Scotland and England had joined in Union in 1706.

made by his Irish speaking tenants of County Sligo in 1808 to secure a hedge school education for their children: "The thirst for education is so great that there are now three or four schools upon the estate. The people join in engaging some itinerant master: they run him up a miserable mud hut in the roadside, and the boys pay him half-a-crown, or some five shillings a quarter." There were even cases where desperate parents kidnapped a hedge schoolmaster from another area. In one case the teacher was forbidden to travel a mile from his new home until he had trained a replacement. The imprisonment lasted five years, at the end of which the schoolmaster had no desire to leave the people to whom he had become so attached.

While hedge schoolmasters remained key figures in local communities, promoting traditional customs such as festival gatherings, the "merry wake," and religious patterns, the local priest began to distance himself from such things.[2] This was initiated early in the 19th century by reforms in the Roman Catholic church. First passed were rules forbidding priests from attending a variety of festive gatherings and places of amusement. The situation deteriorated further when priests were obliged to adopt a distinctive clerical dress, highlighting their difference from the local people, and was not helped by their repeated threats of excommunication against the common people for attendance at patterns and their condemnation of irreverent practices at wakes.

While Britain and the Roman Catholic church struggled for different reasons to submerge the Irish culture, the Irish way of life continued. Hector Urquhart describes how they passed

---

[2] Patterns were outdoor pilgrimages to a religious location, often on the feast day of a local saint, which could attract thousands of people. The rituals carried out at a pattern, often of pagan origins, didn't require the sanction or presence of a priest.

their culture along, outside of the hedge schools, at the beginning of the 19th century:

> It was also the custom when a stranger, celebrated for his store of tales, came on a visit to the village, for us, young and old, to make a rush to the house where he passed the night, and choose our seats, some on beds, some on forms, and others on three-legged stools, etc., and listen in silence to new tales . . . .

Closer to the end of that century James Logan wrote:

> It was usual for the young women of a baile, or hamlet, which consisted of from four to twenty families, to carry their work to the houses of each other's parents alternatively. In these societies oral learning was attained without interrupting industry, and the pleasure of instructing and receiving knowledge was mutual. The matron, visited on one evening, perhaps excelled at genealogy; while another was well versed in general history; one may have been adept at poetry, and another an able critic; etc. The Gael, after his daily occupations, hastened to join the society of the young women, where he met his beloved, or had the pleasure, in her absence, of repeating the last sonnet he had composed in her praise, for which he either received applause or encountered disapprobation.

The daughter of a British army officer stationed in Connacht following the rebellion of 1798 was astonished to find that she could roam the wild mountains of the area without fear of molestation, while in England no girl could ramble in the woods and fields alone, even though at this time Irishmen who had taken part in the rebellion were being hanged by the British on a nearby (Ballina) bridge. She would, she wrote, "have fearlessly trusted" the Irish peasantry "in any circumstances." The intelligence of the people surprised her.

I never met a solitary peasant in my rambles but I addressed him, and by this means got stores of legendary lore. One man I remember told me the subjects of most of Ossian's tales, in his own version of English." Returning to England five years later she was "greatly struck by the vulgarity of everyone . . . we happened to stop opposite a cottage and . . . asked for a glass of water. It was brought . . . and the woman asked for payment. An Irish woman would have considered it an insult to be offered such. The cottages were clean and neat and the country looked clean in comparison but the manners were far inferior."

Though the Irish were ridiculed and oppressed by the British to the point of starvation, when S. C. Curwen visited Ireland in 1818 he was surprised by their high spirits and the warm atmosphere that filled their miserable cabins. They exhibited a "warmth of heart – an overflowing of the kindest domestic affections, and of the purest joys of life." He was amazed by the Gaelic veneration for family and remarked, "In no country are conjugal and parental affections exceeded more warmly or powerfully felt, or more sincerely and unaffectedly exhibited, than in Ireland." Another Englishman named Young commented, "the circumstances which struck me most in the common Irish were, vivacity and a great and eloquent volubility of speech . . . . They are infinitely more cheerful and lively than anything we commonly see in England, having nothing of that incivility of sullen silence with which so many Englishmen seem to wrap themselves up, as if retiring within their own importance." Young was also struck by the fact that such an impoverished people thought so highly of the arts that they would actually pay dancing masters to teach their children.

In 1829, J. E. Bicheno, a political servant of Britain, traveled across Ireland even though he had been warned against this by his Protestant friends and said:

We traveled in spite of our forebodings, and had never the slightest reason to regret our determination, our only care being not to be mistaken for Irish gentlemen [of the Protestant Ascendancy]. Not a finger was ever lifted against us, but the most cheerful assistance was afforded to us in every difficulty; and although we traveled in the most disturbed districts, and among people who were sheltering murderers, and some of them murderers themselves, I am satisfied they might have been trusted with untold gold; and it is certain, that they are ready to share their scanty meal with the needy, and to relieve one another by acts of kindness, to which the more civilized poor of England are strangers.[3]

While the Irish culture remained, many realized that it was in jeopardy. After rebellion had failed, cooler heads turned to political reform. Daniel O'Connell, who was to become known as "the Liberator," effectively organized the Irish Catholics during the early 19th century and pressured the government into giving them more rights. After decades, he succeeded dramatically when the Roman Catholic Emancipation Act, allowing Catholics to hold office, was passed in 1829, repealing the last of the Penal Laws.

The Act contained more than just emancipation, however. It also included a small change in voting laws that had devastating consequences. Previously anyone leasing lands worth 40 shillings (£2) a year was qualified to vote. The new Act bumped this amount up to £10, which reduced the number of Catholic voters to 92,000 males, barely 1% of the population, and removed politics from their landlord's priorities. Before 1829, the landlord purposely settled 40-shilling tenants thickly on his land to exploit them as a voting block. After 1829, these

---

[3] J. E. Bicheno, *Ireland and Its Economy; Being the Result of Observations Made in a Tour through the Country in the Autumn of 1829* (London, 1830).

smaller tenants lost their political value so landlords introduced grazing animals, always more cost effective, to take their place.

Through all this the Irish kept their self-respect. J. G. Kohl, a teacher from Germany, visited Ireland in 1842 and wrote, "In many countries, when a stranger visits the huts of the poor, he must undergo a long and scrutinizing stare before they feel comfortable in his presence. With the Irish it is quite the reverse. Poor and half-naked though they may be, such accommodation as they have is instantly offered to their well-dressed visitor without embarrassment; and though they never forget to address him politely, as 'your honour,' they always appear to consider him . . . their equal."[4]

The British, belatedly recognizing their previous plan of charter schools was a total failure and realizing emancipation gave the Catholic Irish a chance to fight politically for their culture, created a national education system for Ireland in 1831. They had improved their concept of charter schools by enlisting the aid of a segment of the Irish population who were envious of the respect accorded the hedge schoolmasters, the teachers who fueled the life of the Irish culture. Britain enlisted the aid of the Catholic priest, who would now share managerial power and the right to catechize in Irish schools on equal terms with his Protestant counterpart. The churchmen eagerly opened their schools to British trained schoolteachers, who "will aid us in a work of great difficulty, to wit that of suppressing hedge schools."[5] The hedge schoolmaster, attacked by both Church and State, still managed to survive until a third, far more devastating adversary appeared in the 1840s.

In 1843, a British government commission reported that the agriculture of Ireland was good with three quarters of the land being used to cultivate wheat and other crops. The health of

---

[4] J. G. Kohl, *Travels in Ireland* (London, 1844).
[5] P. J. Dowling, *A History of Irish Education* (Cork, 1971).

the country, however, was not rated so highly. Living conditions of country people in Ireland had suffered such a grievous decline that one commission concluded people had lived better in the 1770s than their grandchildren did now.[6] Well over two million, almost a third of the population, subsisted on the verge of starvation for eight months of the year, getting enough to eat only in the four months following harvest. A commission warned that if a severe failure of the potato crop were to occur, it could result in extreme hardship to these people. It criticized the system whereby landowners paid their laborers with a scrap of land on which to throw up a hut and plant a potato garden. Because the laborers weren't paid in cash, they were tied to this scrap of land, unable to leave no matter how much work the landlord required from them.[7] The system discouraged self-improvement, thereby encouraging idleness.

> Countless were the cases of tenants renting uncultivated poor ground at the foot of the mountain at a few shillings an acre. After a few years, when by their own labor they had raised the value of the land, they were forced to leave their farms and move higher up the mountain to begin again on uncultivated land. This went on until those who began to cultivate the soil at the foot of the mountain were, by progressive removals, forced as near the top of the mountain as the land allowed. They were thus defrauded of the fruits of their early hard labor and forced to end their days in want and misery, with the added mortification of daily seeing the ground they had in their youth brought into cultivation occupied by others. Yes, it was difficult to help a country whose laws made a mockery of self-help and instilled in the peasantry the conviction that it was better to leave squalor well

---

[6] Those living in the 1770s lived in a far worse situation than their ancestors had in the 1170s. See the previous chapter entitled "A 12th-Century Commoner" for a description of living standards then.

[7] Donald MacKay, *Flight from Famine* (Toronto, 1990).

enough alone.[8]

Britain paid little heed to these commissions because by 1843 another generation of Irish was again preparing to battle the Protestant Ascendancy. The government garrisoned Ireland with an army so large that by 1844 the number of troops in Ireland was greater than the number in India, a country with thirty five times the population and almost fifty times the area. Britain, the most powerful government on earth, was terrified of another Irish uprising.

In 1845, another government commission wrote they could not "forbear expressing our strong sense of the patient endurance which the laboring classes have exhibited under sufferings greater, we believe, than the people of any other country in Europe have to sustain." By the late summer of 1845, a blight struck the potato crop in several areas of Ireland, appearing first in Counties Wexford, around Gorey where the Kinsellas were concentrated, and County Waterford. A local paper wrote in September of 1845, "a most extensive failure of the potato crop . . . particularly between Gorey and the sea."[9] Unlike previous blights, which were attributable to either bad weather or to diseases that destroyed only a few potatoes in any given farmer's field, this was a new disease which spared no potatoes once it entered a field system. Its devastation of a farmer's crop was total. This crisis would test the union of Ireland and England – a test that the union failed.

By October it was discovered that between a quarter and a third of the yearly average for the potato crop was lost, with the blight concentrating in diverse areas, allowing those not affected to help those in need. A good potato crop the next year would allow Ireland to recover. For now, Britain ordered

---

[8] Thomas Gallagher, *Paddy's Lament: Ireland 1846-47* (New York, 1982).
[9] *Conservative*, Wexford paper, 9/27/1845.

enough Indian corn from America to feed the country over the next three months, enough to cover the starvation period until the crop came in for 1846. While Britain was inclined to cautious optimism with this news, deep pessimism was characteristic of a broad spectrum of Irish public opinion. It struck many as scandalous that while the potato crop was melting away, the abundant oat crop, widely touted as a partial substitute, was rapidly being exported out of the country, a situation the government refused to stop.

> If the people were more fully and effectually represented, we cannot believe that such things could be. If Ireland had a Parliament of her own, we are convinced that the lives of the Irish people could not be held as a matter of endless and unproductive discussion.[10]

Eviction, more than starvation, became the terror in 1845. With the little money a laborer earned from the sale of garden goods going toward food and the family pig slaughtered to the same end, there was no money left to pay exorbitant rents. Historians have generally credited the British government under the Tories with reacting promptly to the partial potato failure of 1845. Unfortunately for Ireland, the Tories were voted out of power in the summer of 1845, and the Whigs took over.

The potatoes of 1846 grew lush and green in the early summer. A month before harvest, in August, blight much worse than in 1845 struck again. To use the adjectives "total" and "universal" in reference to the failure of 1846 is hardly exaggeration. Since much of the potato usually used as seed had been eaten after the failure of 1845, fewer potatoes had been planted for 1846, which strengthened the calamity. This

---

[10] *Independent*, Wexford paper, 2/25/1846.

of course would be an even larger problem for the following year, 1847.

Charles Trevelyan, the head of the British Treasury, insisted that the government should not respond with major relief efforts because "the supply of the home market may safely be left to the foresight of private merchants." He did, however, propose minimal intervention: government food depots were set up on the west coast, where the land was poorest, but they were not to compete with local merchants, i.e. they were only to be opened to the public in the advent that local food supplies were inadequate. Trevelyan was urged to purchase Indian corn in late July but he ignored this warning. By the end of August almost all of his depots were out of food. He scrambled to increase the official stocks of food but even then his initial purchases, each which would take months to deliver, were quite small.[11]

By the fall of 1846, Irish landlords were exporting grain out of Ireland again, regardless of the obvious famine looming. Trevelyan's decision, never questioned by his political masters, was to rigidly adhere to the economic doctrine of laissez-faire. His expressed concern, that stalling or reducing exports of grain from Ireland would paralyze trade, was unbelievable. He only needed to delay the export for the few months it would take to fill the fateful gap in domestic food supplies until the Indian corn ordered from America began to reach Irish shores in December.

---

[11] Initially the government allowed foreign food aid into Ireland only through British ships, so ships from America had to arrive in England where the food could be taken off and put on British ships. This created jobs for England's unemployed. By early 1847 world opinion, together with the obvious scale of the disaster, caused this to be retracted.

An eviction

The true famine, later to be called the Great Famine, began to show itself in the fall of 1846. Some resident landlords refused to evict their tenants who were unable to pay rent. The same was rarely true of absentee landlords, who were in the majority during the Great Famine, because they neither witnessed nor had any emotional involvement in the evictions. One absentee landlord served notices to his tenants to pay the November rent. The tenants asked for time, saying they had only a few black potatoes left. "What the devil do we care about you or your black potatoes?" replied the rent collector. "It is not us that made them black. You will get two days to pay the rent, and if you don't you know the consequence."[12]

Sir Charles Wood, chancellor of the British exchequer, said in a letter to Lord Monteagle, a landlord in Ireland: "I am not at all appalled by your tenantry going. That seems to me a neces-

---

[12] Thomas Gallagher, *Paddy's Lament* (New York, 1982).

sary part of the process . . . . We must not complain of what we really want to obtain." Sheep and cattle were more cost-effective on the land than tenants. From 1847 to 1850, fifty-thousand evictions took place in Ireland.[13]

Grisly stories of the starvation that quickly set in, and first affected the young and old, began to circulate. One was of a boy dying on the floor who could not be helped because those around him were too close to his own weakened condition to stand. Yet the father of such a family walked, or tried to walk, in his bare feet six to ten miles to the public works in order to obtain the necessary food to keep his wife and children alive, until he too fell and died, often with the food his family needed in a bag beside his body.

With the arrival of the Indian corn months later, the depots were once again full, but they operated under Trevelyan's inflexible view that unless prices were allowed to attain the full market rate, Ireland would be worse off. Of course the depot owners over-charged. From one inspecting officer in County Leitrim came the report that "the miserable condition of the half-famished people is greatly increased by the exorbitant . . . price of meal and provisions, insomuch that the wages gained by them on the works are quite inadequate to purchase a sufficiency to feed many large families." Feeding the starving peasants who weren't strong enough to work was discouraged for fear they would become accustomed to such handouts and grow lazy. Foreign shipments of free food were turned away.

Trevelyan's plan to feed the starving Irish who couldn't pay for food at the depot was to set up a well-funded system of public works. The Irish were to be paid for improving their country as long as these improvements didn't interfere with the economic status quo. As an example, building a new road or bridge that helped one landowner bring his crops to market

---

[13] R. F. Foster, *Modern Ireland 1600-1972* (London, 1989).

cheaper than before would hurt those he competed with and so had to be avoided. Numerous roads leading nowhere, bridges on dry land, etc. can still be found today as memorials to this effort. Part of the Poor Law Relief Act stipulated: "All able bodied males receiving relief must work eight hours each day." (Stone breaking was the most common form of employment for such people.) An Irish paper in 1848 states:

> Rising from the ground reeling like men recovering from sea-sickness and having steadied themselves by an effort and brushed off the perspiration of death from their pallid brows, resumed their labour and remained at their post until the ten hours task was completed. Then and not till then 'for such are the Commissioners instructions' they received their tickets for food. With fainting heart and trembling frames they sit down to their scanty meal at evening tide – the first food of the day. What a system of relief?[14]

The winter of 1846-47 was "the most severe in living memory" and the longest.[15] Frost was continuous and icy gales blew hurricanes of snow, hail and sleet, creating appalling conditions in north Wexford which were described in the local and national press:

> Our accounts from the northern parts of the county [Wexford] are most deplorable. What the poor people earn on the public works is barely sufficient to support them. All their earnings go for food and the consequence is that they have nothing left to buy clothes. Since the extreme cold set in, sickness and death have followed in its train. Inflammation of the lungs, fever and other maladies resulting from excessive privation, have been bearing away their victims, many died in the course of last week

---

[14] *Independent*, Wexford paper, 8/23/1848.
[15] Cecil Woodham-Smith, *The Great Hunger* (New York, 1962).

. . . . The Government should prevent exports, put a stop to distillation and buy the corn remaining in the country, bring in more as required, form provision depots and supply food to the people at such prices as they can afford . . . the maxim of political economy must be cast to the wind.[16]

Unsanitary housing, over crowding, poverty, and dirt created the right environment for typhus, and the fever flared up whenever additional hardship such as shortage of food or fuel or severe weather prevailed. When reports of mass deaths began coming in during the spring of 1847 the British Whig government, in a terribly belated confession of failure, performed a total about face and began distributing free food.

James H. Tuke, an English Quaker philanthropist who had visited the United States and spent several weeks in Ireland in 1847, had this to say:

I have visited the wasted remnants of the once noble Red Man on his reservation grounds in North America, and explored the "Negro quarter" of the degraded and enslaved African . . . but never have I seen misery so intense, or physical degradation so complete, as among the dwellers in the bogholes of Ireland.[17]

In the spring of 1847, though urged to buy and distribute seed, the government refused to do so for a variety of reasons, one being the fear that farmers would be discouraged from preserving their own. In fact, with Indian meal selling at famine prices in the winter of 1846-47 and the subsequent spring, laborers and smallholders had no choice but to consume their seed potatoes if they wanted to stay alive. When they should have planted, they could not. Only 1/7 of the total planted for

---

[16] *Independent*, Wexford paper, 12/12/1846.
[17] James Hack Tuke, *A Visit to Connaught in the Autumn of 1847* (London, 1847).

1846 was planted for 1847. The cruel irony of this situation
was that the warm, dry weather of the spring and summer of
1847 kept the destructive blight at bay, and the national average was excellent. But because of minimal planting, the total
crop was no larger and perhaps even smaller than in the cata-
strophic season of 1846.

Christine Kineally writes in *The Great Calamity*:

> The response of the British Government to the famine was in-
> adequate in terms of humanitarian criteria, and increasingly after
> 1847, systematically and deliberately so. The localized short-
> ages that followed the blight of 1845 were adequately dealt with
> but, as the shortages became more widespread, the government
> retrenched. With the short-lived exception of the soup kitchens,
> access to relief – or even more importantly, access to food – be-
> came more restricted. That the response illustrated a view of
> Ireland and its people as distant and marginal is hard to deny.
> What, perhaps, is more surprising is that a group of officials and
> their non-elected advisers were able to dominate government
> policy to such a great extent.
>
> This relatively small group of people, taking advantage of a
> passive establishment, and public opinion, which was opposed to
> further financial aid for Ireland, were able to manipulate a theory
> of free enterprise, thus allowing a massive social injustice to be
> perpetrated within a part of the United Kingdom. There was no
> shortage of resources to avoid the tragedy of a famine. Within
> Ireland itself, there were substantial resources of food which, had
> the political will existed, could have been diverted, even as a
> short-term measure, to supply a starving people. Instead, the
> government pursued the objective of economic, social and agrar-
> ian reform as a long-term aim, although the price paid for this
> ultimately elusive goal was privation, disease, emigration, mor-
> tality and an enduring legacy of disenchantment.[18]

---

[18] Christine Kineally, *The Great Calamity, The Irish Famine, 1845-52*
(Boulder, Co., 1994).

Many British officials viewed the Great Famine as a God-sent solution to the Irish problem. Nassau Senior, a professor of political economy at Oxford and a staunch supporter of the views of the British treasury, had a discussion with his Oxford colleague, Benjamin Jowett, during the Great Famine. Jowett later remarked, "I have always felt a certain horror of political economists, since I heard one of them say that he feared the famine . . . in Ireland would not kill more than a million people, and that would scarcely be enough to do any good."

William Bennett, a well-to-do Englishman, writes of his six-week stay in Ireland in 1847:

> My hand trembles while I write. The scenes of human misery and degradation we witnessed still haunt my imagination, with the vividness and power of some horrid and tyrannous delusion, rather than the features of a sober reality. We entered a cabin. Stretched in one dark corner, scarcely visible, from the smoke and rags that covered them, were three children huddled together, lying there because they were too weak to rise, pale and ghastly, their little limbs – on removing a portion of the filthy covering – perfectly emaciated, eyes sunk, voice gone, and evidently in the last stage of actual starvation. Crouched over the turf embers was another form, wild and all but naked, scarcely human in appearance. It stirred not, nor noticed us. On some straw, sodden upon the ground moaning piteously, was a shriveled old woman, imploring us to give her something – baring her limbs partly, to show how the skin hung loose from the bones.

Another severe winter followed 1847's famine, causing more deaths than ever as the people, weakened by starvation and disease, were unable to withstand its rigors. An extraordinary effort in the spring of 1848 was mounted to bring the potato back from near-oblivion even in the face of the continuing scarcity of seed. But in contrast to the previous season, the summer of 1848 was exceptionally wet, and blight again raged all over the country. In the path of famine, plague spread also, so typhoid fever and dysentery became another cause for death.

The response of the citizens of the United States to the appeal for starving Ireland was "on a scale unparalleled in history." In spite of anti-Irish feeling, huge sums of money and large amounts of food were sent to Ireland, although much was diverted into the pockets of greedy merchants. Another source of aid was the Irish themselves. The Gaelic clans, now spread throughout the world, consistently sent money home. "I am proud to say," wrote Jacob Harvey, "that the Irish in America have always remitted more money, ten times over, than all the foreigners put together!" Between 1848 and 1867 an estimated £34,000,000 was sent back from America to Britain, 40% of it in the form of pre-paid tickets.[19]

The British government began referring to the Great Famine as Divine Providence. This was a clever ploy to avoid responsibility while accepting the loss of millions of Irish who were no longer needed on the estates in Ireland. It also was an attempt to placate the starving Irish themselves who should see this "visitation of Providence" as an opportunity to inspire them "with confidence in Divine mercy and thus enable them to endure their sufferings with patience, to be resigned to the appointment of the Almighty and to bear every stroke, even that of death by hunger in humble submission to the Will of God."[20]

"They call it God's famine!" cried a distraught Bishop Hughes from a pulpit in New York City. "No! No! God's famine is known by the general scarcity of food which is its consequence. There is no general scarcity – but political econ-omy, finding Ireland too poor to buy the produce of its own

---

[19] R. F. Foster, *Modern Ireland 1600-1972* (London, 1989).
[20] *Independent*, Wexford paper, 7/17/1848.

labor, exported that harvest to a better market, and left the people to die of famine, or to live by alms."

Arrival of the funeral cart

At this moment, the funeral cart with its attendant came to-wards us; it stopped opposite the cottage; a deal coffin of a large size, in order to suit the dimensions of all persons, lay jolting at the top . . . We learnt that the coffin was for a woman who lay dead in that house, and that four others of the same family lay sick of the fever, unable even to assist in removing the body of their relation. The man with the cart called to another [and] both disappeared within the shadow of the doorway. Presently they returned, bearing between them the dead body, over which a scanty tattered yellow rag had just been thrown, not sufficient however to cover the whole length of the figure, or to prevent one's seeing the livid lifeless arms as they hung down swinging and knocking against the ground. They hastily flung it into the shell, the cart drove off, and the remains were hurriedly con-

342

signed to the earth without a coffin, and without the offices of religion![21]

The reprehensible conduct of the British government during this calamity is difficult to understand, but their antipathy and fear of the Irish must be taken into account. As always, even in their want, the Irish began an insurrection in 1848. Led by a small band of idealists, it came to nothing. It was the British government's response that was more revealing. In 1846, the government declared that there was no money to help the starving Irish, yet in 1848, on hearing that a small group of Irish were arming themselves, huge numbers of soldiers were sent to Ireland.

It is not characteristic of the English to behave as they behaved in Ireland. As a nation, the English have proved themselves of generosity, tolerance and magnanimity, but not when Ireland is concerned. The moment the very name of Ireland is mentioned, the English seem to bid adieu to common feeling, common prudence and common sense, and to act with the barbarity of tyrants and the fatuity of idiots.[22]

In the spring of 1849, the British officially declared the Great Famine over.[23] To celebrate, Queen Victoria of Britain arrived in Dublin amidst great fanfare and pomp. Fluttering high above the fastidiously clad soldiers and colorful marching bands was a huge Union Jack. Kitty (Kinsella) Coffey remembers being told how one of her ancestors, William Kinsella,

---

[21] Frederick Temple Blackwood, *Narrative of a Journey from Oxford to Skibbereen* (Oxford, 1847).

[22] By the English author C. W. Smith.

[23] It's difficult to tell how they determined this since the crop hadn't been fully planted yet, let alone harvested. As it turns out, there was a partial failure of the crop again this year.

managed to cut the flag's ropes so it dropped on the heads of the lead marching band. (He promptly emigrated to America.)

During the Queen's visit no expense was spared to make the tour a success. At one banquet, £5,000 was spent on food and wine alone. The Duke of Leinster, one of the more compassionate Irish landowners, was disgusted with this extravagance. He wondered how in this land when hundreds of thousands were starving, where a family of six could be kept alive for a week on less than £1, the Queen's government could justify such opulence for a privileged few.

During the period of the Great Famine, which officially lasted for four years, the population of Ireland dropped from 8 million to around 6 million through starvation and emigration (mostly to North America), almost all of these being poor Catholics. As for the Protestant Ascendancy, in Cork, as elsewhere, "large farmers holding more than thirty acres not only escaped almost unscathed but in fact strengthened their position during the Famine years."[24] By 1881 the population of Ireland would drop further to about five million.[25]

Ireland was not the only country suffering famine at this time; Scotland and Belgium[26] had their own. However, Ireland was the only country in Europe that was exporting food when its own population was starving. Industrialized England, which did not produce enough food for its own population, required the crops grown in Ireland. The words of Dr. Samuel Johnson,

---

[24] J. Donnelly, Jr., *The Land and the People of Nineteenth-Century Cork: The Rural Economy and the Land Question* (London, 1975).

[25] It's impossible to get an accurate figure because the British neglected to keep records concerning their Irish serfs. This also makes it nearly impossible for Irish people researching their genealogy to trace it back before the beginning of the 1800s.

[26] The Belgian government purchased food for distribution, organized public works, and removed tariffs. Their population recovered quickly with few scars.

"Do not make an union with us, Sir. We should unite with you only to rob you," had come true with striking accuracy.

> Ireland [after the Union] lost the income raised from her own taxation and was still subjected to taxation for England's expenditure and she became responsible for a share of England's debts expended for England's glory and use . . . . Yet now in Ireland's extremity we are told that on our own resources alone are we to depend for our famishing people.[27]

A leading English historian, A. J. P. Taylor, writes that the men of the British government "were gripped by the most horrible, and perhaps the most universal, of human maladies: the belief that principles and doctrines are more important than lives. They imagined that rules, invented by economists, were as 'natural' as the potato blight."[28] The British, and perhaps more accurately the Protestant Ascendancy, had only themselves to blame for this terrible calamity. Under the system by which they had forced the Irish to live, it was only a matter of time before mass starvations occurred.

In County Wexford, where the majority of the Kinsellas were located, fifty years previously the people had proudly proclaimed the birth of the Wexford Republic. Now, though the effects of the Great Famine were less than in the west of Ireland, the people were broken. Thanks to the aid of a number of landlords who had done their utmost to shoulder the burden of the famine, for which they earned the gratitude of the people, the population of County Wexford declined by only 11% from 1841 to 1851, though considerable emigration continued for the rest of the century, largely from the area populated by the Kinsellas. The population of County Carlow, the

---

[27] *Independent*, Wexford paper, 12/19/1846.

[28] A. J. P. Taylor, *Essays in English History* (Harmondsworth, 1976).

county containing the second largest group of Kinsellas, declined by 21% over the same time period. The population wasn't the only thing that declined because of the Great Famine: in 1835 the number of native Irish speakers was estimated at four million, but in 1851 only two million spoke Irish as their first language. In four years the Great Famine had succeeded where almost six centuries of British pressure had failed.

During the Great Famine, and for several generations after, a combination of anglicizing intention and the effect of the new national school system, with the determination of Irish-speaking parents that their children should learn English, led to an extraordinary endeavor. The parents would not speak their own language to their children; the children, at the primary school, learned another language. In some schools, the "tally stick" was used. A child wore a cord around his neck, from which was suspended a small stick. Each time the child broke into Irish, a notch was placed on the stick, and the child was punished at the end of the day according to the number of notches on the stick. The Gaelic language was disappearing along with the Irish population.

The millions of Irish who emigrated after the Great Famine carried with them one thing in common besides their culture, a bitter hatred of Britain. They could never forget seeing wagonloads of wheat, vegetables and dairy products being loaded on ships bound for England while they had nothing to eat. These bitter memories, heirlooms of their past, they passed on to their children and they to theirs. "Between Ireland and England the memory of what was done and endured has lain like a sword. Other famines followed, as other famines had gone before, but it is the terrible years of the Great Hunger which are remembered and only just beginning to be forgiven."[29]

---

[29] Cecil Woodham-Smith, *The Great Hunger* (New York, 1962).

Irish Emigration

In the past 350 years, more than ten million Irish left their homeland, a figure almost three times the present-day population of Eire. In the 17th century the figures are vague, but as many as 50,000 indentured servants were sent out as virtual slaves to the Barbados and Jamaica, or to Virginia, Maryland and the Carolinas. We know of one Kinsella who emigrated during this time:

Cornelius Kincheloe (1693) as related by his descendant John Kincheloe III

The earliest record of Cornelius Kincheloe appears in 1693, in Richmond County, Virginia. Oral history passed down through the family speaks of Cornelius as coming from Scotland, and while this may be true, he or his ancestors originated from Hy Kinsella as Kincheloe is a variation of the name Kinsella (during the period he arrived in America there were many spelling variations on the name Kinsella). By 1695 Cornelius had received a 100-acre parcel of land on which he raised his family. Cornelius' son John ended up selling this land in 1724 and moved the family.

In 1996, after years of painstaking research, John Kincheloe III had identified where the 100 acres of Cornelius Kincheloe, his 8th-generation grandfather, was located. That very year a parcel of the land was auctioned off so John drove from his North Carolina home and managed to buy 3.5 acres of the original tract.

In the 18th century almost 80% of emigrants from Ireland were Protestants, mostly disaffected Scots Presbyterians from

Ulster. The Protestant Ascendancy, who were Anglican, trusted them only slightly more than Catholics, persecuting them almost to the same extent. During times of rising land rents and depressions they left, not feeling the same tie to the land that the Irish Catholics did. The majority of these Scots Presbyterians emigrated to North America where they were fundamental in establishing the United States of America.

America had been a convenient place for England, whose prisons were overcrowded, to transport convicts, but after 1776, this option was closed. They turned to Australia where Captain Arthur Phillip arrived in 1788 with almost 1,000 convicts. Transportation of convicts to Australia continued for the next eighty years, though on a much reduced scale after 1840. While many of the original convicts were hardened criminals, the vast majority were victims of difficult times, often being forced to poach a trout or rabbit from the landlord, to steal a sheep to feed the family, or perhaps take a piece of linen to sell for the same purpose. Many of these people were granted pardons in Australia after serving a period of good behavior, with a large number going on to become respectable citizens. Here are the stories of two Kinsellas sent to Australia:

Martin Kinsella (1824) as related by his descendant Shirley Duckworth

My Great Great Grandfather, Martin Kinsella, was born about 1792. He committed the crime of stealing a pot of glue for which he was tried in Dublin on February 9, 1824 and sentenced to seven years in the Australian penal colony. His age at the time was listed as 32. In 1825 he was transported to Australia on the ship "Anna & Amelia." In 1833 his wife and daughter joined him while his son remained behind in Ireland.

Timothy Kinsella (1836) as related by his descendant Noelene Hoysted

Timothy Kinsella was born in County Kildare around 1810, the son of Terence Kinsella of Castledermot, whose family is shown in official records to have lived in this area "from generation to generation." By the mid-1830s, Timothy, Terence and his family were living at Nicholastown, near Athy, in County Kildare and were said to be "of excellent character, honest, industrious and well conducted."

In many ways Timothy was a victim of these difficult times, which led him to become a political activist with one of the proscribed secret societies formed during this period. In July 1836 he was arrested whilst "searching for arms" in a local house, was charged, tried at Athy, and given the mandatory sentence for political offences – death by hanging.

Since he had no previous convictions and violence wasn't involved in the crime, the sentence was commuted to transportation to Australia for life. His 70-year old father Terence had a moving petition circulated in the hope that Timothy's sentence could be shortened to seven years banishment allowing him to return to his family "a wiser and better man." Despite the signatures and excellent character references from many respected local identities, the petition failed. After spending one month on the old rotting hulk *Essex,* Timothy was placed aboard the ship *Earl Grey* in Cork Harbour and sailed for Australia on 27th August 1836, never again to see his native land or his family.

Conditions on the ship were cramped, steamy, and appalling, and many men had come aboard directly from the hulks in poor health and quickly succumbed to illness and scurvy. Fortunately the surgeon insisted that a stop be made for fresh supplies at the Cape of Good Hope and from this point onwards cases of illness dropped dramatically. From a complement of 384 passengers, only three men died during the voyage of over four months, a relatively small number for this period.

Timothy survived the voyage, arriving in Sydney Cove on 31st December 1836. His character references stood him in good stead, and rather than being placed on one of the dreaded "chain gangs," he was employed privately by a widow who was the owner of a large flour mill. Timothy went on to become a respected and valued member of Colonial society, gaining a Pardon from Queen Victoria in 1850.

A ship of emigrants about to embark

There are usually a large number of spectators at the dock-gates to witness the final departure of the noble ship, with its large freight of human beings . . . As the ship is towed out, hats are raised, handkerchiefs are waved, and a loud and long-continued shout of farewell is raised from the shore, and cordially responded to from the ship. It is then, if at any time, that the eyes of the emigrants begin to moisten with regret at the thought that they are looking for the last time at the old country – that country which, although, in all probability, associated principally with the remembrance of sorrow and suffering, of semi-starvation, and a constant battle for the merest crust necessary to support existence is, nevertheless, the country of their fathers, the country of their childhood, and consecrated to their hearts by many a token.[1]

Irish emigration steadily increased throughout the 18th and 19th centuries, mainly to North America, but it was only in 1815, after the Napoleonic Wars, that the major emigration began, culminating in a flood tide during the Great Famine of 1845-50. Throughout the 19th century the mechanisms of emigration became more efficient: brokers, entrepreneurs, and subagents made their appearance, manipulating increasingly professionalized propaganda to lure the Irish from Ireland. Even when emigration had become established as an almost automatic part of rural life, it conflicted sharply with the high value that Irish country people put on communalism, kinship and a sense of place. Estimates reveal that as many as eight million left Ireland between 1801 and 1921. No other country lost so large a proportion of its people during the 19th century.

For ship owners and their captains, the emigrant trade began as a grudging afterthought, a means of making profit on the westward run to North America before they loaded timber bound for England. Emigrants, however inconvenient, were more profitable than ballast of sand or bricks.

Few emigrant ships had been built to carry passengers. Most were aging cargo vessels, three-masted barks and two-masted brigs, the workhorses of the North Atlantic, vessels of 350 tons or less with holds so shallow and wide that unless

---

[1] *Illustrated London News*, July 6, 1850.

they were well loaded with ballast they rolled in the slightest breeze. No matter how leaky and decrepit these coffin ships, a cargo of timber, it was hoped, would keep them afloat long enough to get home.

Once a ship discharged its timber, loose boards were laid over the bilges as temporary flooring and rows of rough berths little bigger than dog kennels were fitted in place and covered with straw for bedding. A couple of rickety wooden privies nailed to the foredeck completed the transformation from timber scow to emigrant ship, where hundreds of women, men, and children were fated to live for a least a month and a half, and sometimes as long as three months if contrary winds blew a ship off course. Even in fine weather with the hatches off there was little light or ventilation, but in rough weather with hatches battened the steerage was like a dungeon lit with smoky kerosene lamps and filled with a fog of sweat, spilled chamber pots, rotting scraps of food, and the vomit of seasick humanity. All around lay luggage, bags, sacks and boxes.

To the emigrant, the evils began before a ship left port. Speculators chartered steerage space at the cheapest price they could and sent commission agents into the countryside to recruit as many emigrants as possible to fill the space. These men, paid by the number of emigrants they could produce, spun fanciful yarns of shipboard facilities . . . glibly assuring the potential passengers that the voyage would be short, three weeks at most, and a kindly captain would look after their needs like a father. Passage could be purchased with or without provisions. If an emigrant's small stock of food – potatoes, oatmeal and perhaps some bacon or salt herrings – ran out on the voyage, as it usually did, there was nothing to do but buy whatever the captain had to offer at exorbitant prices. Unlike slavers, who had a vested interest in getting their human cargoes from Africa to American plantations in working condition, Irish emigrants were left to fend for themselves once their fares were collected.

From the hour of his departure to the hour of his settlement on his final resting-place, the emigrant is a prey to human vultures. At the great ports where emigrants embark in the Old World – Liverpool, Limerick, Glasgow, Belfast, Bremen, Amsterdam, Havre – a brood of hungry rascals earn a fat livelihood by cheating them. The business is most profitable at Liverpool – which is the largest emigrant depot of the Old World – and the chief dupes are the Irish.[2]

Patrick and Rose Kinsella (1854) as related by their descendant Rose Quaid Munsch

Patrick and his wife Rose emigrated from Dublin to New Orleans, a trip of three months, before continuing on to Pennsylvania with their 11 children. At that time free passage to America in freighting vessels could be arranged if the head of the family signed up for a certain number of years labor. The destination of families was often the factories and mines of Pennsylvania. One of Rose's granddaughters still has the roll-

---

[2] *Harper's Weekly*, June 26, 1858.

ing pin she used in the bottom of a sailing vessel to make the bread for her eleven children. One little daughter about five years old died shortly before the ship reached port. The family kept the death secret so that the child would not be buried at sea.

There was a vast difference between American and British ships. American ships were required by law to carry 100 pounds of breadstuffs, 100 pounds of salt meat and 60 gallons of water per passenger; there were heavy fines if a ship carried too many passengers. This drove up the cost of passage to the States and had the effect of forcing the poorest Irish, the majority, to the British colonies. Many Irish therefore sailed to Canada and then traveled south to the United States. In some years two thirds of all emigrants followed this route.

Immigrant ships entering the United States also had to be sanitary. A last minute scrub down before entering a U.S. port was never necessary on an American ship, where weekly and sometimes even daily scourings with the help and cooperation of the immigrants were standard procedure. Scrub downs were considered unnecessary on English ships carrying Irish people, because the emigrating Irish were looked upon as the dregs of an overpopulated country, a primitive people. Diseases that thrived on filthy English ships were curtailed on clean American ones, so the death toll was much higher on English than on American ships.[3]

The Irish, especially those emigrating during the famine, could not afford unsanitary conditions in their weakened states. Figures from the *New York Post* showed that the total number of emigrants who landed in New York in 1847 was 166,000. The numbers of German and Irish were almost equal at about 60,000 each. Of this number 6,932 were received into the hos-

---

[3] Donald MacKay, *Flight from Famine* (Toronto, 1990).

pital of whom 6,376 were Irish, 330 Germans, 173 from all other countries.

Since emigration had the same effect on a family as death, the loss of a loved one forever, the custom of the American Wake sprang up in Ireland. It was often called American because this was the destination of the majority of the Irish.

> I remember still with emotion the emigration of the young peo-
> ple of the neighborhood to America. In those days the farmer's
> children were raised for export. There were times of the year –
> in spring or fall – when there would be a sort of group emigra-
> tion; that is, a dozen or so would start off together once or twice
> a week for a few weeks to take the train to the boat at Queens-
> town or Derry. Generally each group was bound for the same
> town in America where they had friends or relatives who had
> paid their passage money beforehand or sent them their tickets.
> The night before their departure there would be a farewell
> gathering called an American wake in one of the houses of the
> emigrating boys or girls. There would be singing and dancing
> interlarded with tears and lamentations until the early hours of
> the morning, when, without sleep, the young people started for
> the train, the mothers sometimes keening as at a funeral or a
> wake for the dead, for the parting would often be forever and the
> parents might never again see the boy or girl who was crossing
> the ocean. There was, I remember, a steep hill on the road near
> our house, and when the emigrating party reached the bottom of
> it, it was their habit to descend from the sidecars and carts to
> ease the horses, and they would climb the height on foot. As
> they reached the top from which they could see the whole coun-
> tryside, they would turn and weepingly bid farewell to the green
> fields, the little white houses, the sea, and the rambling roads
> they knew so well. The hill was called the Hill of Weeping in
> Gaelic, because of all those who had wept their farewells from
> the top of it.[4]

---

[4] Mary Colum, *Life and the Dream* (New York, 1947).

Peter and Elizabeth Kinsella (1850) as related by their descendant Janice Smith

It was unusual for the Irish to come as a family, often they came alone or as siblings, but the family of Peter and Elizabeth[5] Kinsella arrived from County Carlow around 1850. They purchased a farm a few miles from Lockport, N.Y. in a German settlement. Peter pronounced Kinsella with the accent on the first syllable, KIN'sella (as it's pronounced in Ireland today), and the guttural German accent of those among whom they lived slurred it to Kinsler.

Kinsler was the name all the children of Peter and Elizabeth used until their son, Moses, had some difficulty over the deed to a piece of property and in tracing back the legal documents, found the real spelling of his family name was Kinsella. The other children were established as Kinsler by that time and Moses was the only one who changed back to Kinsella. The ancestors of these Kinsler's can be found in Indiana and Illinois.

The following recounts the fairly typical emigration of a number of American-Irish. They came alone or in small groups, enticed to a location by friends or family. They began humbly but often rose in their social rank over time. It also illustrates the truth rather than the myth; the typical Irish immigrant did not settle in the large cities but instead followed the flow of unskilled jobs that were most commonly found in the country, especially transportation projects such as canal building, railroads, or motorways.

---

[5] It's uncertain if the wife's name was Elizabeth.

Martin Kinsella (1851) as related by his descendant Jack Kinsella

In the mid-19th century Auburn, N.Y., located along the Erie Canal, was a booming town with plenty of work but not enough workers. The need for labor was so great that the Auburn city fathers sent representatives to Ireland looking for recruits. These representatives painted a beautiful picture of life in Auburn and probably offered financial incentives to those interested. One of those from Kildare who listened was John McGarr. He had arrived in Auburn by 1837 when laborers earned 50 cents a day, incredible pay compared to what could be earned in Ireland. John wrote friends and relatives back in Ireland and probably sent money to pay for transportation. His signature is on numerous naturalization records of Irishmen from County Kildare. Terence Kinsella, who arrived in 1846, was one of those he encouraged to come over. The witness for Terence's U.S. citizenship papers, which he signed with an "X", was John McGarr. Terence Kinsella was not only surrounded by friends he had known back in Ireland, but a number of his first cousins had arrived also.

Five years later, after writing letters describing the benefits of Auburn where Terence worked as a railroad laborer, Terence's brother Martin, who was thirty-one and escaping the potato famine, arrived. By 1852 Martin, illiterate and without any skills, applied for citizenship. Two years later another of Terence's brothers, Michael, arrived. Martin Kinsella went on to marry Bridget McGarr (a relative of John McGarr) in the local Catholic church. By 1860 Martin and Bridget had moved to Manchester, about 40 miles away, where they were recorded in the census as the Kinslers. Martin was working for the railroad at the time while his brother Terence was a stationmaster and his other brother Michael was Auburn's chief of police. In

1872 Martin Kinsella bought five acres of land which he farmed with the help of his wife and nine children. By 1880 the census was back to recording them as Kinsellas.

Very few of the Famine Irish emigrants were destined to achieve prosperity and success themselves. The condition to which they had been reduced not only by the Great Famine but by the centuries that preceded it was too severe a handicap. These emigrants were destined to be regarded with aversion and contempt. Not until the second or third generation did the Irish intelligence and quickness of wit reassert themselves. Along with these attributes, the emigrants brought their culture. Irwin Cobb, the famous American author and humorist, told of Gaelic hospitality:

> The son of an Irish refugee, Pat Cleburne of Arkansas, one of the most gallant leaders that the Civil War produced.[6] Pat Cleburne died on one of the bloodiest battlefields of Christendom[7] in his stocking feet because as he rode into battle that morning he saw one of his Irish boys from Little Rock tramping barefooted over the frozen furrows of a wintry cornfield and leaving tracts of blood behind him. So he drew off his boots and bade the soldier put them on, and fifteen minutes later he went to his God in his stocking feet. Raleigh laid down his coat before Good Queen Bess, and has been immortalized for his chivalry, but I think a more courtly deed was that of the gallant Irishman Pat Cleburne.

The Irish Diaspora has flooded the globe over the centuries. Some 70 million people in the world call themselves Irish today though Eire contains only 4 million of them. While the

---

[6] Although he had no sympathy for slave owners, he fought for the community where he had made friends.

[7] The battle of Franklin, Tennessee.

majority reside in North America and Europe, healthy proportions of Irish can be found in each of the other continents. Writing in the *Irish Times* (March 20, 2000), Conor O'Clery, the paper's Asia correspondent, remarked on the fact that everywhere he traveled – in Beijing, Tokyo, Kuala Lumpur, Manila, Hong Kong, Jakarta, Singapore – he came across "interesting Irish people in a variety of occupations."[8]

Ireland's emigration was initially equated with blood gushing from a wounded artery. With hindsight it's more appropriate to compare it to the scattering of seed in spring. Mary Ambrose, a Canadian journalist said: "The love affair with things Irish continues around the world – unless you live in England . . . being Irish in England is still a liability."

---

[8] Tim Pat Coogan, *Wherever Green is Worn: The Story of the Irish Diaspora* (London, 2000).

Ireland – A Nation

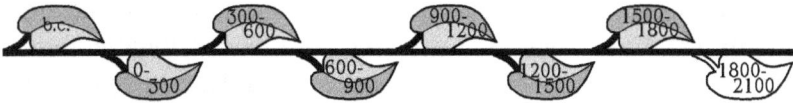

he terrible years of the famine succeeded in bringing disparate groups together. Kitty (Kinsella) Coffey remembers a story about her uncle Paddy Kinsella who around 1900 worked as a laborer on the estate of Lady Nesta Fitzgerald in County Carlow. One day as Paddy was working in the stables, Lady Nesta came by and decided to chat with him. When she offered him a drink, Paddy quickly accepted. As they were sipping their drink, Nesta said, "Paddy, we've known each other for several years and I don't know your last name." When Paddy told her, Nesta exclaimed, "Oh dear, who could ever imagine it, a Fitzgerald and a Kinsella drinking together in the same stable!"

Destitution followed the Great Famine in Ireland, and the Catholic church increased its presence by assisting the unfortunate. This increased the power it wielded. In 1850 Paul Cullen, recently made Ireland's Cardinal, called an Episcopal synod, the first to be held in Ireland since the 12th century. As a result, the Church's hierarchical structure was strengthened in an effort to allow Rome more control in Ireland. While this brought much needed economic aid, it also further injured Gaelic practices kept alive through religion. Irish Catholicism even into the 19th century strayed from strict Roman Catholicism.[1] Huge celebrations, called "patterns," were held on the feast of a local saint; holy wells and shrines were visited without the presence of a priest; masses were said in the homes of remote farms. Irish religion tended to be celebratory and life-affirming. Even funerals were enjoyable as the local community arrived and sat up all night, either with the corpse present, or in an adjoining room, drinking and playing games. The reforms installed by Cardinal Cullen actively discouraged such religious expression, focusing instead on events within church buildings.

The 1850s also brought a huge increase in evictions as landlords cleared their land for cattle and sheep, more economical tenants than humans and less likely to rebel.[2] From 1848 to 1878 "In County Wexford alone 366,724 acres of land had gone out of cultivation and within the same period the population of the county had decreased by 69,367 while within living memory 9,203 houses had been leveled in the county."[3] The Irish farmers expressed their frustration through crime, including the killing of their landlords, because with no legal representation, they had no legal alternative. A militant group called the Irish Republican Brotherhood was founded in 1858 by survivors of the 1848 revolt. It linked up with other organizations in America, Australia, South Africa, and Britain which called themselves the Fenians after the Fianna led by Finn. The government followed them closely for years, imprisoning them whenever possible, until finally the Fenians staged an

---

[1] *"The Roman Church gave law, the Celtic Church gave love"* is a revealing Irish proverb.

[2] "It has been estimated that, excluding peaceable surrenders, over a quarter of a million people were evicted between 1849 and 1854. The total number of people who had to leave their holdings in the period is likely to be around half a million and 200,000 small holdings were obliterated." Cathal Poirteir, *Famine Echoes* (Dublin, 1995).

[3] *Independent*, Wexford paper, 10/2/1878.

ineffective rebellion that was quickly put down in 1867. While Britain believed the threat was over, the Fenians would resurface to more dramatic effect early in the 20th century.

The following is an example of Irish retribution:

On the 18th of May, a beautiful bright sunny day at noon, I was riding with a friend to the sessions at Borrisokane. I heard a faint report at a little distance in the fields as of a gun or pistol, but took no notice of it, when almost immediately afterwards a man came running up a lane to meet us, saying,

"Oh! Sir, Mr. Hall has just been shot."

"Shot!" cried I, pulling up my horse, "do you mean murdered?"

"Oh! Yes, Sir," replied the man, "he is lying there in the field."

"Is he dead?" I asked.

"Stone dead!" was the man's reply; and as he said so, I never shall forget the strange mixture of horror and of triumph which pervaded his countenance.

We rode on rapidly down the lane, and just where it emerged upon a little grass lawn, was the body of Mr. Hall. He was a man apparently about fifty years of age, and his bald head lay uncovered on the ground. He was quite warm but 'stone dead', lying in the open field. Numbers of people were working all around, planting their potatoes; but not a trace of the murderer could be found.

It was a sessions day at Borrisokane, and several other gentlemen who were also going there joined us almost immediately afterwards. There were a few country-people standing by. I shall not easily forget my feelings on this occasion. There lay the body of a murdered gentleman, with whom I had been on terms of friendly intercourse – dead on his own estate, and in his own field, in the noonday, whilst on the faces of the peasantry could be plainly seen an expression of triumphant satisfaction; and there we stood, several mounted horsemen – every man of us armed, burning to avenge his death and to arrest the murderer, and yet we looked like so many fools not knowing what to do, though it was scarcely more than ten minutes since the fatal shot had been fired.[4]

The Irish farmers, with few rights, began to demand land reform.[5] By 1879 political forces had combined to create the National Land League party, which organized the tenant farmers in their demands and encouraged controlled agitation against landlordism. The party's other aim was Home Rule.[6] The Land League chose a young Protestant of uncertain ability, Charles Stewart Parnell, to serve as their president in Britain's Parliament.

Charles Stewart Parnell was born in County Wicklow in 1846 to an upper-class Protestant family living on an estate of 5,000 acres. Early on he developed a hatred for Britain and the injustices it had perpetrated in Ireland. Upon being elected president of the National Land League party he immediately began to show his promise. No other man was to disturb the scene of British democratic politics so profoundly or for so long as Parnell. In the 1880s he dominated British parliamentary life, and no British prime minister could govern with-

Charles Stewart Parnell

---

[4] William Steuart Trench, *Realities of Irish Life* (London, 1869).

[5] This land reform became known as "the 3 Fs": free sale, fair rent and fixity of tenure.

[6] Home Rule meant that Ireland would manage her internal affairs while still allowing Britain supreme control over trade, the army and navy, foreign policy and all imperial matters.

out taking into account how Parnell might react. Parnell helped bring about a great social revolution: the change in relations between landlord and tenant in Ireland. He also raised the demand for Home Rule among the Irish.

Parnell, with the help of his subordinates, had the inflexible will, the unbeatable tenacity, and the instinct of command required to face the British. His reserve and silent personality impressed even the British House of Commons, "the finest gentleman's club in the world." Irish leaders had often tried to flatter Britain, but Parnell always spoke as an equal and never apologized either for Ireland or himself. To the mass of Irish people, still accustomed to aristocratic leadership, he became "The Chief," a name taken from their Gaelic culture.[7] He found a tremendous supporter in the leader of the British Liberal party, William Ewart Gladstone. Together, the Protestant Irishman and the Englishman fought for the Catholic Irish to have land reform and Home Rule.

> The Land League's policy was to prevail upon tenants to pay no rent at all unless the landlords agreed to the reduction which they demanded. If a landlord retaliated by evicting tenants who refused to pay, the League endeavored to make it impossible for anybody else to take their holdings by the method which came to be known as boycotting after being used in 1880 on Captain Charles Boycott, an English farmer and land agent in County Mayo. The activities of the League inevitably led to violence, and there was a sharp increase in agrarian crime.[8]

The Land League was the most important political development in the second half of the 19th century. The slogan "the land for the people" united a broad front in pursuit of the prin-

[7] The Irish had accepted the anglicizing of righ as chief.
[8] Mark Bence-Jones, *Twilight of the Ascendancy* (London, 1993, 1987).

ciple of the occupier owning the land he worked. This well-organized campaign achieved a remarkable triumph – the relatively bloodless transfer of ownership from the landlord minority to the tenant majority. The powerhouse behind this campaign was the use of the press to mould public opinion; the Brooke Estate at Coolgreany in northeastern Wexford was chosen by the Land League leaders in 1887 to focus national and international attention on the injustice of the landlord system.[9] Coolgreany (the sunny corner), a small town located on the slope of Croghan Kinsella, was planned and built in 1610 to serve the English settlers of the original plantation in North Wexford; it had long since reverted back to being overwhelmingly Irish.

In 1887 a tenant could be evicted for any reason, the most common being missed rent payments, or for no reason at all. John O'Neill, a blacksmith who had faithfully paid his rent, was among this last category. The landlord, George Brooke, and his bailiff, George Freeman, were in debt to him for his services, but what proved to be O'Neill's undoing was his refusal to do work for a friend of the landlord.

Before an eviction, notice was given to the tenant with the expectation that they would remove all their goods from the house and leave willingly. In reality the notice gave combative tenants time to barricade themselves inside in preparation for a pitched battle over the house. A typical maneuver was to bury the trunks of large trees behind the door so it couldn't be opened, large boulders or rocks were embedded in the earthen floor so maneuvering around was difficult for those unfamiliar with the placement, and thorn bushes or branches choked the windows making entry difficult.

---

[9] Our thanks to Justin Rossney who informed the authors about the source *Croghan to the Sea* by Fiachra O'Lionain. One of Justin's ancestors was among those evicted from this estate.

On the day of the first evictions in Coolgreany a detachment of 100 men from the Suffolk Regiment and 150 police armed with crowbars went to each house. They were followed by several hundred local people to cheer on the family being evicted. To gain a feeling for those times, some of the evictions will be summarized.[10]

♣

James Garvey, a well-to-do farmer, had carefully barricaded all entrances to his house so the police were forced to attack the walls of the house itself. Eventually, amid the hooting of the crowd, they made a breach in the building with their crowbars. After a strenuous effort the bailiffs, having suffered cascades of boiling water thrown in their faces, rushed in and ejected James Garvey and his five girls.

The police then proceeded to the residence of Thomas Kennedy, a typical one-story thatched house. He had driven large pieces of timber into the ground behind the door, while huge pieces of hawthorn were placed in the windows. The police, unable to gain access by the door, spent a great deal of time attempting to break through the thorns. Finally they succeeded, and upon entering the house, they wantonly destroyed everything inside before throwing all of it out the windows. When the furniture had been removed Mr. Kennedy cried out, "You may evict us from our homes, but you cannot evict the spirit of nationality from our hearts." These words were greeted with loud applause by the people assembled.

---

[10] The information is taken from *Croghan to the Sea* by Fiachra O Lionain.

An eviction

The police then proceeded to Thomas Kinsella's mud cabin where they met the most determined opposition. When the slight barricading was removed from the window, a policeman, thinking the coast was clear, poked his head in but he received such a scalding that he was unable to continue further duty that day. At some eviction sites the tenants were beaten with crow-bars by the police who, upon entering the house, were themselves attacked by tenants wielding wooden bats.

A few days later the eviction party, now consisting of 18 armed men, arrived at the entrance to the farm of Michael Kavanagh. As the estate bailiff talked to Kavanagh over the entrance gate those who lived with Kavanagh began gathering around. When a policemen began climbing the gate, John Kinsella, one of those living with Kavanagh, struck the gate with the two pronged fork he held in his hand. The estate

368

bailiff said, "Do that no more, or by God I'll shoot you, Kinsella." The bailiff then drew his revolver and fired. As all watched John Kinsella fall dead at the knees of his son, Myles, the bailiff shouted, "Now, boys, fire," starting two volleys of ten or twelve shots each. During the ensuing trial the Wicklow Grand Jury, twenty-two of twenty-three members being land-lords or land-agents, found the estate bailiff innocent.[11] A Celtic cross stands over John Kinsella's grave with the inscription:

> The monument was erected by the men of Wicklow and Wexford as a testimony of their respect for his many Christian virtues and as an indignant protest against the cruelty and injustices of those who before God are guilty of his innocent blood.

On the final day of the evictions a huge crowd had gathered. Mrs. A. Darcy, a widow, aged 70, was lying in bed in the far end of her house when a bailiff called inside asking her to leave without a struggle. Weak in frame but strong in spirit her defiant reply was "you may cast me out on the dunghill, you may put bullets through my breast, but death before dishonor!" A cheer rent the air and the bailiff left saying he would let the landlord deal with this case. The evictions were carried out over a period of 2 weeks and 60 families were evicted (a total of 300 people).[12]

---

[11] Years later when John Kinsella's grandson was brought back in this home his proudest and most treasured memory, passed on to his children, was of the words spoken to him by his parents on crossing the threshold – "This is a day you'll never forget." The ancient Irish sense of place had been passed on to this generation.

[12] After the evictions the estate landlord, George Brooke, brought in several loyalist planters to occupy the farms. They were boycotted by the local people and most went away after a few years. The Land Commission then

♣

By 1891 so much progress had been made on land reform because of Ireland's Parnell and Britain's Gladstone that the great Irish estates owned by Protestants were now largely a thing of the past. The ownership of most of the arable and grazing land was transferred gradually from the landlords to the tenant farmers – the farmers being subject to payment of annuities to reimburse the British Government for its purchase of the land. The Protestant Ascendancy landlords were cut off at the roots, and the tenants, who often fancied themselves the inheritors of some immemorial original ownership, moved in. Ireland was on its way to becoming a land of peasant proprietors. However, the progress on Home Rule had not been so significant. Even though Gladstone had championed it along with Parnell, the British government and the crown would not allow it. Ireland could not be ruled by her own people.

A major casualty occurred on the way to the victory of land reform. Parnell was discovered to be in love with a divorced woman. The effect of this affair on Catholic Ireland, even though the woman had not lived with her husband for years, was devastating. The Land League party debated whether Parnell should remain as their leader. The national issue of Home Rule was shelved while, in a country where the influence of the Catholic Church was so powerful, the debate over whether an adulterer could be allowed to lead the nation's party raged. Parnell thought he should, but the Catholic church called for him to step down. Then Gladstone, the British prime minister and Parnell's ally, dealt the final blow; if Parnell were to remain leader, Gladstone would step down as head of the Liberal party. Without Gladstone and the Liberal party, Ireland

---

took over the estate from Brooke and most of the tenants returned under new terms of settlement.

would get nowhere, so Parnell was replaced as head of his party. Overcome by the stress, he did not survive the year.

After the fall of Parnell a disillusioned and embittered Ireland turned away from parliamentary politics. They refocused their energy, and an amazing artistic and cultural rebirth emerged termed the Celtic Dawn. This Gaelic revival was most evident in the foundation of two organizations: Douglas Hyde's Gaelic League, which he founded in 1893, and the Gaelic Athletic Association (GAA), begun by Michael Cusack in 1894. The former brought people of all ages and both sexes into classes where they learned the Irish language and Irish dances, and acquired an interest in Irish history. It pushed for inclusion into the educational curriculum at all levels. The Gaelic Athletic Association was aimed at reviving Irish games such as hurling and Gaelic football. Thomas Kinsella was among the founders of the GAA in northeastern County Wexford.

Literature also saw a resurgence. It had begun earlier, though less obviously, with a band of mid-century scholars whose work was prodigious both in its ambitions and in its accomplishments. John O'Donovan's massively annotated translation of the *Annals of the Four Masters* (1851), Eugene O'Curry's two sprawling volumes on the history and literature of ancient Ireland, George Petrie's study of ancient ecclesiastical architecture and his collections of songs, along with the linguistic and historical researches of university teachers who were associated with them demonstrate an unprecedented burst of scholarly energy.

Building on the work of these scholars, a group of Anglo-Irish writers including W. B. Yeats, Lady Augusta Gregory, and J. M. Synge popularized many of the country's myths and legends. Although they wrote in English, their writings were based on an awareness of a new Irish nationalism. Yeats, together with Lady Gregory and Edward Martyn, founded the Abbey Theatre in 1904 to spread the ideals of the literary revival. Few independence movements in the world can be said to have been so strongly influenced by the work of theater and its playwrights as was the Irish one by the Abbey. The Irish Literary Revival was responsible for the production of an exceptionally strong body of work, which not only stimulated Irish nationalism but also gave Ireland a place on the international stage. The writers of the revival were responsible for developing and articulating a new national consciousness.

The Irish had achieved a great deal in terms of cultural awareness, but as the historian Paul Bew has pointed out, their professional status lagged. Between 1861 and 1911 the percentage of Catholic barristers and solicitors rose from 34% to 44% and that of doctors from 35% to 48%. This still left the Catholics, who comprised 80% of the population of Ireland, with something of a professional mountain to climb. The Irish realized that political action was required to go further. Sinn Féin, meaning "ourselves alone," was the most important political movement to emerge from the Celtic Dawn. Founded in 1905, its members believed Ireland should have its own independent assembly, such as a parliament, in Dublin. From its beginnings there was a close connection between Sinn Féin and the Irish Republican Brotherhood because they both sought the creation of an Irish republic; the major difference was that Sinn Féin did not advocate violence. Sinn Féin attracted little support during the first decade of its existence.

By 1907 Home Rule for Ireland appeared a very real possibility and was championed by Parnell's party, now renamed the Irish Parliamentary Party. The province of Ulster had other ideas. With its huge plantation of foreigners started back in 1609, Ulster had diverged from the rest of Ireland after Cromwell. Instead of the troops and violence Britain had offered the rest of Ireland, the government had offered Ulster money and advice during the 18th century because of its large population of Protestants. Britain encouraged Ulster to join the dawning industrial revolution, creating an infrastructure of roads and canals, while actively discouraging the rest of Ireland, which needed to remain rural in order to feed England. Great industries had sprung up so that in 1900 Belfast was the second largest city in Ireland[13] and alone in Ireland had industries as powerful as those of England with a very large and highly-skilled artisan class made up almost exclusively of Protestants.

Upon seeing the possibility that Ireland might gain Home Rule, the Protestant aristocracy of Ulster proclaimed they would use "all means which may be found necessary to defeat the present conspiracy to set up a Home Rule parliament in Ireland, and in the event of such a parliament being forced upon us to refuse to recognize its authority." A visit by Winston Churchill's father, Lord Randolph Churchill, only made the situation more difficult when he uttered the words "Ulster will fight and Ulster will be right." The Protestant Ascendancy was worried about losing the power it had enjoyed for more than two hundred years to the Catholic majority.

The Ulster Protestant Ascendancy did not merely play the Orange card, they played the German one also. In 1913, Bonar Law said in the House of Commons that rather than be ruled by Irish Nationalists, the Ulster Unionists would "prefer to accept the Government of a foreign country."[14] In spite of these threats from Ulster, Home Rule was finally passed by the British parliament in 1914, but with the outbreak of World War I, its execution was to be delayed for a minimum of twelve months. More delays were to follow until it appeared Home Rule, though agreed upon in theory, would never take effect.

---

[13] Dublin had a greater population.
[14] Tim Pat Coogan, *Ireland in the 20th Century* (New York, 2006).

Irish Citizen army led by Pearse

Now the militant Irish Republican Brotherhood (Fenians) that had sprung up in the 1850s, for which Sinn Féin acted as a political arm, dramatically reentered the world stage. On Easter Monday of 1916, 1,000 Irish led by Padraic Pearse took over the General Post Office and other buildings in the heart of the Irish capital. They began by hauling down the Union Jack and replacing it with two potent emblems. One was the customary green Irish flag, emblazoned with a golden harp but now accompanied by the extraordinary legend "Irish Republic." The other was the flag of today's Irish Republic, the tricolor: green for the Gaelic tradition, orange for the Unionists, and white for peace between them. Finally, they read the document that was to cost its signatories their lives – the 1916 Proclamation declaring an Irish republic.

Pearse had left hints he would attempt an uprising like this. In a poem written the previous Christmas he stated:

> Here be ghosts that I have raised this Christmastide, ghosts of dead men that have bequeathed a trust to us living men. Ghosts are troublesome things, in a house or in a family, as we knew even before Ibsen taught us. There is only one way to appease a ghost. You must do the thing it asks of you. The ghosts of a nation sometimes ask very big things and they must be appeased, whatever the cost.[15]

Years later W. B. Yeats, the defining Irish poet of the twentieth century, recalled the event this way.

> When Pearse summoned Cuchulain to his side,
> What stalked through the Post Office?[16]

A large British force landed, and after a bombardment of four days the main body of the rebels surrendered. By the next Monday, 450 had been killed and 2,614 wounded. Immediately the British convened a court martial to which Pearse was summoned. "When I was a child of ten," he told them, "I went on my bare knees by my bedside one night and promised God that I should devote my life to an effort to free my country. I have kept that promise." He added as he was being walked out of the room, "You cannot extinguish the Irish passion for freedom. If our deed has not been sufficient to win freedom, then our children will win it by a better deed." Pearse, who had talked in the past of a blood sacrifice needed to purify Ireland, was the first to be killed. He had at times used the analogy of Christ sacrificing himself for humanity, and it was not a coin-

---

[15] Patrick Pearse, Christmas Day, 1915.

[16] *The Collected Works by W. B. Yeats*, ed. Richard Finneran (New York, 1996). The poem is "The Statues," published in 1933.

cidence that the rebellion took place on Easter. Fourteen other executions followed at intervals over the next week and a half, until international public opinion (largely from the United States) forced their halt. Britain imposed martial law indefinitely throughout Ireland and reprisals against the innocent and defenseless mounted ominously.

Rather than the Easter uprising itself, it was what came after that changed the feelings of Irish citizens. British retribution was more than severe, including executions, wholesale arrests, and deportations, reminiscent of Cromwell.

Edward MacLysaght, a home rule supporter, wrote in his diary shortly after the Easter Rebellion: "My heart is with them and my mind is against them." The executions caused him to write that he was, "completely and absolutely pro them." Britain had succeeded in creating martyrs and yet again galvanizing Ireland against her.

It was announced in the British House of Commons that "The government has come to the conclusion that the system under which Ireland has been governed has completely broken down." Sinn Féin represented the Easter rebellion soldiers who had held the British army at bay for nearly a week. Nothing like this had happened in Ireland for well over a century. However much people might deplore the violence, at the same time they felt some pride in the rebels. Sinn Féin rose in prominence until it soon was considered the most important Irish political organization.

Douglas Goldring, a magazine writer for England, wrote about a Dublin funeral in 1917 for Thomas Ashe, one of the executed rebels:

> The Sinn Féin colours were everywhere in evidence, but anything less revolutionary in appearance than this sober and peaceable gathering of citizens it would be difficult to imagine....

Immediately behind the clergymen came the hearse, with the coffin wrapped in a Republican flag and half buried in an avalanche of flowers. The hearse was flanked by a picked guard of Irish Volunteers in their dark green uniform, the men carrying their rifles reversed and their officer marching behind them with drawn sword.

"Ah, they always kill the ones we love best," said a woman near me, who had known Pearse and MacDonagh and the O'Rahilly....

It was not until the bands struck up the extraordinary inspiring 'Soldier's Song' that it came over me in a flash that in the eyes of the Irish Government all these people must be 'criminals', just as the dead man was a 'criminal'! Technically the bands-men were breaking the law by playing 'rebel' melodies. Hundreds of people had been punished for doing nothing more than this. Then again I remembered that the bearing of rifles by civilians was expressly forbidden. I knew that a conviction on this charge brought a long term of imprisonment; and there just before my eyes was a firing party, fully armed, with a policeman gazing at them benevolently! Again, all drilling was illegal. Just as I recalled this fact a volunteer officer blew a whistle immediately in front of me and a thousand men stopped as one. Another short whistle, the words 'left, right, left' and the procession had started again. Then surely, the carrying of hurleys was prohibited? I noticed an entire contingent go by, armed with the forbidden weapon. As for the volunteer uniform, Dublin was plastered with the proclamations threatening pains and penalties to those who might have the temerity to put it on. Yet during the ninety minutes which the procession took to pass, I expect I saw very nearly every volunteer uniform which exists in Ireland. What a situation! I suppose the futility of Castle government was never more pitilessly shown up than it was on that Sunday....[17]

---

[17] Douglas Goldring, *A Stranger in Ireland* (London, 1918).

377

Over 3,000 people, most of whom were in no way con-nected with the violence, were arrested in the wake of the 1916 Rebellion on the word of informers. Initially the prisoners were scattered throughout a variety of British prisons, but soon a prisoner-of-war camp was established in north Wales. This became the principal "Republican University" of the period. Men were brought together in a ferment of new books, ideas and interchange, and left revolutionary graduates who would change the course of Irish history. Michael Collins, the best known of these, began to reorganize the Irish Republican Brotherhood inside the camp, using the wide variety of inmates to ensure that the doctrines of Wolfe Tone would be carried to the four corners of the land when internment ended.

By the end of World War I in 1918, Home Rule was forgot-ten. All of Ireland except Ulster was now convinced that an Irish republic, free of Britain, was the only acceptable answer. In the general election that year Sinn Féin won in a landslide victory. The Irish Parliamentary Party was left with only six seats, and it was obvious that the Irish had chosen to leave Britain, whether they allowed it or not. Sinn Féin, stating that its elected members would not sit in Britain's Parliament, set about establishing an independent government, called Dáil Éireann, in Dublin. Early in 1919 the members of the Dáil declared Ireland a republic. Britain responded by declaring them rebels.

Éamon de Valera,[18] the president of the Dail and leader of Sinn Féin, traveled to America where he raised $10,000,000 between 1919 and 1921 for the new Irish Republic.[19] Mean-while the Irish Republican Brotherhood had become the Irish Republican Army (IRA) and, led by Michael Collins, was

---

[18] He was the senior surviving officer of the Easter Rebellion.
[19] R. F. Foster, *Modern Ireland 1600-1972* (London, 1989).

committed to looking for a solution to the British problem through force.

The British government sent the first of a series of ex-servicemen taskforces to Ireland in 1920. Ruthless and violent, they became known as the Black and Tans from the colors of their uniform. They were given a free hand to shoot, loot, and carouse as they wished, and for support, they could call on the more elite Auxiliaries who were ex-British army officers. The IRA responded by setting up guerrilla-like flying columns – small groups of men who were able to move easily throughout the country while local people supplied them with food and shelter.

"What probably drove a peacefully inclined man like myself into rebellion," recalled one Clare man, "was the British attitude towards us, the assumption that the whole lot of us were a pack of murdering corner-boys."

There was a series of atrocities and reprisals committed on both sides. On November 21, 1920, a date that became known as Bloody Sunday, nineteen British intelligence officers and soldiers were shot in Dublin by Michael Collins' gunmen. Crown forces reacted by shooting into the crowd at a GAA match in Croke Park, Dublin, that afternoon, killing fourteen people and wounding sixty. Marital Law was declared in Cork, Kerry, Limerick, and Tipperary and the following day a group of Auxiliaries went on the rampage in Cork, burning down a substantial part of the city center. Britain began formulating plans for deploying 250,000 troops.

A showdown was avoided when the British Prime Minister declared a truce with Sinn Féin. A conference, held in London, was called to discuss Ireland's constitutional status, Britain's security interests in Ireland, and future links with Britain along with a partition of Ulster between the predominantly Catholic and Protestant counties. The negotiations lasted two months.

The Treaty that resulted was signed on December 6, 1921. A compromise had been reached whereby British rule in Ireland was at an end: Ireland had Dominion status and the twenty-six counties were to be called the Irish Free State.[20] One of the concessions that Ireland had to make in order to obtain this treaty was that the six counties in the province of Ulster that had a majority of Protestants were separated from the rest of Ireland and remained under the control of Britain. The Irish delegation believed this was only a temporary situation.

The Treaty divided the Irish into two opposing groups: those who were pro-Treaty, led by Michael Collins, and saw it as giving Ireland independence, and those who were against it, led by Éamon de Valera, believing that the Treaty was a betrayal of what the men of 1916 had died for because it did not immediately create a Republic. While a provisional government was created under Michael Collins to oversee the transfer of power to the Irish, civil war broke out between these two groups. On December 6, 1922 the Irish Free State became a reality as Ireland's people fought among themselves. The following year when Éamon de Valera ordered his followers to lay down their arms the civil war ended.

Immediately the new Irish government drew up a constitution for the country and formed a parliament. In regards to moral or religious views, the politicians deferred to their revered Catholic Church. A film censor was appointed who could cut a film or refuse a license if he felt it to be "subversive of public morality." This was followed a few years later by the creation of a board that had the power to ban any book or periodical because it was "indecent or obscene." In 1924

---

[20] Britain retained access to three Irish ports for defense (Berehaven, Queenstown [Cobh] and Lough Swilly) and all Irish leaders had to swear an oath of allegiance to the crown.

Cardinal Logue set the ground rules for public morality in the new Irish state. He declared war on women's scant clothing as well as dancing, "the outcrop of the corruption of the age" which stood in the way of making Ireland "what she ought to be, a good, solid, Catholic nation." Not only was the Catholic viewpoint on divorce strictly enforced but an Act followed which prohibited the dissemination of literature advocating birth control and formed the basis for legislation which ultimately outlawed contraception altogether. The Catholic bishops favored a puritanistic approach more sympathetic to Rome than to their own traditional Irish culture.

It wasn't only in moral matters that the traditional Irish culture was abandoned. The ancient Irish respect for women was disregarded, and legislation restricting women's right to serve on juries was enacted. Then a women's right to sit for any civil service examination was limited. In 1932 compulsory retirement was enjoined on female teachers who married, and this was subsequently extended to the civil service. Finally the state restricted the employment of women in industry.

While the new government struggled with laws to govern itself, it quickly established Ireland as an international presence. Ireland became a member of the League of Nations in 1923, and was elected to the Council of the League in 1930.

Ireland was free of its oppressor. John Gibbons, an Englishman, writes of his visit to an Irish pub in a small town during this time. He sat down next to an old Irishman who started singing

> . . . some of the old Irish songs in English, and this time I understood very well indeed. Some of them must have come down from the Rebellion times of 1798, and one of them was about the potato famine of the eighteen-forties and how we English starved the Irish. The odd thing was that the old man apologized to me before each song, and then went on to sing it.

All about English soldiers being tyrants and despots and things, and once, I know, we were 'demons'. And to nearly all these things the people knew the chorus, and sang it. There was one bit about 'England quaking' that went with such a swing that only just in time did I pull myself up from joining in it. Real pep they put into the business, and to one bit about hating England I put it genially to the man next to me that he sang the verse as though he really meant it. "But I do mean it," he said, "and so does every one else in this room." It made me jump a bit, for, after all, though a joke is a joke there is a limit. I am English and I must not for very decency listen to everything. And yet if I walked out into the one-horse village ten miles from anywhere, where on earth was I to spend the night? I was fumbling uneasily for my hat when the atmosphere cleared again. "But," the man went on, "my hating England does not mean that I hate the English." I tell you it was all most peculiar.[21]

A significant event took place in 1932 when, through a general election, de Valera was voted into power. The government transferred power smoothly between the two groups who had opposed each other so violently during the civil war. From the outset Éamon de Valera was determined to pursue an Irish Republic instead of simply a Free State. He began by removing from the Constitution a great psychological barrier required under the initial British treaty, the Oath of Allegiance taken by all Irish politicians. He also declared forfeit the land annuities still owed to the British. Dating from the 1880s, these annuities were repayments on loans given to Irish farmers to buy out landlords of which annual installments were still being sent to the British. The British reacted with a trade war that would last six years.

In 1937 Éamon de Valera introduced a new constitution. The Irish Free State was renamed Éire and declared a "sover-

---

[21] John Gibbons, *Tramping through Ireland* (London, 1930).

eign, independent, democratic state." In all but name Eire was a republic.[22] De Valera, obviously envisioning the end of partition, laid claim to both North and South Ireland "pending the reintegration of the national territory." Britain, still enforcing its trade war with Ireland, responded by calling for a conference. Éamon de Valera entered the talks with three priorities – the end of partition, the handing over of the Treaty Ports to Ireland and an end to the trade war. He was successful in two of his demands, the Treaty Ports were restored to Ireland and a trade agreement put an end to the economic war with the stipulation that Britain would write off the £104 million owed by Ireland for land annuities in return for a one-time payment of £10 million. Ulster, however, would not accept an end to the partition.

When World War II broke out, the Prime Minister of Britain, Winston Churchill, demanded that the Treaty Ports of Cobh, Lough Swilly, and Berehaven be at the disposal of the British Navy. Éamon de Valera, determined that the country should remain neutral, refused. As the war dragged on, despite opposition from both Churchill and President Roosevelt of America, he never wavered. The psychological effect for Eire, with Britain unable to control them, was inspiring to the people. Though Britain was furious with this public stance, privately Ireland helped. Any British planes forced to land in Ireland were returned to Britain or Northern Ireland with their crew while the crews of German aircraft that crashed in Ireland were interned in the Curragh until the end of the war. British over flights of Irish air space and "hot pursuit in Irish territorial waters" were sanctioned as well as the use of Shannon Airport by the British. According to the Secretary of the Irish Government, Maurice Moynihan, "we could not do more if we were in

---

[22] He dared not call it a republic for fear it would create a country devoid of Northern Ireland.

the war, all our surplus production going to them [Britain]."[23]

In his victory broadcast of 1945 Churchill could not restrain himself from making an attack on de Valera and Irish neutrality.

> Had it not been for the loyalty and friendship of Northern Ireland we should have come to – we should have been forced to come to close quarters with Mr. de Valera or perish forever from the earth. However with a restraint and poise with which I say history will find few parallels His Majesty's Government never laid a violent hand upon them though at times it would have been quite easy and quite natural. And we left Mr. de Valera's government to frolic with the German and later with the Japanese representatives to their hearts' content.

Several days later de Valera responded, justifying his policy and winning himself many supporters by the calm and statesmanlike way in which he refuted Churchill's accusations. He concluded by saying:

> There is a small nation that stood alone not for one year or for two, but for several hundred years against aggression: that endured spoilations, was clubbed many times into insensibility, but that each time on returning consciousness took up the fight anew; a small nation that could never be got to accept defeat and has never surrendered her soul.

The years following World War II were an economic boom for Northern Ireland, but snubbed for its neutral position by Britain (who dominated as their trading partner) and the other allies, Eire did not share in this. Bad harvests as well as strikes in the public and private sectors fueled a growing depression. Inflation, unemployment, and emigration wracked Ireland's

---

[23] Tim Pat Coogan, *Ireland in the 20th Century* (New York, 2006).

economic situation. Politicians, eager for a distraction, chose to promote a bill declaring Eire a Republic in 1949. On Easter Monday, April 18, 1949, the anniversary of the Easter Rebellion, Eire became the Republic of Ireland, formally free of allegiance to the British crown and no longer a member of the Commonwealth. In the following month, the British Parliament confirmed the status of Northern Ireland as part of the United Kingdom until its own parliament chose otherwise.

The Republic became a member of the United Nations on December 14, 1955. It declined to join the North Atlantic Treaty Organization (NATO), however, since this would have entailed entering into an alliance with the United Kingdom, which retained possession of Northern Ireland.

The economic conditions in Ireland slowly improved through the 1950s, but it wasn't until 1959, under the innovative leadership of Seán Lemass, that the climate in the Republic of Ireland dramatically improved. Foreign investors were attracted to Ireland, living standards rose, and there was a resurgence of national spirit. Educational opportunities for Irish children were expanded. In 1966 free secondary education and transportation for children was introduced which resulted in an immediate increase in the number of children attending school. Lemass also put Ireland on the world stage when, despite opposition, he agreed to send Irish troops to join the United Nation peacekeeping forces in the Belgian Congo. Ireland had never before been involved in an international situation like this. It was the beginning of Irish involvement with United Nation peacekeepers throughout the world, marking the end of its neutrality policy. Lemass's attempts to facilitate better relationships between Northern and Southern Ireland, however, were not so successful. Northern Protestant extremists accused their own leader of selling out whenever a compromise seemed possible.

Ireland Today

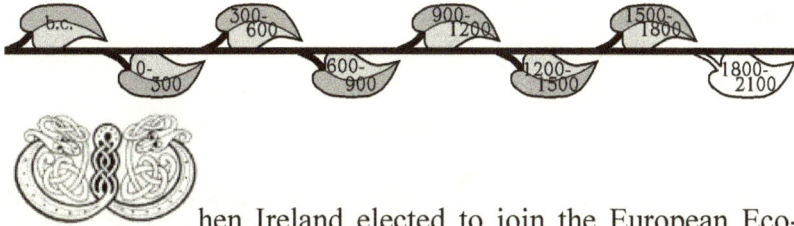

hen Ireland elected to join the European Economic Community in 1973, it appeared to be exchanging its policy of self-reliance for dependency. As Denis O'Hearn put it, a "country which had virtually clothed and shod itself in 1960 imported more than seventy-one percent of its clothing in 1980." Europe, still viewing the country as poor and backward, authorized funding for the construction of Ireland's first modern infrastructure. Within a few short years the choice to join the European Economic Community had transformed Ireland. By shedding its isolationist policy, however, Ireland exposed itself to globalization.[1] The poor global economic growth of the 1980s was therefore mirrored in Ireland. When the global economy rebounded in the 1990s, so did Ireland's.

Ireland's economy began to grow so rapidly that, in 1994, Kevin Gardiner of the Morgan Stanley investment bank in London compared it to the "tiger" economies of south-east Asia and called it the "Celtic Tiger." Throughout the 1990s, Ireland's levels of growth soon became the envy of every other western state. Over the decade as a whole, gross domestic product (GDP) per capita grew on average by seven percent each year. In 1996, an important psychological barrier was

---

[1] The influential US magazine *Foreign Policy* issued a "Globalization Index" in 2001 that, for the second year in a row, found the Irish Republic to be number one among the 62 states surveyed. Ireland's economy is tied very closely with the global one.

breached when the economy of the Republic of Ireland overtook that of the United Kingdom for the first time and far outperformed that of Northern Ireland.

At the close of the 20th century Ireland was the fastest growing economic power in Europe. According to the Organization for Economic Co-operation and Development:

> Many U.S. businesses find Ireland an attractive location to manufacture for the E.U. (European Union) market, since it is inside the E.U. customs area . . . . The availability of an educated, well-trained, English-speaking work force and relatively moderate wage costs have been important factors. Ireland offers good long-term growth prospects for U.S. companies.

While the era of the Celtic Tiger has brought modernization and prosperity to Ireland, destroyed the British "stereotype of the drunken, hotheaded, garrulous Irishman that had been common on the English stage since the time of Shakespeare,"[2] and greatly increased women's equality, not all of Ireland has benefited. Increased productivity, necessary to feed the Celtic Tiger, requires both parents to work therefore impinging on quality family time. Recent statistics also suggest that the Irish Republic has the second greatest concentration of poverty in the western world. Among the developed countries only the United States has a larger proportion of people who are poor.[3] "Few will disagree that while the quality of the things we own has improved, our quality of life is declining."[4] Irish society, and therefore culture, appears to be in jeopardy.

---

[2] http://www.fact-index.com/i/ir/irish_theatre.html
[3] P. Cullen, "Statistical Snapshot of a World Divided by Poverty," *Irish Times*, July 24, 2002, p. 7. The concept of economic stratification was found in the Brehon laws, however, and goes back to ancient Celtic independence. Those who work hard can improve, those who don't won't.
[4] *Irish Times*, November 1, 2002.

A great deal of this book has examined Irish culture, but before looking at modern Irish culture, three common misconceptions about the word should be cleared up. The first misconception believes culture is a geographic term, that only those born in Ireland can have Irish culture. This misconception means the child of an Arab immigrant born in Dublin has Irish culture while a second generation Irishman born in the Irish section of Boston doesn't. A second misconception believes culture is transferred purely through language. As fewer and fewer Irish speak Gaelic, so goes the culture. This implies that Jamaica and England must have the same culture since they have the same language, although different dialects. A third misconception is that as physical examples of a culture disappear, such as thatched roofs, pastoral living, and digging peat, so does the culture. If this is true then none of the industrialized countries of the world have survived with their culture intact. These misconceptions err by creating a structure for culture, but culture is the way a group sees and interacts with the world, which by nature is fluid. Geography, language, and physical objects are only a means of maintaining and transferring culture, along with other means such as traditions, folklore and history.

Will modernization destroy Irish culture? Modernization, conveyed throughout the world in the form of American media, invades a country economically as well as politically and culturally. Ireland has suffered invasions before – the Catholic Church, the Vikings, the Normans, and the Tudors – yet its culture has reemerged, albeit altered as any healthy culture should be. Even with the loss of its language,[5] which weak-

---

[5] Those claiming an ability to speak some Irish in the 20th century have grown from a low of 18% in 1911 to a figure at the close of the century around 30% (350,000 people). One of the significant developments in Irish education has been the growth of the Gael scoileanna in which Irish is the

ened the sense of distinctive Irish identity and culture, "Irishness" remains. This modern invasion, like all previous ones, will surely alter Irish culture, but not overwhelm it. Old Irish proverbs, succinctly conveying the wisdom of Gaelic culture, can still be applied today, as the following account suggests.

In 1996 Jim Kinsella launched the Kinsella homepage[6] and began planning a visit to Ireland for research on Ireland's 12th century. Coincidentally, Jim received an email from Denis Kinsella of Ferns, Ireland, who was planning a Clan Kinsella assembly for that summer, the first such assembly in almost 400 years. Excited by this prospect, Jim posted the date of the assembly on the Kinsella homepage, then asked whether Denis would mind if he stopped by beforehand. Denis agreed.

Jim, arriving in Ferns by bike since his headquarters for the next month was in nearby Carlow Town, booked himself into a B&B before arriving at Denis Kinsella's house. When Jim met Denis, he was also soon introduced to Denis' wife, Marion, and their four children. Almost immediately Denis called the B&B and cancelled Jim's reservation – he would be staying with the Kinsella family that night.[7] Discussions ranging from biking to pop stars and clan history soon filled the air.[8] Only the oldest child, Sarah, was missing. She was in Donnegal for the summer to learn Gaelic through the Gaeltecht program.[9]

The next morning, over a wonderful breakfast of oatmeal and sausages, Denis asked, "Would you like to take out the bikes today?

---

sole medium of instruction. It is commonplace for middle-class families to send their children to Gaeltacht districts (those that speak Gaelic exclusively), principally in the west of Ireland, for summer immersion courses in the language, music and dancing.

[6] www.kinsella.org.

[7] "A generous man, they say, has never gone to hell." Always have your house open to a guest.

[8] *"It is a sign of nobility to listen to art."* The arts, especially music, are highly respected. They add another dimension to one's life.

[9] Learning the Gaelic language.

I'd bring you by some of the cousins if you'd like." He then added shyly, "I also have to speak to Patrick, my second cousin down the road, about borrowing a tool."[10] Jim nodded his assent, and since his bike equipment was already set up from yesterday's ride, he waited outside while Denis prepared. Ferns, situated on a low-lying hill, affords a spectacular view of the River Slaney basin.

The oldest boy, Shane, came out also. Jim looked over at the young lad and asked, "Are you looking forward to school this year, Shane?"

"I suppose so," he began, but then added with a grin, "though I'm not looking forward to climbing Mount Leinster."[11]

"You don't have to climb it do you?" Jim asked a little incredulously (Mount Leinster is 2,160 feet above sea level).

"Yes. Everyone from the third year class must climb it unless they have a doctor's excuse. It takes all day. You can see it right over there." He pointed across rolling farmland in the valley below to the mass of land that abruptly rose from amidst a scattering of hills. He continued by naming many of the surrounding close hills, turning around as he did so. "That's Black Rock Mountain, Gibbet Hill, Sleiveboy, Tara Hill, Carrigroe Hill...."[12] A few days later Jim traveled to one of these nearby hills, Knockavoca, where he found at its summit a plain cement marker. The inauguration site of Hy Kinsella had not been forgotten.[13]

---

[10] *"There is luck in sharing a thing."* The sharing of material goods such as tools, equipment, etc. with friends and kin is expected. This helps form a close bond in the Gael's neighborhood.

[11] "Three candles that illume every darkness: truth, nature, knowledge." Nature is respected, especially mountains and water.

[12] *"A man lives long in his native place."* The land one grows up in is like a mother, always to be revered. The Gaels became intimately familiar with their local land.

[13] *"Truth is the historians food."* Education, especially history, is highly respected.

Surrounding hills of Ferns as seen from Knockavoca

Jim, between his other obligations and research, visited the Kinsellas frequently. A week after his initial visit he returned to attend the All Ireland Semi-Finals with the Kinsellas, a hurly event at Croke Park in Dublin. County Offaly was playing County Wexford and Offaly was highly favored to win. Before arriving at the Kinsellas' house, Jim grabbed a bite at a local restaurant, so as not to take advantage of the Kinsellas' hospitality, then walked down to their house.

After greeting Jim, Marion asked, "Do you like turkey, chicken, or ham, James?"

"I'm not very picky," he replied. "I like all three, but I've already eaten."

"What?" she said with surprise and slight indignation. "Surely you didn't. You must eat with us." No amount of convincing would change Marion's mind; Jim had to sit down with the family and eat. Never again would he make that mistake.[14]

The next day they all drove to Croke Park. It struck Jim as odd that their side of the road was full of traffic but the other side was empty. "They're all going to Croke Park," Jim joked.

---

[14] "*A generous man, they say, has never gone to hell.*" Hospitality is highly regarded.

"That they are," the youngest, Donnacha, replied. Jim was stunned. Was everyone from County Wexford driving to this game? The lanes leading south, into Wexford were empty. The game of hurly, if you haven't watched it, is fast and exciting with few dull moments. This semi-final was no exception. When the end of the game drew near, as predicted, Wexford was losing and the entire family was crestfallen.

In the last few minutes of the game, however, the warriors of Wexford surprised everyone and pulled off a dramatic victory. The stadium erupted as the crowd cheered and applauded; some even ran out onto the field to congratulate their players. The Kinsellas drove back to Ferns on a high, replaying the game through their conversations until they reached County Wexford. As soon as they reached the county line everything changed. People stood along the roadside cheering. Banners were hung from house windows congratulating Wexford on its victory. Every corner had a bonfire blazing. Rather than losing the sense of excitement engendered by the game, it was heightened.[15]

On the way home Jim mentioned to the Kinsellas, "I would like to take you all out to dinner tonight. I will not accept any excuses." He paused and noticed Marion about to say something but then he firmly added, "You've all been so warm and accepting of me that I feel the need to reciprocate."

"James," Marion finally managed, "you needn't do such a thing. I already have a meal planned and it wouldn't be right to waste it."

"You can have that meal tomorrow, Marion. Where would you like to go tonight?"

"It's sometimes easier with the children," began Denis, "to eat at home."

"Then we can order the food and bring it home," Jim countered. "I won't take no for an answer." After debating the issue for a while longer, finally Denis and Marion hesitantly accepted.

---

[15] *"There has not been found, nor will there be found, a juster judge than the field of battle."* Fighting was glorified – the modern Gaelic culture has transformed this into a love of sports.

"The Celtic Arms," immediately blurted out Ciara. Like the other children she had tried to conceal her excitement over the proposal. After dropping the car off at home, they walked down to The Celtic Arms together where they had a wonderful time and a great meal.[16]

A few weeks later Jim's parents and a sister arrived in time to attend the Clan Kinsella Assembly at Ferns. People who had never met came together for a mass, dinner, and history talk. Throughout the entire evening, stories of personal as well as family histories predominated.[17] For the first time in almost 400 years, a leader of Clan Kinsella was elected: Eddy Kinsella, a historian.[18]

To those who believe the Irish culture was vanquished by the English occupation, the authors agree that 12th-century Irish culture disappeared, as did 12th-century English culture in England. To those who believe Irish culture no longer exists, the authors would ask them to visit 21st-century Ireland and spend a few weeks with a family.

"Wexford is largely undiscovered, we call it the 'secret island,' an authentic experience of the people as we are. Distinct, we are a combination of three different cultures: Gaelic, Anglo-Irish and Norman. Indeed Wexford was the first soil touched upon by the Norman's when they first invaded Ireland in 1169.

The county enjoys a rare mix of mountains, valleys, flora, fauna and breathtaking beaches spanning 200 km of coastline. This delightful melange provides for active resorts, scenic

---

[16] *"Money is a poor substitute for reciprocity."* Paying for a favor circumvents pride, honor, and familiarity with neighbors.
[17] *"You would make a story out of the stones of the strand."* Stories should be told and retold at any gatherings. Great attention to the truth is essential; details shouldn't be altered simply because they make a better story.
[18] *"Three candles that illume every darkness: truth, nature, knowledge."* Hold learning, especially history, in high esteem.

villages and pretty harbours dotted around the coast. Serviced by two major rivers, the Slaney and Barrow, the county has become a well-recognised fishing paradise. The county is host to one of the busiest ferry ports in Ireland at Rosslare, servicing both the UK and mainland Europe; we are also within easy access of three major airports: Dublin, Cork and Waterford.[19]

While Kinsellas can still be found in northern County Wexford, what ties us together now is no longer geography. It's a name. Long ago a clan's name identified its members with certain characteristics, histories and ideals: their ancestor's values. The relationship between the generations with these values was considered reciprocal. Clan members derived pride from stories of ancestors who demonstrated them, but each clan member was expected to add to this oral history through feats of his or her own. The authors hope you have derived pride from these stories of the Clan Kinsella, but . . .

---

[19] http://www.wexfordtourism.com/.

Appendix A

Kinsella Coat of Arms

KINSELLA

The emblems of heraldry recognized today were introduced by the Normans; they were not considered a matter of importance by the Gaelic Irish who had their own symbols and flags. Heraldry only became important to the Gaels when they found themselves banished to continental Europe after their defeat by William of Orange in 1691.

Official Description
Argent a fess gules between in chief two garbs of the last and in base a lion passant sable.

Explanation
The white background stands for sincerity. The red band signifies a military belt and stands for a clan of warriors who esteem honor. The black lion means constancy. The sheafs of wheat represent the fertility of the area the Kinsellas live in.

Crest's History
According to Ireland's Herald of Arms, the Kinsella arms "were probably assumed rather than granted and at some later time confirmed to a petitioner descended from the first user . . . in all likelihood someone in France in the 18th century."

Kinsella Motto
Mo dhuthaidh ro bais = My home territory to die

Kinsella Battle Cry
Kinchelagh Abu = Victory to Kinsella

Appendix B

Kinsella Genealogy Listing[1]

In this listing of the Kinsella genealogy, the first thirty-five generations, which include biblical names and the names of the Gaels that wandered all over the Mediterranean Sea, are purely the invention of enthusiastic monks who were trying to make Irish genealogy agree with biblical information.

The story of the landing in Ireland around 1,000 B.C. as recorded in the Book of Invasions is considered mythology, similar to the Greek and Roman ancestor myths. The next fifty-odd generations after the Milesians are likewise considered to be mythological, although it is conceded that the activities of these people in some cases may refer to actual historical events.

All the leading families in Ireland trace themselves back to one of the four Milesian chieftains who supposedly led the Gaelic invasion of Ireland. Douglas Hyde in *A Literary History of Ireland* concludes that the long list of descendants from these chieftains should be discarded until we reach names of people who lived in the 3rd or 4th century A.D. At this time most of the noble genealogies converge. He believes that genealogy lists after this time should be considered authentic.

Hyde goes on to state that there is one family line that appears to be much older than the rest. He says that the most ancient of all Irish pedigrees is the line of Leinster righs that goes back to around 300 B.C., at which point it joins the

---

[1] John O'Hart, *Irish Pedigrees* (Baltimore, 1976, 1892); and Patrick Laurence O'Toole, *History of the Clan O'Toole: and Other Leinster Septs* (Dublin, 1890).

artificial list of names that leads back to the Milesians. The Kinsellas descend from this line.

Biblical portion
1.   Adam: his wife was Eve
2.   Seth: son of
3.   Enos: son of
4.   Cainan: son of
5.   Mahalaleel: son of
6.   Jared: son of
7.   Enoch: son of
8.   Methuselah: son of
9.   Lamech: son of
10.   Noah: son of
11.   Japhet: eldest son of Noah, who had 15 sons, among whom he divided Europe and the part of Asia his father had allotted him.
12.   Magog: his son, from whom descended the Parthians, Gadelians, Amazonians, etc.; also Bartholinus, the first planter of Ireland, about three hundred years after the flood.
13.   Baoth: one of the sons of Magog, to whom Scythia came as his lot upon the division of the earth by Noah and subsequently by Japhet of his part among his sons.
14.   Phoeniusa (Fenius) Farsaidh: inventor of letters.
15.   Niul: after his father's return to Scythia, continued some time at Aeothania, teaching the languages and other laudable sciences, until, upon report of his great learning, he was invited into Egypt by Pharaoh, the king who gave him the land of Campuss Eyrunt, near the Red Sea, to inhabit, and he also gave him his daughter Scota in marriage, from whom their posterity are ever since called the Scots. It was this Niulus who employed Gaodhal (Gael) son of Eighor, a learned and skillful

man, to compose, or rather refine, the language called Bearla Tobbai, which was common to the posterity of Niulus, and was afterwards called "Gaodh-ilg" from the said Gaodhal, who composed and improved it, and for his sake also Niulus called his eldest son "Gaodhal."

16. Gaodhal: the son of Niulus, was the ancestor of the Clan na Gael, that is, the children or descendants of Gaodhal. In his youth this Gaodhal was stung in the neck by a serpent, and was immediately brought to Moses, who, by laying the miraculous rod on the wounded place, cured him, and, in addition to this cure, he obtained a further blessing, which we enjoy to the present day – namely, that no venomous beast can live at any time where his posterity should inhabit, which privilege is verified in Candia, Getulea, and Ireland.

17. Asruth: his son, continued in Egypt, and governed his colony in peace during his life.

18. Sruth: his son, soon after his father's death, was set upon by the Egyptians, actuated by their former animosities towards his predecessors, for having taken part with the Israelites against them, and which animosities had, until then, lain raked up in the embers, but which now broke out into a flame, to that degree that, after many battles and conflicts, wherein most of his colony lost their lives, Sruth was forced, with the few remaining, to depart the country, and after many traverses at sea, arrived at the Island of Crete, or Candia, where he died.

19. Heber Scutt: after his father's death, and a year's stay at Crete, departed thence, leaving some of his people to inherit the island, and where some of their posterity likely remain, as the islands harbor no venomous serpents ever since. He and his people soon after arrived in Scythia, where his cousins, the posterity of Nenuallus

(eldest son of Farsa), refused to allot a place of habitation for him and his colony; they fought many battles, wherein Heber, being always the victor, at length forced the sovereignty from the reigning king, and settled himself and his colony in Scythia where they continued for four generations. Heber Scott was afterwards slain in battle, by Noemus, the son of the former king.

20. Beouman: son of
21. Oghaman: son of
22. Tait: were kings of Scythia, but in constant war with the natives, so that after Tait's death, his son . . .
23. Agnan: and his followers betook themselves to sea, wandering and coasting upon the Caspian for several years, in which time he died.
24. Lamhfionn: and his fleet remained at sea for some time after his father's death, resting and refreshing themselves upon such islands as they met with. It was then that Cachear, their magician or Druid, foretold that there would be no end to their wanderings and travels, until they would arrive in the western island of Europe called Ireland, which was the place destined for their future and final abode, and that not only they but their posterity after three hundred years should arrive there. After many traverses of fortune at sea this little fleet arrived at last with their leader at Gothia or Gethulia, more recently Libya, where Carthage was afterwards built, and soon afterwards Lamhfoin died there.
25. Heber Glunfionn: his son, was born in Getulia where he also died. His posterity continued there to the eighth generation, and were kings or rulers for one hundred and fifty years and upwards.
26. Agnan Fionn: son of

27. Febric Glas: son of
28. Nenuall: son of
29. Nuadhad: son of
30. Alladh: son of
31. Arcadh: son of
32. Deagh: son of
33. Brath: was born in Gothia. Remembering the Druid predictions, and his people having increased considerably during their abode in Getulia, he departed thence with a numerous fleet, to seek out the country destined for their final settlement by the prophecy of Cachear. After some time he landed on the coast of Spain, and by the strong hand settled himself and his colony in Galicia, in the north of that country.
34. Breoghan (Brigus): from which the "Brigantes": was king of Galicia, Andalusia, Murcia, Castile, and Portugal, all of which he conquered. He built Breoghans Tower, or Brigantia, in Galicia, and the city of Braganza, in Portugal, called after himself. The kingdom of Castile was then called Brigia after him also.
35. Bile: was king of those countries after his father's death, and was succeeded by his son Milesius (Galamh). This Bile had a brother named Ithe.

Foundation Myth portion
36. Milesius of Spain: From whom all the nobility of Ireland are descended.
37. Heremon: his son. He had the following sons:
a. Muimne: This Monarch was buried at Croaghan, situated near Elphin, in County Roscommon. In the early ages, Croaghan became the capital of Connacht and a residence of the ancient Ard Righ of Ireland; and at Croaghan the states of Connacht held conventions, to

make laws and inaugurate their righs. There, too, about a century before the Christian era, the Monarch Eochy Feidlioch erected a royal residence and a great rath, called Rath Cruachan, after his queen, Cruachan Croidheirg, mother of Maeve (famous from Red Branch stories).

b. Luigne
c. Laighean
d. Trial or Eurialus (Irial Faidh). He asserted his rights to his father's crown, and succeeded in gaining it in a pitched battle.

38. Irial Faidh (a prophet): his son, was the 10th Monarch of Ireland; died 1670 B.C. This was a very learned righ; he could foretell things to come; and caused much of the country to be cleared of the ancient forest. He likewise built seven royal palaces (Rath Ciombaoigh, Rath Coincheada, Rath Mothuig, Rath Buirioch, Rath Luachat, Rath Croicne, and Rath Boachoill). He won four remarkable battles over his enemies: Ard Inmath, at Teabtha, where Stirne, the son of Dubh, son of Fomhar, was slain; the second battle was at Teanmhuighe, against the Fomhoraice, where Eichtghe, their leader, was slain; the third was the battle of Loch Muighe, where Lugrot, the son of Moghfeibhis, was slain; and the fourth was the battle of Cuill Martho, where the four sons of Heber were defeated. Irial died in the second year after this battle, having reigned 10 years, and was buried at Magh Muagh. During his reign a great part of the country was laid open, and freed from woods.

39. Eithrial: his son; was the 11th Monarch; reigned 20 years. This prince was distinguished for his great learning; he wrote, with his own hand, the history and travels of the Badelians; nor was he less remarkable for

his valor and military accomplishments. He was slain by Conmaol, the son of Heber Fionn, at the battle of Soirrean, in Leinster (1650 B.C.) leaving only one son.

40. Foll-Aich: his son; was kept out of the Monarchy by Conmaol, the slayer of his father, who usurped his place.

41. Tigernmas: his son; was the 13th Monarch, and reigned 50 years.

42. Enboath: his son. It was in this prince's lifetime that the Kingdom was divided in two parts by a line drawn from Drogheda to Limerick.

43. Smiomghall: his son; in his lifetime the Picts in Scotland were forced to abide by their oath, and pay homage to the Irish Monarch; seven large woods were also cut down.

44. Fiacha Labhrainn: his son; was the 18th Monarch; reigned 24 years, slew Eochaidh Faobharglas, of the line of Heber, at the battle of Carman. During his reign all the inhabitants of Scotland were brought in subjection to the Irish Monarchy, and the conquest was secured by his son the 20th Monarch. Fiacha at length (1448 B.C.) fell in the battle of Bealgadain, by the hands of Eochaidh Mumho, the son of Moefeibhis, of the race of Heber Fionn. He was called Labhrainn because during his reign the stream of Tubher Labhrainn began to flow.

45. Aongus Olmucach: his son; was the 20th Monarch. He was named for having a breed of swine of a much larger size than any in Ireland, the words "oll" and "mucca" signifying "great swine." He was a valiant and warlike prince, and fought the following battles: the battle of Claire, the battle of Moigen Cgiath, in Connacht; the battle of Glaise Fraochain, where Frachain Faiah was killed; and in his reign the Picts again refused to pay the tribute imposed on them 250 years before, by Heremon,

but this Monarch went with a strong army into Alba and in thirty pitched battles overcame them and forced them to pay the required tribute. Aongus was at length slain by Eana, in the battle of Carman, 1409 B.C.

46. Main: his son; was kept out of the Monarchy by Eadna, of the line of Heber Fionn. In his time silver shields were given as rewards for bravery to the Irish militia.

47. Rogheachach: his son; was the 22nd Monarch for 25 years; slain 1357 B.C. by Sedne (Seadhna) of the Line of Ir at Rath Cuchain. Silver shields were made, and four-horse chariots were first used in Ireland during his reign.

48. Dein: his son; was kept out of the Monarchy by his father's slayer, and his son. In his time gentlemen and nobleman first wore gold chains round their necks, as a sign of their birth; and golden helmets were given to brave soldiers.

49. Siorna "Saoghalach" (long life): his son; was the 34th Monarch who reigned 21 years; he was slain (1030 B.C.) at Aillin, by Rotheachta, of the Line of Heber Fionn, who usurped the Monarchy, thereby excluding Siorna's son, Olioll Aolcheoin, from the throne.

50. Olioll Aolcheoin: son of Siorna Saoghalach.

51. Gialchadh: his son; was the 37th Monarch for 9 years; killed by Art Imleach, of the Line of Heber Fionn, at Moighe Muadh, 1013 B.C.

52. Nuadhas Fionnfail: his son; was the 39th Monarch for 21 years; slain by the son of Art Imleach, Breasrioghacta (961 B.C.), his successor.

53. Aedan Glas: his son. In his time the coast was infested with pirates; and there occurred a dreadful plague (Apthach) which swept away most of the inhabitants.

54. Simeon Breac: his son; was the 44th Monarch; he

inhumanly caused his predecessor to be torn asunder; but, after a reign of 6 years, he met with a like death (903 B.C.), by order of Duach Fionn, son to the murdered righ.

55. Muredach Bolgach: his son; was the 46th Monarch for 4 years; killed by Eadhna Dearg (son of Duach Fionn) in 892 B.C. Had the following sons:

a. Duach Teamhrach, who had the following sons:
   1. Eochaidh Framhuine, 51st Monarch of Ireland.
   2. Conang Beag-eaglach, 53rd Monarch of Ireland.

b. Riacha Tolgrach, who is described below.

56. Riacha (Feachus?) Tolgrach: son of Muredach; was the 55th Monarch for 5 years. His life was ended by the sword of Oilioll Fionn of the line of Heber Fionn, 795 B.C.

57. Duach Ladhrach: his son; was the 59th Monarch for 10 years. He was distinguished by the name Duach Lagrach by reason of his being so strict and hasty in the execution of justice; that he was impatient and would not admit of a moment's delay until the criminal was seized and tried for the offense; the word "Lagrach," means speed and suddenness. He was killed by Lughaidh Laighe, son of Oilioll Fionn, 737 B.C.

58. Eochaidh Buadhach: his son; was kept out of the Monar-chy by his father's slayer. In his time the kingdom was twice visited with a plague.

59. Ugaine Mor: his son. This Ugaine (Hugony) the Great was the 66th Monarch of Ireland for 40 years.

60. Laeghaire Lorc, the 68th Monarch of Ireland: son of Ugaine Mor: began to reign, 593 B.C.

61. Olioll Aine: his son. Slain by Cobhthach Caolmbreag, lest he should disturb his reign.

62. Labhradh Longseach: his son. Around 250 B.C. (*See*

the chapter "The Origins of the Leinstermen," p. 53.)

63. Olioll Bracan: his son.
64. Aeneas Ollamh: his son; the 73rd Monarch for 18 years. He fell by the sword of Iaran Gleofathach.
65. Breassal: his son.
66. Fergus Fortamhail: his son; the 80th Monarch. He was known by that name because he had great strength of body, and brave beyond any of his time. He reigned 12 years and was slain 384 B.C. in battle by Aongus Tuirmeach.
67. Felim Fortuin: his son.
68. Crimthann Coscrach: his son; the 85th Monarch for 7 years. He was distinguished by that name because he behaved with such bravery at the head of his army, that he was victorious in every battle he fought; "Cosgrach" signifies "slaughter" and "bloodshed." He was slain by Rogerus, the son of Sithrig.
69. Mogh-Art: his son.
70. Art: his son.
71. Allod (Olioll): his son.
72. Nuadh Falaid: his son.
73. Fearach Foghlas: his son.
74. Olioll Glas: his son.
75. Fiacha Fobrug: his son.
76. Breassal Breac: his son. Had the following sons between whom he divided his country:
a. Lughaidh, who is described below. He was the ancestor of the Righs, nobility, and gentry of Leinster. He inherited all the territories on the north side of the river Barrow, from Wicklow to Drogheda.
b. Conla. He was the ancestor of the Righs, nobility, and gentry of Ossory. He inherited the south part, from the Barrow to the sea.

77. Lughaidh (Luy): son of Breassal Breac.
78. Sedna: his son; built the royal city of Rath Alinne (now Allen in County Kildare).
79. Nuadhas Neacht (Neass): his son; the 96th Monarch. The royal city of Naas is named after him. He was killed by the sword of Conaire, the son of Eidersgoil. Had the following sons:
  a. Fergus Fairge, who is described below.
  b. Baoisgne, who was the father of Cubhall (Coole) who was the father of Fionn, commonly called "Finn MacCoole," the general in the 3rd century of the ancient Irish Militia known as the Fianna Eirionn, or "Fenians of Ireland."
80. Fergus Fairge: his son.
81. Ros: son of Fergus Fairge.
82. Fionn File (a poet): his son.
83. Conchobhar Abhraoidhruaidh: his son; the 99th Monarch of Ireland for 1 year. His name came from the fact that the hair of his eyebrows was red; the word "abrudhruadh" means "red eyebrows."
84. Mogh Corb: his son.
85. Cu-Corb: his son; Leinster righ. He had the following sons:
  a. Niadh Corb, who is described below.
  b. Messincorb, from which Dal Messincorb.
  c. Cormac, from which Dal Cormaic, and who was the ancestor of Quirk.
  d. Cairbre Dluitheachar.
86. Niadh Corb: his son. He was a most valiant and warlike prince, "Nia" signifies hero. Had the following sons:
  a. Cormac Gealtach, who is described below.
  b. Ceathramhadh.
87. Cormac Gealtach: his son. He succeeded his father and

was a great general, and led the Irish army into Scotland, to assist the Picts and Scots against the Romans, who were commanded by Agricola. The battle with the Romans on the Grampian Hills was fierce and bloody; but the superior discipline of the Roman legions made it decisive in their favor. At his death he was succeeded by his son.

88. Felim Fiorurglas: his son. Had the following children:
a. Cathair Mor, who is described below.
b. Main Mal, the ancestor of O'Kelly of Cualan (in Wicklow), O'Tighe, and O'Cuallan.
c. Eithne.
89. Cathair Mor, 109th Monarch of Ireland in the beginning of the 2nd century: son of Felim Fiorurglas.
90. Fiacha Baicheda: youngest son of Cathair Mor; died 220. His father praised him for his bravery and spirit, and for the universal love he gained. He was called "the lame" on account of a wound he received in the battle of Moigh Acha, where his father was slain. From his posterity came the majority of the Leinster righs.
91. Breasal Bealach (large lipped): his son; was the 2nd Christian Leinster righ. Had following sons:
a. Labhradh, who is described below.
b. Enna Niadh, who begins family of O'Tooles.

The ancient righs of Leinster (Ui Cinnsealaigh = Hy Kinsella) had fortresses or royal residences at Dinn Righ, near the river Barrow, between Carlow and Leighlin; at Naas, in Kildare; and, in after times at the city of Ferns in Wexford, which was their capital; and also at Old Ross in Wexford; and at Bally-moon in Carlow. The Ui Cinnsealaigh were inaugurated as righs of Leinster at a place called Cnoc-an-Bhogha, attended by O'Nolan, who was the righ's Marshal, and Chief of Forth in

Carlow; by O'Doran, Chief Brehon of Leinster; and by
MacKeogh, their Chief Bard.

The major Leinster families began to split off at this point

92. Labhradh: son of Breasal Bealach. Had the following
    sons:
a. Eanna Cinnsealaigh, who is described below.
b. Deagh, from which Ui Deagha Mor; in Ui Cinnsealaigh
    lands.
93. Eanna Cinnsealaigh: elder son of Labhradh; married
    Conang; was named Ceann-Salach by Cednathech the
    Druid, whom he slew at Croghan Hill, in the King's
    County, where Eanna defeated Eochaidh Muigh
    Meadhoin (Eochy Moyvone), the Monarch, 365. (*See
    the chapter* "The Ui Cinnsealaigh Clan," p. 81.) Had the
    following children:
a. Feidhlimidh (Felim).
b. Eochu (Eochaidh) Cinnsealaigh, who was exiled to
    Scotland by the Irish Monarch Niall of the Nine
    Hostages, whom Eochu later assassinated near
    Boulogne, on the river Leor (now the Lianne).
c. Crimthann Cass, who is described below.
d. Earc.
e. Aongus.
f. Conal.
g. Trian.
h. Cairpre.

Historical portion

94. Crimthann Cass: 3rd son of Eanna Cinnsealach; was
    Leinster righ for 40 years; baptized by St. Patrick at
    Rathvilly around 448; slain in 484 by his grandson
    Eochaidh Guinech of the Hy-Bairche. Married Mell,

daughter of Erebran of the Desies in Munster (son of Eoghan Bric, son of Art Cuirb, son of Fiacha Suighde, son of Felim Rachtmar). (*See the chapter* "Saint Brigid to Crimthann," p. 109.) Had the following children:

a.   Ingen, wife of Daire MacErcadh of the Hy-Bairche.

b.   Nathach (Dathi), who is described below.

c.   Fiacra the Fair, made first bishop of Leinster by St. Patrick.

d.   Eithne Uathach, wife of Aongus MacNadfraech, Munster righ.

e.   Fergus, who defeated Diarmuid MacCearbhaill at Drum Laeghaire, by the side of Cais in Hy-Faelain, defending the Boromha Tribute.

f.   Aongus.

g.   Etchen.

h.   Cobthach.

95.   Nathach: son of Crimthan Cass; was Leinster righ for 10 years; baptized in his infancy by St. Patrick. Had the following children:

a.   Owen Caoch, who is described below.

b.   Cormac.

c.   Faelan, who had a son named Fergus.

d.   Olioll.

96.   Eoghan (Owen) Caoch: eldest son of Nathach. Had the following sons:

a.   Siollan, who is described below.

b.   Fergus, ancestor of O'Ryan.

97.   Siollan (skinny person): son of Eoghan Caoch.

98.   Faelan: his son; was Leinster righ for 9 years.

99.   Faolchu: his son. Had the following sons:

a.   Elodach, Leinster righ for 7 years.

b.   Onchu, who is described below.

c.   Aongus, slain in 721 at Maisden, Mullaghmast.

100. Onchu: son of Faolchu.
101. Rudgal: his son. Had the following sons:
a. Aodh (Hugh), who is described below.
b. Flann, slain at Allen, in the County Kildare, 722.
102. Aodh: son of Rudgal. Had the following sons:
a. Diarmuid, who is described below.
b. Bruadar, slain in 853.
103. Diarmuid: son of Aodh. Had the following sons:
a. Cairbre, who is described below.
b. Tadhg, slain in 865.
104. Cairbre: son of Diarmuid; slain in 876.
105. Ceneth: his son; slain by the Danes of Wexford; was Leinster righ for 13 years. Had following sons:
a. Echtighern, Leinster righ for 9 years; slain in 951 by the sons of Ceallach, his brother. He had the following sons:
   1. Cairpre, abbot of Clonmore, who died in 974.
   2. Aodh, who slew Donal Cloen in 983.
   3. Bruadar (Bran?) who died in 982, and was Leinster righ for 4 years.
b. Ceallach, who is described below.
106. Ceallach: 2nd son of Ceneth; was slain by the Ossorians in 945, at Athcliath (Dublin). He had the following sons:
a. Doncadh, Leinster righ for 6 years.
b. Donal, who is described below.
107. Donal: 2nd son of Ceallach; was Leinster righ for 9 years; slain by the Ossorians in 974. Had the following sons:
a. Aodh.
b. Doncadh, slain by Donal Cloen in 983.
c. Diarmuid, who is described below.
d. Maolruanaidh, who was Leinster righ for 13 years.

108.   Diarmuid: 3rd son of Donal; was Leinster righ for 13 years; died in 997.
109.   Donoch Maol-na-mBo: his son; was Leinster righ for 9 years. Had the following sons:
a.   Donal Reamhar, slain in 1041 at Killmolappog, County Carlow. He had 3 sons:
1. Donchadh, slain in 1089 by O'Connor Failghe (Faley).
2. Donal, who was a hostage of Tirlogh O'Brien.
3. Ruadh, who gave Clonkeen, near Kingstown, to Christ Church in Dublin.
b.   Diarmuid, who is described below.
110.   Diarmuid: 2nd son of Donoch Maol-na-mBo; was the 47th Christian Leinster righ, and the 177th Milesian Monarch of Ireland; was slain on February 23, 1072, at Odhba, near Navan; married Darbhforgal (died 1080), granddaughter of the Monarch Brian Boromha. (*See the chapter* "Dermot MacMaelnamBo," p. 165.) Had the following children:
a.   Murcha, who is described below.
b.   Glunairn, who in 1071, was slain by the Meath men at Donlah, and buried at Duleek.
c.   Enna, who had a son Diarmuid, slain in 1098.
111.   Murcha (a sea warrior, also called Morough): eldest son of Diarmaid; was the 50th Christian Leinster righ; invaded the Isle of Man in 1070; died in Dublin on the 8th of December, 1090. Had the following children:
a.   Donal, who was King of Dublin, died after 3 days illness in 1075.
b.   Gormlath, who was Abbess of Kildare, died in 1112.
c.   Donoch, who is described below.
d.   Enna, who had a son Diarmuid, died 1113 in Dublin.
e.   Glunairn, whose daughter Sadhbh (died 1171) was

Abbess of Kildare.

f.   Murcha (or Moragh).

112.   Donoch MacMorough: the third son of Murcha; was
       King of Dublin and the 56th Christian Leinster righ; slain
       in 1115 by Donal O'Brien and the Danes at Dublin. He
       had 3 sons of whom Dermod was his second. Had the
       following children:

a.   Enna, Leinster righ, died in Wexford in 1126.

b.   Murrough, Hy Kinsella righ while Dermod was away in
       1166.

c.   Dermod, who is described below.

113.   Dermod naNGhall: 2nd son of Donoch MacMorough;
       died 1171; was the 58th Christian Leinster righ. (*See the
       chapter* "Dermot MacMurrough," p. 173.) Had the
       following children:

a.   Eanna Cinnsealach. The Kinsella family line springs
       from Eanna.

b.   Dervorgilla. She married into the MacGilleholmock's of
       Dublin.

c.   Donal Kavanagh (fostered with Kavanaghs). The
       Kavanagh family line springs from Donal.

d.   Orlacan, who married Donal O'Brien.

e.   Aoife, who married Strongbow.

f.   Conor who was killed by Rory O'Connor.

114.   Eanna Cinnsealaigh: 2nd son of Dermod na nGall,
       Leinster righ; first assumed the surname Kinselagh. He
       was blinded by Ossory.

115.   Tirlach: his son.

116.   Morach: his son.

117.   Thomas Fionn: his son.

118.   Dermod: his son; had an elder brother named Art, who
       was slain by MacMorough in 1383, and from whom
       descended Slioght Thomas Fionn.

119. Art: his son.
120. Donoch: his son.
121. Arthur: his son.
122. Donoch: his son.
123. Edmund Kinselagh: his son.
124. Dermod Dubh: his son; Chief of the clan in 1580.

Appendix C

Hy Kinsella Righs[1]

1. Enna Cennselaig
2. Crimthann, son of (1)
3. Findchad
4. Fraech, son of (3)
5. Nath I, son of (2)
6. Oengus
7. Faelan Senchustal, son of (5)
8. Eogan Caech or Goll, son of (5)
9. Muiredach, son of (6)
10. Faelan
11. Eochaid
12. Forannan
13. Brandub, son of (11)
    Died in 605.
14. Conall, great-great-grandson of (2)
    Ruled for 20 years.
15. Crimthann, grandson of (9)
    Ruled for 17 years.
16. Dunchad, son of (14)
    Ruled for 15 years.
17. Ronan, great-grandson of (5)
    He ruled for 20 years. (If so his three predecessors
    couldn't have reigned.) Died in 624.
18. Crumdmael, son of (17)
    Ruled for 3 years.

---

[1] Donnchadh O Corrain, "Irish Regnal Succession, A Reappraisal," *Studia Hibernica* 11 (1971): 7-39.

19. Cummuscach, son of (17)
    Ruled for 16 years.
20. Colgu, son of (18)
    Ruled for 11 years.
21. Colum
    Ruled for 39 years. Probably an ecclesiastic who was chosen as a neutral party between warring factions.
22. Bran
    Ruled for 3 years. Killed by the Hy Kinsella themselves in 712, probably in a dynastic struggle.
23. Cu Congalt
    Ruled for 5 years. Died in 724.
24. Laidcend brother of (23)
    Ruled for 10 years. Slain in battle by northern Leinster in 727.
25. Elothach, grandson of (10)
    Slain by Aed Mend, his successor, in 732.
26. Aed Mend, great-great-grandson of (18)
    Extremely able righ who defeated Munster in 732 and became Leinster Righ. Slain in battle against the Hy Neill in 738.
27. Sechnassach, brother of (26)
    Listed as a Leinster righ. Died in 746.
28. Cathal hua Con Mella, son of (23)
    Died in 758.
29. Dondgal, great-great-grandson of (17)
    Slain by Ossory in 761.
30. Dub Calgaig, brother of (29)
    Slain at battle of Ferns by his successor in a dynastic struggle in 769.
31. Cennselach
    Slain by his successor in a dynastic struggle in 770.

32. Etarscel, son of (26)
    Died in 778.
33. Cairpre, brother of (29) and (30)
    Attacked Hy Neill in 780. Died in 793.
34. Cellach Bairne, son of (29)
    Slain in a dynastic struggle in 809.
35. Cathal, grandson of (23)
    Attacked and defeated the monastery of Ferns in 817.
    Died in 819.
36. Cu Congalt, son of (35)
    Ruled for 2 years.
37. Cairbre, son of (35) and brother of (36)
    Died in 844.
38. Echthigern, great-great-grandson of (25)
    Slain by his successor in 853 who had the help of
    Cerball Ossory righ.
39. Bruatar, grandson of (33)
    Slain in 853 within 8 days of killing Echthigern. Not
    recorded as Hy Kinsella righ by some.
40. Cellach, brother of (38)
    Died in 858.
41. Tadc
    Slain in a dynastic struggle in 865.
42. Donnacan
    Slain in a dynastic struggle.
43. Cairpre, brother of (41)
    Ruled for 7 years. Slain in a dynastic struggle in 876.
44. Dungal, son of (47)
    Ruled for 2 years though not called a righ in some
    annals. Died in 876.
45. Flannacan, brother of (44) and son of (47)
    Probably righ with opposition. Died in 880.

46. Riacan, son of (38)
    Ruled for 14 years. Died in 893.
47. Faelan, brother of (38)
    Probably chosen as a compromise candidate for the throne. He died in 894.
48. Dubgilla, son of (32)
    Ruled for 9 years. Died in 903.
49. Tadc, son of (47)
    Probaby had to face opposition from dynastic struggle before 911. Ruled for 19 years and died in 922.
50. Cinaed, son of (43)
    Ruled for 13 years. Slain in 935 by the Vikings.
51. Brutar, son of (46)
    Probably killed in a dynastic struggle in 937.
52. Cellach, son of (50)
    Killed in battle with Ossory in 947 while in alliance with north Leinster.
53. Echtigern, son of (50)
    Killed by his nephews in dynastic struggle in 953.
54. Donnchad, son of (49)
    Hy Kinsella was attacked and defeated in 957 and 960 by north Leinster. Deposed in 965 after ruling for 10 years.
55. Domnall, son of (52)
    Ruled for 9 years. Killed in battle with Ossory.
56. Mael Ruanaid, grandson of (49)?
    Ruled for 4 years.
57. Donnchad, son of 52
    Ruled for 3 years. Probably a weak righ because of dynastic struggles.
58. Muiredach, grandson of (39)
    Slain by the Vikings in the battle of Bithlann in 978.

59. Bruatar, son of (53)
    Ruled for 4 years.
60. Diarmait
    Ruled for 14 years. He was killed by the men of Dublin in 996.
61. Donnchad Mael namBo
    Successfully fought off a dynastic struggle in 1003. Killed in another one in 1006.
62. Mael Morda
    Ruled for 17 years. Of uncertain ancestry but appears to be from one of the subject people of Hy Kinsella rather than the royal line. Slain with his son and the Leinster righ (from Hy Murray) by the Hy Faelan righ in 1024.
63. Tadc, brother of (62)
    Died on his pilgrimage to Glendalough in 1030.
64. Dermot MacMaelnamBo, son of (61)
    Was Leinster righ. Died in 1072.
65. Domnall, grandson of (64)
    Probably set up as a puppet righ by O'Brien. Died in 1075.
66. Donnchad, grandson of (61)
    Ruled as Hy Kinsella righ for 17 years. Ruled as Leinster righ for 3 years. Died in 1089.
67. Enna Bacach, son of (64)
    Ruled as Leinster righ while dynastic struggle was tearing Hy Kinsella apart. Died in 1092.
68. Diarmait, son of (67)
    Died in 1098.
69. Donnchad, grandson of (64)
    Ruled as joint Leinster righ for 2 years with Offaly. Killed by O'Brien and Dublin Danes during Battle of Dublin in 1115.

70.   Diarmait
      Died in 1117.
71.   Enna, son of (69)
      Died in 1126.
72.   Dermot, son of (69) brother of (71)
      Ruled as Leinster righ for 37 years. Died in 1171.

The line of officially recognized Hy Kinsella righs ends here, when the Normans arrived in Ireland.

The following families held hereditary positions at Hy Kinsellas' court:

>   *Brehon*: O'Doran whose law school was probably at Ballyorley.
>   *Marshal*: O'Nolan.
>   *Standard bearer*: O'Molloy of Offaly.
>   *Royal file*: MacKeogh.
>   *Physician*: O'Lea.
>   *Seanchie*: O'Dunn and O'Daly.

Appendix D

Tour of Kinsella History

For those interested in searching out their "Kinsella Roots" in Ireland, here is a recommended itinerary, one that includes many of the places made famous over the centuries by our Kinsella ancestors.

The trip starts in Dublin, and after doing the sights of that great Irish city, we drive northwest to our first stop, Newgrange, situated on the banks of the Boyne River in County Meath. Newgrange is a large pre-historic passage grave that is not very well known in spite of the fact that it is much grander than the famous Stonehenge megaliths in England and is a thousand years older. Recent DNA evidence suggests that the people who first populated Ireland around 9,000 years ago were probably proto-Celtic. The builders of Newgrange and the majority of present day Irishmen descend from them. To be able to stand in that 5,000 year old burial chamber built by long-dead ancestors is a moment you'll never forget. It is a must see.

The next stop is Tara, the legendary residence of Ireland's Ard Righ. Tara is approximately 15 miles southwest of Newgrange. Ancient documents state that Tara was the residence of Leinster righs for centuries including some of our illustrious ancestors. The Leinster righs were replaced at Tara by the Hy Neill dynasty in the 4th or 5th century. There isn't much to see at Tara today, but the view is magnificent and just being at such a legendary spot is well worth the visit.

After leaving Tara, we journey 25 miles south to Croghan Hill, a high point just inside the northern border of County Kildare. It was here that Enna Cinnsealaigh defeated Eochaidh Muighmheadhin, leader of the Hy Neill and father of the famous Niall of the Nine Hostages. It was also here that the name Kinsella originated.

Continuing south, our next stop is Rathvilly, just inside the northern boundary of County Carlow. It was here in 448 A.D. that Crimthann, son of Enna Cinnsealaigh, was baptized by St. Patrick, thereby becoming the first Christian Leinster Righ. Near Tullow, a few miles east of Rathvilly, is a wonderful stone fort named Rathgall that may have been the original stronghold of the Hy Kinsella clan. (The historical marker says that it was used by the Kings of Southern Leinster, which as we know were from Hy Kinsella.) The fort consists of three large stone rings, each about 10 feet tall and 8 feet thick. The diameter of the innermost ring is approximately 80 feet! It is a most impressive sight.

In the same area, also near the town of Tullow, is a huge boulder called a "Holed Stone." Legend has it that Enna Cinnsealaigh's son, Eochaidh, was chained to this very stone by Niall of the Nine hostages. Niall's intent was to kill Eochaidh, but he was foiled when Eochaidh broke the chains and escaped. Eochaidh then proved the truth of the old adage, "he who runs away, lives to fight another day"; several years later when the two met again, Niall died of an arrow wound – shot by Eochaidh.

Our next stop is in the town of Leighlinbridge, on the Barrow River. Here long ago stood Dinn Rig, headquarters of the Leinster righs. It was at this spot that Labraid Loingsech, the legendary founder of the Leinster righs, avenged the murder of his father and grandfather by killing the reigning righ.

Next we proceed about 25 miles south to the southernmost part of County Carlow to visit the monastic ruins of St. Mullins. The site includes several churches, a round tower and a high cross. St. Mullins, who founded this monastery in the 7th century, was Bishop of Hy Kinsella.

After visiting St. Mullins, we head east. Proceed through Bunclody and enter County Wexford through a pass in the Backstairs Mountains, probably the very same route the Kinsellas took when they decided to establish a royal seat at Ferns. We continue following their path until we end up at Ferns, the place made famous by Dermot MacMurrough and his illustrious ancestors. It was here, of course, that Dermot's son, Enna Cinnsealaigh, the founder of the surname Kinsella was born. Sights to see here are a ruined castle, an ancient church, monastery ruins and several high crosses. In a grave-yard behind the church stands a cross with a broken shaft that is said to mark the spot where Dermot MacMurrough was buried.

For those who know where their own particular Kinsella family originated, that should be the next spot if for no other reason than to "walk the streets and paths our ancestors once did."

From Ferns, we drive north towards Arklow. As we approach that town, off to the left can be seen a large mountain. It is now called Croghan Mountain but it was formerly called Croghan Kinsella. In fact, it was here that considerable depos-its of gold were discovered in the late 1700s. Just before Arklow, we turn northwest and travel up the Avoca valley. At the end of this valley is Glendalough, one of the most beautiful spots in Ireland. The ruins of the monastery founded by St. Kevin are scattered all over this gorgeous valley. In addition to round towers, high crosses, and ancient churches, there are numerous spots of natural beauty – waterfalls, steep cliffs, clear lakes, etc.

To complete our journey, we drive northeast about 30 miles to Dublin. The total mileage of this "Kinsella Roots" trip in Ireland is about 350 miles. It will certainly be a trip to remember.

Appendix E

Getting Started with Your Own Genealogy

Beyond the obvious reasons for discovering who your ancestors were, there are other more subtle but powerful reasons for conducting genealogical research. Anyone who has delved into the history of their family knows that the more information they uncover about their ancestors the more real these people become, and the more fascinating. The researcher begins to learn more about the times these people lived in: the social, religious and political situations. The expression "Those who are unfamiliar with history are doomed to repeat it" demonstrates itself in every generation and therefore can be applied by the researcher to his or her benefit. But history is not the only facet of knowledge gained by genealogy.

As people research their ancestors, now passed away, they learn about the strengths as well as the idiosyncrasies of these relations, their likes and dislikes, their friends and their enemies. Though the spirits of these people have moved on, their personalities remain – as genes in their descendants. By researching one's ancestors, one may come closer to understanding oneself, "the noblest undertaking of Man."[1]

Irish genealogy is difficult; that's not meant to discourage you, it's meant to prepare you for what is ahead. The difficulty stems from a scarcity of records for the whole of Ireland. Some records are difficult to access while others simply lack important details. Records weren't kept for our poorer ancestors (the vast majority of the Catholic Irish). Other than the

---

[1] Socrates.

parish records, their name listed on a lease may have been the only records generated in their lifetime.

Here's a table of contents listing the steps necessary for your research. Jump ahead to wherever you are in your genealogy research:

Hints for Genealogists

Check repeat sources. Someone may include what another has missed.

♣ Don't go under the assumption that Northern Ireland or the Republic of Ireland records are exclusive to their own country. A large number of the Irish moved from one area to the other because of economic or social reasons (i.e. famine, religious persecution, etc.) Overlapping records occur because of the way some families spread out over the island.

♣ Be thorough. Leave no stone unturned. Information turns up in the most unlikely places.

♣ Be aware of your sources. Things aren't always what they seem.

♣ Study your history:
  • Locality and area history – What went on while they were alive in their townlands?
  • Social history – What lifestyle did or could they have led?
  • Relational history – Family, immediate relations, allied or collateral families, associated families, non-related families. Knowing who, what, when, and where will help you locate and identify particular families – especially in common names such as Kelly, Burns, Maguire, O'Reilly, etc.

♣ Learn social customs and government practices. Occupation or social status such as spinster, widow, gentry, esquire carries with it a load of information with just the one word.

♣ Date or place association. Very important in Irish research.

♣ Find out what records were created when particular transactions took place – such as marriage contracts, land deeds, wills, heraldic grants, marriage bonds, court proceedings.

♣ Take good notes – Note any and all information: surnames and christian names, nicknames, use-names, locality, event and circumstances surrounding event, date (be as precise as possible), occupation or status, religion. All information is "Vital Statistics" when referring to an individual or group of individuals and linking them to a place, date or other people.

♣ Check all resources before taking *No* or *You Can't* or *You Need* as the final say so.

Researching Irish Immigrants

♣ Find out all you can about your family tree from your older relatives.

♣ Fill out your understanding of these ancestors by searching through papers in their local towns or searching through immigrant lists.

♣ Find the townland in Ireland that your immigrant ancester came from. While there aren't a lot of records that survive for All of Ireland, there are many that survive for smaller geographical areas. This one fact alone makes knowing your ancestor's townland in Ireland deeply important.

Finding Your Ancestor's Irish Townland
General Sources in your own Country
♣ Immigration records and passenger lists
♣ Death records
   These often contain the name of parents and their place of birth.
♣ Cemetery records
   The Church of Jesus Christ of Latter-day Saints (LDS Church) has many of the cemetery records available on microfilm. Visit a Family History Center near you.
♣ Funeral home records
   To determine whether or not a funeral home exists in your area of interest, most funeral homes carry a "blue book" of all the funeral homes in their country. Operators seem to feel it a good selling point to advertise the number of years they have been in business. Look through the book until you find a funeral home in the area your ancestor died that shows the most years in business (and particularly in business at the time of the death of your ancestor) and give them a call. I've never found one that couldn't tell you who had the oldest records in their possession. A simple telephone call to them can provide the information you are seeking.
♣ Land records and/or wills

♣ Directories and local histories

Canadian Sources

♣ Archives/Libraries

Almost all Canadian records that have been committed to microfilm are available to US researchers by interlibrary loan.

- The National and Provincial Archives of Canada are very helpful to genealogists.
- In the Research Tips and Resources Library, you will find a file entitled "Ontario Archives" which includes a microfilm catalog of items that may be ordered through interlibrary loan.

♣ Publications

Eric Jonasonn's *Canadian Genealogical Handbook: a Comprehensive Guide to Finding Your Ancestors in Canada* (Winnipeg, 1983) is a good place to start. So is Angus Baxter's *In Search of Your Roots: A Guide for Canadians Seeking Their Ancesters* (Toronto, 1986).

United States Sources

♣ Naturalization Records

They sometimes give a place name, seemingly depending on where the Naturalization was granted. Midwest records seem to have a great deal more information included than do those of the West or East Coast. Those I have seen simply show that the immigrant was renouncing his allegiance to the Queen of England!

♣ Revolutionary War Records

The Revolutionary War pension and bounty land records of the Veterans Administration Archives, in the National Archives, Washington, D.C., include the papers of a very large number of men and their widows who were of

Irish or Scot/Irish origin. See the *Guide to Genealogical Records in the National Archives* by Meredith B. Colket & Frank E. Bridgers (National Archives, 1964).

♣ Directories and local histories

These sometimes give the place of birth. See Clarence S. Peterson's *Consolidated Bibliography of County Histories in Fifty States in 1961* (Baltimore, 1963). This booklet shows what county histories are available and whether they are already available on microfilm through the LDS Church.

♣ Publications

- John W. Heisey's *Works Progress Administration: Sources for Genealogists* (Ye Olde Genealogie Shoppe, 1988). In the late 1930s, the Works Progress Administration (WPA) in their Federal Writer's Project sent many writers into the halls of records in various counties in the US and in many instances the actual records were extracted (these sometimes include cemetery information as well). Not all of these extractions were published, but many were and this book lists all those that were.
  - o Many of these records are available through the LDS Church. Many other of these records are available for you to "rent" through American Genealogical Lending Library.
- *Newspapers in Microform* (LDS Church film # 1145942) is a book carried by most major libraries that lists, among other things, the various groups that owned the newspapers; which issues are available and which issues have been converted to microfilm and are, therefore, available through interlibrary loan; and usually lists which repositories have the original papers. If the US portion of the family knew where the immigrant

ancestor was born in Ireland, this bit of news will usually be found in the obituary.

Researching Irish in Ireland
General

While there are few country-wide sources of genealogy in Ireland, there are a host of localized sources. I've listed all sources I'm aware of but this list is not exhaustive.

♣ Census

Irish Census Returns were taken by the Government in 1813, 1821, 1831-34, 1841, 1851, 1861, 1871, and every ten years thereafter. The early Census Returns 1813-1851 were nearly all burned in the Four Courts fire in 1922 and the Returns from 1861-1891 were "pulped" or destroyed by the Government since they saw no need to keep them.

- The earliest existing complete Return is that of 1901. Another exists for 1911. The burned fragments from the 1821-1851 Census that have survived are available on microfilm through the LDS Church (mostly from County Antrim, see the Locality Catalogue under Census).
- Elphin Diocesan Census
  1749, Elphin Diocesan Census arranged by townland and parish, and listing householders, their religion, the numbers, sex and religion of their children, and the numbers, sex and religion of their servants.
- Scully Census
  1840, Castledermot, County Kildare.

♣ 18th & 19th Century Census Substitutes

Some Census substitutes are available through the LDS Library on microfilm and many LDS film numbers are involved. Just a few are:

- A Census of Ireland 1659 LDS film # 0923639.

- Religious Census 1766 LDS film # 0100173, items 1 & 2.
- The 1821 Census (17 reels), the 1841 Census (8 reels), the 1851 Census (19 reels – mostly Northern Ireland).

♣ The Registry of Deeds

The Registry of Deeds, established in 1708, provided a national office for land registration. Any conveyance of land dated after March 25, 1708 was "deemed and adjudged fraudulent and void" unless it was duly recorded in the Registry. These records have survived intact and can be a most useful genealogical tool when used correctly. The books of memorials are kept in Dublin and the indexes are open to the public. To use the Registry you must know either the name of the landlord who granted land to your ancestor (Grantor's Index) or that ancestor's townland or parish (Placename's Index).

Almost 1,500 wills were also recorded in the Registry from 1708 to 1820. An index published by the Irish Manuscripts Commission includes testators, beneficiaries, and witnesses, the date of probate and registration, and the memorial number of the original transcript in the Registry of Deeds. Memorial numbers are the key for using the microfilm copy of the wills.

♣ The Convert Rolls

The Convert Rolls, ed. Eileen O'Byrne (Irish Manuscripts Commission, 2005). A list of those converting from Catholicism to the Church of Ireland. The bulk of the entries date from 1760 to 1790.

♣ The Religious Survey of 1766

In March & April of 1766, Church of Ireland rectors (on the instructions of the government) compiled lists of householders in their parishes. The lists they compiled were not confined to member of the Church of Ireland,

Catholics were also included. This was known as the Religious Survey of 1766. No rules were laid down on the amount of detail to be collected, nor the manner in which the information was to be presented.

Some rectors produced only numerical totals of population, some drew up partial lists, and others detailed all householders and their addresses individually. All of the original returns were lost in 1922, but extensive transcripts survive for some areas, and are deposited with various institutions. The only full listing of all surviving transcripts and abstracts is in the National Archives Reading Room on the open shelves. However, this does not differentiate between those returns that supply names and those that merely give numerical totals.

♣ Spinning Wheel Premium Entitlement Lists

As part of a government scheme to encourage the linen trade, free spinning wheels or looms were granted to individuals planting a certain area of land with flax. The lists of those entitled to the awards, covering almost 60,000 individuals, were published in 1796 and record only the name of the individual and the civil parish in which he lived. The majority were in Ulster but some names appear from every county except Dublin and Wicklow. A microfiche index to the lists is available in the National Archives and The Public Record Office of Northern Ireland.

♣ Persons who suffered losses in 1798 Rebellion

A list of claims for compensation from the government for property destroyed by the rebels during the insurrection of 1798. Particularly useful for the property-owning classes of Counties Wexford, Carlow, Dublin, Kildare and Wicklow.

♣ National School Records

In 1831, a countrywide system of primary education was established, under the control of the Board of Commissioners for National Education. The most useful records produced by the system are the school registers themselves, which record the age of the pupil, religion, father's address and occupation, and general observations. Unfortunately, in the Republic of Ireland no attempt has been made to centralize these records; they remain in the custody of local schools or churches. The Public Record Office of Northern Ireland has a collection of over 1,500 registers for schools in the six counties of Northern Ireland. The administrative records of the Board of Commissioners itself are now held by the National Archives in Dublin. These include teacher's salary books, which can be very useful if an ancestor was a teacher. (The National School Records are available through the LDS Library.)

♣ Griffiths Valuation

1845-1864, Griffiths Valuations was a taxation program. The valuation began in 1845 in the extreme southern Irish counties where they mapped the land and registered not only the property owner, but the property occupier as well. It was from this Valuation that early Ordnance Survey Maps were created. It ended in the north in 1864.

Note that much of the information for the valuation may have been gathered up to a decade earlier so this will be of value to many researchers seeking Famine emigrants in Ireland.

♣ Church Records

Birth, marriage, and death records covering the entire country.

♣ <u>Irish Land Records</u>

Land records were not required until 1703 when a law was passed in an effort to block the sale of land to Catholics. Usually only the very well to do in the more urban settings registered land transactions. In 1778 the laws were relaxed and many Catholics chose that time to register their land transactions.

See the LDS Locality Catalogue under the subject: "Land/Property" for what is available for use on microfilm. See also Ireland Registry of Deeds with Surname and County Indexes 1704-1929. There is an excellent index but each one covers a 10-year period.

♣ <u>Irish Military Records</u>

The Public Record Office in London has records of service, marriage, deaths and pensions for members of the Royal Artillery and the Royal Horse Artillery. These records are arranged by regiments and cover the time span of 1760 to 1854. Records for 1873-1882 are arranged alphabetically and contain more information of a genealogical nature than do the former.

Check the LDS Locality Catalogue (on microfiche) under the subject: "Military records" for further indexes and records.

♣ <u>Electoral Records 1703-1838</u>

No complete collection of the electoral lists used in the elections of this century exists. The largest single collection of surviving electoral registers is found in the National Archives, but even here the coverage of many areas is quite skimpy.

These will be found in the LDS Locality Catalogue (fiche version) under the subject: "Archives/Libraries" subtitle: "Public Record Office of Northern Ireland in

Belfast and Public Record Office/National Archives, Dublin."

♣ Valuations

Local valuations and re-valuations of property were carried out with increasing frequency from the end of the 18th century, usually for electoral reasons. The best of these record all householders.

These will be found in the LDS Locality Catalogue (fiche version) under the subject: "Archives/Libraries" subtitle: "Public Record Office of Northern Ireland in Belfast and Public Record Office/National Archives, Dublin."

Middle to Upper Class

♣ Estate Records

In the 18th and 19th centuries, the vast majority of the Irish population lived as small tenant farmers on large estates owned by English landlords. The administration of these estates inevitably produced large quantities of records, maps, tenants lists, rentals, account books, lease books etc. Over the course of the 20th century, as the estates have been broken up and sold off, many collections of these records have become public. Though they apply to a rather limited number of families, they are gold mines of information, occasionally supplying whole family relation-ships.

Unfortunately, these records are generally indexed by landlord name, and it is quite rare for a large landowner to have individual rental or lease agreements with the huge number of small tenants on his land. Instead, he would let a significant area to a middleman, who would then sublet to others, who might in turn rent out parts to the smallest tenants. It is very rare for estate records to document the smallest landholders since most of these had no right of tenure in any case, being simply tenants "at will."

There are a number of ways to discover who your family's landlord was so you can search for his estate records:

- If the location of your ancestor is known after the Famine, the Immediate Lessor column in Griffiths Valuations should be examined. If the Immediate Lessor is not the landlord but the middleman, then it can be useful to find this middleman's own holding or residence and see whom he was leasing from. Often the largest lessor in the area will be the landlord.

- It can be very difficult to establish the identity of the landowner before the Famine. Samuel Lewis's *A Topographical Dictionary of Ireland* (London, 1837; available in reprint and cd-rom editions) usually gives details of local landowners and their estates; however, there are omissions.

- Historical and Archaeological societies can offer much help.

Upon finding the name of your family's landlord, you're ready to check the sources for his estate papers:

- The best place to begin looking is in Richard Hayes' *Manuscript Sources for the Study of Irish Civilization*, with supplements, copies of which can be found in the National Library and National Archives as well as on microfilm through the LDS Church. Keep in mind Hayes only indexes manuscripts available through 1976 and many have been made available since then.

- The Public Record Office of Northern Ireland (PRONI) houses several hundred sets of estate records. The Deputy Keepers of the PRONI Reports 1924-1953, which are available through the LDS Church, detail these acquisitions. The Name Indexes of PRONI should also be checked. Note that many of the estate records have still not been catalogued and thus remain completely inaccessible.

- The card index at the National Archives may also be checked. This is second only to PRONI in the size of its estate record collection.
- After the Famine, a great deal of land was sold by bankrupt landlords and these you will find listed in the Encumbered Estates or Landed Estates Court. Most of the buyers were Catholic merchants and large farmers. Brochures were offered which gave details of the property, occasionally listing the tenants, the rents paid, and the terms of the lease. These brochures are available at the National Archives in Dublin and are keyed to the townland index.
- A number of the most ancient and extensive estate papers have been published in 6 volumes by the Irish Manuscript Commission.
- If your landlord had the major portion of their estate in England, you should check the Probate Records and Wills in England. Some Irish lands are to be found in these English documents.
- The following publications may be of value:
  o U. H. Hussey de Burgh, *The Landowners of Ireland* (Dublin, 1974, 1878). Provides a guide to the major landowners, the size of their holdings, and where in the country they are situated.
  o *Analecta Hibernica* publication, issues 15 and 20. This may be available through interlibrary loan at your local library.
  o *Landowners in Ireland: Return of Owners of Land of One Acre and Upwards...* (London, 1876).

Reissued by the Genealogical Publishing Co., Baltimore, 1988. This records 32,614 owners of land in Ireland in 1876, identifying them by province and county; the entries record the address of the owner, along with the extent and valuation of the property. Only a minority of the population actually owned the land they occupied, but the work is invaluable for those who did.

♣ Directories for cities and towns

For those areas and classes which they cover, Irish directories are an excellent resource, often supplying information not readily available elsewhere. Their most obvious and practical use is to find out where precisely, in the larger towns, a family lived, but for members of the gentry, and the professional, merchant, and trading classes, they can show much more, providing indirect evidence of reversals of fortune or growing prosperity, of death and emigration. In many cases, directory entries are the only precise indication of occupation. The only classes totally excluded from all directories are, once again, the most disadvantaged, small tenant farmers, landless laborers and servants. Virtually all classes other than these are at least partly included. This file categorizes the Irish directories into:

• Dublin Directories
• Country Wide Directories

Paying for Irish Genealogy Researchers

♣ Irish Family History Foundation
[http://www.mayo-ireland.ie/roots]

The Irish Family History Foundation is the coordinating body for a network of government approved genealogical research centers in the Republic of Ireland (Eire) and in

Northern Ireland which have computerized tens of millions of Irish ancestral records of different types.

Services Provided:
- Record Searches
- Family History Reports

♣ Irish Heritage Centers
[http://www.kinsella.org/genealogy/research/irhercen.htm]
Centers undertake two types of commission:
- Full family history research leading to a detailed report on a particular family
- Searches of specified records for specified items of information.

♣ General Register Office (GRO)
The public does *not* have direct access to the records themselves. Researchers must first consult an index to identify a reference number for a record that is then photo-copied or transcribed by the staff in the office. The records in this repository include the following:
- Non-Catholic Marriages from 1 April 1845,
- All Births/Marriages/Deaths from 1 January 1864,
- Marriages in the German Protestant Church in Dublin 1806-1837,
- Adoptions from 10 July 1953.

The Address of the Office is:
GENERAL REGISTER OFFICE
The Research Room at Irish Life Centre, Lower Abbey Street
Dublin 1, Ireland

Mailing Address:
General Register Office, Government Offices
Convent Road
Roscommon, Ireland   Tel: +353 (0) 90 6632900

Appendix F

Gaelic Culture

Culture, though commonly associated with ethnic groups, doesn't have to be; witness the case of an Asian whose family has lived in England for generations. They consider themselves English. Culture is a choice, not a blood type, and anyone can become a member. A Gael alive in the early part of the 19th century recalls:

> My heart still burns with delight when I remember the traditions and customs of the [Gaels] . . . What person, who was raised in a Gaelic community, did not experience in their early youth the mental excitement that comes when the tales of the Fianna are heard. I will never forget for as long as I live the enjoyment with which I listened to the lore of the old people when they would speak about the exploits of the warriors from whom they were descended. I'm sure that this enabled the Gaels to be endowed as they grew up with qualities superior to other people of the world – since their ideas were elevated by constantly hearing references to the fame and excellence of their ancestors . . . Those who know the love with which the Gaels listen to the lore of their ancestors will not be surprised that they are remembered. . . .[1]

The following ideals or values, as saved in their proverbs, are cherished by Gaelic culture:

---

[1] *An Teachdaire Gaidhealach* (1836): 228-9.

1) *"Remember the people from whom you descend"*
The Gaels believe help can be gained from your ancestors, even those who have long since passed away, if they are remembered and honored.

2) *"Honor is more noble than gold"*
Living an honorable life is always to be strived for. This may lead to defending your honor whenever it's disparaged.

3) *"This life is but a vapor"*
The world is comprised of reality, as judged by your senses, and spirituality, as judged by your heart. Both worlds are just as "real" and should be respected. This also includes the Gaelic belief in magic so common in their superstitions.

4) *"Three candles that illume every darkness: truth, nature, knowledge"*
Nature, being sacred, requires respect, as does the pursuit of truth and knowledge.

5) *"Seldom is there a champion who does not meet with some reverse"*
Life, like the seasons, is cyclic. For example, human beings die but are reborn again, generosity will be reciprocated, etc.

6) *"Truth is the historian's food"*
Education, especially history, is highly respected.

7) *"It is a sign of nobility to listen to art"*
The arts, especially music, are highly respected. They add another dimension to one's life. Music, considered an important part of everyday life, was practiced constantly by all in the form of work songs, play songs, entertainment, and support for

the community. Another one of the arts, dancing, was enjoyed spontaneously by all the community. Few examples of Irish visual art remain, but it's known the Gaels loved multiple colors in their clothes, houses, crosses, etc.

8) *"A man lives long in his native place"*
The land one grows up in is like a mother, always to be revered. Gaels became intimately familiar with their local land.

9) *"Three glories of a gathering: a beautiful wife, a good horse, a swift hound"*
The coming together of the community was a desirable common occurrence.

10) *"You would make a story out of the stones of the strand"*
Stories should be told and retold at gatherings. Great attention to the truth is essential, however. Details should not be altered simply because they make for a better story.

11) *"A generous man, they say, has never gone to hell"*
Always have your house open to a guest.

12) *"Money is a poor substitute for reciprocity"*
Paying for a favor circumvents pride, honor, and familiarity with neighbors.

13) *"The covetous man is always in want"*
Greed and hoarding are greatly disparaged. Don't make more money than you need, especially if it comes at the cost of reducing human relationships.

14) *"Conversation is the cure for every sorrow"*

The Gaelic language is an important component of Gaelic culture.

15) *"Burning embers are easily kindled"*
Gaels are very emotional, "wearing their emotions on their sleeves."

16) *"There has not been found, nor will there be found, a juster judge than the field of battle"*
Fighting was glorified though the modern Gaelic culture has transformed this into a love of sports.

17) *"It is a good horse that pleases every rider"*
Gaelic culture loves horses and has raised them almost to sacred levels.

18) *"There is luck in sharing a thing"*
The sharing of material goods such as tools, equipment, etc. with friends and kin is expected. This helps form a close bond in the Gael's neighborhood.

19) *"Blood is thicker than water"*
Extended family, the clan, are close and stay together, even through disagreements.

20) *"A man never fails among his own people"*
The clan takes care of its own in every sense of the word though never if it requires breaking a just law.

21) *"Every bird goes along with its own flock"*
Extended family spends time together. Not only are gatherings of the clan frequent, but vacations are spent visiting friends and family.

Appendix G

The DNA Evidence

Laoise Moore, a member of the genetic research group at Trinity University, Dublin, recently published an article on DNA that received world wide attention, including a long article in the *New York Times*. Interest was sparked by data that suggested a single male, who lived in Ireland around 1,500 years ago, today has two to three million descendants worldwide. Moore reached this conclusion because the 5th-century man had a very rare "signature marker" that was passed on through his y-chromosome to his descendants and that was detected in the DNA of the subjects of her study. If one progenitor for millions was not startling enough, Moore identified who she believed that prolific man was. Her data shows a clear peak in this marker in northwest Ireland. This is where Niall of the Nine Hostages, High King of Ireland, was supposed to have lived in the 5th century.

Ancient chronicles identify Niall as the powerful founder of the Ui Neill dynasty, the most dominant and long lasting of all Irish dynasties. But some scholars have called into question the reliability of these early chronicles as history, suggesting that Niall's exploits were exaggerated, and that Niall may be more a figure of myth than of history. Here, however, is new evidence that suggests Niall was very real, and very successful. This newfound support for Niall's historical authenticity should be kept in mind when reading our description of the enmity between the early Kinsellas and the O'Neils. If Niall existed, then surely so did Eochaid.[1] And if they both lived,

---

[1] For the full story see the chapter "The Ui Cinnsealaigh Clan."

perhaps it's true that Niall chained Eochaid to a hole stone, that Eochaid managed to escape to Scotland and then Europe, and that Eochaid killed Niall with a bow shot across the River Loire. We must presume that Niall was cut down in the prime of life so we might ask, if he were responsible for 2-3 million descendants, how many more would he have had if not for Eochaid's good aim?[2]

This is one example of the ways that DNA studies are beginning to shed new light on Ireland's early history and culture. Over the past decade, scientists at Trinity University in Dublin have tested the DNA of Irish men with Gaelic surnames with startling results. Focusing on the DNA of the y-chromosome, which is passed from father to son practically unchanged over thousands of years, they found that over 90% of the men tested carried a "signature marker" also carried by over 90% of the Basques in northern Spain.

The conclusion of this study is that these Irishmen are the direct descendants of the group of Stone Age hunters who arrived in Ireland from Spain 9,000 years ago. There were no later "invasions" as the ancient manuscripts insist and as the archaeologists and historians have believed. These studies suggest that the majority of the people who now live in Ireland are descended from these first settlers.

This conclusion raises some profound questions. It is generally agreed that the Celts are a branch of the Indo-European peoples, who eventually populated most of Europe and whose original home was somewhere near the Russian steppes. Since the 1950s it has been assumed that the Celts, fierce horseman warriors, left their ancient homeland and invaded Europe, conquering the less advanced people who

---

[2] It is worth noting that the rare O'Neill DNA "signature marker" that peaks at 18% in northwestern Ireland is absent from the Province of Leinster, the homeland of the Kinsellas.

lived there. When this happened is debatable. The Greeks first took note of the "barbarians" to their north whom they called the Kelti in the 5th century B.C. Scholars suggest that Celtic people had arrived or developed north of the Alps as early as 1000 to 750 BC. It has been accepted as truth that descendants of these early Celtic peoples were the Celts who Caesar encountered when he took his Roman legions into Gaul.

So what are we to make of new DNA evidence that suggests the vast majority of Irishmen today are descended from people who arrived in Ireland 9,000 years ago, 6,000 years before the Celts arrived in Europe? Several articles have been written lately (foremost being papers presented at the Ulster-Scot Forum) joyously proclaiming, "The Irish aren't Celts!" How can this be true when it is well known that when Ireland was discovered by the outside world its inhabitants were speaking a Celtic language and were steeped in Celtic customs and traditions?

It will be years before this DNA evidence is sorted out and further refinements in this science give us a clearer picture of this puzzle. Recently, however, a theory has been put forth that might provide an answer to this question. This states that when the Ice Age in Europe was at its peak, about 15,000 years ago, the stone-age hunters that had migrated to northern Europe could no longer survive in the extreme cold. Therefore, they migrated south to a more hospitable area – one group traveling to northwestern Spain. There is evidence that this group was Proto-Celtic, i.e. early Celts, or the stock from which Celts were to develop. Evidence of an early infusion of Celtic words into the Basque language may support this theory. It was this group of stone-age hunters who migrated to Ireland after the glaciers melted and, according to this theory, developed Celtic culture.

But what about the strong evidence that Celts were in control of Europe around 750 B.C.; where did they come from? The new theory suggests that Celtic culture migrated into Europe from Ireland! The migration may have been from the west not from the east!

As to the proposition of Celtic culture moving from west to east, consider this: Newgrange, the massive passage grave in County Meath, Ireland was built 5,000 years ago. Stonehenge in England and similar stone monuments in France and Germany were built 1,000 years later. Some scientists believe that the expansion of this advanced building technology was led by Celtic navigators and astronomer-priests who instigated the megalith building in Ireland and then carried it to England, France and Germany. This is all very difficult to believe and it will take much more DNA evidence, along with radical reassessment of the archaeological record, before this conclusion will by accepted by the scientific community.

Lots of questions and lots of disagreements remain, but we can be reasonably certain that the whole subject will be deeply influenced, if not resolved, by future DNA evidence. As one historian stated, "Everything we have believed about ancient people is being proven wrong by DNA evidence."

Selected Bibliography

For those interested in learning more about Irish history, this bibliographical note suggests further reading. Omitted are primary and secondary sources used for this book that were deemed too detailed and/or tedious. The titles in this section, we hope, will lead the curious reader to the other, omitted sources. For ease of use, we've categorized the titles.

The Catholic Church

Gwynn, Aubrey, S.J. *The Irish Church in the Eleventh and Twelfth Centuries.* Dublin: Four Courts Press, 1992.

Harbison, Peter. *Pilgrimage in Ireland.* Syracuse, NY: Syracuse University Press, 1992.

Morris, Colin. *The Papal Monarchy: The Western Church from 1050 to 1250.* Oxford: The Clarendon Press, 1989.

O'Rahilly, Thomas F. *The Two Patricks: A Lecture on the History of Christianity in Fifth-Century Ireland.* Dublin: The Dublin Institure for Advanced Study, 1942.
An excellent source on this subject.

Gaelic Culture

Danaher, Kevin. *The Year in Ireland.* Cork: Mercier Press, 1972.

Dunlevy, Mairead. *Dress in Ireland.* New York: Holmes & Meier, 1989.

McClintock, H. F. *Old Irish and Highland Dress.* 2nd ed. Dundalk: Dundalgan Press, 1950.

Newton, Michael. *A Handbook of the Scottish Gaelic World.* Dublin: Four Courts Press, 2000.

O'Rahilly, Thomas F. *A Miscellany of Irish Proverbs.* Dublin, The Talbot Press, 1922; reprinted, 1977.

Genealogy
O'Hart, John. *Irish Pedigrees*. 2 vol. Baltimore: Genealogical Pub. Co., 1976, 1892.

Ancient Celtic History
Cunliffe, Barry. *The Ancient Celts*. London: Penguin, 1999, 1997.
Covers Celts largely from 8000 BC to 1 BC.

Ancient Irish Tales and Myths
Cross, Tom Peete and Clark Harris Slover, eds. *Ancient Irish Tales*. New York: Barnes & Noble, 1969, 1936.
Flood, J. M. *Ireland: Its Myths and Legends*. Port Washington, N.Y., Kennikat Press 1970, 1916.
Gantz, Jeffrey, ed. and tr. *Early Irish Myths and Sagas*. London, Penguin, 1981.
Glassie, Henry. *Irish Folktales*. New York: Pantheon Books, 1985.
Gregory, Lady and W. B. Yeats. *Complete Irish Mythology*. London: Chancellor Press, 2000.
There are two other recent editions: Smithmark, 1996; Slaney Press, 1994. Originally published by John Murray Publishers, London, in separate volumes: Gods and Fighting Men (1904) and Cuchulain of Muirthemne (1902).
Jackson, Kenneth Hurlstone, ed. and tr. *Celtic Miscellany: Translations from Celtic Literatures*. Harmondsworth: Penguin, 1971.
Scott, Michael. *Irish Folk and Fairy Tales*. New York: Penguin, 1989.

General Irish History
Byrne, Francis John. *Irish Kings and High Kings*. London: Batsford, 1973.

De Paor, Liam. *Ireland and Early Europe: Essays and Occasional Writings on Art and Culture.* Dublin: Four Courts Press, 1997.

Edwards, Nancy. *The Archaeology of Early Medieval Ireland.* London: Batsford, 1990.
Very comprehensive outline of all areas of Irish society and culture that can be discovered from archaeology up to 1990.

Kee, Robert. *Ireland: A History.* Boston: Little, Brown, 1982.

Lydon, James F. *Lordship of Ireland in the Middle Ages.* Dublin: Four Courts Press, 2003, 1972.
Solid book but with only one chapter covering the pre-invasion period.

McCullough, David Willis. *Wars of the Irish Kings: A Thousand Years of Struggle from the Age of Myth through the Reign of Queen Elizabeth I.* New York: Crown, 2000.

Moody, T. W. and F. X. Martin. *The Course of Irish History.* Cork: Mercier, 1984; and several other editions.

Nicholls, Kenneth. *Gaelic and Gaelicised Ireland in the Middle Ages.* Dublin: Gill and MacMillan, 1972.

O'Croinin, Daibhi. *Early Medieval Ireland 400-1200.* London: Longman, 1995.

Social Structure of Ireland

O'Riordan, Michelle. *The Gaelic Mind and the Collapse of the Gaelic World.* Cork: Cork University Press, 1991.
Covering the 13th to the 17th centuries. Focus is largely on the 16th century and how foreigners have affected the country.

Patterson, Nerys. *Cattle Lords and Clansmen: The Social Structure of Early Ireland.* Notre Dame: University of Notre Dame Press, 1994.
A rich and wonderful source for those interested in the details of Irish society.

Stout, Matthew. *The Irish Ringfort*. Dublin: Four Courts
   Press, 2000.
   A wonderful source for those interested in details of Irish homes.

Specific Irish History
Cahill, Thomas. *How the Irish Saved Civilization*. New York:
   Doubleday, 1995.
   *About the Catholic missionaries who transformed Europe after
   the fall of Rome.*
Flanagan, Marie T. *Irish Society, Anglo-Norman Settlers,
   Angevin Kingship: Interactions in Ireland in the Late
   Twelfth Century*. Oxford: The Clarendon Press, 1989.
   *Excellent book that describes some of Dermot MacMurrough's
   life with few errors, describes a fair amount about Strongbow
   and some of the other important invaders. The author tries to
   prove all her points with historical facts.*
Furlong, Nicholas. *Dermot King of Leinster and the
   Foreigners*. Tralee, Co. Kerry: Anvil Books, 1973.
   *Covers the life of Dermot MacMurrough in a very readable
   fashion.*
Gallagher, Thomas. *Paddy's Lament: Ireland 1846-1847
   Prelude to Hatred*. New York: Harcourt Brace Jovanovich,
   1982.
   Excellent readable source on the Great Famine.
Morgan, Hiram. *Tyrone's Rebellion: The Outbreak of the Nine
   Years War in Tudor Ireland*. Rochester, NY: Boydell
   Press, 1993.
   *About Hugh O'Neill and Ireland's history during the late 16th
   century. The author corrects many mistakes Sean O'Faolain
   made but the story isn't as readable as O'Faolain's.*
O'Faolain, Sean. *The Great O'Neill: a Biography of Hugh
   O'Neill, Earl of Tyrone, 1550-1616*. New York:
   Longmans, Green & Co., 1942.

About Hugh O'Neill and Ireland's history during the late 16th century. The author admits he's not a historian, but he weaves a great story.

Roche, Richard. *The Norman Invasion of Ireland.* Dublin: Anvil Books, 1995, 1970.
Covers the period after Dermot MacMurrough invited the Normans to Ireland. Very readable.

Woodham Smith, Cecil. *The Great Hunger.* London: Penguin, 1991, 1962.
Excellent readable source on the Great Famine.

History of Hy Kinsella

Culleton, Edward. *Celtic and Early Christian Wexford, AD 400-1166.* Dublin: Four Courts Press, 1999.

Kavanagh, Art. *In the Shadow of Mount Leinster.* [Ireland?]: A. Kavanagh, 1993.
From the Kavanagh point of view.

O'Byrne, Emmett. *War, Politics, and the Irish of Leinster, 1156-1606.* Dublin: Four Courts Press, 2003.
From the O'Byrne point of view.

Image Credits

23 Photo copyright Maggie and Keith Davison of www.megalithics.com.
24 Courtesy of www.knowth.com.
26 Thanks to David Soren.
29 Thanks to Wayne Narey.
33 Courtesy of http://sabreteam.free.fr/prefortif.htm.
34 Thanks to www.irishmegaliths.org.uk.
44 Courtesy of the Department of Heritage Ireland.
54 Author's drawing based on Hall's, *Ireland*, i, 413.
56, 57 Thanks to Jim Dempsey.
61, 218, 224 Courtesy of Irish National Heritage Park.
66 Courtesy of Ragnar.
70 Courtesy of http://www.irishmythology.com.
72 Failte Ireland Copyright ©.
85, 93, 105, 244, 298, 392 Authors' pictures.
91 Author's drawing based on O'Hanlon's, *Lives*, iv, 488.
98 Thanks to Kieran Convery and his father.
100 © Copyright The British Museum.
103 Courtesy of Liam Lyons ©.
107 Courtesy of *An Atlas of Irish History* 2nd edition by Ruth Dudley Edwards (Methuen & Co. Ltd. 1981): 140.
111 Thanks Mary!
113 Courtesy of John Paterson.
145 Thanks go to Cron Mackay.
146, 163 Courtesy of Dover Publications.
187, 194 From *Topographia Hibernica* by Giraldus Cambrensis.
202 Thanks to Elen Models Limited.
206, 368 Courtesy of J. S. Hylind and Co.
211 Courtesy of Myra VanInwegen.
237 From www.grenada.ru courtesy of Grenada Studio.

238, 270, 300 Maps from http://www.ireland-information.com/irelandmaps.htm.
259 From Art Kavanagh's *In the Shadow of Mount Leinster.*
274 Author's drawing.
275 Thanks to The Arnold Bernhard Library of Quinnipiac University.
287 Courtesy of John Caldwell.
289 © Courtesy of the British Library.
293, 320 Map from http://www.rootsweb.com/~irlkik/ihm/ire1600.htm.
335 *Illustrated London News*, December 16, 1848.
342 *Narrative of A Journey from Oxford to Skibbereen*, 1847.
350 *Illustrated London News*, July 6, 1850.
353 *Harper's Weekly,* June 26, 1858.
364 Courtesy of Joycean.org.
374 Thanks to Lorcan Collins.

Colophon

Kinsellas have always passed on stories. For those continuing the tradition, we describe the mechanics of this book.

All text in Times New Roman font
Title 14 pt bold
Subtitle 12 pt bold
Body of text 12 pt
Indented quotations 11 pt
Authors' stories 11 pt
Footnotes 10 pt
Picture titles 10 pt bold
Headers 12 pt italic

The top margin of this book is 1 inch; the bottom is 1.5. The left and right hand margins are both 0.75 inches with an alternating gutter of 0.25 inches. The pages were set with Microsoft *Word*, saved as pdf files, then uploaded to the Lightning Source site: www.lightningsource.com. The book paper is 55 lb acid free, natural shade opaque; paperback covers are printed on a bright white 80# cover stock.

In preparing a book, the thing that surprised the authors most was the amount of time required to gather permissions for images. If your book has many pictures, set aside nearly a year to gain permissions. The use of the internet speeds this process up, but the quality of picture is often a tradeoff.

Index

Waterford, 146, 157, 200
Wexford, 157, 197, 296
Wild Geese, 304
William III, 303
William the Conqueror, 155,
 168, 170, 185

Wolfe Tone, Theobald, 316,
 317

Yeats, W.B., 371, 375